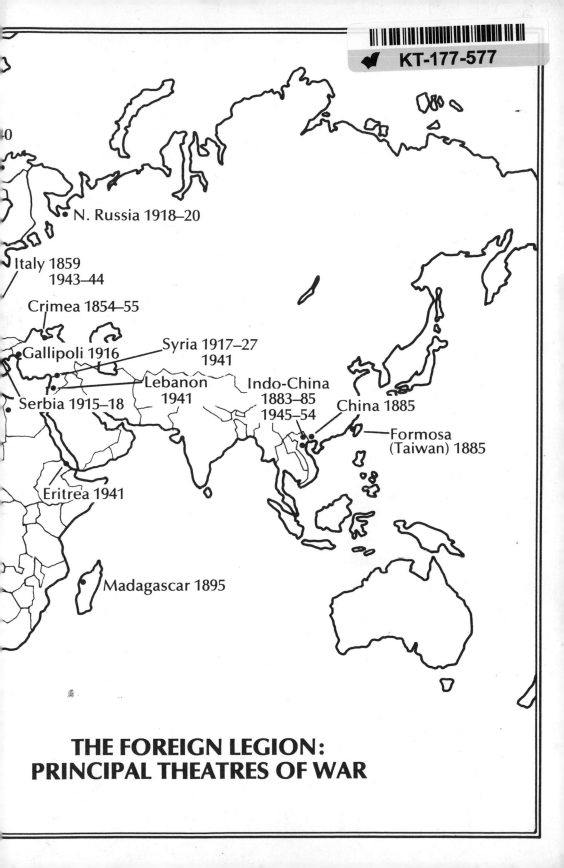

N. Russia 1918–20

Italy 1859
1943–44

Crimea 1854–55

Syria 1917–27
1941

Gallipoli 1916

Lebanon
1941

Indo-China
1883–85
1945–54

China 1885

Serbia 1915–18

Formosa
(Taiwan) 1885

Eritrea 1941

Madagascar 1895

THE FOREIGN LEGION:
PRINCIPAL THEATRES OF WAR

MARCH OR DIE

France and the
Foreign Legion

By the same author

MARCH OR DIE

France and the Foreign Legion

TONY GERAGHTY

GRAFTON BOOKS

A Division of the Collins Publishing Group

LONDON GLASGOW
TORONTO SYDNEY AUCKLAND

Grafton Books
A Division of the Collins Publishing Group
8 Grafton Street, London W1X 3LA

Published by Grafton Books 1986

British Library Cataloguing in Publication Data

Geraghty, Tony
   March or die: France and the Foreign Legion.
   1. France. *Armée. Légion étrangère* – History
   I. Title
   355.3'5   UA703.L5

ISBN 0-246-11975-6

Photoset by Rowland Phototypesetting Ltd
Bury St Edmunds, Suffolk
Printed in Great Britain by
Mackays of Chatham Ltd., Kent

CONTENTS

ILLUSTRATION CREDITS

Emir Abd-el-Kader. Photograph by Gustave Le Gray, courtesy of Jean-Loup Charmet, Paris

Abd-el-Kader's cavalry in action, Algeria 1840. Képi Blanc

François-Achille Bazaine. Engraving from *The Franco-German War* by Maj-Gen. J. F. Maurice and others

Battle of Camerone, Mexico, 1863. Painting by E. Detaille, courtesy of the Musée de l'Armée, Paris

Major Paul Brundsaux. Photo: Foreign Legion Archives, courtesy of Documentation Tallandier, Paris

Five Legion heroes of the First World War. Photo collection of Etablissement Cinématographique et Photographique des Armées (ECPA), courtesy of Martin Windrow

Blockhouse at Bou-Denib. Photo: Foreign Legion Archives, courtesy of Documentation Tallandier, Paris

A desert patrol at Sidi-bel-Abbès. Popperfoto

Rollet at Sidi-bel-Abbès. Popperfoto

Death of Bruno Garibaldi. Foreign Legion Archives, courtesy of Documentation Tallandier, Paris

Colonel Duriez. Foreign Legion Archives, courtesy of Documentation Tallandier, Paris

Legion pioneers march in a Bastille Day parade. Private Collection

Bastille Day parade in Paris, 1939. Popperfoto

Bren Gun carrier at Bir Hakeim. ECPA/ICARE

General Koenig. ECPA/ICARE

Susan Travers. Courtesy of Susan Travers

Bird's-eye view of Dien Bien Phu. John Hillelson

Vietnamese soldier taken prisoner. John Hillelson

Operating theatre, Dien Bien Phu. Photograph from *Doctor at Dien Bien Phu* by Major Grauwin; Hutchinson, London 1955

Algeria 1960: troop-carrying helicopter. Photograph courtesy of Jim Worden

57mm recoilless rifle. Jim Worden

Legion's First Paras behind a barrage of napalm. Képi Blanc, photo courtesy of Col. A. Hunter-Choat, OBE

Mine clearing on Tunisian border. Jim Worden

The 'stop' team in a rare patch of marsh. Jim Worden

Death of 'Amirouche'. Jim Worden

Field cooking in Algeria. Jim Worden

Lieutenant-Colonel Pierre Jeanpierre. Képi Blanc, photo courtesy of Col. A. Hunter-Choat, OBE

English Legion sergeant Tony Hunter-Choat. Col. A. Hunter-Choat, OBE

Captured Algerian enemy flag in the Sahara, 1958. Col. A. Hunter-Choat, OBE

The human ferret, Ouled. Col. A. Hunter-Choat, OBE

Sergeant Albert Dovecar. Documentation Tallandier, Paris

Men of 2 REP hurl themselves from a helicopter into the sea. Jim Worden

Bob Craigie Wilson at the piano. Robert Craigie Wilson

Djibouti, March 1967. Rex Features

Colour party of the 4th Compagnie Portée. Képi Blanc/Col. A. Hunter-Choat, OBE

The Foreign Legion's most precious relic. Popperfoto

The modern Legion: paras of 2 REP training at Calvi, Corsica. Gamma/Frank Spooner Pictures

Operation Manta, Chad 1984. Sipa/Rex Features

Beirut, September 1983. Gamma/Frank Spooner Pictures

FOREWORD

by Colonel A. Hunter-Choat, OBE

Legio patria nostra

The Legion is Our Country: the motto of the French Foreign Legion and of the French Foreign Legionnaire. Yet it is an odd fact that most of the many books about the Foreign Legion, particularly those written by French authors (some former Legion officers themselves), assert that the legionnaire has chosen to make France his country. Without any doubt every legionnaire owes a great and unpayable debt to the France who provided him with the escape and refuge he sought so desperately; every legionnaire owes a great debt to France for the comfort and succour she gave him when he needed it most. France in turn owes an inestimable debt to her legionnaires for repeatedly and unstintingly saving her bacon. And her face. Despite this mutual indebtedness the legionnaire's loyalty is to his country and its officers, his love is for his country and its officers, and his country is the Legion.

The notion that he chose France rather than the Legion is a peculiarly French one and engendered by France's view of her importance to the average legionnaire. It was by chance blended with genius that France created the Foreign Legion in 1831. Having done so, France – or rather French governments dominated by the mercenary dictates of Paris – never quite came to terms with their unique military formation. The legionnaire knows only too well the extremes of feeling France can have towards her foreign offspring, and adulation and hate – no, worse, detestation – flicker back and forth with confusing rapidity.

None of this should be taken to mean that the legionnaire is ungrateful to France. France and the Legion both give him a sense of purpose in life which, at the relevant time, no other organization could offer (for legionnaires are self-selecting). That sense of purpose shows very vividly. It always has done. In 1895, Colonel de Billebois-Mareuil wrote:

> In the hybrid circle into which a man enters blindfold, passportless, without recommendation or any mention of his past, there is a strange mixture of good and bad, of latent heroism and bitterness . . . but from this amorphous whole emerges an iron will, an instinctive passion for adventure, an amazing fertility of invention, a supreme contempt for death, in fact all those sublime virtues which go to the make-up of a true warrior.
>
> And this quality of the whole is reflected in the individual legionary; whether one sees him passing by in the street, his waist tightly girt by his broad belt, or rigidly at attention on a ceremonial parade, one notes that determined air, that insolent male pride of the man of action: virile, superior. No other soldier has his superb bearing.

It is symptomatic of something about the times that a growing number of young Englishmen are discovering what they need in such a setting. As France and Britain grow closer it would be appropriate in any case to re-examine the British connection with the Legion as well as that of France.

France's other Anglo-Saxon neighbour, Germany, has always provided the Legion with volunteers, so many indeed as to seem at times to dominate the institution. The British, by contrast, have kept their distance (and, historically, had a reputation for being too ready to desert after they had joined).

Times change. During a recent visit to the Legion's parachute regiment at Calvi, Corsica, I formed the impression that more young Britons are joining the Legion. Many are victims of unemployment. Others are starved of adventure. A former British soldier now with the unit believes that there are about 350 'Englishmen' (of all kinds) now serving in the 2nd Foreign Parachute Regiment. His educated guess is that the number throughout the Legion's eight major units now exceeds a thousand. If true, British citizens constitute almost one-eighth of the Legion's current strength. This is in remarkable contrast with the experience of preceding generations of British legionnaires. As a young Legion paratrooper in Algeria just under thirty years ago, I was unable to discover more than twenty 'Brits' serving among a total Legion strength of about 26,000, or fewer than one in a thousand.

The superficial facts of Legion history have been copiously documented in official and unofficial reports and in personal memoirs. Tony Geraghty's incisive inquisitiveness has led him to cut through the mass of military records, unit histories and individual recollections to discover the forces which motivate the two heroes (or villains) of this book in their relationships with each other: France and the Legion. I believe that much that he discovered surprised him, and that it all intrigued him. Every chink of light indicating a partly open door drew him like a voyeur. The result is a work which opens up to the public eye this Legion nestling like a transplanted organ in the body of France, vital to her existence but constantly on the brink of being rejected.

The average Frenchman might not recognize the story it tells and would probably find much unwelcome. But most legionnaires, including those who are French-born (by blood received, rather than by blood shed for France), will welcome the fact that this book says publicly what most of them have always known in private . . . that France still believes she emerged victorious at Waterloo.

A. Hunter-Choat, OBE
(Formerly Legionnaire No 116798)
Mons, Belgium
December 1985

ACKNOWLEDGEMENTS

My thanks are due first to my friend Colonel Tony Hunter-Choat, OBE, President of the Foreign Legion Association of Great Britain, who encouraged and sometimes provoked me into finishing this book; his wife Lyn, whose kindness mattered during my sojourn in France; to the cheerful, sometimes bibulous members of the Foreign Legion Association for their readiness to accept an outsider at successive Camerone Day celebrations; to those officials of the Defence Ministry in Paris who (in time) gave me the clearances I needed to approach the Legion itself; to those Legion officers and senior NCOs who welcomed me into their respective messes at Aubagne; and to the many excellent writers in French and English on whose work, wisdom and experience I have drawn. None of these sources is in the tiniest degree responsible for the work that has resulted.

INTRODUCTION

'A nation which cannot confront its own past
honestly is a nation with problems'

– Neal Ascherson, writing in the *Observer*, 1985,
about contemporary France

France employed mercenaries long before it had an empire. In 1346, Genoese crossbowmen who had been put into an impossible position by their French commanders at Crecy, broke before the English longbows. The Genoese were then made scapegoats for the defeat and massacred by their employers. Successive French monarchs recruited a Scots Guard, a Swiss Guard, Polish Lancers and Ireland's Wild Geese. Like the multi-national force that followed Napoleon on the road to Moscow in 1812, all of these units fought in pursuit of European campaigns.

It is in its colonies outside Europe that France has most consistently used the Foreign Legion. Because of this the Legion has suffered, along with the colonial peoples it controlled on behalf of France, from an unfortunate habit of betrayal as described by the nineteenth-century scholar Alexis de Tocqueville. Professor Xavier Yacono, in his *Histoire de la colonisation française*, quotes de Tocqueville as follows: 'In general in Africa, like everywhere else, all our alliances have led to the destruction or the diminution of those who have placed their confidence in us.'

Thus, when one French general (Galliéni) said in 1896, 'I am asking for 600 men of the Foreign Legion who are able, if need be, to die decently,' or when another (de Negrier) asserted in 1883, 'You legionnaires are soldiers in order to die and I am sending you where you can die,' they spoke the unvarnished truth. In French eyes, the legionnaire – sometimes the entire Legion – is expendable. And as many legionnaires discover, most good French parents, conscious of the market value of everything, do not take kindly to the idea that a legionnaire might marry their daughter before he dies for France.

France's refusal to learn from history is another of the keys to understanding its relationship with its foreign mercenaries. One might ask – though the French tend not to – why did France need a foreign legion in the first place? Why does it still retain the Foreign Legion, a unique fighting force of men drawn from 100 nations and no common culture? Perhaps most interesting of all, why do they need France? Many books have been written about the Legion but few ask such questions since this runs the risk of spoiling a good story. True, there are the brilliant monologues, those individual memoirs which capture the smell of fresh blood under powerful suns from the Sahara to Tonkin and back again; there are the heroic general histories, painted on huge (but two-dimensional) canvases, full of cloned infantrymen, obedient as lemmings as the end approaches; there are also excellent military, political and social histories of France covering the 150 or so years of the Legion's attachment to that country.

This work seeks to bridge the gap between those brilliantly told but entirely insular stories from the Legion on the one hand and the French dimension on the other, to trace the Legion's evolution as a rational process shaped by French politicians who tended to be rather less noble than the men under their control. It also endeavours to analyse the legend without seeking to destroy it, so as to make it comprehensible to those soldiers (and others) who have never been touched by the sort of emotional commitment the Legion uniquely requires. And it examines the careers of exceptional individuals who were loyal to their military oath and yet defied all efforts to make them conform to a regimental pattern.

Collisions with reality (the phrase might have been an apt sub-title for this work) are a regular feature of French military history, and the soldier – particularly the foreign legionnaire who is an outsider in a society which prides itself on '*l'esprit de clocher*', or 'parish pump' – has customarily been made the scapegoat for failure. Indeed, the very phrase '*French* Foreign Legion' is a cultural contradiction in terms. No surprise, then, that the foreign legionnaire has not only been made the scapegoat for failure but equally (as in Mexico and Algeria), has been blamed for military success against all odds when that success became politically inconvenient. By the 1960s the practice of penalizing the successful fighting legionnaire for *not* failing was enshrined in a memorandum issued by the High Command in Algeria on the subject of medals. This, according to one Legion officer, apparently proposed a limit of two citations a year for combat troops in order to reduce the number of decorations won by men who were described by the desk soldiers as '*scandaleuse-ment distingués*'. The scapegoat is an essential part of a mechanism which would rather bury historical embarrassment than learn from it. Thus, scapegoatism – which sustains the French myths about themselves – is a service performed for France second only in value to the Legion's actual military achievements. Indeed, the Legion came into being because France needed colonies not only for plunder and prestige, but also as a convenient political carpet beneath which to brush out of sight the disaffected and dangerous, the subversive and the criminal.

In 1830, a revolution had driven the French king, Charles X, to abdicate and left an insecure Louis-Philippe, Duke of Orléans, the inheritor of a war in Algeria as well as enemies at home who included many unemployed soldiers, the remnants of Napoleon Bonaparte's officer corps on half-pay since the 1815 defeat by Wellington at Waterloo. In *The Damned Die Hard*, Hugh McLeave has written one of the most lively accounts of the problem and its solution:

> The revolution that replaced Charles X with the frock-coated bourgeois king, Louis-Philippe, also filled Paris with a wrack of dissidents who had risen vainly against their masters in Belgium, Germany, Italy, and Poland; in the French capital, bombs and broken glass reverberated as hungry mobs joined disbanded mercenaries to ravage and loot shops or public buildings.
>
> 'So they wish to fight,' murmured the War Minister, Marshal Joseph Soult. 'Then let them bleed or shovel sand in the conquest of North Africa.'

Soult it was who insisted that the new force he created – largely through a purge of soldiers sympathetic to Charles X with the addition of exiles from political persecution in Italy, Spain and Poland, economic deprivation in Switzerland, and both in Belgium, Holland and Ireland – should not be employed in mainland, metropolitan France. When his advice was ignored for the first time, it was to use the Legion in the hopelessly mismanaged war against Bismarck's army in 1870–71, and then – following France's defeat by Prussia – to assist in the massacre of rebel communards still resisting in Paris. The estimate of 20,000 Parisians slaughtered by their fellow-countrymen is acknowledged by historians to be the minimum figure. What is certain is that another 1,600 were killed by firing squads while thousands more went to prison or were banished to New Caledonia. For this the army was blamed (and is still, implicitly) just as it would be blamed for its impact on Algiers in 1957.

When Louis-Philippe signed the royal warrant authorizing the creation of a Foreign Legion, France had already won and lost an empire, much of it to the British. Between 1533 and Napoleon Bonaparte's defeat in 1815, that lost empire included much of Canada, Louisiana, the Caribbean, slices of North and West Africa and India. With few exceptions, expansion of empire was about the search for loot rather than permanent occupation. The colonists' search was not always successful and a French synonym for disappointment was minted: 'As false as Canadian gold.'

The new golden age of French imperialism started in 1830 at a time when France's population was starting a long decline in comparison with those of other European powers. Yet the expansion was remarkably successful until France's surrender in 1940 destroyed her mystique among subject peoples far removed from the conflict in Europe. Large numbers of French soldiers, including Legion units loyal to Vichy France in North Africa and Indo-China, simply 'sat out' the most critical phase of World War II, only to join the allies when it was clear (after America's intervention) that Hitler would lose.

In these deflating circumstances France's subject territories – with Syria at the front of the queue – began to demand their independence. However, this should not diminish the astonishing fact that during 110 years of expansion, starting almost from scratch, France acquired an empire of approximately 68 million inhabitants – of whom only 1.5 million were European – girdling the earth from North Africa via the Middle East and the Indian Ocean to Indo-China, Polynesia, Central America and

Africa. It was a remarkable achievement, reflected in the romano-imperialist architecture of nineteenth-century Paris. That expansion into what is now called the Third World was the Legion's golden age also. It is after 1940 that regimental veterans and historians start to describe their predecessors as the 'Old Legion', one which had served the empire of a France whose invincibility was intact. In the days of the Old Legion, the emperor did have clothes, and splendid they were too.

After 1940, that small fraction of the Legion which joined the Free French would win glory by restoring some of France's military credibility in Norway and, most famously, at Bir Hakeim in 1942 with other non-French soldiers from Africa and the Pacific. But this would be the *Legion's* glory, not France's. Predictably, when a post-war army – largely controlled by men who had served the collaborationist Vichy regime in preference to the 'renegade' Free French – took control of the military bureaucracy after the Allied victory, former Free French officers were, in the words of Alistair Horne (in *The French Army and Politics*) 'shunted off into dim staff jobs'. The other source of criticism of the post-war legionnaire was the New Left, inspired by Jean-Paul Sartre. It was a bizarre conjunction, reflected in Britain in a similar blend of criticism against the Special Air Service from the military establishment on the one hand and post-war radical journalists on the other.

The Legion's participation in distant colonial wars during its first 100 years had an advantage which became apparent only on those isolated occasions when the unit came directly under the heavy hand of government in Paris. While soldiering on in Tonkin or Algeria or Madagascar, it was out of sight of warring politicians, military and civilian. Colonial expansion, as we have noted, was dynamically successful. It also appeared to have a momentum of its own, unrelated to what was going on (which was frequently total confusion) at the centre of the empire.

After Napoleon's final defeat at Waterloo in 1815, the French switched from monarchy to republic and back again. There were nineteen governments and sixteen war ministers in Paris between 1870 and 1888.

Towards the end of the nineteenth century, the French army

asserted the right to belong to France rather than to any given government, so as to be 'above existing institutions'. As General Gallifet put it, 'The Army belongs to no party. It belongs to France.'

French public attitudes to the army have been volatile throughout the whole period covered by this history, as one policy is discredited and abandoned, a scapegoat discovered and a new policy adopted, usually without much forethought. For some years before World War I professional soldiers, particularly officers, were a despised minority in society. In 1911, when it became apparent that war was probable, patriotic fervour took over France just as it had done at the outset of the disastrous Franco-Prussian war in 1870. The army was out of favour in 1917 when a number of units, sickened by the carnage of the Western Front, mutinied and threatened Paris itself; back in favour after victory in 1918; out of favour through the 1920s until 1934; in favour again after the liberation of 1944; out of favour during the post-colonial wars of the 1950s and 1960s.

The periods when the army was out of favour were often punctuated by the sound of firing squads of one sort or another as the latest scapegoat was discovered, the 'guilty' ones punished and the latest collision with reality satisfactorily explained away. So, after the failure of the French army in 1870, it was Maréchal de France Bazaine, a former Legion sergeant, who was cast in the role of Guilty Man and impeached. In the next round of Franco-German hostilities, the 1917 affair created an unusually charismatic sacrifice for France's reputation in the form of Mata Hari shot at Vincennes for spying after the British had released her. It was said of her that she 'lived dangerously, died courageously and was shot into fame', unlike the hundreds of rebellious but anonymous French soldiers who also died before firing squads that year.

Most of the time, the Legion was well out of France. When the unit was lured from its long-term empire-building in Africa or South-East Asia and made answerable directly to the ruling regime – whether monarchist or republican – the result was usually not good for the reputations and prospects of those involved, even when the legionnaires succeeded militarily.

So why be a legionnaire? If the regiment's identification with the overseas empire was one long historical shadow cast by its origins, then another was the sanctuary it provided, of a sort, for able-bodied outcasts. Since its creation it has always reflected the tidal waves of disaster sweeping across Europe and many other areas. With the loss of Alsace-Lorraine after the Franco-Prussian War, the Legion attracted excellent fighting men from that region, who now considered themselves stateless persons. Following the Spanish Civil War, many Spanish republicans signed on for Legion service. After World War II, defeated Germans and Hungarians joined former French enemies in the Legion's epic campaigns in Indo-China. With the loss of Indo-China, many loyal Vietnamese joined the Legion to fight in Algeria.

At other times volunteers have come forward as a result of economic hardship. Demographically, the Legion has always provided a ready chart of the hardships of the Northern hemisphere. Just now, there is a noticeable increase in the number of Poles (for political reasons) and British subjects (unemployment).

This essentially prosaic process is still given a touch of theatre, for those who like that sort of thing, by the right to adopt a *nom-de-guerre* for the period of service with the Legion, even if that is a lifetime. French authorities try these days to ensure that they know the man's real name. The choice of a new name, like that of the novice monk born again as 'Brother Dominic', is symbolic of much more: it is about the risks and joys of a new identity within a new community. The non-military cynic might argue that it is also a control mechanism, but for this theory to have merit, one must assume, wrongly, that all recruits to the Foreign Legion are fools, or weak-minded, or both.

'All legionnaires are romantics at heart,' a hard-bitten sergeant at the Legion's depot near Marseilles suggested to me in 1984. There is some truth in this. While Piaf sang 'Mon legionnaire', they – on their way to prison after the Algiers putsch of 1961 – repaid the compliment and sang, with a flourish before their regiments were disbanded, 'Je ne regrette rien!'

But the search for a new identity, one which is paradoxically within the individual already but can find expression only under the protection of the Legion, is more than romanticism. It is a psychological imperative, a passion which overrides the problems of language and alienation of every other sort. (Many good legionnaires speak only halting French and some are illiterate in their own tongues. The Legion is tailor-made for the inarticulate in a world where articulacy is a badge of success.) For some legionnaires, the regiment is the religious brotherhood of the military world. Successive generations of young men in search of absolutes (because that is the only way they know how to make sense of the world) and pilgrims who insist upon asking the unanswerable know that the Legion's promised rendezvous with death has an irresistible appeal. Some veteran Legion recruiters, who have been there themselves, drily describe such men as 'types sportifs', to distinguish them from those driven by hunger or scandal.

Like any other religious brotherhood, the Legion has a domestic dimension which is just as important to it as the bigger issues of life, death and glory. When, within a week in 1959, three famous Hungarian sergeant-majors were killed in action with different Legion regiments, it inspired some illuminating comments about the Legion from within its own ranks. The veteran depot commander, Colonel Brothier, reflected:

> These three boys were not yet twenty years old at the end of the Second World War and found themselves at the heart of a Europe in ruins, without country, without reason for living. They did not know one another. Their brotherhood started one day when each refused to accept his fate and live in an enslaved country. The Foreign Legion opened its ranks to them. They were looking for a refuge and they found a family.

The head of the family, the officer, is invariably French. By tradition the officer leads from the front, in the debonair tradition of one of Napoleon's best cavalry generals, the Comte de Lasalle, who declared: 'Any huzzar who is not dead at thirty is a blackguard.' The roll of Legion commanding officers who died young, in action, from 1831 onwards, is long. It includes Combe (Constantine, 1837); Conrad (Barbastro, 1837); Vienot (Sebastopol, 1856); de Chabrières (Magenta, Italy, 1859); Guilhem (Paris vs Prussia, 1870); Pein (Western Front, 1915); Duriez (Western Front, 1917); de la Tour (France, 1940); Guéninchault

(France, 1940); Amilakvari (Western Desert, 1941); de Sairigné (Indo-China, 1946); Segrétain (Indo-China, 1948); Raffalli (Indo-China, 1950); Gaucher (Indo-China, 1953); Jeanpierre (Algeria, 1958). This list is not exhaustive.

Such commitment intimidates. It challenges the legionnaire to desert, or to follow his leader through the gates of hell. Many desert. Those who do not are dedicated men. Colonel Brothier again:

> One of the exceptional characteristics of the Legion is the dog-like devotion of the men to their officers. It is from them that they find the structure and balance that civilian life did not give them. Thus, they transfer all their attachments and affection to their officers. For they have no critical sense. In their officers they will forgive everything, even the most extravagant actions. [Quoted in Hugh McLeave]

Visiting generals inspecting Legion guards-of-honour learn not to ask: 'Which country did you come from?' Such a question will assuredly elicit the stock answer: 'The Legion is my country, general.'

A more macabre explanation of the legionnaire's motivation was offered to the military medical establishment of France in 1912 by one Jean Robaglia, supported by Dr Paul Chavigny, a major. Noting that the Legion's suicide rate was then four times greater than the army average and twice the average for the army in Algeria, the study reaches the somewhat sweeping conclusion that the born soldier, the sort who joins a high-risk, élite unit is also a born suicide. What was more, Robaglia continued:

> The man who pushes hard to join the Legion is very often of abnormal psychology, a degenerate subject to morbid influences, a misfit. If one imagines what fate would befall any of these 15,000 unfortunates of the Legion up to the day they no longer exist, one should also reflect that these rejects would not be able to choose between crime, suicide or depression. One should understand the full beauty and grandeur of France's redemptive role; the Legion is not only the most admirable of military elites but also a school of expiation and oblivion.

Thus, the authentic voice of Paris when the French empire, whose spearhead was the Legion, was at its peak.

It is explicable that for some men the life of a legionnaire is not merely desirable, but – in spite of the dangers and hardships – essential. It is less clear why the officers (who are French and therefore, unlike the foreign volunteer, potentially less susceptible to Gallic rhetoric and self-deception) also join a club whose membership fee is often life itself. Such officers tend to remain with the Legion throughout their military careers and are self-selecting. Often they are the best of their year to emerge from the military academies of St Cyr and elsewhere. In my view, there is one theory which fits the known evidence better than any other. This is that the France which such an officer serves in the Legion is an altogether different entity from the everyday, cynical society into which he was born. An English equivalent, perhaps, would be based upon a hunting print in which the red-coated horsemen (foreground) are cheered on by besmocked, loyal, ruddy-faced country folk (background). In spirit, hidden away in rural corners, such an England might still exist but it is not the norm, any more than the Cockney spirit of the Blitz ('We can take it!') represents contemporary London.

What matters is that the legionnaires, officers and men, *believe* in their France, a place dedicated to martial courage of a decidedly medieval kind at the hub of its culture. In such a culture, it is no surprise to discover that there are only two kinds of French soldier: those who serve French arms as of birthright, and those who are French not by blood inherited, but by blood shed in battle. The lines by the Legion poet Pascal Bonetti, written in 1914:

N'est pas cet étranger devenu fils de France
Non par le sang reçu mais par le sang versé?

('Has not this foreigner become a son of France, / Not by blood inherited, but spilled?') are among the most frequently quoted by the Legion about itself.

The French officer, faced with some of the world's most dedicated soldiers, is unlikely to turn iconoclast. He and his soldiers buttress one another's illusions which are mutually reinforcing and, by total commitment, capable of turning dross into real gold. The alchemy unfortunately requires liberal quantities of young blood.

The process by which the faith is maintained, as in any religious order, is through ritual. The Legion is strong on ritual, a ritual heavy with German melody and deep, masculine voices singing – initially compulsorily, on the march, as part of basic training – to the slow, sand-slogging rhythm of eighty-five paces to the minute. ('March or die!' was the watchword, if not the official motto, for generations of legionnaires; anyone who could not march would be taken by the enemy or die of thirst.)

Much of that ritual, and many of the songs, are about death. The subject is approached with a lack of inhibition, a passion even, which would seem indecent to the undemonstrative British. Certainly it is not possible to understand the Legion without appreciating its attitude to the last and most profound of life's mysteries. As human beings, the legionnaires are afraid of death, if they have time to think about it. As legionnaires, however, they have to come to terms with it as part of their cultural equipment. Some forms of death, like the Christian martyrdom, are highly desirable since they involve a deliberate sacrifice of one's life in order to be there, with one's comrades, when the end comes. It was in this spirit, in the last, doomed days of Dien Bien Phu that many legionnaires, making their first and only parachute descent, jumped into a situation which they knew to be militarily hopeless. They were no longer fighting in earthly terms, they were making a metaphysical gesture.

Since 30 April 1863 – that day in Mexico when one captain, two sergeants and sixty-two legionnaires held off 2,000 enemy soldiers – the Legion phrase for it has been 'To do a Camerone'. At the end of that day the five survivors still fit to fight but with no ammunition left, charged their enemy with bayonets fixed. Theoretically, they were defending a consignment of gold. In practice, facing adverse odds of forty to one, they were making a statement about the value of duty, of courage and their own identities. Every year, the Camerone anniversary is solemnly, and then less solemnly, commemorated wherever legionnaires gather, including the Maréchal Foch statue near London's Victoria Station.

The Legion's defiance of numerical inferiority, its rejection of fear as if it were a pollutant of the spirit, is closer to Zen than to the fatalism of Islam and, in most cases, light years away from the pointless self-indulgence of suicide.

Its most eloquent expression in English was written by the American poet Alan Seeger, who died fighting with the Legion's Marching Regiment on the Somme in 1916. These are the last two verses:

> God knows 'twere better to be deep
> Pillowed in silk and scented down,
> Where Love throbs out in blissful sleep,
> Pulse nigh to pulse, and breath to breath,
> Where hushed awakenings are dear
>
> But I've a rendezvous with Death
> At midnight in some flaming town,
> When Spring trips north again this year,
> And I to my pledged word am true,
> I shall not fail that rendezvous.

Seeger and his comrades made their regiment the second most decorated of any in the French army during World War I. Although France's national military museum, Les Invalides, says nothing of that, or of the Legion on the Western Front, something more than an appetite for self-destruction is required to create such a record of physical courage.

The Camerone spirit has been expressed many times, often in actions from which no survivors emerged to catch the historian's eye. Occasionally the enemy, if he is more generous than France, fills in the gap. History, they say, is written by the victors. So it was at Les Aides, a suburb of Orléans, on 10 October 1870, during the Franco-Prussian War. In all, said the victorious Prussian General von Heinleth: 'The French lost about 4,000 men in killed, wounded and prisoners, among these the Foreign Legion of 1,300 men alone lost its Commanding Officer, 19 officers and 900 rank and file.' That is, a quarter of the French losses.

The attitude of the rest of the French army to such soldiers has always been equivocal. The differences show up most clearly during those crises of conflicting loyalty to which France's armed forces are more prone than most in the Western world. The Legion, for example, was almost alone in *not* participating in one of the many mutinies in 1917 (and enjoyed pride of place in the Bastille Day parade in Paris that summer as a result). In 1940 Legion officers including Pierre Messmer, a future Prime Minister of his country, were among a tiny minority who refused to surrender and followed de Gaulle (then a mere brigadier) into exile to salvage France's military honour in the teeth of French opposition. The Legion's commitment to duty makes it a less than comfortable companion in adversity, except among those who share its conscious acceptance of early death as a natural outcome of soldiering. So at best, less dedicated soldiers (particularly civilian-oriented conscripts) would rather applaud the legionnaire than follow him. This is what happened, for example, when Legion officers sought support in their trial of strength with President de Gaulle in 1961. The Legion's representatives were entertained with champagne at many of the messes they visited in Algeria, but left without any of the backing they had requested in opposing de Gaulle's U-turn on Algerian independence.

There is another dimension of alienation between legionnaires and the rest of the French army. This is the existence of two types of commission, or engagement, to distinguish 'real' French officers from the others. The precise terms of a foreign commission in the French army were not even defined until the end of World War I, but long before then such a title could be recognized by inferior pensions and other conditions of service attached to it. Occasionally, French officers came to the Legion with foreign commissions only after some personal or professional catastrophe which had led to their resigning a regular French commission. Others, their regular commissions intact, chose to serve with the Legion for most of their careers because they preferred hard soldiering far from Europe to armchair manoeuvres and preferment in Paris.

Indeed, for some of the golden years of colonial expansion prior to 1939, a tradition developed of sending the cream of graduates from France's military colleges to the Legion, often as a first posting to get them blooded. In 1964 Simon Murray, an English NCO serving with the Legion, noted in his diary (later published as *Legionnaire*): 'We no longer draw on the first six who pass out of the French military academy for our source of officers as we used to. The Legion is now open to all French army officers, even those doing national service. The result has been a marked decline in the quality.' When he was offered an officer-cadetship himself later that year he wrote: 'As a foreigner I would never get beyond the rank of captain and to adopt French nationality is not on as far as I am concerned. I am a son of England . . . I have no wish to be a captain in the Foreign Legion for the rest of my life.'

These days the Legion has a modern look. It has its own song-book and markets an excellent recording of songs which bear such titles as 'But the Devil Marches With Us'. At Aubagne, on the hills above Marseilles, facing nostalgically towards Algeria, the organization also has an elaborate, modern editorial and printing plant, run exclusively from within its own ranks, to produce a multi-coloured monthly journal, *Le Képi Blanc*. In an important sense, the Legion remains self-contained, out of reach of researchers including even those French officers who seek to construct a history of the regiment which is neither an apologia nor a demolition job. Having encountered numerous obstacles, Lieutenant-Colonel (E.R.) Pierre Carles concluded wearily in *Revue Historique des Armées* (by Col. Villaume, et al.) in 1981: 'One day it must be hoped a researcher will perhaps be tempted to do a real history, neither hagiographic nor iconoclastic, of the Foreign Legion.'

Elsewhere on the same campus at Aubagne, hardened paras are also trained to operate computers along with the best of modern infantry weapons. Yet such modernity only barely conceals a Franco-German military culture which is unself-consciously Roman as well as medieval-troubadour in its expression. At a critical point in the Algiers rebellion by 1st Legion Paras (1 REP), those involved described it as 'a centurions' revolt', and – as a programme note to accompany the main production – they circulated in French a protest by Marcus Flavinius, centurion of the 2nd Cohort of the Legion Augusta, serving in North Africa. As reported by Suetonius, the protest asserted: 'If we must leave our bones to bleach uselessly on the desert road, then beware of the legions' anger!'

The reminder was 2,000 years old. Its function was to give historical legitimacy as well as credibility to the Legion's concept of France and this, one suspects, is what infuriated de Gaulle more than anything else, provoking a threat to disband not just one or two regiments – which he carried out – but to wind up the entire organization.

The Legion's anger after Algeria was responsible, among other things, for a profound change in the literature produced by the regiment's articulate veterans, particularly those of the 1 REP. Until then, throughout the regiment's long and eventful history, the story repeatedly was one of calm acceptance of Seeger's deadly rendezvous. But the betrayal of the pledged word destroyed the value of martyrdom and polluted the sacrifice of life which civilian, political France, ever rapacious, demanded to compensate for its rhetoric, its muddle-headedness and its lies. The padre of 1 REP, Father Delarue (a man dedicated to obedience as a priest as well as a soldier) started the questioning at a famous funeral in 1960. 'We no longer know what we are dying for,' he declared, and in that one sentence shattered the illusion that legionnaires died not only bravely, but unquestioningly also. Afterwards, the 'lost paras', as de Gaulle described them, took up authorship as readily as soldiering and spoke about their experience with a new voice, cynical in its battleground humour, radical in its questioning of the Legion as mere cannon-fodder.

So what is it that the Legion does for France, aside from sitting on strategically sensitive bits of real estate in Djibouti in Arabia, Guiana in Central America (formerly French Guiana) and the Pacific? It preserves a martial ideal, an essential part of the nation's self-esteem. The Legion believes in glory. France also believes in glory, so long as the cost to France is not too burdensome. It was an official French army historian who expressed dismay that prosperous farm people living near Orléans refused help to legionnaires – fever-prone veterans of wars in Africa who were now lying in the wet of a bad November – while they fought the Prussians. The historian Lieutenant-Colonel Henry Dutailly contributed the following account to a collection of essays commemorating the Legion's 150th anniversary in 1981:

The men's suffering was sometimes aggravated by the indifference, if not the hostility, of the population whom the soldiers were defending. The supply of goods against official chits was honoured with extreme ill-will. At the beginning of November, the Mayor of Loir-et-Cher even refused to supply wood and fodder needed by the regiment.

This, then, was the Legion's first experience of fighting for France on French soil, in 1871. Several wars later, things had not improved much. Thus, the historian of another foreign army of liberation, shedding its blood in Normandy seventy-three years later, noted: 'Soldiers were puzzled, sometimes angered, by the sight of French civilians tending their fields or going about their business with their little carts, apparently indifferent to the claims of their liberators to gratitude.' The writer, Max Hastings, then describes how dead British soldiers were robbed of their boots by civilians who were in turn shot by a military policeman with the crisp comment, 'Bloody bastards'.

Because of their complementary needs, France and the Legion are made for one another. France's cynicism (a vice of maturity) and the pilgrim's youthful mysticism are the improbable bed-fellows which combine to create, and re-create the Foreign Legion. Over the past 150 years the two have discovered a sort of symbiosis which works so long as their separate illusions do not collide. When that does happen, as it did in Algeria, the firing squad tends to be French and the victim's last words, '*Vive la Légion!*'

In 1989, France celebrates her bicentenary as a republic, to become a middle-aged state in the prime of life. As she reflects upon the mirror of history she could do worse, if she wishes to learn something to her advantage from the first 200 years, than examine her relations with the world outside France beginning with her own, beloved Légion Étrangère.

CHAPTER 1
'The Legion is Our Country'
(1831–47)

The turbulent spirit of our nation needs some
unusual circumstance to occupy its ardent
imagination.

– Count Clermont-Tonnerre,
French Defence Minister, 1830

From this time, the legionnaire's total
dedication to his contract was established.

– Legion historian on transfer of first
Foreign Legion to Spain, 1835

We have burned everything. How many women
and children have died of cold and fatigue!

– Colonel Leroy de Saint Arnaud,
Algeria, 1845

By 1808, Napoleon's armies were striding across Europe with the
leonine arrogance of Roman legions. France's only recent defeats
had been at sea, at the hands of the British: at the Nile in 1798 and
Trafalgar in 1805. Mindful of this, the Emperor was already
turning his ambitious and clever strategist's mind towards North
Africa and the route to France's old colonies in India. In 1807 he
invaded Portugal. An attack on Spain, ultimately disastrous to
his military strength, followed a year later.

Possibly he had in mind the creation of an entirely Gallic
western Mediterranean from which the dangerous English fleet
could be excluded by hostile guns based on both coasts. The
example of the Barbary Coast, whose organized piracy had been
hallowed by time and custom into a protection racket which
did not even oblige the pirates to put to sea much of the time,

was a vivid illustration of the deterrence Napoleon was seeking.

At any rate, a full seven years before the final defeat at Waterloo, Bonaparte had sent a sapper officer named Major Boutin to Algiers. The Major discreetly walked about a bit, chose a promising beachhead at Sidi Ferruj and drafted a detailed plan for an advance on Algiers. Naturally, he said nothing to the Turks who had asserted intermittent control over the Maghreb's main population centres for about two centuries.

When the French finally landed at Sidi Ferruj, Napoleon was dead. The expeditionary force was led by a nobleman – Count Louis de Bourmont – Napoleon's Minister of War, who had deserted to the enemy three days before Waterloo. Soldiers have long memories and as de Bourmont's men waded ashore, muskets held high, fifteen years later it is said that they sang a rude song about their Commander.

Historians still disagree about the reasons as well as the timing for France's move against Algiers on 14 June 1830. Whatever the cause, the events of that day were to spawn a whole new army – the Armée d'Afrique (Army of Africa). This was composed of 'exotic' regiments among which the Foreign Legion was for some years one of the least distinguished. Yet it is useful to try to answer the question 'Why Africa?' if only because it makes France's attitude towards its legionnaires more comprehensible. Also – since the Legion's reaction to French administration was a formative influence on the regiment – the events leading up to the creation of the Armée d'Afrique are an important element in the history of the Legion.

The Bourbon monarchy was brought down by the Jacobin revolution of 1789. Napoleon emerged from the internecine chaos which followed to unite the country and overrun all of Europe except Britain. He inaugurated the First Empire by solemnly crowning himself before a less-than-convinced audience, an event recorded in oils and still hung in a chamber of the Versailles palace. Napoleon was defeated, imprisoned on Elba, escaped to bewitch Europe again for a hundred days, finally lost to Wellington at Waterloo and died in 1821 on far-away Saint Helena, amid rumours – subsequently rebutted – of arsenical poisoning.

By 1830, when the French army landed in North Africa, the Bourbon line had been restored. The new King Charles X, it is said, wanted to punish the *Dey* of Algiers (a Turkish governor) because of the 'fly-whisk episode'. This had occurred during a diplomatic reception held to mark an Islamic festival. The governor, Khodja Husein, nagged the French consul, Monsieur Pierre Duval, about a debt owed by France to Algiers for grain and money supplied during the lean days of the French Revolution. Duval brushed the matter aside somewhat impatiently and Husein struck Duval with the fly-whisk. It was an assault on French honour of a kind which Bismarck copied in order to provoke the Franco-Prussian war some forty years later. On both occasions the French responded with all-out war. However, King Charles's response in 1830, his assault on Algiers, took place a full four years after the Turkish insult to French dignity.

Some historians, Frenchmen among them, have concluded that the pirates of Algiers were the root cause of France's first military adventure since Waterloo. There could be no doubt that the pirates were as much a menace of the Maghreb as they were to the British in the Arabian Gulf. In the Gulf the British reacted by making arrangements with local puppet rulers supported by an occasional show of force. It was more cost-effective than putting huge expeditionary forces ashore for long periods.

The western Mediterranean, however, was a more international thoroughfare along which loss of goods was compounded by the enslavement of European prisoners sold at auction in Algiers and Tripoli. Until the French intervened, Algiers was the principal market for slaves brought up by caravan from Equatorial Africa along with gold, ivory and ostrich feathers. Most maritime nations found it expedient to have an 'agreement' with Algiers through which an indemnity – protection money – was paid to the *Dey*. One of the foreign consul's regular tasks was to be on hand to accept responsibility for nationals freed when the indemnity was honoured. The Barbary Coast pirates were not always over-fastidious about honouring agreements made between a foreign *Dey* and a foreign government, and some European women ended up in harems. The youthful, idealistic United States was one of the governments which readily participated in the undignified commerce of buying protection. It had no choice. Seeking moral purity with new-found political independence, it had no standing army or navy – until the Barbary Coast pirates betrayed one contract too many and obliged the Americans to react. The US then raised a real navy and sent several men-o'-war to attack the city of Tripoli in 1801. (A line about 'the shores of Tripoli' can still be found in the Marine Corps hymn.)

A quarrel about a stale debt, a consul struck with a fly-whisk one hot afternoon in Algiers, even occasional acts of piracy hardly seem enough, in retrospect, to justify embarking an expeditionary force of 37,000 men in 600 ships. The reasoning of King Charles's Minister of Defence, Count Clermont-Tonnerre, is more plausible: 'The turbulent and light-hearted spirit of our nation needs some unusual circumstance occasionally to occupy its excessively ardent imagination.'

But there are two other, complementary, reasons for the Algiers expedition. First, the French thirsted for empire again. Defeated by the British first in the Americas and then in Europe, France turned to Africa and Asia. Initially, conquest was cost-effective. Five days after an unopposed landing, de Bourmont's forces defeated a Turkish force on the Staouëli Plateau and then, still following the twenty-two-year-old plan provided by Bonaparte's spy, they hit a strongpoint known as Emperor's Fort. Inside, the desperate Turks blew up the place themselves. The *Dey* surrendered and the contents of his treasury more than covered the cost of the adventure. Valuable artefacts plundered from mosques and shipped home to France also provided individual officers with something to show for their trouble.

Second, besides the appetite for expansion to restore something of France's former glory, there was the need to export some of the country's dissidents. Among the first to be disposed of in this way were the men formed into the first Foreign Legion who in 1835 were moved lock, stock and barrel to Spain, and forgotten.

Count de Bourmont sailed from Toulon in May 1830 and landed at Sidi Ferruj at 3 a.m. on 14 June. He seized Algiers twenty days later on 4 July. Charles X received the news of de Bourmont's victory on 9 July, and the next day he approved an order nullifying the effects of a democratic election and dissolving Parliament. By the end of the month Charles was forced to abdicate in a coup supported by Parisian mobs and fled to Britain. He was replaced as head of state by Louis-Philippe, Duke of Orléans, by blood a Bourbon, by political instinct a manipulative, middle-class bourgeois. To head off the renewed threat of republicanism, he saw to it that monarchy would provide a radical alternative to itself. Press censorship ended, for a time, and sixty-five out of seventy-five top generals – the hard core of the professional army – were removed from the active list. Military power shifted in metropolitan France away from the professionals, the *armée de métier*, towards a citizens' National Guard.

News of the Paris coup did not reach Algiers until 11 August, about the time General de Bourmont also received word of his promotion to Maréchal de France. And so on 2 September, General Bertrand Clauzel (another Count), arrived to take command from the now-dismissed de Bourmont, who was thus the unwitting political victim of his own military success.

Paris was by now plagued by the rabble that had brought the new King and his radical friends to power. Louis-Philippe set about exporting the trouble as rapidly as possible. One gang of street toughs was formed up as the Paris Volunteers and exported to Algeria where, after some unsuccessful attempts to blend them with indigenous troops, they were reorganized yet again as the 67th Infantry Regiment. So much for his embarrassing allies. Louis-Philippe next turned his attention to potential enemies in the army and at court. As the French historian (and former legionnaire) Erwan Bergot has noted:

The creation of the Foreign Legion (which Marshal Soult, the Minister of War, decreed 'should not be employed in the continental territory of the Kingdom') was intended to remove from France those officers and soldiers, French or foreign, who were felt to be awkward, excitable or frankly dangerous subjects for the new monarchy. [John Robert Young, et al., *The French Foreign Legion*]

Certainly what followed seems to sustain this conspiracy theory. The Legion was sent first to Algiers in 1831, a year after the invasion, and when it failed to get itself annihilated in the North African war which followed, it was handed over in 1835 as a gift to Queen Isabella II of Spain to help her fight a civil war against her uncle, Don Carlos. The Queen was a three-year-old child at the time and the war was undertaken on her behalf by her mother, Queen María Cristina. In their history of the Armée d'Afrique published in 1977 a group of senior French army officers comment:

> France . . . took the strange decision to give away to Spain the Foreign Legion which, according to a regulation dated 20 June, 1835, ceased to be part of the French army. Under the name 'Auxiliary French Legion', it brought honour to France in giving proof of its military valour. [General R. Huré et al., *L'Armée d'Afrique*]

An official Legion publication hardly disguises its contempt for what happened:

> On 29 June, 1835 a new regulation 'ceded' the Foreign Legion to the Spanish government . . . For good or ill, the officers and men had to accept this. They fought no less fiercely, in deplorable conditions [in fact, without pay, rations or uniforms] in an adventure which ended three years later. Of the 4,000 Legionnaires who took part in this campaign, little more than 500 survived.

With soldierly irony, the commentary concludes: 'From this time, the legionnaire's total dedication to his contract was established.'

Nothing, be it noted, is said about France's fidelity to the signed contract.

This, then, was the origin of the Foreign Legion, a unit unlike any other mercenary regiment to fight under the French flag if only because, from the very beginning, France's lack of gratitude or even interest was manifest. For the most cynical of political reasons the regiment was devised as a plausible military and political coffin for France's outsiders. Louis-Philippe thus turned on its head the existing concept of a royal guard (Scottish, Swiss, German) composed of foreign troops. It was a characteristic symbol of the man: a 'democratic' royal who would engage in a popular gesture strictly for self-interest.

Very well, said the Legion in reply, it would serve France in spite of that, to demonstrate what integrity was. But the regimental motto, '*Honneur et Fidélité*', made no mention of 'la patrie'. On the contrary, the unofficial motto became, 'The Legion is my Country'.

Having willed as its strategic end the occupation of Algiers, Oran and Bône, France was unwilling to provide the means required to sustain such a campaign. General Clauzel was ordered to cut his force by 10,000 men. As the American writer on French history, Douglas Porch, points out in *The Conquest of the Sahara*:

> French colonial campaigns tended to follow a monotonously regular pattern. The initial invasion succeeded in breaking the back of local opposition. The invasion force then withdrew, leaving behind a few garrisons. As soon as the bulk of the French troops had disappeared, the inhabitants recovered their courage and revolted, requiring a second invasion. This is what had happened time and again in Algeria, Tunisia, Tonkin and Madagascar.

Clauzel's way out of his difficulty was to raise local, tribally-based regiments, first from among the non-Arab mountain people, the Kabylie, who had traditionally provided military manpower for the occupying Turks. From these 'volunteers' emerged the soldiers known as Zouaves, to provide at least two battalions of infantry plus a cavalry regiment. Each Zouave company had attached to it two French officers, three senior NCOs and two corporals. Under a famous French soldier, Duvivier, the totemic magic of uniform was exploited: the 1st Zouave cavalry wore red turbans; the 2nd, green.

The Zouaves came into being in 1831, the same year as that other new regiment of the new Armée d'Afrique, the Foreign Legion. Both were intended to serve permanently outside France, a resolution which held good only until France was invaded by the Prussians in 1870. For adventurous French officers seeking rapid promotion such units had the same lustre as, say, the Bengal Lancers among their British counterparts in India. Names which appeared as lieutenants and captains in North Africa at this time in France's first post-Napoleonic army – Bazaine, Saint Arnaud, Espinasse – were those of future generals and marshals of France.

Within the Legion also, the 'tribal' system was adopted. Each of the battalions created before the regiment was sent on its doomed enterprise to Spain comprised a single nationality. The Germans, dominant from the very beginning, provided two battalions. The 1st battalion were Swiss: the 2nd, German: the 3rd, German; the 4th, Spanish. In 1833 another three battalions augmented the Legion strength: the 5th Italian, 6th Belgian and 7th Polish. There were no French battalions as such. Other new regiments accommodated them.

In spite of such rapid recruitment of foreigners, the total strength under French command in North Africa was down to 11,000 men and 400 officers by December 1831, and this in a country where every tribe regarded itself as an independent statelet entitled to impose its own laws; where guerrilla warfare against any occupying force was endemic. So after six months the new commander-in-chief, General Savary (Napoleon's former police chief), authorized the creation of yet another new regiment, the African Light Infantry, also known as the Bats d'Af (Bataillons d'Afrique) or again, with mordant humour (for these were really penal battalions manned by accredited military criminals), as 'Les Joyeux'.

Later came another cavalry unit, the Spahis; then the exclusively French Chasseurs d'Afrique; the Gendarmerie d'Afrique; native sharpshooters such as Tirailleurs (from Algeria, Morocco, the Sahara and Senegal); wildly irregular, nomadic Goum; solid – and, in post-independence Algeria – the doomed Harkis . . . The list is long and at the outset the ragbag of European veterans known as the Foreign Legion were nothing special. Yet after 132 years' campaigning including two world wars and many smaller ones, the Legion was the only remnant of this vast Armée d'Afrique to survive France's withdrawal from Algeria in 1962. The rest – like the Dublin Fusiliers and the Sepoys in the service of Britain – were swept away into oblivion.

The Legion's career started uneventfully enough. After landing in Algiers in August 1831, Swiss volunteers of the 1st battalion (former members of the now-disbanded royal bodyguard under the Swiss Colonel Stoffel) were put to work to drain a marsh and build a road which became Legion's Way. It was the beginning of a tradition of civil engineering equal to that of the Roman army. Roads, houses for incoming settlers, barracks, even harvesting were among the spare jobs handed to this new, untried regiment.

It was almost a year before the unit came under fire. On 27 April 1832 the Swiss and German battalions led an assault across open ground on the walled, well-defended township of Maison Carrée, a few miles east of Algiers. News of this success filtered back to Paris to remind the government that this group of foreigners had no colour of its own to demonstrate whom it was fighting for. Hurriedly a flag was stitched together and decorated with the somewhat deadpan message, 'The King of France to the Foreign Legion'.

A few months later it was the turn of the Spanish battalion, part of the garrison holding the enclave of Oran. By now the Arabs had agreed to bury their differences, if temporarily, to serve under the leadership of a chieftain whose unifying influence was to be as great as that of Ibn Saud in the twentieth century. This was the handsome, twenty-five-year-old Abd-el-Kader, son of an influential sheikh and a young man already touched by the lustre of the hadj, or pilgrimage, thousands of miles across the desert to Mecca. El-Kader was a superb horseman and a natural soldier who dreamed of uniting all the Maghreb tribes under a federal government. Clad in the patriotic green of Islam, astride a white horse, he was endorsed by hundreds of imams preaching holy war against France.

The tribes responded readily to his call to arms. A passion for soldiering, paradoxically, was the one real point of contact they had with the French invader. They also had a good, meaty reason for their quarrel in spite of the peace treaty signed soon after the French landing. Had not General Savary executed two Muslim leaders whose safety he had personally guaranteed? What the tribes would not accept, however, was an ordered, disciplined government which reduced their right to rob one another as well as passing strangers.

On 11 November 1832, on a hill above the entrance to Oran, el-Kader led a characteristically tempestuous cavalry charge of 3,000 horse supported by 1,000 infantry. The first wave was stopped by artillery. As the second came in the French counter-attacked, supported by the Spanish legionnaires on foot. These veterans of the Peninsular War – guerrillas who were most at

home in close-quarter fighting with knife and bayonet – knew
about cavalry charges. They weaved into the mass of enemy
horseflesh, cutting saddle straps, disembowelling horses,
bayoneting the riders' legs and underparts and, when they could
dismount a rider, slitting his throat. The battle flowed back and
forth through the day but Oran was never seriously threatened.
At dusk, el-Kader's force withdrew leaving its dead. The lesson
was obvious: hit the French from the flank or the rear, but never
from the front, in the open.

In June 1835, el-Kader had his revenge just twenty-five miles
south-east of Oran in a shallow mountain pass shaded by trees.
Under General Trézel a punitive column of twenty heavy car-
riages escorted by 2,000 men and six horse-drawn guns was
ambushed by Arab cavalry. General Huré's team records:

> Units were seized with panic; carriages abandoned; the wounded left
> with throats cut. Yet some groups and individuals showed great
> courage, among them the 1st Bataillon d'Afrique [the criminal
> 'Joyeux'] who cut a way through for the column to escape; a
> rearguard spontaneously formed by 40 Chasseurs d'Afrique, gun-
> ners and about 50 soldiers of all arms saved the column from
> annihilation.

This version, in a history of the Armée d'Afrique, makes no
mention of the Legion's role. After the initial attack, at a spot
known as Moulay-Ismael, Trezel's column made a ragged retreat
towards the coast and the sanctuary of Arzew, a small town
recently occupied by the French. The most direct route lay across
a flat, gleaming, hardened salt marsh. It took forty-eight painful,
limping hours to cover the twenty miles or so to the marsh but at
least Abd-el-Kader's men had withdrawn. Or so it seemed. In
fact, word was spreading through the hills that the French were in
trouble, an easy target for blood sport and loot, not at all like the
formidable, organized defence before Oran. Their courage raised
by this knowledge, Arab volunteers flocked to join the attacking
force which swept down in the full heat of day to overrun the
remnants of Trezel's team. By now, probably sent out as an
emergency reinforcement, two battalions of the Legion were also
on hand, one Italian, one Spanish, to which were attached one or
two companies of the 7th Polish. The Italians lost Lieutenant

Boldini; the Poles, Lieutenant Josevitch; the Spaniards, their leader Major Horain.

So much is certain. The rest is a matter of intelligent speculation since no Legion historian agrees about the regiment's true role in the events of that day. The hagiographers assert that the legionnaires were all, without exception, heroic. Others believe that, while some men held their ground and fought with the inhuman doggedness that was subsequently to make the Legion a by-word for courage, this was not true of everyone on the Macta salt marsh on 28 June. In particular, it is alleged that the Italians broke ranks and abandoned the wounded to be emasculated by Bedouin women; further, that the Spaniards, who had fought well, at the end of the day turned upon their Italian comrades and murdered a number of them as a reprisal for their desertion. The retreat became a rout, however, and those who could save themselves, did so. Soon afterwards, under a new commanding officer, monolingual units ceased to exist, while the Spanish battalion, as such, was disbanded.

The survivors of the Legion who marched back into Oran were immediately packed aboard waiting ships to take them across the Mediterranean to another war in Spain. From Oran, their ships sailed first to Algiers, where no one was allowed to go ashore; then on to Palma, Majorca, where the other battalions, which had sailed from Algiers before the battle of the salt marsh, were waiting. The rank and file probably did not yet know it, but they were no longer part of the French army. Under an agreement signed by Louis-Philippe in June the preceding year (1834), they had been handed over to an infant Spanish queen and her regent-mother, for use in a civil war. The French king undertook 'not to recall the legionnaires to the service of France unless Her Majesty the Queen-Regent formally consented to this'.

Pay, pension rights, the cost of feeding and clothing the 4,000 men of the first Foreign Legion, were also bestowed upon the new proprietor, who never honoured them. The men were now doubly exiled, with no rights left to them. None of their achievements in Iberia would be recorded in regimental journals or on regimental colours. They were that most ludicrous product of the military world, the unpaid mercenary. Even the criminal Joyeux received a better deal at French hands. The Foreign Legion, in French eyes, no longer existed. It had to be reinvented from scratch, with a brand new royal decree, on 16 December 1835. The most compelling reason for this was that the Armée d'Afrique had taken a punishing reverse at Arab hands in an unsuccessful effort to seize Constantine. France needed more new blood.

The cause for which the Legion fought in Spain was not a good one. A Spanish king had decided to change the rules of succession so as to ensure that the throne would pass to his only child, a daughter, Isabella. His younger brother, Don Carlos, was thus deprived of the legal right to succeed and so the civil war began, with Britain and France vying with one another to curry favour with Isabella's mother, María Cristina. The opposing ends in the deadly game which followed were thus the Carlists versus the Cristinos. The Carlist stronghold was the natural fortress of the Pyrenees and the regions immediately below them – from Navarre on the Bay of Biscay to Catalonia overlooking the Mediterranean – and it was here that the first French Foreign Legion died slowly and painfully between August 1835 and December 1838. Tarragona, where they disembarked, is a Catalan port. No surprise, therefore, that among the applauding crowd as they swaggered ashore – 123 officers, 4,021 Other Ranks – there were Carlist agents present to note the style of this new, alien opposition.

There were some surprises. The commander, Colonel Joseph Bernelle, was a Napoleonic veteran whose notoriously short temper had considerable impact on Legion discipline. For this adventure he had surrounded himself with a bodyguard of pioneers, large, bearded men wielding axes as a symbol of their calling. Yet more colourful was the Colonel's lady, Madame Tharsile Bernelle. She also wore a sort of uniform and was surrounded by her personal staff of young, handsome officers. No one who was with the unit for longer than a day or so was unaware that in Bernelle's Legion the way to promotion and preferment was through the Colonel's lady. The men called her 'Queen Isabella III' or, more simply, '*La Putain*', the whore. Her imperious manner anticipated Lewis Carroll's Queen of Hearts as she passed instant sentence ('Eight days in the cells!') on any legionnaire who caused her offence. Officers were demoted and

ORs flogged as her appetite for control of the regiment grew. It was not an ideal recipe for good regimental morale unless Bernelle — like some other commanders — believed that aggravation made men fighting mad.

Those who wanted relief from such insanity could serve with the Alsatian Colonel Conrad, Bernelle's junior, a small man whose men adored him. They adored his command of five languages, his ability to remember everyone's Christian name and, most of all, his personal courage. He led from the front, always on a white horse, armed only with a swagger stick. At the start of operations, Conrad commanded an advance guard of three Legion battalions whose first job was to halt an advance by 5,000 Carlists on the Aragon hills overlooking their port of disembarkation.

When Conrad arrived at Lérida, a hill town that was the main operations centre, his force was promptly divided by the Spanish high command into penny packets to reinforce static defensive positions in a series of mountain outposts. The pattern of this war was already bearing some resemblance to Algeria. The regular, government forces could hold population centres but everything else was under the control of enemy guerrillas. Yet by offering themselves as bait, and raising the temperature, the Legion lured the guerrillas into pitched battles which cost them dear.

It was also, from the outset, a dirty war: an outpost of thirty legionnaires led by Second Lieutenant Dumoustier fought for several days against a besieging force ten times that number, and then exploited surprise to break out of encirclement. Betrayed by a guide, Dumoustier's men were taken prisoner. When they refused to change sides they were paraded naked for three days through the area, roped together by the neck. One version of the story asserts that the captive legionnaires' eyes were put out. Dumoustier and three NCOs were then shot. Others were tortured to death. When word of what had happened reached the Legion, the inevitable cycle of matching one atrocity with another was set in motion. Three Legion companies under Captain Ferrary pursued the remnants of a numerically superior force which he had repelled after sixteen hours' combat. About eighty guerrillas took refuge in a local castle. Ferrary invested it.

After a four-day siege the guerrillas surrendered, and were promptly butchered by their Legion captors.

Throughout the bitterly cold winter of 1835–36 the Legion marched up the Ebro valley and then into the Pyrenees proper, lashed by hail and Madame Bernelle's abuse. Even in May, the snow and cold were relentless that year and their boots were wearing out. By now, Bernelle had learned not to trust his Spanish allies (hardly surprising: as one of Napoleon's old guard, he knew what had happened during the Peninsular War). Before he and his men were staked out in Navarre's hostile capital, Pamplona, he forced through a reorganization of the Legion to create an all-arms force including, as an organic entity, its own artillery, sappers and cavalry. The latter job remained the exclusive preserve of the Poles, many ex-Huzzars, all trained horsemen, thus making an exception to the new rule that all units must be multi-national. A mystery surrounds this reorganization. No Legion officer at this time could obtain pay, rations, food or clothes for his soldiers. Yet the reorganization required guns, horses and other valuable stores. How was this financed?

The answer may lie in a desperate measure taken by hungry legionnaires led by Colonel Conrad later that year, just before Christmas, to solve the other basic problems mentioned above. According to Legion historian Pierre Sergent, the unit went on a *razzia*, or looting expedition on a Pyrenean town from which they seized twelve wealthy citizens as hostages. It is a reasonable guess that the horses for the cavalry, the lances, artillery pieces, gun limbers were simply scrounged, or picked up as war booty.

That spring of 1836 was memorable for one other episode in a slogging campaign by the Cristinos forces to hold a defensive line against an enemy who, all too often, had the advantage of the high ground. At an obscure mountain village called Zubiri, Sergeant Samuel-Benoit Berset, a Swiss giant, was in charge of a reconnaissance patrol which was ambushed by enemy horsemen summoned by hostile locals. Berset stood his ground, ramming his bayonet into anything that approached him. He shot, at point-blank range, the Carlists' charismatic cavalryman El Rojo. According to Erwan Bergot's account in *Historia Special No. 414 bis* Berset himself 'received fifteen bayonet wounds, three blows from a lance and two sabre strokes, a total of twenty-two wounds'. As the Carlists broke off the engagement, the legion-naires – now reinforced – chased them, killed 200 in battle and took thirty prisoners. On their side the Carlists 'burned alive five legionnaires whom they had captured and taken back with them'.

Bernelle scourged his men to march from one hot-spot to another and the effect of this mobile brigade group on the front was to multiply the fighting effectiveness of the Legion. Time and again its artillery saved the day. In territory that was unsuitable for cavalry the Poles rode and fought until their horses could stand no longer. They then continued the combat on foot 'without hope of winning, but until death', as one of their enemy conceded (quoted in Pierre Sergent, *La Légion*).

It was from this battle, at Zubiri, that a regimental tradition started to grow: collective death in battle, against hopeless odds on behalf of a lost cause, as a sacramental act. It was to be repeated many times; so often as to become a trademark of the Legion. On this occasion its effect upon the enemy – a tough, guerrilla force fighting on its own, mountain territory – was to force upon it an uncharacteristic prudence. At the end of a succession of running battles that April, the Carlists withdrew, having lost 1,000 men. The Legion's fatal casualties were around 300.

Of greater concern to the old veteran Bernelle, if not to his strange young wife, was the increasing rate of desertion. He made a final appeal to the French and Spanish governments for his soldiers' wages, rations and clothes and when that went un-heeded, offered his resignation. Possibly to his surprise – for he had worked miracles as a tactical fighter – it was promptly accepted. Accompanied (to audible sighs of relief) by his wife, he returned to France. His successor, a buffoon named Lebeau (who wore his sword secured to his body by a piece of rope) was replaced a month later by Conrad, who had himself resigned some months earlier in protest at Madame Bernelle's interfer-ence in regimental affairs. Now Conrad was back, to a unit which was fast disintegrating.

Conrad poured his own fortune into the men's pockets, since no one else would pay them; and his officers dined with him, at his expense also. He could not make good the absent boots or the total indifference of Paris or of war-weary Madrid. It was appropriate, if tragic, that Conrad should meet his end the same day that the first Foreign Legion died as a fighting force. After a winter in the Pyrenees even more debilitating than its predecessor, the legionnaires were half starved and clothed in rags. The Paris newspapers were carrying stories about the scandalous neglect suffered by the Legion. In March 1837, War Minister Maison grudgingly sent a supply of new clothes. This arrived not long before the men were led by Conrad into battle for the last time on 2 June 1837.

Jaunty as ever on a white horse, Conrad pointed forward towards the enemy on the other side of an olive grove above the old town of Barbastro and ordered, '*En avant!*' He spurred his animal and moved off. His Spanish allies stayed where they were. Possibly they knew that Conrad's preferred route was right in the path of the Carlist regular army, and that Don Carlos himself was leading it. Conrad did not look back, did not see that behind him there was a meagre group of legionnaires on foot and a few of his officers, including Bazaine, on horse. A heavy volley of artillery fire sent cannonballs ripping through the trees. Then, from Conrad's right flank, came the enemy infantry. He wheeled his horse to face them, his cap perched on his cane as a signal.

As the two enemy forces came closer, something eerie occurred. Every legionnaire noticed it. The enemy had familiar faces, wore familiar uniforms; they were brothers – or former brothers – in arms. The deserters, it appeared, had not melted away; they had joined the other side. There was a short, strange pause as shouted greetings were exchanged. The greetings gave way to questions about old friends. This Carlist legion included other ghosts: men who had been banished by Louis-Philippe in 1830, or who were determined not to serve that dubious king; Germans and Swiss of the old guard of Napoleonic times, veterans of the Hohenlohe Regiment. They were professionals. They had not been starved by their masters. Now they would go about their work. Even the Carlist officers, however, were surprised by the animal ferocity which boiled out of both sides at that moment, as if the pent-up frustrations of a lifetime were obtaining release. After the first volley or two no one paused to reload. The battle became a brutal, close-quarter affair in which rifles and muskets were used as clubs; knives and bayonets, swords and rocks were used; boots and fists were applied by one group of legionnaires to another in a parody of military science.

Conrad was one of the first victims. A musket ball at close range struck his head. His loyal Lieutenant Bazaine swept him up, pretending to the troops that their beloved Colonel was only scratched, and rode back with the slight figure leaning against him. Conrad lost a lot of blood, much of it over Bazaine's tunic.

Of the Carlist legion of 875 men, only 160 survived, most of them severely wounded; Bazaine was one of a charmed 130 of the official Foreign Legion still alive. For the next eighteen months, this remnant stayed miserably in a camp near Saragossa until, at last, Spain indicated to France that it had no further use for it. They marched six days to Jaca, a town near the Spanish frontier with France, still carrying the regimental colour sent to them by Louis-Philippe. At Jaca they sought permission to rest overnight; begged for a little food. María Cristina's local representative, the Military Governor, had them moved on like vagrants. So, somehow, they marched another three days to the 5,500-foot Somport Pass, and then two more days to Pau. There they presented themselves on 10 January 1839 for further service to France, a Foreign Legion now reduced to just sixty-three officers of whom only twenty-nine were French nationals; and 159 Other Ranks, including a mere twenty-five Frenchmen. Grudgingly, they were given house room by an organization which had all but forgotten their existence. They lost all seniority. In some cases, commissioned officers were reduced to the ranks for having, perhaps, succeeded against all odds.

Some comparative casualty statistics set the Spanish adventure in its real context as a carefully chosen cemetery for those whom Paris regarded as dubious elements. The Legion dead during the three years of the campaign totalled twenty-eight officers, ninety-eight NCOs and 977 legionnaires. In Algeria, between 1831 and official 'pacification' in 1882, the fatalities were twenty-seven officers, sixty-one NCOs and 756 legionnaires. Spain probably cost more Legion lives than any other campaign during the regiment's first 100 years with the sole exception of the Western Front during World War I.

During the Legion's wasted years in Spain, the Algerian campaign continued, relentlessly. There were opponents of French occupation other than Abd-el-Kader, including lesser Arab chieftains and warlike non-Arabs such as the Kabylie tribes of the Atlas mountains. But until 1847 Abd-el-Kader was the most consistent and quick-witted of France's enemies in the region and the war between the two – as Professor Cobban reminds us – was 'bloody and barbarous' on both sides:

> The Algerians massacred their prisoners; the French destroyed crops, orchards, villages and asphyxiated 600 men, women and children who had taken refuge in a cave. Behind the fighting, colonization was slowly but steadily proceeding. By 1847 Algeria had 109,000 Europeans, about half of them French, and the new French Empire, with its promises and problems, was solidly founded. It was the achievement of the constitutional monarchy even though Louis-Philippe had taken no particular interest in it himself. [Alfred Cobban, *A History of Modern France, Vol. 2*]

The dynamic force behind this new French empire, which was to extend well beyond the African continent, was the Armée d'Afrique. As often as the generals were told to occupy no more territory, so they would embark upon a new campaign for the glory of France. Time and again, Paris faced a *fait accompli* and a new territorial acquisition which it could not bring itself to reject.

For the soldiers, the chronic problem of continuous expansion was one of insufficient military manpower. When the first Foreign Legion was arbitrarily handed over to the infant Isabella, its departure created an embarrassing hole in the resources of France's man in Algiers, Count Bertrand Clauzel, who was intent upon revenging the defeat at the Macta salt marsh with new punitive columns. The answer was to resurrect the Foreign Legion as if the first episode (and the men concerned in it) had never happened. So on 16 December 1835 – just four months after the old Legion landed at Tarragona – Louis-Philippe signed a new decree creating a new entity. This date, rather than 10 March 1831, marks the foundation of the regiment still in being.

The new regiment formed up at Pau in the French Pyrenees and was promptly despatched to Algiers. Its re-creation benefited from a brief period in government by the pro-military historian

Adolphe Thiers, France's Prime Minister from February until September 1836. Thiers, stirred by over-optimistic reports sent by Clauzel from Algiers, endorsed a policy of total occupation by France. When Thiers lost office the new administration turned down Clauzel's strident appeals for another 30,000 men. Yet in spite of the fact that he now suffered severe 'overstretch' problems, Clauzel obstinately marched on Constantine, a fortress held by 1,500 Turks and the Kabylie warriors of the *Dey* Ahmad. Clauzel was roundly defeated in this winter campaign, and marched miserably back through hail and snow to Algiers and disgrace.

Contemporary historians of the Legion prefer to celebrate the second, successful assault on Constantine almost exactly a year later on 13 October 1837. When the legionnaires arrived before their allotted position they found it fearfully exposed. Sheer cliffs surrounded the objectives on three sides while from the fourth artillery poured shot upon them. After several days of skirmishing, French artillery breached the walls and at 7 a.m. the first of 20,000 men of the Armée d'Afrique poured into the city led by de la Moricière's Zouaves, Colonel Michel Combe's fighting 47th Infantry, the Legion's only marching battalion commanded by Major Bedeau, and two battalions of Joyeux. In the intense house-to-house fighting that followed, several officers were killed. In spite of two severe chest wounds Combes – who had commanded the old Legion before its despatch to Spain – insisted on delivering his report in person to his brigade Commander, the Duke of Nemours. According to General Huré, the Duke interrupted him: 'But Colonel, you are wounded are you not?'

'No my lord,' Combes replied unblinkingly, 'I am dead.'

He was, just twenty-four hours later. The French lost thirteen other officers including their Commander-in-Chief, General Damrémont, in conquering this Kabylie stronghold. It was not a style of warfare in which the rank and file exclusively took the risks, and the generals the glory. The Legion's assault was led by a furious gambler and hellrake known at that time as Captain Jacques Leroy, who had some colourful things to say about leading a death-or-glory assault on Friday the 13th of the month in an odd-numbered year. His team hurled themselves through two barricades across the winding, narrow streets. Amid smoke, gunshot and confusion Sergeant-Major Doze seized the enemy colour. His feat is commemorated in a famous painting by Benigni and it led to the 1st Foreign Legion Regiment's being awarded the cross of the Legion of Honour to be attached to its own regimental flag . . . sixty-nine years later in 1906. By then, the Legion was becoming half-accepted as part of France's military tradition and Leroy, with the snobbish addition of 'Saint Arnaud' to his name, later became a Marshal of France.

For a short time in 1839 it seemed that Louis-Philippe might pull it off. Until then not even the French would acknowledge him as legitimate inheritor of the throne. He was like Don John of Austria, risen – in Chesterton's phrase – from a doubtful seat and half-attained stall, neither true royal nor commoner, target of a near-miss bomb plot in 1835, an upstart King who whinged to Victor Hugo that other European monarchs 'hate me for myself'.

His credibility needed some exotic triumphs, one of which was a characteristically showy march made in 1839 by his eldest son and heir, the Duke of Orléans, from Constantine to Algiers, across territory accorded to Abd-el-Kader under a preace treaty agreed with the French General Bugeaud two years before. The young Duke (one of four brothers among 'a family of brilliant second lieutenants') [Cobban: Ibid] required an escort of 5,000 soldiers.

The Arab leader promptly declared a jihad, or holy war, against France so, in the event, the young Duke's royal gesture cost seven years of conflict and thousands of lives. Within two years the Armée d'Afrique had expanded from 40,000 to 70,000. At the height of the campaign it consisted of almost 90,000 men. The Foreign Legion would double its strength from one regiment to two. Ironically, Abd-el-Kader's surrender on 23 December 1847 was followed within a few weeks by a revolution in France and the end of Louis-Philippe's reign. One advantage of this was that the royal princelings could no longer dabble in the deadly serious business of guerrilla warfare.

The increase in French manpower at the beginning of the war was the direct result of some near-disasters provoked by the French habit of placing insufficient garrisons in hostile territory. Three of these were immediately besieged for months and most of the men inside them condemned to a lingering death. When the

Spanish War veteran Bazaine (now a major) and other soldiers of the Legion took over one of these outposts, a little town called Miliana seventy desolate miles from the nearest external aid at Algiers, in June 1840, it was already a smoking ruin. The garrison of 1,200 men which was to hold it comprised one battalion of Joyeux, the Legion's 1st Battalion, and five guns. In five months they were reduced by disease and guerrilla warfare to just fifty active men. According to Philip Guedalla:

> It was now the height of summer and their stores were insufficient from the start . . . The whole garrison went down with dysentery and fever, until they could rarely muster more than a hundred men fit for duty on the walls against the daily raids of Abd-el-Kader's waiting tribesmen. Men went mad; a few deserted; the two battalions melted into one; and in sixteen awful weeks nearly three-quarters of them died in hospital. The walls were manned by anyone who could stand; they even had a sing-song twice a week. But their hopes gradually faded until an Italian legionnaire, who had graduated in Abd-el-Kader's arsenal, slipped out of Miliana in native dress with a despairing note in cipher . . . Five weeks later he was back again with word that General Changarnier was on his way to their relief. They held on for another fortnight; and when the dapper general appeared . . . the tricolour still fluttered over Miliana. [Philip Guedalla, *The Two Marshals*]

As a result of such errors, things changed. For once, the policy of singling out a scapegoat (in this case the Governor of Algeria, Marshal Valée) did achieve, with his replacement, a real shift in policy. The new supremo was Bugeaud, who stamped his will all but indelibly on Algeria for the next century. He it was who insisted that 'containment' of the Arab rebels was totally inadequate; that total occupation and colonization were the only alternative to total withdrawal. 'We must lead a great invasion of Africa in the style of the Franks and the Goths,' he declared, and meant it.

Thomas-Robert Bugeaud de la Piconnerie was the son of a prosperous farmer promoted to corporal in Napoleon's army on the battlefield of Austerlitz. For him the Algerian war was a means to an end, the end being the creation of a great French farm full of worthy yeoman-settlers. His approach was not dissimilar from that of other yeoman-farmers who had opened up the

American West, with a similarly patronizing attitude to non-European natives. But, like any professional, he took the war seriously and – in spite of accusations that he was obstinate, or lacked intelligence – rapidly made innovations which destroyed Abd-el-Kader's power base.

First, Bugeaud re-equipped his soldiers. He took off their heavy, European shakos and replaced them with light kepis. He converted the best infantry, including the Legion, into mounted infantry equipped with mules for greater mobility and removed the absurdly overweight, 100lb packs the men were expected to carry in mountainous terrain in the Mediterranean heat. Most significant of all, he replaced the strategy of fixed, defensive outposts with a vigorous policy of offensive sweeps through the countryside. It was effective but, as a sometime Legion officer Saint Arnaud would admit, 'not a pretty nor an amusing war' . . . 'We have burned everything, destroyed everything. How many women and children have died of cold and fatigue!'

Colonel Pélissier, the man responsible for the asphyxiation of 600 people in a cave, is on record describing how Algerian women decapitated wounded French soldiers, 'then allowed themselves to be massacred, with a child at their breast, with the most awful resignation'.

According to the writer Edward Behr, in *The Algerian Problem*, Saint Arnaud learned something about press relations from the row Pélissier's actions provoked in Paris: 'Barely two months later, Saint Arnaud suffocated 1,500 Moslems in another cave, carefully left no survivors to tell the story, and in a confidential message reported to Bugeaud, "No one went into the cave; not a soul . . . but myself".'

Yet for some people, including Louis-Philippe's 'brilliant lieutenants', the war was an exercise in military chic. On 15 March 1844 the king's fourth son, the Duke of Aumale, insisted on taking over command of 2nd Foreign Legion in a high-risk, uphill assault on the Berber mountain village of M'Chounech. Lieutenant-Colonel (later Marshal) MacMahon reduced the risk to the royal hero by sending Louis Espinasse, his most courageous captain, with a small party to act as decoys. Espinasse, hit several times by Kabylie gunfire, survived, and next day received from the young Duke the Légion d'honneur.

Step by step, Abd-el-Kader's men were driven from town to village, village to obscure hamlet, and finally by Bugeaud's scorched-earth strategy into nomadism. The Arab rebellion headquarters became a community – a 'smala' – of 60,000 men and women of all ages as well as camels, mules and horses constantly on the move, its presence betrayed at a distance by a moving cloud of dust. In May 1843 the twenty-one-year-old Duke of Aumale learned that the veteran Colonel de la Moricière was stalking the smala as it moved south towards the sanctuary of a plateau on the edge of the Sahara. The Duke decided to get there first and put together a column of light infantry, cavalry and a section of mountain guns. After several days he divided his forces and took off with a lightly-armed reconnaissance cavalry group. This, by chance, stumbled into the area where the smala was setting up camp. The Duke immediately gave the order to attack without waiting for the infantry and artillery to arrive. The French horsemen struck from two sides, simultaneously. There was much confused fighting during which the Arabs lost 300 dead and the French, nine. The rest of the smala escaped but Paris delighted in the romantic image of a young prince charging so heedlessly into battle, and surviving.

Abd-el-Kader made his way to Morocco, where he set up a permanent base from which to harass the French. France responded with a naval fleet (commanded by another junior royal, the Prince de Joinville) which bombarded Tangier. In August 1844, Bugeaud invaded Morocco with 11,500 men and defeated the Moroccan army at the Battle of Isly. It was not an action in which the Legion participated but it did mark the end of Abd-el-Kader's long fight to keep the French out of Algeria. By the time he surrendered formally in December 1847 he was a spent force. The French were able to betray the terms of his surrender without fear of reprisal. From now on, France was the master of Algeria and – until 1962 – indigenous opposition was a rebellion against the 'official' government.

Fate, and the French, were not so unkind to Abd-el-Kader in the end. After a period of imprisonment in France (in contrast to a promise of liberty outside Algeria, but in the Near East) he was sent to Damascus on a pension. There in 1860 he intervened at the risk of his own life to save 12,000 Christians, many of them

Frenchmen, from the Turks. For this he was awarded the Légion d'honneur. He passed the rest of his life in scholarship, creating a vast library in Damascus, and becoming an international celebrity welcomed to exhibitions in London and the inauguration of the Suez Canal. He died in 1883 and is interred in the Great Omayyad Mosque in Damascus. In Algeria, a million colonists were setting up shop, including ex-legionnaires and a community of Trappist monks. Rarely in history can a fly-whisk have been wielded to such drastic effect.

CHAPTER 2
An Elite Marches Out
(Crimea, Italy, 1848–60)

The Empire Means Peace.

– Napoleon III, 1852

La Légion est dans Magenta: l'affaire est
dans le sac!

– General MacMahon, 1859

From the surrender of Abd-el-Kader to World War I almost seventy years later, the Foreign Legion acquired just three battle honours in Algeria. Starting from scratch, the regiment also built its home at Sidi-bel-Abbès, Algeria. Thus it was physically as well as culturally part of that strange entity the Armée d'Afrique, the French equivalent of Abd-el-Kader's *smala*, a nomadic community condemned to perpetual exile from everything except its own day-to-day survival. Although the regiment's adventures (and cemeteries) during this period truly circle the globe, the unit was never in one place long enough to put down roots.

The list of places where it dug its graves, however, is impressive: 1854–5; the Crimea; 1859, War of Italian Unification; 1863–7, Mexico; 1870–71 France, to fight first the Prussians, then the Parisian Communards; 1882–1907, Morocco's Empty Quarter of South Oranais; 1883, Tonkin; 1885, Formosa; 1892, Dahomey, West Africa; 1893, Sudan; 1895, Madagascar; 1907–14, Morocco.

Louis-Philippe's reign had ended in 1848, as it began, with riots on the streets of Paris. The spark which ignited his pyre was his scheme to reduce unemployment in Paris by ordering all unmarried men drawing dole to join the army. Six days of street combat around the French capital were then ruthlessly suppressed by the National Guard.

His successor was Bonaparte's nephew Louis, elected President on a law-and-order platform. His 'Second Republic' lasted until 1851 when, having decided to ignore the constitutional requirement to submit himself for re-election, he engineered a putsch in which France's 'Algerian' generals were indispensable. Their leader, Saint Arnaud, is alleged by some historians to have been bribed for his participation.

Whatever the truth of that, some 50,000 soldiers seized the key points of Paris and arrested hundreds of MPs on the night of 1–2 December 1851. Protesters manning barricades were summarily executed. Of 30,000 people arrested, 9,000 were transported to Algeria. The Armée d'Afrique was receiving from Napoleon's nephew, now known as Napoleon III, its first lesson in the uses of military muscle in and upon Paris itself and the 'Second Republic' was now the 'Second Empire'.

After the *coup d'état* the army withdrew and the reign of Napoleon III embarked upon a course whose motto was 'The Empire Means Peace'. This was too good to last in the expansionist, acquisitive nineteenth century. In 1853 Russia invaded Turkish territory ostensibly as part of a quarrel about who should guard and maintain shrines in the Holy Land; in fact, to control the Black Sea entrance through the occupation of Istanbul. France believed she was responsible for the shrines of Christendom. More to the point, she did not wish to be elbowed aside by the British, who were sending an expedition to aid Turkey. So, although she had been at war with the Turks elsewhere for much of the preceding twenty years, France also joined in the conflict on Turkey's side. It was a cynical war which would cost the lives of around 300,000 men, most of them from cholera.

Part of that loss occurred during the Charge of the Light Brigade at Balaclava in 1854. Long after the causes of the war were forgotten, memories of British military incompetence in an age when commissions were sold to rich dilettantes lingered to give soldiering a bad name. For the elderly, one-armed Lord Raglan and his team, fighting their first campaign since Waterloo forty years before, the strain of the Crimea rapidly became manifest, not least through Raglan's habit of describing the enemy not as the Russians but as the French. Leading the French, the venal Saint Arnaud, former gambler, deserter and specialist in suffocation, was also a dying man, a walking skeleton who coughed blood. Shortly before this campaign he had been warned by doctors that he had only a few months to live.

As a result of his cholera, Saint Arnaud was by turns hyperactive and incapable of movement. He did not wish his former regiment, the Legion, to take part in this campaign but, at the last moment, the 1st and 2nd regiments totalling 4,500 men had been added to the French contingent. On 20 September 1854, as they marched in a tight formation, uphill towards death and glory on the enemy side of the river Alma, Saint Arnaud shouted: 'Forward, the élite battalion.' He then spurred his horse forward as if to take command of the assault. The officer actually in command of the Legion, Colonel Achille Bazaine, was as imperturbable as usual and the two men led the assault together. Soon they were joined by a third senior officer, General François Canrobert.

The objective beyond this battle was an advance on Sebastopol to seize that great fortress with its vast naval base. If Russia lost that, the back of its power in the Black Sea would be broken and the war decided. Equally, if the Allies did not cross the river Alma to come within gun range of Sebastopol's city walls, then they might as well return home without delay. The Russians had chosen to defend Sebastopol on the Alma. So this confrontation was the most important of the Crimean War.

British historians blame the French for their late start that day, and the French still blame the English fondness for a solid, expansive breakfast. Raglan had ordered his infantry – Highlanders led by their pipers and red-coated guardsmen – to advance at 2.30. They marched as if at a military tattoo before Queen Victoria, one French officer observed. Having waded the river the British, on the left of the line, stormed the highest point held by the Russians, the Great Redoubt, defended by fourteen heavy guns. At the beginning of the assault, a gap had opened between the two allied armies, and Raglan rode through it. He established an observation post and two guns upon a prominent knoll actually inside the Russian lines. The Russians naturally assumed that the French were at least level with him. In fact, some of the fiery Berbers of the 3rd Zouaves were ahead of him. Starting at the extreme right-hand flank, out of sight of the

British, they had scrambled on foot, their rifles with bayonets fixed, to the plateau on the enemy side of the line. Soon they were joined by the legionnaires of the neighbouring Canrobert division. The French lost sixty dead in this action; the British, 362; the Russians, 1,807. The Allies then allowed the Russian Prince Menshikov to withdraw unhindered to Sebastopol across open country, with most of his force intact, thereby imposing upon themselves the deadly obligation of besieging the port throughout a Russian winter and a new epidemic of cholera.

In the leisurely way of a gentleman's campaign, the opposing leaders exchanged bows and decorous salutes when they were not actually engaged slaughtering one another, and their wives came along too. None was more fetching than the young bride of the Legion commander Bazaine, now promoted to the rank of Brigadier. When Bazaine had first met Maria de la Soledad Indria Gregoria Tormo he was a half-colonel in charge of the Arab Bureau in Tlemcen (Algeria) as a change from regimental soldiering. She was seventeen, flirtatious and the daughter of his Spanish landlady, an innkeeper. At his expense she was educated at a good school in Marseilles, where she became an accomplished pianist. They married just before setting off for the Crimea. Her luggage included a grand piano.

So equipped, Madame Bazaine was able to serenade those of the dying who could be brought within earshot. Fashionable Parisians thought this very chic. When she was not comforting the dying she was sometimes to be found entertaining Saint Arnaud's successor and fellow-asphyxiator, General Pélissier. This gallantry continued for months while Bazaine – also promoted to General but still Pélissier's junior – was kept busy by his boss fighting the war. The British high command offered no more inspiring an example. One observer noted at this time that 'Lord Raglan lives in his house for days together and is not visible'. Raglan, like Saint Arnaud, was a cholera victim.

Outside the confines of Madame Bazaine's boudoir and Raglan's sick-room, the Anglo-French force passed a hideous winter in the trenches before Sebastopol. The siege followed a classic routine. Daylight hours were spent in prolonged artillery duels, the night in stealthy patrolling across no man's land, a pattern the Legion would experience almost a century later at Bir Hakeim and Dien Bien Phu. For the besiegers at Sebastopol it was hard to judge which was worse: the temperature well below freezing when there was insufficient warm clothing, or the mud that seeped into the trenches whenever the temperature started to rise.

In such conditions it was not surprising that two legionnaires took an interest in their neighbours of the Royal Welch Fusiliers or, rather, in the goat presented to that regiment by the Queen herself eleven years earlier. Having befriended the official 'Goat Major' with cognac they slipped into the goat's quarter one night and gave it a lethal dose of poison. The creature was dead next morning; buried with full military honours in the afternoon and – under cover of darkness the same short winter day – disinterred and skinned by its assassins who cured the fleece, after a fashion, and created a perfect garment for such a winter. When the weather got warmer they sold their coat to a British officer on the look-out for a souvenir. He was serving with the Royal Welch Fusiliers.

That is the Legion version. The RWF agrees that its goat did die during the campaign, and that something odd might have happened to the pelt on St David's Day, 1 March 1855. The 'goat' which paraded as custom required in the Officers' Mess on that Welsh national holiday surprised everyone by standing up and quaffing a glass of champagne. Closer scrutiny revealed it to be a certain Private Styles dressed up in a *sheepskin* coat with the dead goat's head on his cap. The circumstances of the goat's death are not recorded in the regimental archive.

The nights were full of clandestine activity. Lieutenant Charles Gordon, Royal Engineers (later to become General Gordon of Khartoum) noted that the French soldiers, better cared for by their officers than the British, were in good spirits, particularly the Zouaves who used to drape French flags over the Russian outworks at night.

Reconnaissance generated a demand for courageous scouts – 'enfants perdus' – who foraged no man's land entirely alone. When they were not officially on duty the same heroes carried out equally dangerous missions strictly for profit, robbing the dead of both sides. The Joyeux were particularly skilled at these games, moving with so light a touch that they also became 'Les Zephyrs' or – because of the commerce which followed next morning – 'Stars of the Bazaar'. Dead men's boots were particularly prized. Some hard-drinking legionnaires sold their own as well as the dear departed's to raise the price of a bottle of cognac. This, it is thought, explains the appearance on parade of one legionnaire whose feet were blackened with boot polish to simulate the boots he no longer had.

From time to time each side agreed upon a ceasefire of limited duration so that the dead could be decently buried. A trumpet call signalled the beginning and end of these occasions when the burial parties, with careful exchanges of mutual courtesy, paraded under white flags. Then the two parties retired and the whole cycle of war, death, grave-robbing, commerce and truce began anew.

By the spring of 1856 the Allied siege was becoming very much a French affair. British incompetence in stores management was now such that the French took over the task of supplying the British force, an event which brought down Lord Aberdeen's government. Sebastopol, a fortress defended by 135,000 men, was besieged by 80,000 French, 22,000 Turks and 10,000 British soldiers. The French force contained a minority of true Frenchmen, however, for this was the Armée d'Afrique fighting for France's reputation: the Zouaves, Algerian Tirailleurs, Spahis, Bats d'Af, were all represented as well as the Legion. With the arrival of spring, Napoleon III became impatient about his army's lack of achievement and so, on 1 May, a nocturnal attack went in to secure a single Russian outpost at a cost of 118 dead. One of these, during a hand-to-hand battle fought with bayonet and sword, was the commanding officer of 1st Foreign Legion, Colonel Vienot. To the dead were added another 480 wounded men; almost 600 missing from the morning roll-call after a single operation of dubious value.

Under further pressure from Napoleon III General Pélissier tried again on 7 June. Two forts standing on high ground at the south-western edge of the walled city – the Redan and the Malakoff – were the keys to Sebastopol. They could only be taken the hard way, by frontal assault, which was why the Zouaves told newcomers that the city would fall 'When there are three Thursdays in a week'. This time the Zouaves and Tirailleurs contrived to occupy a high point outside the city known as Green Hillock. They then assaulted the Malakoff itself, occupied it briefly and were repulsed. On 18 June another general assault went in, aimed at producing a resounding French victory on the anniversary of Waterloo. The French, mistaking some random shooting for the signal to attack, crossed the start line ten minutes' prematurely so that when the British moved forward on time towards the Redan, the Russian defenders were alert and waiting. Caught in open ground the British were torn apart by grapeshot. The French assault was also repulsed. Total Allied casualties were 6,000 including 1,400 French dead.

In September, the Allies ground down the Sebastopol defences with a relentless, three-day barrage of 800 guns under cover of which the infantry inched closer to the walls of the Malakoff fort trench by trench, like military moles, until they were a mere thirty yards from the walls. Finally, on 8 September the strongpoint was seized for good by seven regiments of which four were African (three Zouaves, one Algerian). Only a sprinkling of assault pioneers under Sergeant Valliez represented the Legion. While General MacMahon planted his sword on top of the tower, Corporal Lihaut of 1st Zouaves hoisted a tricolour shredded by missiles. Victory had cost the French dear. The dead in this campaign so far included four generals. Yet for a nation still seeking to expunge the memory of Waterloo, it was regarded as worthwhile.

After Sebastopol crumbled, the Legion was sent under Bazaine to the last centre of Russian resistance, 100 miles away on the northern shore of the Black Sea. A force of two brigades, one English, one French, landed at Kinburn under naval covering fire to attack the fortress there. This was no Sebastopol, however, and the commander surrendered after a five-hour battle. Mopping up resistance elsewhere in the area occupied Bazaine and his men for another two weeks. Meanwhile, the French commander Pélissier had been occupied with other matters. As Bazaine's biographer, Philip Guedella, recounts the story:

Pélissier, a Marshal now, was particularly complimentary. Indeed, his sympathy [for Bazaine] had prompted him to visit Madame Bazaine every afternoon during her husband's brief absence, arriving shortly after three o'clock each day in the only carriage on the peninsula, an ancient coach captured from a Russian prince and now harnessed to a gun-team. This picturesque conveyance brought the playful Marshal to pay his daily call on her in sight of the whole army. But she knew what soldiers were; for Miss Nightingale's was not the only reputation made in the Crimean War.

Back in Paris, the Legion was given the customary recognition for its services – disbandment. The men were shipped back to Sidi-bel-Abbès. There they enlisted in the new 2nd Foreign Legion Regiment alongside veterans of Kabylie, while the new 1st Foreign Legion Regiment was composed entirely of Swiss who had not fought in the Crimea, or elsewhere for that matter.

Thus, after their service to France in a bitter winter campaign the veterans of the Crimea found that their existing status, and contracts, were of little value. The regiment for which they had bled, and which so obstinately refused to die, had been eliminated at the stroke of a pen. It was a repetition of the experience of the first Foreign Legion raised by Louis-Philippe, twenty years earlier.

For those who returned from the Crimea, there was always another battle to be fought for France. While Arab resistance to French occupation had crumbled with the surrender of Abd-el-Kader, there were other nations obstinately opposed to a European takeover. In the south, the Tuareg – 'the Forgotten of God' – would remain in control of the Sahara until 1905. For them, 'to pillage' and 'to be free' are synonymous. Likewise among the Berbers of Kabylia, who lived in the Atlas mountains looming over Constantine and eastern Algeria, and who still like to think of themselves as *bandits d'honneur*. In 1857, with the Russians defeated, France now turned its attention to subduing the tribes of the Kabylie with a force of 35,000 men commanded by Marshal Jacques de Randon, Napoleon III's man in Algeria. He was not convinced that this was enough force to suppress tribes which had defied fifteen punitive expeditions already.

By June, seven months after the campaign began, the focus of Kabylie resistance was a village named Ischeriden, nestling in the shelter of a natural fortress 5,000 feet high and separated from the surrounding countryside by a ravine 1,000 feet deep. The task of taking this objective was given to MacMahon's division, including the 2nd Zouaves and the reorganized 2nd Foreign Regiment. The Zouaves descended the precipitous forward slope to begin their advance and were instantly pinned down by accurate Kabylie fire. Now it was the Legion's turn. These Crimean veterans led on foot by Major Paul Mangin marched into battle with even more sang-froid than the British at the Alma, rifles over shoulders in true parade-ground fashion. The tribesmen could not believe this. A sporadic burst of fire was aimed at Mangin who, in the way of such heroes, appeared to have a supernatural ability to defy bullets. One other officer was killed and three wounded, as they came remorselessly on but the French tactics, or lack of them, should have ensured the annihilation of the whole regiment.

The legionnaires paused imperceptibly as they came over the rim of Ischeriden plateau, fired their first volley into the tribesmen and then followed through with the bayonet. The defenders broke ranks and fled. Among the Legion's iron men decorated for gallantry that day was an aristocratic priest from Florence, Prince Mori-Ubaldini. The Legion knew him as Sergeant Mori.

For the time being, the Kabylie were subdued, though they rebelled again in 1871. Meanwhile, Napoleon III rewarded Marshal Randon by stripping him of most of his authority in Algeria. One French account relates that Randon resigned on 31 August 1858, a mere fourteen months after the victory at Ischeriden, 'with dignity'. His emperor, meanwhile, dismissively described Algeria as 'a ball and chain attached to the feet of France'. By implication, France had bigger fish to fry in Europe.

Napoleon III (Louis Napoleon) was nicknamed 'the Well Meaning', a polite way of saying that he was a Quixotic figure. Unlike the original Don, however, Louis had a remarkable run of luck which made his wilder adventures seem almost plausible. He had been sentimentally attached to Italian culture since his youth, when he had flirted with revolution there. He decided that he would support the cause of unifying a country split into a number of statelets, most of them controlled by Austria. 'Italy,' it was fashionable to remark in the Austrian capital, 'is no more than a geographical expression.'

Napoleon III's decision meant making common cause with the Piedmontese against Austria but it promised, in French eyes, the acquisition of some useful territory including Nice and Savoy. In a secret meeting with the astute, machiavellian Italian nationalist Count Cavour, the Prime Minister, in July 1858, Napoleon III dispensed with his ministers. Indeed, the key conversation took place while the French Emperor drove a horse-drawn carriage around the little town of Plombières, with Cavour as his only passenger. For France the war which followed the next year, 1859, lasted a mere eight weeks from the opening of hostilities to the armistice. It had to be relatively brief since Austria, in the last analysis, could depend on its German cousin, Prussia.

Louis set off from the Paris Gare de Lyon amid emotional scenes to take personal command of his 140,000-man expeditionary force. He, along with most of that force, missed the first battle completely in a campaign which was like a game of blind man's bluff. As the French advanced on Milan, the Austrians moved to intercept them. MacMahon's division (Tirailleurs, two Zouaves, two Legion regiments) crossed the river Tessin and the Grand Navigation Canal flowing down from the Alps, across their path. The Austrians, having missed their chance to hold a defensive line on these waterways, now found their right flank being turned by a series of localized but nasty attacks launched on them by the Algerian Tirailleurs, the 'Turcos'. Napoleon III, convinced that the main enemy force was miles away, on the other side of Milan, ordered MacMahon to occupy Magenta.

Magenta was a prosperous little market town about ten miles west of Milan, already a place of sufficient importance to be on a railway line running east-west, at right angles to the waterways. Around Magenta was a densely populated rural environment, teeming with smallholdings and walls to mark their precious boundaries. Like the bocage country of Normandy which the Allied invaders of 1944 hated so much, MacMahon's men at Magenta were frustrated for the same reason: there was no visibility beyond fifty metres or so. The same walls and hedges which hampered vision, made it impossible to construct any big military formation. The French force was sub-divided into penny packets.

After a day of confused fighting on the part of other French divisions, in which these were pushed back to the canal bank by Austrian counter-attacks, the Legion, already in the outer suburbs of the town elsewhere, went on to the attack in the evening. The vanguard was the 2nd Foreign Regiment, composed of hard-bitten veterans of the Crimea and pre-Crimea days, which held the line. The commanding officer, Colonel Granet Lacroix de Chabrières, sabre pointing forward, shouted, 'Forward the Legion!' Seconds later, as his men moved with bayonets at the ready, their Colonel – an obvious target on his white horse – was brought down with a bullet in the chest. He died soon after, in the arms of Sergeant-Major Victor Maire.

Chabrières's successor, Jose Martinez, was already in command, shouting his orders in a patois that was neither quite French nor Spanish. Martinez was a rather special veteran of the Carlist War which had bled the first Legion to death. In that war he was the Legion's enemy as well as Queen-Regent María Cristina's lover. For mysterious reasons of his own, he had then trekked across the Pyrenees with the retreating survivors of the first Legion and joined the regiment himself at Pau.

The Austrians recoiled under the first Legion assault and slowly retreated further back into the town, their nerve far from broken. They were hard mountain men from the Tyrol, and this was their third battle of this campaign. The first two – against irregular Piedmontese – had been clear-cut victories. They saw no reason for their luck to change.

For some hours, MacMahon's force was stalled on the outskirts of Magenta while fierce fighting went on to his rear, as the main body of the French army tried to hack its way from near the river to his position. The Legion regrouped under Martinez's direction behind the useful cover of a railway embankment, advanced behind this and then swarmed over it into the town. They were twice repulsed. Then, at last, a relieving force of Grenadiers appeared. The legionnaires cursed them as poachers and charged into the attack once again. In the furious street fighting which ensued, Louis Espinasse – a Legion officer under MacMahon for at least fifteen years – was shot dead at point-blank range through a window. Espinasse was one of two French generals to die that day, a heavy toll when compared with the four officers of that eminence lost during the whole of the Crimean War. The battle within Magenta went on until just before dusk at 9 p.m. but MacMahon, still not in complete control of the outskirts, exulted as soon as he got word that the foreign regiments had penetrated so far. 'The Legion's in Magenta; the job is in the bag!' he declared.

It was a hard-won victory which cost the Legion 300 casualties including some who, according to Hugh McLeave, drowned in wine vats during the looting which followed. Total French losses were 4,000 killed and wounded and 600 missing while the Austrian figures were, respectively, 5,700 and 4,500. Next day, the Legion occupied pride of place in a victory parade through Milan before Napoleon III and the Italian crowned head, Victor Emmanuel. After the parade, the 1st Foreign Regiment, Napoleon III's personal creation commanded by his long-standing friend Ochsenbein, an honorary Swiss general, and manned exclusively by Swiss soldiers, stayed on in Milan. It was suffering from an embarrassing lack of volunteers which it now tried, without success, to make good. It was disbanded soon afterward.

The battle of Solferino on 24 June 1859 was to leave an unexpectedly benign mark on history. The encounter was a particularly brutal one which caused around 40,000 casualties, most of whom were left to die in agony where they fell. As a result of the pain he witnessed, Napoleon III's warrior pretensions were promptly deflated. A Swiss civilian travelling with him, Henri Dunant, was inspired to take the first steps towards creating the International Red Cross Organization. Solferino was yet another clumsy affair in which two sizeable armies totalling about 400,000 soldiers lumbered about, back and forth like drunken giants on a fifteen-mile front with little science or control by the respective high commands. Napoleon III started the day badly by repeating his mistake at Magenta in believing, optimistically, that the enemy had retreated far beyond its true location. On the Austrian side another monarch – the Habsburg Franz Josef – was in command of a force reinvigorated by new regiments.

In fact, from the defeat at Magenta the Austrians had retreated east, across Lombardy, with the French following. The Austrians halted five miles in front of the Mincio river south of Lake Garda and were about to dig in on a series of hills with more than 700 artillery pieces and around 20,000 cavalry. At 3 a.m. on 24 June the French 1st Army Corps under Marshal Baraguey d'Hilliers foraged slowly forward along a ridge and into a valley leading down to Solferino.

At about 5 a.m. that summer morning soldiers on the French right flank, just outside the village of Fontana, were challenged at an Austrian outpost and overran it. A series of contacts now occurred but it was several hours before the commanders appreciated that their two armies were locked in a fight to the death. By mid-afternoon, having used up most of his reserves, Napoleon III had taken a little high ground, eight cannons, a flag and 1,500 prisoners. Against that the Legion – on his right flank – had twice occupied Cavriana, a village a mile or so south-east of Solferino, only to be repelled following spirited counter-attacks by white-coated Austrian infantry. Worse, Austrian cavalry had penetrated like a sword thrust through the French centre. Incompetence had failed to exploit this breakthrough by a single regiment.

Napoleon III, convinced that he was about to lose, arrived on the flank held by the pride of his Armée d'Afrique, the Algerian 'Turkos', and the Legion. By now the area was under increasing artillery fire. The Emperor asked for a last, all-out assault. The Legion stormed forward into Cavriana for a third time while the neighbouring heights of Fontana were seized by the Algerian soldiers. These men, according to a contemporary account quoted by General Huré, 'hurled themselves like the wildcats of their native country upon the Austrian ranks, cutting their throats for pleasure; the terrified Austrians fled.

In fact, in spite of such hyperbole, the issue was still quite finely balanced at mid-afternoon when the storm of battle was magnified by a spectacular summer storm of thunder, lightning, high wind and torrential rain which ran down the Italian hills to mingle with the blood of men and horses. The storm coincided with a charge by French-African cavalry of the Chasseurs d'Afrique, exploiting the flanking assault made by their infantry comrades. In exchange for heavy losses the cavalrymen created havoc in the Austrian rear as they hit gun crews from behind to hack them to death with sabres. It was the last straw. Suddenly, Austrian discipline, excellent until this moment, snapped and its army melted away in the blinding rain like some gigantic theatrical illusion.

If he had enjoyed some military success, Napoleon III had also pushed his luck politically. The Prussians, disturbed by a resurgence of French power in Europe, placed their army on a war footing. The French took the hint and did a quick diplomatic deal to end their intervention at the beginning, rather than the end, of the process of Italian unification. Nevertheless there was a special victory parade in Paris that summer as if Napoleon III's aims had been fulfilled. Permanent, if modest garrisons of Tirailleurs and Spahis were welcomed to the French capital. The Legion was also allowed to parade through Paris for the first time. Immediately afterwards its soldiers were confined to barracks until the next morning, when they were despatched by train to Toulon and from there, by ship, back to Algiers.

CHAPTER 3
Mexican Gold at Camerone
(1861–67)

I preferred to leave foreigners rather than
Frenchmen to guard the most unhealthy
area . . . where malaria reigns.

– General Élie Forey, C-in-C, French expedition
to Mexico, 1863

Non son hombres, son demonios!

– Mexican Colonel Francisco Milan,
after Camerone, 1863

Napoleon III was one of nature's entrepreneurs. When he spotted a chance to collect bad debts on behalf of his half-brother, the Duke de Morny, and to extend the French empire into the New World, he jumped at the chance. In 1861 the Emperor had his eyes on Mexico, confident that he could invade that country without US opposition because the United States was at war with itself. When the American colonies had rebelled against Britain in 1776, France had backed the anti-colonial Americans. Now that there was civil war in the US, eighty years later, France would seek to benefit from that internecine quarrel also by imposing a whole new monarchy on her southern neighbour.

Napoleon III had yet to discover that the Mexicans have a special talent for financial anarchy. In this affair, as often is the way with the Legion's heroism, political squalor was in stark contrast to the idealism of the soldiers. Ultimately, the reason why the Legion was where it was in the 1860s was that one Mexican President, Miguel Miramón, had covered his debts by selling valueless bonds to greedy Europeans who still believed that there was some sort of El Dorado in Central America. Miramón was swept aside in a *coup d'état* and replaced by Benito

Pablo Juárez, who suspended payment of interest on these debts for two years. Spanish, British and French creditors demanded military action from their governments and, surprisingly, succeeded. Only the French persisted, however. Indeed, Napoleon III went far beyond sending a man-o'-war to exact reparation for the unpaid interest. From the house of Habsburg he conjured up a new monarch for Mexico whom he would control. This was Maximilian, the stylish and popular younger brother of Franz Josef, Napoleon's recent enemy in Italy.

In Vienna, Franz Josef counselled Maximilian against taking the contract. So did the British government. Maximilian, dazzled by the prospect of monarchy in a distant land, ignored their advice and joined Napoleon III's latest doomed enterprise.

The Mexicans proved to be anything but a push-over. They drove the first French expeditionary force back into the sea. A second, larger army was despatched and conquered Mexico City but like many other occupying armies it was trapped by the impossible burden of fighting an endless guerrilla war in a country whose population was universally hostile to an alien monarch imposed from outside. An initial French fighting force of 3,000 men in 1862 grew to one of 40,000 under the Legion veteran Bazaine; then was withdrawn completely in 1867 leaving Maximilian to succumb to a firing squad and his Empress to insanity. The soldiers returned to a France governed by an increasingly introverted Emperor, and much snide criticism for the now-unfashionable war they had just fought. As Professors Grant and Temperley point out, the Mexican adventure was a reflection of its architect rather than any military lobby. Of Napoleon III they comment:

> There is no incident more characteristic of the man and his methods; of his brilliant but uncontrolled imagination; of his way of confusing fancy and fact; of his habit of taking up a project with enthusiasm and then dropping it with disgust when the first difficulties showed themselves. [A. J. C. Grant and H. Temperley, *Europe in the Nineteenth and Twentieth Centuries*]

The Mexican affair cost 7,000 French lives and 300 million French francs. For all that, it was to provide the Legion with its credo, the story of the battle of Camerone, a tale still recounted aloud by the senior officer present at the Legion's commemorative parade on its 30 April anniversary, all round the world. For soldiers in search of glory there was an El Dorado in Mexico after all, yielding a special gold which, as is customary in a sacrificial battle, is the property of brave but dead men.

To begin with, Mexico seemed a poor sort of place to seek immortality. Indeed, Napoleon III seems to have decided that his *régiments étrangers* were best left to continue as a military labour force based at Sidi-bel-Abbès. The regiment's younger officers resented that and petitioned the Emperor for a chance to join the party. Mexico conjured up visions of horsemanship, dancing, girls and hot liquor as well as military glory. On 28 March 1863, more than a year after the first 3,000 French soldiers had landed at Vera Cruz on the Mexican coast, two battalions of the regiment plus a headquarters company, totalling 2,000 men in all, also disembarked there. By now, the campaign had become bogged down. About 150 miles inland, and a cool 5,000 feet above sea level, the forces of President Juárez had decided to make a stand at the town of Puebla, which was now under siege by the invaders. The French supply line from the malarial swamp on the coast and up through the high plateau was under constant challenge by guerrillas. The Legion, with memories of Sebastopol, was cheerfully ready to join the fight at Puebla but found itself, instead, manning a series of local guard-posts near the coast. The initiative, as in the early Algerian conflict with Abd-el-Kader, was with the opposition.

The French commander-in-chief in Mexico, General Élie-Frédéric Forey, made no secret of the reason why he had decided to waste the Legion's fighting spirit in manning the line of communication: 'I preferred to leave foreigners rather than Frenchmen to guard the most unhealthy area, the tropical zone from Vera Cruz to Cordoba, where the malaria reigns.' The general might also have mentioned yellow fever, the 'Vomito Negro' and other less well defined maladies, which rapidly started to take their toll of the regiment. There was some action, nevertheless, even as the legionnaires were getting their bearings during early April. A Mexican guerrilla band which raided a railway work camp under the Legion's protection was badly mauled by the newcomers, one of whom, a Prussian lieutenant, killed the guerrilla leader Antonio Diaz in hand-to-hand combat.

To break the siege up-country at Puebla, Forey had just imported some heavy guns and these, together with ammunition, food, gold pieces and a host of other good things, set off from Vera Cruz in a painfully slow convoy of sixty horse-drawn vehicles on 15 April. On 27 April the Legion's colonel, Pierre Jeanningros sent two companies, their strength diminished by illness, to meet the convoy on its way up towards his base command post on the upper slopes of Chiquihuite mountain. Two days later an Indian spy brought Jeanningros grave news. The convoy was about to be ambushed, and not by enthusiastic amateur soldiers but by several battalions of regular infantry and cavalry, as well as local guerrillas. The man in charge of this operation was a regular army Colonel, named Martinez. Another of the leaders on this operation, Colonel Cambas, had actually studied military science in France.

Jeanningros hastily calculated the odds and sent another company on the same road to try to warn the convoy, or make contact with the enemy force. The company he detailed for this task – the 3rd company of the 1st Battalion – had no officers who were fit so a member of the headquarters staff, Captain Jean Danjou, volunteered to take the team out. Two subalterns from HQ company – both sergeant-majors promoted from the ranks – joined him. The company strength was now down to sixty-two men from its normal complement of 120.

In the early hours of 30 April, with rations and spare ammunition on mules, the men marched from Chiquihuite on a north-easterly bearing towards the coast. They were to patrol as far as Palo Verde, about twenty miles distant, and then return. In the cool of night they marched smoothly and by dawn were able to pause at a post held by the battalion's grenadier company. There they stayed briefly for a brew of coffee and some black bread. Captain Saussier, in charge of the position, offered Danjou more men when he heard of the strength of the opposition waiting to ambush the convoy. But Danjou was anxious to be on his way and declined the offer.

In the first light they saw that the countryside rolled downhill towards the river Jamapa. This was just as well since it was clearly going to be a blisteringly hot day for route-marching. Without seeing anyone, they passed through one or two minor settlements, including Camerone, a ramshackle collection of farm buildings inhabited by vultures. Danjou, a cool veteran of the Crimea, was in the lead, on horseback, with his brother officers, Maudet and Villain. Although he had lost his left hand in an accident with an artillery piece, he had no trouble controlling the horse or anything else. The missing hand had been replaced by a beautifully carved and articulated wooden model which was attached to his wrist with a deep leather cuff. The officers were followed on foot by the company drummer, Legionnaire Lai. On a routine march his drum would mark time for the men but today, on a reconnaissance patrol in potentially hostile territory, this was out of the question. Almost certainly acting as back-marker came the company's most experienced NCO, the Polish Sergeant Vincent Morzycki.

It was 7 a.m. when they arrived at Palo Verde. Like everywhere else in the war zone, it was silent and empty. Sweating, the legionnaires paused to boil up a dixie of water for a brew of coffee. This operation was done quietly, while Danjou placed sentries in a close-drawn perimeter. Somewhere up ahead, towards the east and the sea, the big convoy would be labouring towards them with news from France, and the security of numbers. But it was from their own direction of march, the west, that the dust-cloud marked the approaching horsemen.

'*Aux armes!*' shouted Danjou.

The clearing was no place to fight off cavalry, so the patrol drew off the trail into the entangling scrub and the company made a long detour back to Camerone. Danjou, suspecting a trap, sent scouts in ahead of the main party. There was a single shot and a Legion scout rolled in the dirt, wounded in the hip.

The legionnaires then rushed the hacienda, but found no one. Danjou gathered the men and they marched rapidly in the direction of a nearby Indian village. However, alerted by the sniper shot, the Mexican cavalry was already on its way and legionnaires realized they were about to be caught out in the open.

'Form a square! Prepare to fire!'

The Mexicans divided into two squadrons to attack the square from different sides, and coolly approached at a walk to within sixty metres. Then they charged, sabres flashing. At fifty metres,

Danjou roared, 'Fire!' and the first thirty rounds exploded into the horsemen. He repeated the order and another sixty weapons were shot in unison. Then, as the horsemen backed off, wheeled round and prepared to make a second attempt, Danjou ordered, 'Fire at will.'

There was a moment when the Mexicans appeared to be wavering and drawing off. As they returned, Danjou and his men broke through them to recover the doubtful security of the walls of the deserted hacienda flanking the road. In the confusion the mules carrying food, water and ammunition broke away into the scrub. Sixteen legionnaires were also lost. Danjou regrouped at the farm with two officers and forty-six men. From the surrounding countryside, every able-bodied Mexican who could carry a firearm moved in on the battle. Some occupied the farmhouse, firing through the windows on to the courtyard, where Danjou and his men ducked and weaved across the yard into the skimpy shelter of a wrecked stable block, leaving other legionnaires on the opposite side of the yard crouched in the shelter of the wall which already had gaps in it. From the roof of the stable block Sergeant Morzycki reported seeing 'hundreds of Mexicans' surrounding them.

The fight which then began in earnest was an intimate and sometimes leisurely affair in which Mexican snipers tried to creep up on the legionnaires to pick them off at almost point-blank range or endeavoured to rush the weak spots in the wall. About one hour's march away, the Mexican colonel, Milan, received a report from his cavalry. His force of three infantry battalions then kitted up, ready to move.

At nine thirty the Mexican Lieutenant Ramon Laine approached under a flag of truce, offering honourable surrender and a guarantee that the legionnaires would be treated as prisoners of war. The alternative was pointless slaughter, explained Laine. 'There are two thousand of us.'

Danjou responded: 'We have enough ammunition. No surrender.'

During the brief respite of the truce, Danjou asked each man to give his word that he would fight to the death.

By 11 a.m. the sun was high. Danjou, co-ordinating the defence on both sides of the courtyard, took one chance too many. Second Lieutenant Napoléon Villain, an NCO until four months previously, his tunic bearing a gallantry medal won at Magenta, then took command.

By 12 noon the company's youngsters ('*nos benjamins*') Jean Timmermans and Johan Reuss had died. They were seventeen and this was their first engagement. From somewhere beyond the wall, the survivors heard a bugle. Some were convinced that it had to be a relief column. But Morzycki, still on the roof, announced that the reinforcements were for the Mexicans. He estimated that about 1,000 infantrymen had joined the cavalry surrounding them. Worse, they were armed with the latest American carbine.

Again the Mexicans offered honourable surrender and again the legionnaires refused. The battle resumed and the enemy began to dig holes with pick-axes in the long wall protecting the French soldiers. At 2 p.m. Villain was killed instantly by a bullet between the eyes. Maudet, another ex-sergeant-major, succeeded him at the point at which all his men were being driven half-mad with thirst. Some of the wounded were seen drinking their own blood as they lay exposed to gunfire and the furnace heat of the courtyard. Others drank their own urine.

The deaths mounted as the afternoon wore on. Company Sergeant-Major Henri Tonel, a burly ex-actor; Sergeant Jean Germays; Corporal Adolfi Delcaretto; Legionnaire Dubois; and the Anglo-Saxon Legionnaire Peter Dicken. The survivors rummaged through the pockets and pouches of the dead during each lull, to seek unused ammunition. Towards the end of the terrible afternoon the Mexicans ignited bales of straw piled against the exterior wall. The legionnaires' response was to fire at anything moving towards them through the smoke, but they were shooting into the sun and the enemy were hazy silhouettes.

By five o'clock there were just eleven legionnaires left alive in the stable block. The Mexicans suffered casualties running to three figures. Colonel Milan made an impassioned speech about his country's national honour. Another surrender offer was refused, to be followed by a combined onslaught in which fresh troops shot from every firing point at their command. Within the hour the gallant Sergeant Morzycki had been shot as had three others. The five men left were Second Lieutenant Maudet,

Corporal Maine (still wearing the medal they gave him in the assault on the Malakoff fort at Sebastopol), Legionnaires Victor Catteau, Laurent Constantin and Geoffrey Wenzel. Each man had one round left. Maudet led them out. Catteau, the tallest, hurled himself in front of his officer and died with nineteen bullets in his body. Maudet also fell, gravely wounded. Maine and Constantin were uninjured, and the young German, Wenzel, was still on his feet in spite of a wound.

They stood quite still. Colonel Cambas, sword drawn, thrust his men to one side and stepped slowly, deliberately, between the two groups, a risky manoeuvre in a situation which might have exploded again at any second.

'You now surrender,' Cambas said, in French.

'Only if you allow us to keep our weapons, and treat our Lieutenant Maudet here,' Maine replied.

'One refuses nothing to such men as you,' Cambas responded.

Soon after, they were presented more as honoured guests than prisoners to Colonel Milan. Milan was perplexed, and looked for the others.

'Are you telling me that these are the only survivors?'

'Yes, sir.'

'*Pero, non son hombres, son demonios!*' ('Truly, these are not men, but devils!')

Colonel Jeanningros appears to have remained as indecisive after rumours of the Camerone engagement reached him, as he had been before. On 1 May he set off with a relief column down that same road on which 3 Company had vanished. His actions thereafter can be interpreted either as those of a coward (the view of the British historian McLeave) or of a responsible commander seeking hard information rather than military glory. The loss of an entire company from his slender manpower, at a time when a vital convoy was coming through his area, was a severe blow. His only information being garbled stories told by local Indians, Jeanningros had to learn for himself what had happened and to assess how likely it was that it would happen again. He did not camp at Camerone, and has been criticized for that. He found Danjou's drummer, Lai, who had survived under a pile of corpses – in spite of two bullet wounds and seven lance thrusts – until after the battle and then, seriously wounded, had dragged himself out of Camerone and back along the road towards Chiquihuite for a mile or so before collapsing. Lai was able to confirm the strength and professionalism of the opposition.

Some legionnaires do not accept the charge of cowardice against Jeanningros. Colonel Hunter-Choat observed (in a letter to the author):

> Danjou's company had been away on a route-clearing operation and, as it was their wont to march mostly at night, they would not have been expected back until, at the earliest, first light on 1 May. It is strange to expect Jeanningros to react much earlier than mid- to late morning on that day. Subsequently, he would have been guilty of an elementary error had he chosen to camp at Camerone with his small force, in the full knowledge that some 900 enemy cavalry and 1,500 infantry were in the offing. He withdrew to relative safety. What purpose, apart from burying the dead, would have been served otherwise?

When he reached Camerone, Jeanningros found that the Mexicans had removed virtually all traces of the battle. A quick search of the area revealed the naked bodies of some of the missing men, in a ditch. Fearing that his party would be next, Jeanningros – emulating Danjou's initial manoeuvre – took to the bush to make a covert return to safer territory. The dead were to remain unburied for another two days. In the meantime, Jeanningros returned to his headquarters at Chiquihuite, twenty miles away, to assemble a more formidable force. Down towards the coast at the settlement of Soledad, the convoy commander – also alerted to the presence of Milan's troops – waited until his escort could be beefed up. The two French forces finally met on the road at Palo Verde, scene of Danjou's first contact with the Mexicans, on 3 May. On that day also, the dead of Camerone (or rather, what was left of them after such predators as vulture and coyote had discovered the bodies) were decently buried.

Somewhere amid the detritus a local rancher named Langlais (a Mexican of French extraction) picked up an organ less vulnerable to predators. This was an articulated wooden hand. More than two years later, Langlais offered it to General Bazaine at a price of 50 piastres. After four months' correspondence and haggling, Bazaine paid the ransom. The hand – that of Captain

Danjou – is still a treasured relic at the centre of the Legion's museum near Marseilles.

The five legionnaires still on their feet at the end of the battle were not the only survivors. According to Colonel Hunter-Choat, there were twenty-three in all. They were: Second Lieutenant Maudet; Sergeants Palmaert and Schaffner; Corporals Berg. Mangin and Maine; Legionnaires Segers; Billod; Gaertner; Schreiblich; Verjus; Seffrin; Haller; Van den Bulcke; Schiffer; Jeannin; Merlet; Brunswick; Conrad (Danjou's batman); Gorzki; Zey; Kunassec; and the drummer, Lai.

The Legion was to spend almost four years more in Mexico. These years would yield their share of military gallantry. They would also be overshadowed by intrigue, domestic as well as political. The effect of these off-stage pressures, to which Prussia, the United States and internal French politics all contributed, was to make it inevitable that Napoleon III would finally withdraw his force from Mexico and sulk, nursing the suspicion that the Legion veteran Bazaine – now also a Marshal – had flirted with the idea of a *coup d'état* in Mexico.

At the time of Camerone, as a general, Bazaine was in command of a mixed Armée d'Afrique division under Forey, who continued his laborious siege of Puebla, sitting astride the road to Mexico City. Puebla might have held out for longer had Bazaine not led a flying column of 3,500 men in a dawn attack on the heights of San Lorenzo, north of Puebla, against a force of 6,000 Mexicans on their way to relieve the besieged city. Now the guns for which Legion lives were sacrificed at Camerone could be brought to bear on the defences and the city surrendered on 17 May. The 12,000 prisoners included seventeen generals.

From Puebla, the French war machine rolled on towards Mexico City. President Juárez, like Abd-el-Kader before him, was obliged to abandon his fixed base and become a hunted man in his own land. He withdrew north, towards the border with Texas. But not everyone fled. Two compliant Mexican generals and an archbishop were found to promote Maximilian as their Emperor, though it would be months yet before the monarch dared make the journey from Santa Cruz to his capital. In the autumn of 1863, Forey was withdrawn from a half-conquered country back to France. For his trouble, he was promoted to marshal. General (ex-Legion sergeant and lieutenant) Bazaine was appointed to take over as military supremo. Aside from the complication of a spare emperor, he was now the Bugeaud of Mexico and apparently untouchable.

Back in Paris, however, Bazaine's wife Soledad was having one adventure too many. The man in the case was married to a Comédie Française actress who discovered a cache of Soledad's love letters to her husband. These the actress bundled up and posted to Bazaine in Mexico. Then, after a lapse of several days, she wrote a curt little note to Soledad also, just to let her know what was afoot. Soledad threw herself upon the mercy of Napoleon III, who was sympathetic. Not even his intervention, however, was sufficient to stop the boat that had just sailed from Toulon bound for Madeira, Martinique and Vera Cruz. The letters, it seemed, were now an emotional time-bomb on an eight-week fuse. The stress involved in awaiting the explosion was too much for Madame Bazaine, who committed suicide long before the letters arrived at her husband's private office, where one of the General's trusted subordinates destroyed them without mentioning them to Bazaine, who had a war to fight. The General, when he had word of his widowhood, concluded that it was another case of cholera, grieved decently and then courted and married a seventeen-year-old Mexican girl from one of the country's traditional ruling families. He was aged fifty-four. This marriage, albeit a glittering official occasion, plus Bazaine's fluent command of Spanish, was the probable source of rumours that were to reach Napoleon III about his general's ambition to rule Mexico.

There could be no doubting Bazaine's military efficiency. The Legion, like the rest of the Armée d'Afrique, had no formal training courses for its NCOs. Promotion was invariably on merit. And Bazaine, in the Legion tradition, still led from the front, wherever the action was hottest. After twenty years in Africa he also knew more about fighting a guerrilla war than any product of St Cyr military academy. He brought the Legion north, resurrected the Spanish campaign idea of an all-arms force, and provided the Legion with its own cavalry and artillery. The resulting fast-moving columns struck at Juárez's bases as far as the Texas border. In the south, the regiment triumphed in overcoming besieged Oaxaca. North of Mexico City there was disaster when, defying his orders, Major de Brian with six officers and 168 legionnaires took off in pursuit of a larger enemy force, and was then ambushed by 1,500 Juáristas at Santa Isabel. Only one man returned to the Legion's base. One officer and eighty-one men were taken prisoner of whom forty died in captivity.

After the Santa Isabel affair, in February 1866, desertions from the Legion into the USA (by way of a hazardous journey through hostile territory) probably outnumbered the losses sustained in battle. For some this was because of the promise of the good life in America. For others it could have been that after three years' hard fighting it was becoming obvious to the most meagre intelligence that the steam was going out of the French effort. It was becoming yet another lost cause. But there were no cases of desertion among NCOs. Some who were taken prisoner went to extraordinary lengths to rejoin the regiment. Sergeant Finala, taken prisoner at Parras and held near Mapimi in Comanche Indian territory, swam the Rio Grande – the border with Texas – to return 'home'. Another sergeant, Marius Cecconi, wounded and taken prisoner during the siege of Puebla, escaped north across the same river, made his way to French-speaking New Orleans and reported for duty at the French consulate.

Even the Legion's dedication could not disguise the fact that Napoleon III's Mexican fantasy was doomed. The American Civil War ended in 1864, and after four envenomed years the USA had time to bind its wounds and look to its fences. It did not like what it saw across its southern border and let it be known that unless France pulled out of Mexico, the US would give active support to the fugitive President Juárez. In Europe, meanwhile, the Prussians rounded off a three-week war against the Austrians with a spectacular victory at Sadowa, in what is now Czechoslovakia. A French Marshal, Randon, summed up his country's view of this development: 'It is France that was beaten at Sadowa,' he said. An enlarged Prussia, the emergence of a Greater Germany, was not good for France. It was time to stop poaching in the New World on behalf of a member of a now defeated Austrian Habsburg dynasty. Maximilian was an official loser. Napoleon III wanted his soldiers nearer home.

Bazaine received secret, coded orders from Napoleon to evacuate the army as expeditiously as possible. But the General played for time while Maximilian's consort, Empress Carlotta, travelled urgently to Europe to change Louis-Napoleon's mind. She found the French Emperor in a state of deep depression about the Prussian triumph over Austria; her own, Austrian kinfolk equally unhappy. Her breakdown and lifelong incarceration in a madhouse followed.

Bazaine feared that if the French withdrawal were high-profile and obvious, it would reduce Mexico, a country with which he now had domestic ties, to anarchy and revolution. But Napoleon III, now half-persuaded that Bazaine was running out of control, sent Bazaine's junior, a certain General Castelnau, with orders to supervise an evacuation with or without Bazaine's help. Significantly, for a while, this plan excluded the *régiments étrangers*, as the Foreign Legion was described at the time.

Bazaine contrive to extract the French force, then 28,000 strong, without further loss during an eight-week period early in 1867. He was the last man to go on board the last ship to sail. Six weeks after leaving Vera Cruz he set foot on French soil at Toulon for the first time for four years. He was now a Marshal of France. He had emerged victorious from an apparently suicidal colonial campaign 3,000 miles from home. His shrewdness had saved France an army as well as covering her political blushes. He had exercised enormous political skill, in organizing the French government of occupation and in making French rule seem half-plausible in Central America. He was greeted on his return with empty silence on an empty quayside, by order of the Emperor: no guns, no flags, no escort, no speeches of welcome in a society which set great store by such ceremonial. The campaign had cost 7,000 French soldiers' lives and 300 million francs, making it one of the most expensive debt-collecting operations in history.

While Maximilian was captured and shot by firing squad in Mexico, Bazaine and his military friends in the Legion were implicitly made the scapegoats in Paris for having succeeded — embarrassingly — in a military campaign which France no longer wanted to win. This pattern was to be repeated a century later, in North Africa.

CHAPTER 4
Resisting Prussia, Crushing Paris
(1870–71)

The Foreign Legion [defending Orléans] fought
very stubbornly.

– General Adolf von Heinleth,
Prussian Army, 1870

On 16 June 1874 Marshal Chancy,
Governor-General of Algeria, suggested that
Germans in the Legion endangered security and
demanded that the Legion be suppressed.

– Lieutenant-Colonel Pierre Carles,
French army historian

The Franco-Prussian War resulted from France's arrogant illusions about herself and Bismarck's readiness to manipulate French naivety. After Prussia's unexpected victory over the mighty Austrian army at Sadowa in 1866, Prussia accelerated her preparedness for a modern, high-technology war in Europe. As well as a superb professional army, the German Kaiser Wilhelm I had at his disposal 1,183,000 soldiers within eighteen days of mobilization available as a result of conscripting young civilians for three years' service. Krupp's new breech-loading artillery guns; the use of trains and telegraph to speed mobility to the front and communications with it; the infantry's superior weapon training and discipline all contrasted dramatically with French unreadiness for war. Above all, every German was prepared to die to disprove a 'witticism' coined by the American essayist Ralph Waldo Emerson in 1860 (popular at the time in France) that 'the German and Irish millions, like the Negro, have a great deal of guano in their destiny'; or alternatively: 'The Irish and the Germans are the manure of Nations'.

In France, by contrast, for a modest price a young man could legally purchase a substitute to do his military service. Most did so. Proposals to end such élitism met howls of outrage from the National Assembly and were dropped. The regular army was underpaid, badly trained and, aside from a good rifle which it could not often shoot straight, poorly equipped. Rearmament was opposed by republicans and monarchists alike. To fight a war, if it came, the regular army commanders would rely not upon long-range artillery, but French élan and cavalry charges. No maps of France were issued to the army because the war was to be fought exclusively on German soil. In the real world, however, the coming conflict was to be fought between a medieval army and one belonging to the twentieth century.

The immediate cause of the trouble lay in Spain. Those two queens (Isabella and her mother María Cristina) for whom the original Foreign Legion had been so blithely sacrificed by King Louis-Philippe were successively driven into exile by their own army. In 1869, as part of some general bartering, the Prussian Chancellor Bismarck nominated the German Prince Leopold of Hohenzollern-Sigmaringen to be Spain's new monarch. However, since the prince was also a colonel in the Prussian army, the French reasonably feared that they could now be attacked by the Germans from Iberia as well as from the east by a hostile army.

The French duly protested to Prussia and Leopold withdrew his name as a runner for the Spanish throne. This should have ended the matter but France wanted more. A gathering of courtiers disguised as a council of state, conducted by the ailing Napoleon III's consort Empress Eugénie at a country residence, was attended by just one minister. This cabal ordered the French ambassador to Prussia to make fresh demands of the Germans. At France's behest the elderly King Wilhelm was publicly to associate himself with Leopold's retraction and to promise not to support Leopold if he reapplied for the throne. Wilhelm listened with grave courtesy, then told the envoy, Benedetti, that he could not accept such conditions. The same day, Leopold's withdrawal from the race for the throne of Spain was confirmed. Wilhelm sent a note to Benedetti, drawing his attention to this and saying that the matter was closed. Benedetti now made a nuisance of himself and the King refused three times to see him.

News of these events was officially released to the world's press by Bismarck in a document known – from its origin – as the Ems telegram. Mischievously, the Prussian statesman drafted a message that made it seem as if Benedetti had been treated like an itinerant beggar and sent packing. The French did not pause to check the accuracy of this version. Instead, as the distinguished historians Grant and Temperley have put it, 'the statesmen of France . . . treated a question which involved the lives of millions in the temper of duellists.'

Benedetti had presented Paris's insulting demands on 13 July. The French Council of State voted to go to war on 14 July (the national festival commemorating the Bastille, when the country is not at its most sober). Next day, the National Assembly supported the decision, as did street mobs composed of people who had hitherto exercised some ingenuity in avoiding military service. The French prime minister, Emile Ollivier, absent from Empress Eugénie's original meeting – from which the trouble sprang – declared himself ready to accept war 'with a light heart'. War was duly declared on 19 July. Professor Cobban observed:

> The blunders of Napoleon III's foreign policy ensured that France should enter the war with no allies, but on the side of the government hardly anyone, except perhaps the Emperor himself, supposed that there was any need for them. 'A Berlin', was the war-cry on the boulevards and the password of the army.

After the rhetoric, the reality of military action and the scramble to bring fighting men up to the front. The Armée d'Afrique was immediately invited to supply Zouaves and Chasseurs, Joyeux and Tirailleurs, but no legionnaires. This was not because that regiment's original charter excluded them from operations in France proper, but because the majority of its men were Germans. A periodic inspection of the regiment by General Douay in 1866, shortly before the Legion's departure from Mexico, showed that 58.3 per cent were of German origin. At Belgium's urgent pleading and to preserve that country's neutrality, Belgians serving with the Legion were also to stay out of this war. The gap was temporarily closed by other foreign volunteers, some resident in France, most of whom lacked military training or experience. They included the future Lord Kitchener of Khartoum, then a military cadet at Woolwich. For him, his first war did not go well: he took a ride in a balloon, caught a chill, was discovered by his father 'critically ill at a cabaret in a village which the troops had quitted as insanitary' and was invalided home. (See Sir Arthur George's biography of Kitchener.) Most of the others, hastily trained without the benefit of weapons, formed up as the 5th Foreign Regiment on 22 August at Tours. Approval for the regiment's inauguration, signed by the Empress, was one of the last administrative decisions of Napoleon III's Second Empire. The best of the new volunteers included Sergeant Karageorgevic, a graduate of Cyr who had dropped out of army life. After prolonged Legion service, Sergeant 'Kara' would be crowned King Peter I of Serbia in 1903.

By the time the 5th Foreign Regiment went into action, the war was all but lost and the French regular army had been reduced to a few depot companies whose collective manpower totalled only ninety men. On the front line in Alsace and Lorraine, 500,000 Prussians and Bavarians had launched blitzkrieg offensives against 200,000 Frenchmen, who retreated behind a sacrificial rearguard held with fatalistic courage by the Algerians and their French officers. At Fröschweiler, Colonel Suzzoni, commanding the 2nd Algerian Tirailleurs, told his men in Arabic: 'We will die here if necessary, but will not give an inch.'

Moments later he was dead. In the course of that day his regiment was wiped out.

The German offensive was launched on 6 August. By 3 September, Napoleon III together with thirty-nine generals and an army of 104,000 had surrendered at Sedan and the Empress Eugénie was making hasty plans to spend the rest of her days in England. At Metz, near the German border, Bazaine – now Commander-in-Chief and Marshal of France – was besieged with another 180,000. Paris promptly staged its own revolution, created a Government of National Defence and threw up huge fortifications to prepare for a long siege. This largely civilian team, represented by Gambetta, a flamboyant half-Italian lawyer who escaped by balloon from Paris across German lines, did a phenomenal job in staving off Prussia's final victory for another four months. The unco-ordinated forces cobbled together to operate under three commanders in different parts of provincial France included anyone fit to carry rifle or musket. In October the newly-created 5th Foreign Regiment was put into the front line north of Orléans alongside Zouaves and Tirailleurs to hold off a crack Bavarian division. At its back was the city and the river Loire, across which the rest of the French army was retreating in disorder.

The defence of Orléans had started badly at Artenay, about twenty miles north of the city. The German General Adolf von Heinleth recollected:

> Enticed by curiosity, many of the inhabitants had early in the morning gone to Artenay on horseback and in carriages to witness the delightful spectacle of the total destruction of the foreign barbarians, but being roughly greeted by the German shells, the gay multitude speedily ran home again and terrified the whole city by their terror-stricken countenances and exaggerated reports, declaring that the wicked Uhlans were following close upon their heels . . . Only the rearguard, formed of chasseurs and Turkos, bravely stood their ground at Artenay . . . The fleeing cavalry galloped through the town, shouting 'Sauve qui peut' . . . Undisciplined hosts of infantry threw away baggage and arms, or in a drunken fit, fired off their rifles in the streets of the city. [J. F. Maurice, et al., The Franco-German War]

At dusk, the Germans paused in their advance. By next morning, the French line had been stiffened with fresh troops including the novice legionnaires under Major Arago. From the open countryside and the Orléans forest, the German divisions came cautiously to a half to face the suburbs, a higgledy-piggledy huddle of walled gardens and irregular houses, gasworks and a railway station, all prepared for defence in depth. Artillery and cavalry were of marginal value here. It was a close-quarter butchery job for the infantry. From the suburb of Bel Air les Aides, the legionnaires gradually fell back as their strongholds were bypassed and outflanked. By 5 p.m., the few survivors were completely surrounded. Major Arago had been killed by a shell. Eighteen other officers were also dead. Von Heinleth wrote later:

The Foreign Legion fought very stubbornly. Les Aides soon stood in flames. In the burning and falling houses the gallant Swabians fell upon the brave international mercenaries with butt-end and bayonet . . . The French lost about 4,000 men in killed, wounded and prisoners, among these the Foreign Legion of 1,300 men alone lost its Commanding Officer, nineteen officers and 900 rank and file.

That night the Bavarian bands played by the light of their camp fires in front of the statue of La Pucelle, in the streets of a deserted city. Some people were still easing themselves out of the place, including Sergeant Kara, disguised as a miller. For a future monarch, it was a crash course in personal and political survival.

Under a new commander, the French force was given a task of brutal simplicity by War Minister Gambetta: 'Recapture Orléans.' Already, at the end of October, the severe winter of 1870–71 was baring its teeth. The Armée d'Afrique – the backbone of the army of the Loire – found it hard lying in their bivouacs. Yet the mayors of towns and villages such as Loir-et-Cher, loyal to l'esprit de clocher, refused to provide their defenders with firewood or forage. Others, faced with a requisition order, complied with the worst grace possible. Nevertheless, the French regrouped and gathered new volunteers as word spread that General von der Tann's Bavarians were now isolated in Orléans and could easily be outnumbered. Orléans could be retaken and then the great advance north to relieve besieged Paris would begin.

The odds were looking good: 125,000 Frenchmen and their allies against a Bavarian force (whose size and disposition was relayed by an excellent local intelligence force) of 14,500 muskets, 4,450 sabres and 110 guns. The reinvigorated army of the Loire included two battalions of the 'real' Foreign Legion, totalling 2,000 men, brought from Algeria on 11 October to combine with the few hundred survivors of the 5th Regiment. Many were Germans. None was disloyal to France. Von der Tann's orders permitted him to abandon Orléans and follow his own inclination to fight in open countryside if he could establish beyond doubt that he was completely outnumbered.

The two forces met in a day-long skirmish at Coulmiers, west of Orléans, during which several French units panicked when faced with moderate opposition. This was not the Legion's problem. As spearhead of the attacking force it made a bold assault to break through German lines under heavy local artillery fire but no one backed up this initiative. Watching the legionnaires from the German side was one of their old comrades, Ernst von Milson von Bolt. In Mexico he had been the first Foreign Legion officer to win a gallantry award. Now he was a staff officer with von der Tann. Marching towards his position, wearing their medals, the Legion veterans included a survivor of Camerone, Sergeant Brunswick. According to Legion legend, von Bolt gave an order to the German guns to cease firing when he recognized his old regiment. Whatever the truth of that, von der Tann's force withdrew in good order under cover of darkness and evacuated Orléans on 11 November, giving the Legion its first chance for three weeks to get under cover and dry out.

To the French leadership it seemed that the way was now open for a campaign to relieve Paris. This aspiration was doomed, however, by recent events 200 miles away at Metz, on the German border. There Bazaine, the old fox of the Legion, survivor of innumerable sieges including the cruel episode of Miliana in Algeria thirty years earlier, had now surrendered with 180,000 men to a German force under the Prussian Supremo von Moltke. That collapse on 27 October, one of the most controversial surrenders of France's long military history, released 200,000 enemy soldiers to make a forced march to reinforce their comrades around the French capital. Marching north towards Paris on 1 December the army of the Loire was defeated by a German counter-attack. As it fled south across the river Loire yet again on 4 December, it was the Legion which found itself acting as the disciplined, sacrificial rearguard, alongside a Zouave company, in the same suburbs it had defended in October.

It was now clear that Paris could not be relieved. The army of the Loire was therefore sent to apply pressure elsewhere, by harassing and if possible cutting completely German supply lines near the mountainous eastern border. The 15th Army Corps, including the Armée d'Afrique element, was sent by rail, in a temperature touching minus 18 degrees, on a journey scheduled to last thirty-six hours. For this reason each man was issued with two days' rations. In the event, because of incompetence, the two Legion battalions – reinforced by 2,000 Bretons to make good losses in battle – were obliged to spend two weeks in their trains. On their arrival at Sainte Suzanne, near Montbéliard, in mid-January they became part of the Army of the East commanded by General Bourbaki and were committed to instant action. Yet again, they marched on to the enemy guns, but the castle on a hill withstood their three-day offensive. To add to the gloom as they withdrew, a cash box belonging to their army corps head-quarters, containing 4,341 francs, fell into enemy hands.

No amount of locally injected courage could now save a strategically hopeless situation in which fragments of an irregular French army were spread about the country without leadership or co-ordination. The official capital was to be found in Bordeaux. The people of Paris, with a National Guard of 350,000 all armed and under siege, were about to create their own mini-republic. In Algeria, attempts to draft a squadron of Spahis into the war provoked a mutiny: they massacred their French officers rather than embark for France, triggering off another holy war in North Africa. In the Jura, the Army of the East under General Bourbaki started a slow, doleful slog towards the Swiss border in snow that grew ever deeper, pursued by the German General Manteuffel. The Prussian Lieutenant-General Franz Oberhoffer describes how Bourbaki's force was trapped by his own government's incompetence as well as enemy action:

> Already, the German armies were masters of the most important line of communications in his rear . . . The increasing want of discipline of the troops, and the repeated disregard of orders seemed harbingers of coming disaster . . . The stores at Besançon would not hold out for any lengthened stay at that place. The headquarters at Bordeaux of course took a different view of the state of affairs and even sent . . . orders to support Garibaldi, who was being attacked at Dijon. The French army that was fighting for its very existence was to send support to the very men who ought to have covered its rear and who by their inactivity had facilitated its being taken by surprise! [J. F. Maurice, et al.]

On 22 January, in numbing cold and beyond salvation, Bourbaki made the latest of several unsuccessful attempts to kill himself. He was severely wounded and relieved of his command. His successor General Clinchant left two divisions including the foreign regiments to hold Besançon. The next day, as their comrades of the Armée d'Afrique trudged east, the Legion quietly settled down in bivouacs in the Rhone valley. Less than a week later, following an abortive effort by the Parisians to break out of Prussian encirclement, the French Government of National Defence reached a three-week armistice agreement with the Prussians at Versailles. A new assembly was to be elected to vote on Bismarck's peace terms: Alsace, much of Lorraine, the cities of Strasbourg and Metz, and £200 million (sterling) were to be exacted from France.

The Army of the East was excluded from the armistice and therefore its men were left in a political limbo. The remnants of the force, including most of the African regiments, clambered through the snow towards political sanctuary in Switzerland. The last casualties of the Franco-Prussian war were German soldiers guarding the lonely, treacherous paths across the Alps. A number of them were murdered by the Joyeux. Those who did not perish on the slopes of Mont Risoux arrived on Swiss territory a few miles north of Geneva on 4 February, a gaunt army of 87,847 frostbitten scarecrows. They surrendered with 11,800 horses and 285 guns.

In republican Paris, the end to the Prussian siege found the city in a mood of vexed excitement. The benefits of peace were obvious enough. Normal food started to reappear on tables and restaurant menus, which – if they were lucky – had been able to offer kangaroo, elephant and cat. But while the new assembly at Bordeaux (a coalition of right-wing monarchists) was approving Bismarck's conditions, his final exaction – a ceremonial parade by 30,000 German soldiers through the French capital – was the match to the powderkeg. The new French government, based at Versailles, sought to disarm the left-wingers now in charge of Paris under the collective title of the Commune. Both French factions were able to claim the benefit of election; neither commanded a consensus of national support sufficient to achieve political legitimacy. What they did represent was the historic divide between France's proletariat and peasantry on the one hand and its aristocracy on the other and each sought to replay the savage match of 1789 in which the psychopathic blood-lust of the *enragés* responded to the callousness of monarchy. The

Germans withdrew and left the French to the mercies of the French.

On 6 March, all foreign volunteers who had donned uniform for the war against Prussia and all Frenchmen who had joined up in 1863 or earlier, were demobilized. This left a Legion of 1,003 men – an augmented battalion – composed largely of young Bretons led by a few veterans such as the Camerone survivor, Sergeant Brunswick. Three weeks later this unit, still known as the *Régiment de Marche Étranger*, left Besançon by train for Versailles. It arrived just in time to take part in a new siege of Paris.

At the beginning of this new conflict, during which clumsy skirmishing established nothing beyond a readiness by both sides to shoot prisoners, the Parisians were more numerous and better armed than their opponents. From the city's fortified walls, cannon pointed inwards as well as out towards the official enemy. But, as the Communards wasted precious weeks in political debate, the Versailles noose was tightening. On 2 May the city was bombarded by artillery and the forts began crumbling. On 21 May a reconnaissance patrol discovered the city gate at St Cloud totally unguarded and the army of Versailles now poured through it, with the Legion in the vanguard. During the seven terrible days which followed, both sides were guilty of many atrocities. The Communards shot hostages including the Archbishop of Paris. The Versailles army shot 147 Communard prisoners after a macabre battle among the graves of Père-Lachaise cemetery. In a city scorched by fire and slippery with blood, 20,000 Parisians (not all Communards) died. Thousands more were transported to penal colonies including New Caledonia in the Pacific.

In the fullness of time the soldiers were rewarded for their loyalty to the emerging government of the Third Republic. However, immediately after the war, German NCOs came under public suspicion. In June 1871 the Minister of War decided that in future only volunteers from Alsace and Lorraine would be accepted into the Legion. On 16 June 1874, Marshal Chancy, then Governor-General of Algeria, suggested that the number of Germans serving in the Legion endangered security on his territory and he demanded that the Legion be suppressed.

This suggestion was rejected but in the reorganization of the French army which followed the civil war of 1871, French veterans were encouraged to fill the Legion's key NCO posts. Not until many years later did these volunteers discover that because they were considered to be foreigners they were not eligible for their pension rights until after twenty-five years, rather than fifteen which was the norm for soldiers in other French regiments.

Such prejudiced treatment ignored an obvious fact. While the specially-composed Legion regiments were bleeding to death in France, fighting Prussia, the Legion's Germans of the 3rd and 4th Battalions were in Algeria helping to suppress the latest Arab and Kabylie uprising. But by 1882, some 45 per cent of those lined up for promotion to NCO were from Alsace-Lorraine, in a pointed political gesture. Another 5 per cent were French citizens. The balance against foreigners in the Foreign Legion had tipped decisively and from now on Frenchmen, including refugees from Alsace-Lorraine, would be in a majority until after 1920.

The Legion's German NCOs were less spectacular scapegoats for the 1870 débâcle than that other ex-Legion sergeant turned Commander-in-Chief, Achille Bazaine. When news of his surrender with 180,000 soldiers at Metz reached Paris (which also surrendered subsequently with 400,000 to defend it) Gambetta instinctively spoke for France in declaring Bazaine's action a betrayal. As Bazaine's English biographer, Guedella, has commented:

> It was essential, as Gambetta saw it, for Frenchmen to believe they had not been defeated, that it was all due to some dark transaction between the Marshal and the enemy, in which the Emperor had somehow been involved . . . For then France would realize that the Empire was solely to blame for their unhappy situation and rally cheerfully to the Republic.

The triumphant Germans did not share Gambetta's opinion. An eye-witness, Colmar, Baron von der Goltz-Pasha, contributing to the *The Franco-German War* said of the French army surrendering at Metz:

It left the dungeon in which it had held out so long and steadfastly, received by its conquerors with respect and sent on to Germany. The sorrows and hardships they had endured were clearly seen in the forsaken camps. The buildings were mostly destroyed, the gardens and plantations swept away, fences and hedges had vanished. Of vegetation there was not a trace left. The starving horses had gnawed off everything, even the bark of the trees. Many of these animals were seen in piteous condition between the houses and the walls, motionless awaiting death by hunger; half broken down, some sat on their haunches, others licked the slime at their feet, and many had sunk down in harness by the carts. The ground of the camps formed extensive swamps, in which men, horses and carts sank ankle deep. This mud had served as a bed of rest for some time to officers and men; of straw not a trace was to be discovered. Scarcely to be distinguished from the universal grey of the soil, carcases of horses lay in the morass. Also corpses of soldiers were found. These unfortunate men probably had died just before the surrender, and nobody had thought of burying them. It was a hell on earth that these brave defenders had quitted. Indeed one could not but respect an enemy who, under such circumstances, had held out so long. [J. F. Maurice, et al.]

All this was well known at the time, yet France grasped at the myth of Bazaine's treachery with the desperation of a guilty man seizing an eleventh-hour alibi. The myth grew and became a political force in its own right, which no prudent politician or soldier would ignore. If there was a final lack of nobility in France's conduct of the war, it was in the judiciously vague court-martial charge brought against Bazaine, that he had failed to do 'all that duty and honour prescribed'.

As Bazaine would explain, his oath was to the Empire, not a Republic which had failed even to make formal contact with him across the 200 miles of German-held territory that separated Paris from Metz. He did not know what was going on at Orléans. His seventy-day resistance (longer, in fact, than any other element of the regular army which was in the war from the beginning) had tied up 200,000 enemy troops long enough for resistance to be organized elsewhere. There came a moment when, with four days' rations left, it was clear that his army was going nowhere. He could have sacrificed it on the altar of military glory, or kept it intact as a force to guarantee public order. He told the court martial:

When the final moment came and it was clear that a last effort was impossible, I sacrificed myself with a memory of my own feelings as a private in Africa forty years ago. I did not feel that I had the right to make a vain sacrifice for empty glory of those lives that were so precious to their country and their families.

There would be those in the Great War to come who would wish that there were more 'traitors' like Bazaine. But, in the spirit of the time, he was sentenced to death by a military contemporary whose career was in every respect less distinguished than that of the accused. Reluctantly another old comrade, President (former Marshal) MacMahon (a prisoner of the Prussians long before Bazaine's surrender) commuted the sentence to twenty years' imprisonment. Bazaine, now aged sixty-two, was imprisoned on the Ile Sainte Marguerite, off Cannes. Two years later he made a daring and physically testing escape by rope-ladder down a sheer cliff into a waiting boat. He stepped ashore at Genoa even as his gaolers were discovering their loss. He died in poverty in Madrid after an exile of fourteen years.

CHAPTER 5
France's Expanding Empire:
Death in Indo-China (1884–85)

The basis of the colonial idea cannot be other
than self-interest . . . The sole criterion to apply
to any colonial enterprise is the sum of
advantage and profit to be had for the
mother country.

Eugène Etienne, MP for Oran and Organizer,
Colonial Party in Paris, 1885

It's our captain who remembers us, and counts
his dead.

– Captain de Borelli, 1st Foreign Legion Regiment,
Tuyen Quang, 1885

On the rebound from its loss of territory and self-esteem in
Europe, France fell in love with colonization, encouraged by the
wily Bismarck. Still anxious to direct French ambition away from
the German border he proposed that France occupy Tunis.
France did so, in 1881. By then Senegal, Cotonou, the Indo-
Chinese Delta, New Caledonia, the New Hebrides and Tahiti
were in the bag. In 1882 France also began a conquest of what it
called 'South Oranais', a vast territory linking the Sahara with
Algeria and Morocco. Next year Tonkin was added. Not for
nothing did the Colonial Party in Paris – led by a settler, Eugène
Etienne, MP for Oran – subtitle itself '*le parti qui dine bien*' ('the
party which dines well') from 1885 to 1904. A minority party of
102 MPs, it nevertheless enjoyed the sort of influence in the
French parliament that Unionists once had at Westminster. But
the armed services needed little encouragement to expand. As
Paul Johnson has put it:

Algeria was acquired as a result of army insubordination; Indo-China had been entered by overweening naval commanders; it was the marines who got France involved in West Africa. In one sense the French Empire could be looked upon as a gigantic system of outdoor relief for army officers. It was designed to give them something to do. What they actually did bore little relation to what most of the ruling establishment wanted or decided . . . Jules Ferry (a leading colonialist) probably came close to the real truth when he described the imperial scramble as 'an immense steeplechase towards the unknown'. [Paul Johnson, *A History of the Modern World*]

In 1885 it was the turn of Formosa to be absorbed into the French community, and then Madagascar, through the latter conquest had to be reinforced by a punitive expedition ten years later. In 1892 Dahomey; 1893 part of Sudan and from 1907 onward, Morocco. France was on its way to creating an empire of 50 million people, a military larder which would provide the mother country with a cheap army of 500,000 men for the next war against Germany. It was a cultural and economic explosion which produced such extraordinary ambitions as the trans-Saharan railway and licensed such heroic eccentrics as the rake-turned-mystic, Charles de Foucauld (see Chapter 7).

In France, political fashions changed with bewildering speed: the country was governed by nineteen separate administrations between 1870 and 1888. In spite of its defeat in 1871 the regular army enjoyed a honeymoon of public popularity for one generation after the Franco-Prussian War. France still lusted after the lost border provinces for which a re-equipped army would be indispensable. Then – after twenty years without a war on the doorstep – the country underwent one of its periodic bouts of anti-militarism. In some measure this was because successive governments had used the professional army to break strikes within France and then made the soldiers scapegoats for being the tools of oppression. The contrast between the continuity of colonialism (which seemed to have a political life of its own) and the absence of continuous government in France proper could not have been more marked. And just as there were two Frances, so there were two armies. The Armée d'Afrique was not affected by Bismarck's rules limiting the size of France's regular army at home. It was ultimately self-financing through taxation imposed on the colonies which it governed. In Algeria, the model chosen for the future was that of ancient Rome. As Count Molé (briefly Prime Minister under Napoleon III) had put it in 1838: 'France is going to revive Roman Africa.'

In this great expansion beyond Europe, the Legion was an obvious front-runner both in its capacity as a fighting, conquering army and – more pervasively – as a builder of roads and communities at a time when France's population was declining drastically. Yet for ten years after the 1871 débâcle the regiment became little more than a labour corps. Its luck changed with the appointment of a new Commanding Officer, François de Negrier. He was a St Cyr man, courageous enough to have escaped from beleaguered Metz in spite of his wounds; a *'perceur'* ('penetrator') ruthless enough to shoot dead two guards as he rode through the lines. De Negrier decided that some changes were in order. Mobility was a weapon he favoured even more than the rifle in the great empty space of Africa. As he would write later: 'The problem is not to travel fast but to go for a long time and a long way . . . Rifle shots are rare here. We fight best by knocking off the kilometres. It is a question of marching.' But how could men march with full kit, rifle and ammunition and still cover up to forty-five miles a day? De Negrier's solution was the mule, whose six kilometres per hour could be easily matched by a man who had to carry only his own rifle and belt kit. Better still, two men could share one mule and take turns to ride the animal, an hour at a time, as well as marching. The mounted infantry was born on 8 December 1881, comprising the Legion's hardest-marching men plus fifty requisitioned Arab mules which could go places beyond the reach of the cavalry's thirsty horses in a waterless wilderness. The mules learned to drink, like the legionnaires, from a metal canteen. In one of its first actions, the new unit surprised a desert warrior named Si-Slimane, a lieutenant of the Moroccan-based bandit and holy man, Bou-Amama. The tribesmen lost their tents and 4,000 sheep. Soon afterward, Bou-Amama had his revenge.

It so happened that a survey party led by a Captain de Castries was exploring the borderland between the desert and mountains south of Oran, escorted by two rifle companies of the Legion and a new mounted company under Lieutenant Massone. Using the

ground to maintain cover and surprise, about 900 enemy cavalry
and 1,600 riflemen swooped on the French column near Chott-
Tigri on 26 April 1882. The mounted companies would learn in
due course that this was their most vulnerable moment in any
battle. They had to tether their mules, which carried water and
ammunition, and fight back at the same time. This was the first
time they had faced such a problem and they bungled it. They did
not dismount but tried to engage the Arab cavalry on equal terms.
It was a gallant but misplaced gesture and a savage reminder to
their successors that they were infantry, not cavalry. The legionnaires, about 300 of them, were scattered in at least three
separate groups which belatedly formed squares and defended
themselves coherently, fighting off repeated charges. The
mounted company, having lost both officers and all its NCOs,
was the most isolated of all during the seven agonized hours
which followed. Legionnaires unfortunate enough to be caught
in the open were tortured to a slow death within sight of their
comrades but out of rifle range, so that it was not even possible
for anyone to bestow death as an instant release from the horror.
The survivors reached the little post of Gelloul with some of their
wounded and finally encountered a relief column led by de
Negrier. Their casualties were two officers and forty-nine Other
Ranks dead, three officers and twenty-eight men wounded.
Bou-Amama's band fled to sanctuary across the Moroccan
border.

'You legionnaires are soldiers in order to die and I am sending
you where you can die,' de Negrier would tell his men. As a
soldier himself, he did not shirk the logic of this statement. He led
from the front. When, as General de Negrier, he was posted to
Indo-China in September 1883, he promptly sent a signal to
Algiers calling for Legion volunteers to join him. On 8 November
the Legion's 1st Battalion came ashore at Haiphong along with
two battalions of Algerian riflemen before moving north to
Hanoi. From this date the Legion was to have an unbroken
succession of men serving in Tonkin until France's final withdrawal from South-East Asia in 1955.

    With other elements of the Armée d'Afrique, the legionnaires
were to assault enemy fortresses at Son Tay and Bac Ninh. But

who *were* the enemy? For twenty years, since 1862, France had sought to colonize South-East Asia with priests as well as soldiers only to encounter opponents who seemed ubiquitous as well as invisible. Many were regulars disguised as irregulars, deniable if required on the part of the power they really represented, which was to be found in Peking. They were known as 'Black Flags' from the numerous ensigns they carried into battle. Son Tay was held by 15,000 of them together with 10,000 regular Chinese soldiers. The attacking force totalled 5,000.

Under cover of darkness, the legionnaires nibbled through the fort's elaborate outer defences ten days or so before Christmas. A moat had to be crossed and defensive ditches drained. Huge bamboo stakes forming a stockade had to be uprooted. All this work was done with such stealth that the defenders appear to have been unaware of it. Just before dawn, two legionnaires crept up to the fort's west gate and forced it with the expertise of professional burglars. Inside, one of the two men stood guard, while the other – a tall, cocky Belgian of bull-like strength whose kepi was invariably worn at an irregular angle – shinned up to a point where the most prominent black flag was draped. The Belgian, Legionnaire Minnaert, replaced it with a French tri-colour in much the same way as his predecessors had decorated the enemy walls at Sebastopol.

Minnaert's action was more than good for morale. It was an excellent reconnaissance with which to start the day's assault on the fortress from within. But although they were caught by surprise the Chinese hit back and fought so hard that the battle continued for about fifteen hours. After the fort had fallen, more angry words were exchanged in Paris (where China had an ambassador) and another Legion battalion was despatched to Tonkin. About a month after it disembarked at Haiphong in February 1884, both battalions participated in the capture of another Black Flag fort at Bac Ninh. The Chinese arsenal there held the latest rifles and new German artillery pieces.

Playing a mean game of diplomatic poker, the Chinese now signed an agreement through which they recognized Annam – a province of what is now Vietnam – as a French protectorate. This required a Chinese evacuation of their forts there, which the French took over. Towards the end of June, one of these French

garrisons, slogging along the road through the jungle towards
Lang Son, was ambushed by a force ten times stronger. The
column of 600 men was massacred. The war which now developed between France and China was conducted by naval
forces on both sides as well as ground troops. It was a conflagra-
tion which consumed Formosa – where the 3rd and 4th Legion
battalions fought – and brought down the latest government in
Paris (that of Jules Ferry) which had lasted longer (three years and
a few months) than any other of the Third Republic. For the
Legion, the Tonkin campaign was to give rise to a battle as
legendary as that of Camerone.

The Chinese had sent three separate columns of up to 20,000
men each to infiltrate Tonkin. On 2 February 1885 de Negrier led
his men from the Delta to intercept one of these at Lang Son, the
gateway to China. The two Legion battalions in Tonkin were
combined with a battalion of Joyeux to form the *4me Régiment
de Marche* (an ad hoc, and usually temporary, unit). With this
force, in which the officially criminal were blended with those
whose principal offence was to be other than French, plus some
naval infantry and another *régiment de marche* thrown together
from French metropolitan units, the staff created an instant
expeditionary force. Led by the fatalistic de Negrier, it was to
fight with extraordinary self-control against much larger forces
partly, perhaps, because it had little choice. Yet it is to the
soldiers' credit that they seized Lang Son on 13 February and then
advanced into China itself. At Bang Bo in Kuang Tung province,
2,000 French soldiers charged up a forward slope to dislodge an
enemy force of 6,000. Next day, as a Chinese counter-attack by
20,000 men lumbered into position, de Negrier withdrew behind
a screen of legionnaires. The original force of 700 foreign volunteers now numbered 400 but, reinforced by 1,400 more men as he
pulled back towards the border, the French general prepared for
a pitched battle at Lang Son.

The Legion occupied high ground to the north-west, on the
right flank, as masses of Chinese, led by their buglers, came like a
tidal wave to roll over the thin defensive line. It is uncertain how
many Chinese were killed in this frontal assault. French artillery
was already ranged on the killing ground of the Kilua Plain. By
mid-afternoon the battle was finely balanced. Then de Negrier

himself was wounded by a bullet in the chest. He handed over command to Lieutenant Colonel Herbinger, who ordered a fighting retreat during which the Legion units, already isolated from the main force, were left to make their own way back to the sanctuary of the south by a jungle route entirely different from the easier, safer Mandarin Road followed by the rest of the force.

Hasty and less than accurate reports of this action in Paris provoked a rush of self-righteousness to the heads of various opposition politicians, none more so than that of the great Georges Clemenceau. Then a backbencher, Clemenceau accused Prime Minister Ferry of high treason. The hysterical debate which provoked Ferry's resignation took place on 30 March, just two days before a badly-mauled Chinese force started to trek back across its border as a prelude to new peace talks with France.

The French were unashamedly ambivalent about the new colonialism. Memories of the highly publicized massacre of Colonel Paul Flatters by Tuareg tribesmen in the Sahara only four years before were green enough to convince many in France that defence, like charity, should begin at home along the 'blue line of the Vosges mountains', facing Germany. For this reason vociferous opponents of colonialism were Conservatives as often as they were Jacobins such as Clemenceau. But that profoundly cynical organization, the Colonial Party in Paris, knew that it could offer the lustre of military glory and national self-esteem to make up for the humiliation of 1870–71. And for some influential civilians there was much else to play for. Eugène Etienne, MP for Oran at the time, put it this way: 'The only criterion of any colonial enterprise is the sum of advantages and profit to be had for the mother country.' So long as Etienne and his fellow colonialists could manipulate France's lust for '*la Gloire*', they would not lack support.

While de Negrier marched north into China, thousands of Chinese regulars of the Yunnan army together with Black Flag irregulars infiltrated south, to de Negrier's left, following the line of the Red River, to surround the settlement and fort of Tuyen Quang deep in what is now northern Vietnam. The fort had deep brick walls buttressed by earth, one of which overlooked the river Claire. The walls surrounded a bald hill 230 feet high on the top of which perched a pagoda used as the officers' sleeping quarters. Outside the wall was a bamboo fence, a series of trenches, a local village and, beyond that, the most dense wall of all – the jungle rising implacable and dark from the river valley in every direction. To hold this position and its 1,500-yard perimeter in December 1884 there were just thirteen officers and 597 men, including 1st and 2nd companies of the 1st Foreign Regiment (1 RE), under Major Dominé. The senior Legion officer was Captain Cattelin with captains Borelli and Moulinay as his company commanders. On the river itself the French had moored the gunship *Mitrailleuse* with an ensign and his crew of thirteen. The number was insufficient to mount a continuous, coherent defence.

One day early in December a fighting patrol from the fort encountered armed men emerging from the jungle. The encounter seems to have passed off comparatively peacefully. Possibly it was part of a war of nerves on the part of the Chinese. Dominé's response was to send his sapper Sergeant, Bobillot, with an eight-man team to construct a blockhouse on a high point 350 yards away before the Chinese could use the position. Bobillot, a former journalist and writer, went further. He laid mines, organized defensive trenches and burrowed into the hillock inside the wall to create a shell-proof command post. The work was interrupted on 31 December when several hundred Chinese marched as if on parade in a semi-circle round the fort.

On 26 January they made their first mass assault and were mown down by the French who counted fifty enemy corpses and about a hundred wounded. Some of the worst damage was wrought by cannon fire from the gunship. French casualties were two men, slightly wounded. It was the first and last time the Chinese would be foolish enough to advance across open ground in this way. Under the guidance of an illiterate but shrewd commander, Liu-Xan-Phuc, they started tunnelling very expertly in the direction of the walls of the blockhouse outside the fort, and the fort itself. Within three days, the twenty legionnaires holding the blockhouse had to withdraw to the fortress. They did so under heavy covering fire on 30 January. The Chinese promptly placed an artillery piece on the newly evacuated hillock and began a bombardment that would continue throughout the daylight hours of every day of this long siege. As a result, French casualties mounted steadily. Hasty prayers and the committal of the dead to a communal grave became routine, though one or two officers were dignified with coffins made from biscuit boxes.

By now the siege was being fought as tenaciously under the spongy, black jungle earth as on the surface. On 11 February one of the Legion's 'tunnel rats', Legionnaire Vaury, drove his pick-axe into a hole and found himself face to face with an enemy soldier who fired first, then disappeared. Vaury, wounded in the arm, was sent to the makeshift barrack hospital. At 5.45 a.m. next day about 200 lb of gunpowder blew a hole in the main wall. Whooping triumphantly and beating gongs, the Chinese swept through the gap only to be halted by a powerful defensive mine planted by Bobillot. A French counter-attack drove the Chinese back and in the pause that followed, Legion pioneers hastily repaired the gap with bamboo stakes.

About thirty-six hours later another explosion blasted the south-west wall, some of which was apparently swallowed up by a deep trench. Through the smoke and dust the figure of a Chinese soldier appeared to plant a black flag on the wall. Immediately, Captain Moulinay ordered his bugler to sound the charge. In the initial, lethal blast Legionnaire Schelmann had been lofted into the Chinese trenches. To recover Schelmann's body Corporal Beulin and three comrades hurled themselves into the enemy position. In spite of heavy fire from both directions, they succeeded. Beulin was promoted to sergeant next morning.

The pattern of the battle was now established: artillery fire by day; close-quarter combat after dark; tunnelling and mining, twenty-four hours a day. The number of infiltrators into the French position was growing fast: on the night of 15 February, Beulin and twenty-five men launched a bayonet charge to hold off Chinese sappers. They returned with two enemy flags, and four dead legionnaires. Next day the Legion lost Captain Dia, who was duly dressed in a biscuit-box and buried. Another twenty-four hours later and the engineering wizard, Bobillot, was hit by a bullet in the neck which condemned him to a lingering death in the sick bay several days later. The commanding officer, Dominé, made a characteristically laconic note in his diary: 'The Chinese are now digging towards us along four underground tunnels. I believe they could blow up 150 metres of the wall at a single stroke.'

After 20 February the Chinese bombardment was stepped up to a point where there was no hope of holding the position unless it was made more compact. The commanding officer, Dominé, ordered his men to build yet another defensive wall inside the existing one. This flimsy barrier of bamboo and pieces of rock had to be erected under cover of darkness. When the Chinese barrage was lifted, it was to deliver the enemy's message to Tonkinese riflemen serving the French, telling them to change sides, after executing their officers. They declined. Next the Chinese made Dominé an offer: if he evacuated the fort, he could march out with weapons and dignity intact. Dominé ignored this also.

Next day, 22 February, started with a touch of theatre. An overture of Chinese gongs and trumpets at 6 a.m. was the signal for a huge mine to be exploded, sending a shower of rock and earth over the thin line of men defending that part of the wall. A twenty-yard gap was created and Chinese soldiers appeared with flags. In response, Captain Moulinay with a mixed group of legionnaires and other soldiers at his back charged through the gap and straight into the same sort of trap that the French had used themselves ten days earlier. The second mine, laid in the path of the French counter-attack, killed Moulinay and twelve legionnaires and wounded another twenty-six. The survivors were then hit by yet another detonation as they groped their way back towards the fort, deafened and blinded by the horror about them. The Chinese *coup de grâce* was prevented by a party of legionnaires emerging from the fort who vented their anger through the points of their bayonets. Legionnaire Hinderschmitt, meanwhile, was recovering the bodies of his friends, clambering from trench to trench, ignoring the bullets whining round him like angry hornets. On his fifth trip he too was killed. Twenty legionnaires shouting *'Vive la France!'* followed his example, watched by an increasingly bewildered enemy until no French corpses were left to the mercy of the enemy or to the appetites of big carrion crows which now flew daily over the battlefield.

Second Lieutenant Edward Husband, a Paris-born Anglo-

Frenchman and his sergeant, Thevenet, were the next important casualties. After dark on 23 February a group of Chinese appeared from a trench only fifty yards from the nearest breach in the walls. Husband and a handful of his men held the situation, but at a cost. Thevenet died early in the attack. Husband, although gravely wounded, survived (to become, finally, a French general of World War I). After dark, Captains Borelli and Cattelin led bayonet charges, their buglers beside them, to drive the enemy off. Little more than twenty-four hours later another big mine exploded alongside the battered fort, whose bruised, pulped earth – like so many battlegrounds – now resembled a large piece of cheese in which two parties of opposing mites fought one another from hole to hole. Yet it was also the day which was put new heart into the beleaguered garrison.

Almost from the beginning the earnest and systematic Major Dominé had despatched messengers with reports, most of them remarkably phlegmatic, back to his headquarters down-river about events in Tuyen Quang. None of these messengers had returned. This was not particularly surprising. So, having no reason to believe that the outside world was aware of their plight, and taking their cue from the boss, the defenders had slipped into that dour, fatalistic determination to sell their lives as dearly as possible, a state of mind experienced uniquely by soldiers who know that their cause is lost. Doubtless some of them recollected de Negrier's words of welcome. But on this day the unexpected happened. A native messenger whose courage matched his anonymity – he was, in military patois, just another 'cooly-tram' – made the perilous journey out and back. The message he brought was that the French 1st Brigade had been formed up as a relief column and was approaching Tuyen Quang up the river Claire. Dominé convened a meeting of his surviving officers and relayed the good news, but with a characteristic word of caution: no one could be sure how long it would be before the column arrived. There was no guarantee that they would still be alive when that happened.

For the next two days it was war as usual. The latest mine created a fifteen-foot hole in the south wall. There was then another savage nocturnal battle in which Captain Cattelin and

Sergeant-Major Proye drove off the Chinese and seized some of their flags. The regimental journal records the few moments' respite which enabled some hasty dispositions to be made. Cattelin was worried most about losing a lot of men to another big explosion. Instead, hundreds of enemy infantry hurled themselves into the fortress, throwing detonators, grenades and even sacks of ignited gunpowder in front of them as they came into the French line. The legionnaires, picking off their targets as silhouettes, could never be sure that they had made a hit, for there were always more silhouettes coming towards them. At 3 a.m., shortly before daylight would make French marksmanship count for something, the Chinese retired in good order taking their wounded with them. In their wake, however, they left forty dead and a quantity of weapons.

With the morning of 28 February and the customary dawn chorus of hostile artillery, none of the survivors quite believed in the relief column. Like rumours about being posted 'home' for Christmas, it seemed like another comforting, morale-boosting myth. And yet there he was, the second messenger to reach them. The column, under Colonel Giovaninelli, was accompanied by the commander of land forces and an ex-Governor of Senegal, General Brière de l'Isle. This relief was a tantalizing six miles away, encountering fierce Chinese resistance. But at Tuyen Quang, towards the end of that day, the Chinese barrage slackened noticeably. A Legion Sergeant, gripped with some private horror – possibly grief and guilt about the loss of his comrades – turned his pistol on himself and committed suicide. In the calm that followed that single shot the carrion crows circled lower and closer to the corpse-laden trenches. There was no significant action that night though, in the distance, signal flares indicated the presence of Giovaninelli's column. Then, soon after first light on 1 March, the sound of a battle somewhere towards the next reach of the Claire river in the direction of Hoa-Moc.

> Our hearts went out to our liberators [the regimental journal records]. We would wish to go and join them but any sortie is impossible with the strength of our garrison reduced to a mere 180 rifles now defending a mile of wall of which 200 yds are breeched and four or five new mines are ready to blow up.

The Chinese forces, later estimated by the French to be around 20,000, were not ready to give way easily to a relief column of 3,000. The jungle battle went on throughout that day and the next, the Chinese fighting hard from well-dug defensive positions overlooking the river. But at the beleaguered fortress, there was a remarkable change. At 3 a.m. on 4 March French sentries, detecting stealthy movement outside, made a cautious reconnaissance. They could not believe that the Chinese had abandoned the trenches and strongpoints for which they had fought so tenaciously. Some brave souls actually walked outside the walls, standing erect, without becoming targets. At this news the veteran Captain Borelli, revolver in hand, led a small patrol including the burly Legionnaire Thiebald Streibler, to confirm that the Chinese had indeed quit.

As they scrambled cautiously over the broken and tortured ground they heard Chinese voices, chanting softly. One enemy strongpoint was still occupied, possibly by a rearguard deliberately left there, or perhaps because of a failure of communication. Suddenly Streibler shouted something and thrust himself in front of his captain as a fusillade of bullets sliced through the cool morning air. From a hole in the ground a tell-tale wisp of smoke identified the source of the gunfire. In the action which followed, the Chinese stay-behind party was annihilated. Streibler was dead by the time his Legion comrades, faces blackened by powder, opened the gates of the fortress at 2 p.m. that day to present arms as Giovaninelli and the General and 3,000 others swung into the wrecked fortress. Major Dominé, firmly at attention, delivered a characteristically terse welcome, begging to report forty-eight dead including captains Moulinay and Dia, and 200 wounded. Casualties among Giovaninelli's column were more severe: 500 dead and wounded including twenty-seven officers.

On parade next day General de l'Isle told the siege survivors – twenty of whom were crippled for life – that they could say with pride: 'I was with the Tuyen Quang garrison.' But the most moving memorial of the siege was created by the poet-soldier Borelli in memory of Streibler, the legionnaire who had saved his life by sacrificing his own when the battle was all but finished. To be the last casualty, as all armies know, is the least desirable fate of all.

You soldiers who sleep under the earth so far away,
Whose flowing blood leaves so much regret,
Tell them only, 'It's our captain
Who remembers us, and counts his dead.'

Borelli became France's public conscience, reminding the nation what it owed its soldiers, particularly those who were, in his often-quoted phrase, Frenchmen not by blood received but by blood shed for their adoptive country. France was not grateful for such reminders and Vicomte Borelli, although he served for some years after Tuyen Quang, was not promoted. He remained a captain. The souvenirs he brought back, two black flags, were solemnly placed in the Legion's chapel at Sidi-bel-Abbès. In the light of his experience, Borelli declared that these symbols of a high-cost victory did not belong to France. With remarkable foresight he left instructions that if ever the Legion were to leave Africa, the flags should be burned. They were ceremonially incinerated by the Legion in 1962, just before the regiment left Algeria.

The siege had another curious echo in the Legion's later history. In 1954 some seventy-three survivors of Dien Bien Phu – now formed up as Prisoner Convoy No. 42 – were marching to a rendezvous where they were to be handed back to a defeated France. They paused at a town entirely destroyed by the Vietnamese which some of the regiment's amateur historians identified as Tuyen Quang. Sure enough, a Polish legionnaire discovered among the wreckage the remains of a monument erected by Colonel Maire in 1927 in memory of Bobillot and other heroes of the siege. It gave the prisoners food for thought, for Tuyen Quang was not only the site of the victory which had given France almost unchallenged power in that part of South-East Asia for seventy years. It was also the scene of France's first military victory since the great defeat of 1870–71. The prisoners of 1955, as they tramped past, were on their way to a war in Algeria and a new round of promises to allies which would be dishonoured. As one of the Legion prisoners of war put it, 'This is where we came in.'

CHAPTER 6
Hearts of Darkness
(Dahomey, Madagascar, 1892–1907)

We soldiers know only that there are territories
in Africa which ought to belong to us, but the
English and the Germans are taking them. We
are trying to beat them to it.

– Colonel (later General) Joseph Gallieni, 1891

The Army's barracks pollute France with
alcoholism and syphilis.

– Urbain Gohier, anti-colonialist writer, 1898

By 1890 France and Britain were set upon a familiar collision
course in territory belonging to neither of them, far from home.
After Canada and India in the eighteenth century, they now
discovered a new rivalry which even the African continent was
too small to contain. In the scramble for Africa, French entrepreneurs, military as well as civil, sought to open up a colonial belt
stretching from the Niger delta in the west to Djibouti in the east.
There was also a grandiose scheme, never put into effect, to create
a trans-Saharan railway linking the Mediterranean to Timbuktu.
The British had similar dreams of domination all the way from
Cairo to the Cape. The Germans, Italians, Dutch, Belgians,
Portuguese and Spaniards were also active players in the profit-
able game of colonizing (and, as some believed, 'civilizing')
Africa.

It was in this context that the Legion found itself in Dahomey,
West Africa, pitched against a fanatical army whose black
monarch required elaborate human sacrifice to satisfy his passion
for ritual, an army whose corps d'élite were women indoctri-
nated to kill for pleasure. The monarch, Behanzin, was supplied

with gin by the English, wine by the French and Mauser rifles by Germans who put into his mind the idea that 'since 1870, France has ceased to exist'. The king tore up his agreement with the French and tried to run a French coastal trading settlement into the Atlantic. In late August 1892, under the command of Colonel Alfred-Amédée Dodds, a punitive expedition of 4,000 set off into the jungle. It was led by 800 legionnaires freshly disembarked from Algeria under the command of Major Paul Faurax.

In a country where the swiftest and easiest movement is by boat, the Dodds expedition preferred to cut a path alongside one of the main rivers and to march along at a painful five miles a day or less. Faurax encouraged his men from horseback, a command and control facility which was soon to make him a ready target. In mid-September the column paused at Dogba for several days while a bridge was built across the river. The legionnaires followed their usual drill in hostile country of erecting firm defences before they ate and slept. In this case, they dug a ditch and used the waste earth to erect a barrier on three sides. On the fourth, at their backs, the river provided a natural moat.

The jungle at night is a naturally noisy place so that the Marine and Legion sentries on the perimeter had no reason to suppose that the snapping of wood somewhere out in the darkness was not caused by water buffalo or wild pig or monkey. Just before dawn, as they fought off sleep, the sentries on two sides of the square started to see something strange. The blackness of the forest was moving inwards like an enveloping blanket. People emerged from this collective blanket, and battle was joined. The African warriors came on at a rush, paralysing the still-sleeping mass of French soldiers with high-pitched, ululating battle cries while the sentries fired off a ragged burst before the spears overwhelmed them. For a time, much of the French square was immersed, but the Legion force included some very hardened practitioners of warfare for whom Dodds's often-repeated advice, 'Win or die', was no more than a domestic truism. Such men included the dour six-feet tall Captain Paul Brundsaux, he of the flowing beard and Annamite nickname given to the beard, 'Loum-Loum'; a veteran of Tonkin who once had his daughter committed to the cells back in Sidi-bel-Abbès following a minor act of disobedience on her part.

Rising above the screams of Behanzin's warriors the Legion bugle and bull-like voice of Loum-Loum shouted orders. Men turned out of their sleeping rolls, rifles in hand, to pick a target and aim even before they were certain this was not a dream. The fire discipline was as good as ever in a crisis and it cut swathes through the attacking force. True, Behanzin's warriors of both sexes had some firearms, Winchester repeaters as well as Mauser rifles, but they used these as if they were a sympathetic magic, closing their eyes as they pulled the triggers. So there was an element of maverick ill-luck in the death of the Legion commander, Major Faurax, as well as the predictable risk that accompanied his prominent position on horseback. Some say his last words were to his deputy, Antoine Drude, 'Leave me Drude, I'm done for!'; others, that he asked Colonel Dodds who had been summoned to the scene, 'Were you satisfied with my men?'

The bayonet charge had its effect, but there were four more mass attacks after dawn, suicidal waves of Dahomeyans who had yet to learn that courage plus numerical advantage counted for little in such a contest. For some legionnaires, the greatest problem was to clamber over enemy dead in order to get into a satisfactory firing position. Only a few tribespeople were taken prisoner, including two of Behanzin's amazons, their bodies naked from the waist up, glowing with oil, decorated with animal and human teeth. Both were executed along with the other prisoners as the last casualties of that day. French losses were forty-five dead and sixty wounded. Behanzin's army, it is said, lost 832 warriors that day. Some of the bodies were fed to crocodiles in the Oueme, but most were disposed of by burning. The odour of burning flesh lay under the windless jungle mantle, long after the French column had continued on its way. As it did so, always going north towards the hidden heartland of Behanzin's kingdom, there were sudden flurries of action as parts of the winding convoy were ambushed from the cover of jungle and swamp.

On 4 October, as they came to the village of Poguessa a few days' march from the sacred shrines of Kana, the column's advance guard of Senegalese infantry was swept away by a massive attack of men firing rifles from the hip and women brandishing spears and knives. The Legion counter-attacked

with a bayonet charge, losing one of its younger officers, Second
Lieutenant Amelot, on the way. The battle continued sporadi-
cally for most of the day. The Dahomeyan dead numbered 250.
But the steam was going out of the French also. The jungle
seemed as endless as the enemy were numerous and, surprisingly
in a rain forest, fresh drinking water was becoming a problem.
The wells at Koto, some twenty miles away, might satisfy their
thirst if only they could overcome the natural and human enemies
barring the way.

The column now paused for eight days, as more and more men
were struck down by malaria and other diseases. Then came the
rain, a downpour which swept many of the tents away. Their
water-bottles were now full but the wounded could not be left
there much longer. The fittest of the French were about to shoot
their way into the village of Akpa, but for the time being no fight
was left in them. On 16 October, Dodds took the morally difficult
but brave decision to turn back to give his casualties a chance of
survival and the others some respite from the jungle war. During
a harsh retreat, while inexperienced Senegalese infantry showed
signs of demoralization, the Legion carried many Senegalese
casualties as well as their own. The trek back lasted a week and
was punctuated by the graves of men dying of their wounds.

On 25 October, reinforced by new troops marching up from
the coast, the column turned back again towards the Dahomeyan
capital. Horses now hauled a series of artillery pieces and, five
days later, on 30 October, these guns were brought to bear. The
Dahomeyan will to resist started to crumble at last and the French
entered the place of shrines, Kana, to discover a macabre death
cult. Human skeletons were commonplace ornaments. Other
artefacts created from human organs so horrified the Senegalese
infantry that they dared not glance at them for fear of evil magic
entering their souls. Some ten days later, on 16 November, the
column marched through the main gate of Behanzin's walled
capital, Abomey. Everything that could be ignited was already
ablaze, but of the monarch of death and slavery himself, there
was no sign.

That night, legionnaires looted the palace cellars and made bad
jokes about Abomey's skull-encrusted throne. Everywhere, it
seemed, human bones – particularly skulls and teeth – were used

as furniture. Even the royal goblets were adapted from human remains, the heads of former enemies. Abomey was one enormous ossuary, a temple of African paranoia. King Behanzin, stalked for months through the wilder reaches of his former kingdom, surrendered on 26 January 1894. A Legion detachment escorted the monarch – a pensive, clerkly young man – on the first stage of his journey into French exile across the Atlantic, on the Caribbean island of Martinique.

The morning after they seized Abomey, the Legion called the roll. Of the 800 legionnaires who had landed in this grim part of Africa three months before, only 450 were still present to answer their names. Among them was 'Loum-Loum' Brundsaux, newly appointed Chevalier of the Légion d'honneur. Brundsaux was to give France exceptional service and dedication in spite of an explosive temperament. He had come to the Legion – like many another good professional soldier – after a false start elsewhere. But whereas Leroy de Saint Arnaud had arrived smelling of gambling debts and while Prince von Milson von Bolt had trailed behind him a small but troublesome history of duelling, Brundsaux's problem was an excess of personal integrity.

He had graduated from St Cyr in 1874 and did well as an orthodox infantry officer. As a bright young captain serving in Tunisia he fell in love with a young woman in Bizerta. The army refused him permission to marry. When he protested that his fiancée was already the mother of his infant daughter he was promptly posted back to France. He resigned his commission, married his lady and rejoined the army. This time, his commission was not a Regular one but 'Foreign', initially good for service only with the Legion or some other African regiment. He also lost three years' seniority but when he finally retired, still suffering from the malaria he had contracted in Dahomey, it was as Major-General Brundsaux, commanding 136 Infantry Brigade on the Western Front in 1916.

A grateful nation finally rewarded his forty-two years' soldiering for France, including twenty-one years' active service and nine wars, on 30 August 1929. On that date a committee of civil servants in Paris drastically reduced his pension as a military invalid. Brundsaux died a year later, aged seventy-four, leaving an unexpected mark on Legion history. The regiment celebrated its centenary in 1931 by unveiling a large and impressive memorial guarded by four stone statues. The memorial stands still on the Legion parade ground at Aubagne. One of the four guardian figures, at each corner of the globe, representing the empire builders of the Third Republic, is unmistakably the face and broad-shouldered figure of the man known to legionnaires as 'Loum-Loum'.

The Dahomey campaign was part of a larger pattern of French infiltration into Africa and, furthermore, one of the more disciplined pieces. For while Dodds's column was moving north from the Niger delta, other French officers, with stylish disregard for their own government's instructions, were setting out eastward from the Bight of Africa and up the Senegal river to Kayes, across country to Segou and thence north, up the Niger to Timbuktu. As related by Douglas Porch in his excellent history, *The Conquest of the Sahara*, Colonel Louis Archinard's robust policy of carving up slices of Africa was based upon the belief that 'the absence of instructions from the colonial administration may be taken as a tacit authorization to use your own judgement'.

Africa was a long way from Paris, or any other French post office for that matter, and such instructions as were sent out did not always get read, officially, by the officer to whom they were addressed. After Archinard, pushing his luck too far, was recalled to France, his friend Lieutenant-Colonel Eugène Bonnier set off from Segou to seize Timbuktu without government authority. Along the way he was pursued by a civil governor, Grodet, whose instructions Bonnier ignored. The expedition was doomed by indiscipline and rivalry among the French and arrogance (before a massacre of the French by Touareg warriors) about the opposition's fighting ability.

The Legion played no part in this misadventure though two of its companies were on stand-by for it. The men concerned included Sergeant Minnaert, the hulking Belgian legionnaire who had planted the tricolour on Son Tay fort twelve years earlier. In this campaign, however, the Legion's role was to prepare the way into what is now Mauritania and Upper Volta. On 3 May 1893, seven months before Bonnier began his ill-starred journey north, a column of exhausted soldiers marched into the lonely town of

Kayes on the Senegal river. The fighting heart of this group was a party of four Legion officers and 120 of their men acting as a company of mounted infantry. In eight months, this group had covered 1,875 hard miles and fought fourteen battles in the north of the Ivory Coast and Guinea. These exertions together with the various kinds of fever they had collected (swamp, black water, yellow, malaria) had reduced most of the men to a skeletal condition and they were repatriated to Sidi-bel-Abbès. Between February 1894 and January 1895, other mule-mounted Legion companies ranged as far afield as the Sudan.

In controlling parts of the Sudan, both the British and French sought also to control the Nile and Egypt. For the British, the importance of Egypt was its position on the route to India. The French were dragged along by their enthusiastic soldiers. As Porch has put it:

> French colonial policy was made outside the government, in the banquets of the parti colonial and by French soldiers in the field. French soldiers followed a slash-and-burn policy in Central Africa, and everyone kept quiet about it, everyone that is, except the British . . . At one point, British and French troops actually exchanged shots.

That exchange occurred in Nigeria, already a British colony. Subsequently Kitchener – the same Kitchener who had fought so ineffectively for France in 1870 – faced a small but obstinate French force at Fashoda on the upper reaches of the Nile. Under Captain Jean Baptist Marchand, a force of Senegalese infantry had taken two years since July 1896 to reach its objective, a journey of 3,000 miles from its base at Libreville on the Congo river. Marchand's confrontation with Kitchener in the autumn of 1898 made a war between Britain and France a real possibility, defused only by a graceful withdrawal by the French and – several uneasy years later – the negotiation of the friendship agreement known as the 'Entente Cordiale'. Meanwhile, Marchand's epic journey continued across Africa to Djibouti and Suez.

The Foreign Legion was inevitably influenced by all this diplomatic jostling. In 1890, Britain and France agreed a deal in which

British control in Zanzibar was traded off against French domination of Madagascar. Four years later, at a most inconvenient time for France – then saddled with troubles elsewhere – the dominant Hova tribe rebelled in Madagascar.

The French landed an expeditionary force on the 'wrong' side of their island. The beachhead was separated from the ultimate objective, the capital city of Tananarive, by mountains rising to 2,600 feet, and deep, fast-running rivers. Caution underpinned this strategy: an unopposed amphibious operation a long way from home against a sophisticated enemy could not be taken for granted. The Malagasies had a royal family, a queen as head of state (converted to the Protestant religion by a London mission), a court, an elaborate system of justice, rifles supplied by British arms-dealers and a number of British mercenaries as advisers. In time, it became obvious enough to the French that the environment was a far more dangerous enemy than the Hova army but only after the expedition, with 5,000 two-wheel carts and no roads for them to travel on, had been put ashore. The only way to Tananarive, 300 miles away, was to 'yomp' it.

The team serving under General Charles Duchesne which now faced this task was mixed even by French standards: 30,000 men including 7,000 Berber porters (duped into believing that they were to be an élite light infantry) at one extreme and at the other, a regular French line regiment, the 200th, brought from the motherland. Elements of the Armée d'Afrique included some of the French-African light cavalry as well as a Legion battalion (twenty-two officers, 818 legionnaires commanded by Major Barre) which, together with two battalions of Algerian infantry, was temporarily relabelled the 'Algerian Regiment'.

After disembarking at Majunga the expedition was rapidly immobilized by the paucity of usable tracks, combined with a variety of fatal, fast-spreading illnesses among which dysentery and malaria were prominent. Anyone who could wield pick and shovel was mobilized into the labour corps to build a road. The legionnaires dug, watched by spectators including man-sized lemurs, and with mordant humour described their shovels as 'the 1895 model rifle'. On 10 June, seven weeks later, with only a quarter of the distance covered, the French army paused at Suberbieville to build a temporary hospital. The nearby cemetery was for permanent occupation. As well as deaths from natural causes, the suicide rate in the 200th Infantry was growing noticeably. Out of 800 men only 583 were still fit to march. One staff officer, Captain Roulet noted in his diary:

> Every time a European swings a pickaxe here, he's exposed to fever. Even though we are already in the highlands, the men are falling like flies. It is a pity to see these unfortunate men who set off in high spirits now dying without a word of complaint, pickaxe in hand, either of the fever or heat exhaustion which can kill you in three to four hours. Their graves are our milestones. [*Historia Special No. 414 bis*]

At Andriba on 26 August one burst of artillery fire from the French in response to a barrage of enemy cannon was sufficient to put the enemy to flight. The French were now on the high plateau with a clear road ahead of them to the capital, 125 miles away. Yet it was equally clear that at their present rate of progress – two miles a day – very few men would be left alive to march into the Malagasy capital even if it were undefended. So a flying column was put together under General Voyron to bring the war to a rapid conclusion. The fittest soldiers were sorted out, medically examined and counted. There were just 5,000 with 3,000 mules or horses to back them up. The Legion's tally of men cleared for action by the doctor was nineteen officers and 330 Other Ranks compared with a disembarkation strength of twenty-two officers and 818 legionnaires. Additionally, the Legion had just been reinforced from Algeria by three officers and 147 men. The new arrivals included some familiar faces: Brundsaux, Tahon and Martin, all survivors of Tonkin and Dahomey.

The order of march for the advance was that the flying column would set the pace carrying little more than side arms, belt kit and water-bottles. The beasts followed, led by one Berber muleteer for every two animals (a challenging task, since the mules were untamed). The fighting contingent was split into three echelons. The Algerian Regiment, including the Legion at the sharp end, moved off on 14 September to muttered chants from some of the veterans, 'March or croak'. Leading from the front were the tall, bearded figure of Loum-Loum Brundsaux with the two lieutenants, Tahon and Martin.

Malagasy resistance, where it was encountered – as at Tsynainondry the second day of the renewed offensive – seemed to consist of one or two ragged volleys followed by rapid retreat. Abandoned positions contained unused weapons and stocks of ammunition. At the last hill before the capital the French turned loose a locally recruited force of soldiers who knew the terrain and made use of that knowledge to take a short cut to the high points ostensibly defended by the army of Queen Ranavalona III. This reconnaissance alone sufficed to secure evacuation of the last defensible high point before Tananarive. On 28 September a symbolic artillery salvo which put one shell through the roof of the royal palace elicited a white flag of truce and an orderly surrender.

The French lost just seven men killed in action during this conflict, of whom five were legionnaires. Deaths attributed to 'various other causes' totalled 5,736 and four-fifths of these were European. From France proper, the 200th Regiment, including its commanding officer, was all but wiped out by malaria. But there were enough legionnaires on parade in the newly conquered city to be addressed by Duchesne, the military supremo, who told them: 'It is assuredly due to you, gentlemen, that we are here. If I ever have the honour to command another expedition, I will want to have at least one battalion of the Foreign Legion with me.'

In Madagascar as in Tonkin, the Legion was to become a permanent presence so long as there was a French empire. In both territories the end of the big campaign did not extinguish all resistance. In Tonkin, for example, columns of legionnaires were still being unleashed to carry out one-off punitive expeditions ('*colonnes punitives ponctuelles*') up to 1907. But the pick, the shovel and even the hoe were becoming tools as familiar as the rifle, and more often in use. Parallel with the growth of empire, was the belated acceptance of the Legion by France as part of its military tradition. However, at the turn of the century, France had acquired its empire but it no longer loved its soldiers. The most shrill voices raised against the army were those of the anti-colonialists of whom Urbain Gohier was among the most prominent. His book, *The Army Against the Nation*, declared: 'The Army's barracks pollute France with alcoholism and syphilis.'

A year after its publication in 1898, the book was into its fifteenth edition. Clearly, many Frenchmen agreed with Gohier. Since Louis Napoleon's 1851 *coup d'état*, aided and abetted by military chieftains, the French Left had been convinced that the only good army was an amateur one composed of fellow-citizens. The problem of such a *'levée en masse'* was that it tended to be defeated by professionals such as the Prussians. The alternative, the professional *'armée de métier'*, satisfied the average Frenchman's not-so-hidden chauvinism in out-facing the detested foreigner. But it simultaneously aroused his disquiet as a force for imposing law and order upon himself. For Parisians and other city-dwellers, memories of how the Commune had ended with military firing squads, following defeat at the hands of a foreign army, meant that both nightmares could occur.

Further, the use by various governments since the 1860s of the army (particularly the cavalry) to break strikes, as well as the incorporation of the Gendarmerie Nationale into the military structure were potent sources of anxiety about whose side the army was on. To make matters worse, some senior army officers made no secret of the fact that they did not serve the government of the day except where it reflected the 'general will' of France, as they saw it. National honour, such generals believed, was too serious a matter to be left in the hands of politicians.

Public discontent was at last given a focus when a Jewish captain, Alfred Dreyfus, was court-martialled for espionage on flimsy evidence in 1894 and given a life sentence on Devil's Island. When the real culprit was discovered the War Ministry attempted a clumsy cover-up. Emile Zola wrote a demolition of the army's case under the title, *J'Accuse*. The principal prosecution witness, a colonel, was revealed as a forger and killed himself. A re-trial took place in 1899 and Dreyfus was pardoned. As the historian Alistair Horne has recently reminded us, the impact of 'The Affair' on French public life was traumatic and long-lasting.

Across the nation attitudes polarised and hardened, with the Dreyfusards seen as Republican and progressive, standing for justice and individual liberty and supported by the intelligentsia; on the other hand, the Army – from whose closed ranks the scandal had sprung –

partly Monarchist and largely Catholic, dedicated to hierarchical order, tradition and obedience . . . The point came when the Army had reason to feel its whole being was under attack from its Republican foes and there was talk of a right-wing military coup . . . but the Army, once again, did nothing more disloyal than to grumble. [Alistair Horne]

The army, for ideological reasons as well as an implicit assumption that it was less venal than the politicians running the country, was not easily forgiven – at great cost to France. The election as Prime Minister of the ultra-republican Émile Combes in 1902 unleashed an indiscriminate political attack on the army's morale and organization as part of a programme to republicanize both the Catholic Church and the army. In the name of republican reliability the new War Minister, General André, purged the officer corps, using the freemasonry movement to provide gossip about brother-officers' private lives and religious beliefs. Mere attendance at church on Sunday could result in a report which impeded further promotion. The effect on army efficiency generally was disastrous. As Horne describes it:

Inevitably, standards slumped; sluggish bureaucracy thrived. Even by 1910 34.5 per cent of captains in the infantry department of the War Ministry were promoted major, compared to 1.5 per cent from line regiments; while 31.9 per cent of all officers joining the Pay Corps became brigadiers and generals, compared with 9.6 per cent for combat arms. Smart officers flocked to join the administrative branches.

This process – to select for high office soldiers who were not fighting soldiers, but safe, politically reliable placemen – left the officers risking their lives with the Legion a long way out of the promotion race from 1902 onwards. Such men as Brundsaux remained captains for years. There were just twelve years left before the German guns would roar over France's smug, petit-bourgeois frontier once more to start a conflict in which – by no coincidence at all – the much-abused African regiments led by the Legion would win the greatest number of gallantry awards made to French soldiers on the Western Front. Meanwhile, during the first decade of the twentieth century, the Legion fought another colonial campaign which, in a curious way, gave clear early warning of the disaster that was to come in 1914.

CHAPTER 7
Milestones on the Road to Armageddon (1900–1914)

The most beautiful feat of arms in Algeria for
forty years.

– Charles de Foucauld, 1903

A milestone on the road to Armageddon

– Winston Churchill on events of 1906

The first months of the twentieth century were busy ones for
France's empire-builders and desert rats. There was a growing
sense of urgency about the process of colonization, for Germany was also taking an interest in North Africa. In 1887, for
instance, Bismarck promised the Italians German armed support
for Italy's claim upon Tripoli, and opposition to France in
Morocco, in exchange for Italy's assistance in opposing French
interests in Europe. By 1900, most of Africa was either occupied
or pre-empted by treaty. The exception was Morocco, an independent kingdom with an ill-defined border with Algeria to the
east and the Sahara to the south. Successive Moroccan sultans
had laid claim to settlements they could not control, such as
Timbuktu in 1590, and many of the oases on the way. To begin
with, the French were not interested in hard military conquest of
the Sahara as such, but its pacification to enable French influence
to stretch from Dunkirk to Tamanrasset and beyond, to French
West Africa. Since efforts to drive peacefully through Touareg
country in the nineteenth century had failed, the task became one
of real domination of the area.

In March 1900, a column of Joyeux and Algerian sharpshooters, backed by artillery and led by Lieutenant-Colonel
Clement d'Eu, blew their way at point-blank range into the

walled oasis town of In Rahr, deep in the Sahara. Once inside, they used dynamite to scythe their way through the thick kasbah walls. This was firepower on a scale never seen before in the Sahara. For the time being the people of the oases accepted that they were the equal of the French in mobile, skirmishing guerrilla warfare but not big, set-piece battles. Colonel d'Eu's initiative was already being emulated by his brother officers, Bertrand (commanding 1st Foreign Regiment) at Igli, and Ménestrel at the strategically placed oasis of Timimoun in May.

The French sweep to the south through an enormous swathe of Moroccan borderland was carried out at a speed which bewildered the tribesmen. The offensive required thousands of impounded camels – a quarter of which would die – as well as food and water for thousands of tired, tense soldiers. Bertrand's force, for example, included 4,500 camels and 2,000 men. Their survival in a hostile environment peopled with resentful tribesmen required marching of a special and heroic order. The nine officers and 400 men drawn from *2me Régiment Étranger* (2 RE) under the command of Major Letulle, which assisted in the capture of Timimoun on 7 May, set off on a zig-zag route back to their base 360 miles away at the height of summer. On 26 July the column marched back into Géryville on the southern edge of the Atlas range after surviving shade temperatures of 48 degrees Centigrade. In seventy-two days since leaving the base it had covered 1,140 miles. Rock and sand had cut the men's boots to pieces so that many of them ended the journey barefoot.

By then, the Saharans had recovered sufficiently to strike back. Two weeks after Letulle's epic march another Major, Bichemin by name, was escorting a convoy of 4,000 camels north along a border trail, together with a battalion of Algerian infantry. The mounted company of 2 RE, with its mules, was about 1,000 yards in front of the convoy as a protective screen. At dawn the legionnaires were warned that they were about to be attacked. Captain Serant sent the camel train back the way it had come, guarded by a mere section of mounted legionnaires. When this group was at El Moungar, just beyond instant help from the main force, it came under attack from 300 enemy cavalry and 600 men on foot. Within seconds, before the legionnaires could tether their mounts, eight of them had been shot dead and another eight lay wounded. The survivors formed a defensive square and held on until another element of the main column, the mounted Spahis, charged to their rescue.

Three years later, on 1 June 1903, the civilian Governor of Algeria, Célestin Jonnart, was ambushed while making a tour around Figuig, well within the ambiguous border area between Morocco and Algeria. A week later the French sent a punitive column including 2 RE into the shattered, waterless rocks between Wadi Guir and Wadi Zisfana. In the oasis area of Touat, south of this conflict, 200 Berber warriors hit a French camp on 16 July. These actions were a mere curtain-raiser for what was to follow.

At the mid-point between the two incidents, in a desolate place called Beni Abbès, there now lived one of the most exotic men the French ever sent to Africa. Charles de Foucauld had started life as a military hellrake and dilettante who smuggled his mistress in a crate from France to Algeria. He was a cavalry officer, assigned to the Chasseurs d'Afrique. Bored by military life and in search of absolutes, he had resigned his commission at the age of twenty-four, learned Arabic and explored Morocco. At the time, Morocco was closed to outsiders and executed unwanted strangers. Foucauld toured the country disguised as a Jew and then undertook a spiritual pilgrimage which led him to Rome, to the priesthood, the Sahara, asceticism, an insanitary hermitage and a violent death in 1916.

From the time he returned to Africa as a priest in 1901, his old comrades-in-arms held Foucauld in something approaching awe, this man in friar's garb with the Sacred Heart flamboyantly emblazoned on the chest; the lean, bearded martyr's face and deep-set, abstracted eyes that seemed to be fixed on some far desert horizon deep within the man himself. They gave him extra food. He gave it to the poor, the despised outcasts of the tribes and the ex-slaves who came to him each day between his long, punishing periods of prayer and meditation. One of these desert visitors had confidences of a non-spiritual variety to impart: Foucauld was informed that a war party led by Sharif Mouley-Moustafa from Matrara was riding to Taghit against the tribes paying tribute to France.

Foucauld, not without some annoyance, interrupted his pater-nosters and hurried to see young Captain de Susbielle, running the Arab Bureau, or civil administration, at Taghit. The information was good and for four days, from 17 to 20 August, 470 men with two 80mm mountain guns for support held off a series of assaults by 4,000 tribesmen. The defenders included 1st platoon, 22nd Mounted Company of 2 RE under Lieutenant Pointurier and a platoon of Joyeux. The legionnaires had covered forty miles in a forced night march to join the battle. The garrison lost nine dead and twenty-one wounded and the enemy, 1,200. Foucauld recorded in his diary: 'This is the most beautiful feat of arms in Algeria for forty years.'

More dramatic events were just around the corner. At the end of the month a huge convoy was put together near Figuig: a total of 3,000 camels escorted by 2,000 men under Major Bichemin set out in three groups to resupply isolated forts and oasis garrisons to the south. The second group, consisting of 573 camels, was escorted by the 2nd platoon of 22nd Mounted Company and thirty Algerian Spahi cavalrymen. On 3 September, on the rocky, undulating plain of El Moungar the legionnaires broke for coffee. It was 9.30 a.m. The men had marched through the night as rearguard for a wayward, slow-moving and noisy caravan. Sentries from the Spahi were posted to keep watch. First these sentries, then the legionnaires also were overrun by a wave of enemy horsemen who emerged from nearby dead ground at a gallop. In the ensuing mess the animals stampeded. These included the legionnaires' mules which carried most of their ammunition and all their water. The company commander, Captain Vauchez, snapped an order to some surviving Spahis: 'Ride like hell to Taghit or El Morra. Get help back here.'

The enemy were now charging at will through the French soldiers who divided into two groups, each on its own hillock. One of these was commanded by a tall, handsome friend of the Danish royal family, Lieutenant Christian Selchauhansen; the other by Vauchez himself. The Dane was an easy target and was hit by several rounds early in the action. He died slowly, out of reach of would-be rescuers, his blood drying into a cake on the sand beside him. Two of his legionnaires who tried to reach him preceded him into death. This group was now brought under the control of Corporal Tisserand. Tisserand, an old desert hand, knew the tribes; the relish with which they allowed death to come only gradually to a doomed enemy. He and his men were now surrounded by the Berber, the Doui-Menia, the Oulad-Djerir, the Chaamba . . . all circling the legionnaires like jackals. The conflict became a battle in slow motion. Tisserand ordered the men to conserve their ammunition. They were to shoot to kill or not at all. The men knew that they were engaged in the soldier's last earthly transaction. But one's own life could be paid for, and dearly, when all hope was gone. As the tribesmen moved in for the kill, so Tisserand led a bayonet charge by way of counter-attack. The tribesmen backed off.

French casualties among the second group included Captain Vauchez. Sergeant-Major Tissier took over only to be gravely wounded, then killed outright by a second bullet. Then Tisserand was also hit. He died just before the first relief column – a group of locally raised volunteers led by de Susbielle, the Arab Bureau Captain at Taghit – appeared at 4.20 p.m. On the heels of this rescue party was another Mounted Company of the Legion, this one from 1 RE under Captain Bonnelet. The tribesmen now finally broke and fled.

The battle had lasted eight hours. Only thirty-two legionnaires out of 113 comprising the original escort were still on their feet. The dead included two officers, two NCOs and thirty-two legionnaires. Later, the French authorities rewrote the casualty list by awarding Corporal Tisserand a posthumous commission and – following the tradition that an officer newly promoted from the ranks must join another regiment – they formally posted the now-dead Second Lieutenant Tisserand to 1 RE. The wounded comprised five NCOs and forty-two legionnaires. Next day, the company buried its dead in a collective grave. Above it, the surviving legionnaires piled a cairn of desert rocks, carved by the same desert wind that had created this lonely hillock. The commemorative plaque described the enemy as 'Moroccan dissidents'.

As Foucauld nursed the surviving wounded legionnaires at Taghit, news of the loss rapidly spread to Paris where the anti-Catholic, anti-army campaign was at its height. Some were inclined to shrug off the massacre, though the French government did not go quite that far. It agreed to a suggestion by its Governor in Algeria, Monsieur Jonnart, that a certain Colonel Hubert Lyautey should be appointed military supremo in this deadly border zone.

Lyautey was told firmly that he was not to invade Morocco, whose international status was guaranteed by treaty. Lyautey, a veteran of Tonkin, China and Madagascar, had his own ideas about that. He was going to ensure that whatever conflict was to be fought would take place on hostile territory and not that of recently pacified, now friendly tribes, accepting French protection and therefore abusively known to the enemy as 'roumis', or 'emasculated ones'. At a prudent distance inside Moroccan territory, Lyautey would build a *cordon sanitaire*, defended by three posts about 100 miles apart and – appropriately in all the circumstances – manned by the Foreign Legion's fast-moving mounted companies. To fudge the location of the new bases he simply gave new names to the Arab locations on which they were imposed. Ras-el-Ain, about a hundred miles inside Morocco, was renamed Berguent on French military maps in 1906 and was the third such base. The others were Bechar, between Wadi Guir and Wadi Zisfana, opened in November 1903, and Forthassa in spring 1904.

Some historians believe that Lyautey simply thumbed his nose at his own government in engaging in this creeping invasion, but this seems unlikely when set against the geo-political background outside France. Lyautey's unannounced invasion started only five months before the Entente Cordiale between Britain and France was signed in April 1904. The most significant clauses of that agreement were kept secret until 1911. Publicly, in exchange for leaving Britain free rein in Egypt, France 'stated she had no desire to alter the political status of Morocco and Great Britain promised not to obstruct her action there' (Grant and Temperley). But the secret clauses allowed that if the Sultan of Morocco should cease to exercise authority in his own land then – aside from the slice of the Moroccan coastline to be handed to Spain – France could annex the rest.

French incursions into Morocco in advance of April 1904 merely anticipated events and it seems at least plausible to believe that Lyautey's apparent defiance was, in fact, in line with his government's secret strategy to seize control of the last independent land in Africa. From being a mere tactical nuisance on the flank of France's advance across the Sahara, Morocco was now seen as a rather desirable property. Thus, by a quite remarkable coincidence, the Sultan was overthrown within four years by his brother, who presently demanded military support from France. An inevitable consequence of this policy was to reduce German influence in Morocco. The Entente – in part an Anglo-French plot to elbow the Germans out of Morocco – was already setting in train some momentous events, in which the Legion would be intimately involved. By the beginning of 1905 the German government was becoming suspicious about French designs in Morocco. Early in February a French envoy was known to be making new demands on the Sultan, which indicated that France was attempting to obtain more control over the country, thus altering the status quo. The German response was to send Kaiser Wilhelm in person to Tangier, where he made a speech declaring German dedication to the integrity of 'a free Morocco'. Then the Germans demanded an international conference to reaffirm this integrity.

The conference duly took place the following year at Algeciras, but not before the Sultan had revoked all agreements with France. It was a replay of events in Dahomey but on a larger, more dangerous scale and much nearer to the rivals' home territory of Europe. Events now started moving steadily out of everyone's control. Churchill described Algeciras as 'a milestone on the road to Armageddon' because it hardened, for the first time, the impending confrontation between the Anglo–French–Russian Entente on the one hand and the Austro–German alliance on the other. It was during the Algeciras negotiations that French and British naval authorities discreetly agreed to co-operate for the first time since the Crimea, opening the way to a one-sided treaty through which Britain – in defending France's northern coasts – was certain to be involved in any future land struggle.

Germany got nothing out of Algeciras except a promise of participation in trade in Morocco on equal terms with France, Spain and England. France, meanwhile, gained effective control of Morocco's internal and external security, plus the conference's approval to engage in 'a peaceful penetration' of Morocco at once. The blood which would flow from this peaceful penetration, much of it supplied by the Foreign Legion, would still be staining the countryside in 1934.

Within a few months of the new agreement a French official was shot dead in Tangier and a French doctor murdered in Marrakech. In June, Sir H. Maclean, instructor to the Moorish army, was kidnapped. In July, French navvies engaged on port works at Casablanca were slaughtered by Muslim zealots for allegedly damaging a cemetery. To this the French responded with a naval bombardment and occupation of the territory round the city. One objective of this operation was to rescue Europeans who had taken refuge in the French consulate. In August, the modest party of Marines put ashore from the warship *Galilee* was followed by 'a little expeditionary force' of 3,000 men including hundreds of legionnaires. As usual, the number initially sanctioned by Paris proved too few. By January the following year, 1908, there was a total force of 14,000 to pacify an area of fifty miles around Casablanca.

In the rancid political atmosphere left by Algeciras, another quarrel was fabricated between France and Britain on one side and Germany on the other. This time, the Legion was involved to an embarrassing degree. German residents of Casablanca, with the complicity of their consul, created an organization to convert legionnaires belonging to the Moroccan expeditionary force into civilians. For almost two years this clandestine desertion agency spirited away hundreds of soldiers before its activities came to light in 1908. In September of that year, two Germans, as well as a German naturalized as a French citizen, a Russian, a Swiss and an Austrian were persuaded to desert together. The German consulate provided them with civilian clothing and hid them in the city for some days until, on 25 September, a regular mailboat, the *Cintra*, came by. The steamer dropped anchor in the harbour, but some distance offshore.

At noon, the deserters arrived dressed in civilian clothes, carrying false papers issued by the consulate. A Legion corporal, on the look-out for the missing men, promptly called the French vice-consul, a certain M. Maigret, and the naval officer in charge of the harbour, Lieutenant de Soria.

The German consulate's Chancellor, Herr Just, and his Moroccan bodyguard bundled their six charges into a rowing boat and clambered in after them. It was at this point that the adventure took a farcical turn. Great desert warriors no doubt, the legionnaires were no sailors. They contrived to capsize their craft. Some unkind souls have speculated that they were suffering from the effects of several pre-emptive celebrations during their days in hiding. Whatever the cause, their noisy curses rattled round the harbour like rocks in an echo chamber and they were welcomed back ashore by a French posse, which promptly arrested the legionnaires. In the brawl which followed, the Moroccan bodyguard was roughed up and the French naval lieutenant, de Soria, drew his revolver. The deserters, considerably the worse for wear, were removed to the French military prison at Fort Provost.

The diplomatic farce which now followed in Europe's capitals was wilder and more dangerous still. The German Chancellor, von Bülow, leaned on the French ambassador to Berlin to demand liberation of the three Germans (who had not been arrested on French soil) and compensation for two of his mauled consulate staff. The French refused. The German Crown-Prince Wilhelm, heir-assumptive and the army's Hotspur, wrote to von Bülow on 2 October: 'The Casablanca incident is a test of force . . . Our honour is heavily involved in this and it is high time for this insolent group in Paris to experience anew what the Pomeranian Grenadier can do.'

A week later, the German Chancellor replied that Germany had no need of new Slav or French territory. He added, 'Furthermore there would probably be no war against France without a war against England.' This proved to be entirely correct. Colourful evidence that the Casablanca incident was now dangerous to peace in Europe emerged from the columns of the *Daily Telegraph*. On 28 October the newspaper published a long article describing the Kaiser's views about this and other issues, submitted, the paper claimed, by an 'unimpeachable authority'. The anonymous interviewer, the 'unimpeachable authority', was the German Emperor himself. Thus, in the novel format of the Kaiser interviewing himself, Wilhelm told the British public:

You English are mad, mad, mad as March hares. What has come over you that you are completely given over to suspicions quite unworthy of a great nation? . . . In my speech at Guildhall I declared that my heart is set upon peace . . . There is nothing in Germany's recent action with regard to Morocco which runs contrary to the explicit declaration of my love and peace . . .

Both this extract and the following exchange (quoted from the Royal Archives at Windsor with the gracious permission of Her Majesty the Queen), reflect the deepening crisis. On 4 November Sir Charles (later Lord) Hardinge, permanent Under-Secretary of State at the Foreign Office and the King's 'trouble-shooter', wrote to King Edward:

The Germans have again rejected arbitration in the question of the deserters from the Foreign Legion at Casablanca after having accepted it . . . This action . . . is a very dangerous step to take at the present time when the international situation is distinctly critical. Ever since the publication [in the *Daily Telegraph*] of the Emperor's alleged interview, I have greatly feared the consequences of His Majesty's exasperation and his desire to vindicate his own personal position in Germany. The subject of contention is also dangerous as it involves the honour of military and naval officers and national dignity . . . If matters should assume a serious turn, publicity would probably be the only means of avoiding a catastrophe. As the Germans proposed arbitration and the French accepted, the whole of civilised public opinion would be on the side of France . . . Fortunately, the French appear to be quite cool and not disposed to lose their heads and start a panic.

King Edward's response, noted at the top of the letter, was crisp and to the point: 'Answer: Trust French Gov: will remain firm ER.'

Edward had adored France long before Parisian crowds had greeted him with the cry: 'Long live *our* king!' He also detested his nephew Kaiser Wilhelm. Outraged by Wilhelm's appeal, via a British newspaper, to his own subjects, Edward now demonstrated how firm he was prepared to be. As described by the French historian Tardieu (author in 1909 of *Le Mystère d'Agadir*):

On 6 November Bülow made a final and equally fruitless attempt to procure an apology for the arrest of the deserters before the arbitration began. 'King Edward,' writes Tardieu from inside knowledge of the French Foreign Office, 'let the French Government know that he would place at its disposal on the Continent, if peace were broken, five divisions of infantry and one division of cavalry to hold the left wing in the second line.' [Quoted in G. P. Gooch, *History of Modern Europe, 1871–1919*]

On 7 November, more publicly, the British and Russian ambassadors to Paris informed the French Foreign Office that their governments supported France in the deserters' row. It is clear from this just how close the scandal had come to triggering off World War I in 1908. Had it been left to the English monarch of the day and his German relatives, there is no doubt that each part of a divided royal family would have taken up arms in order to assert – or demolish – the Legion's right to reclaim deserters on non-French soil. It is plausible to think that had the war started in that year, Germany would have emerged as victorious as in 1871, though von Bülow did not think so.

At the eleventh hour, on 8 or 9 November, soon after the British intervention (made not only because of Edward's fondness for France, but also because Britain was increasingly uneasy about the burgeoning German battle fleet) – Kaiser Wilhelm was persuaded by his Austrian counterpart to let the matter be settled through international arbitration after all. In due course the Hague Tribunal censured the 'grave and manifest fault' of the Chancellor of the German consulate in promoting the escape of legionnaires who were not German nationals. The French authorities, the tribunal found, had acted correctly 'except that needless violence had been displayed in the arrest of the deserters'.

Behind the scenes, meanwhile, the Legion itself had suffered a blow to its credibility. Two weeks before the brawl, and probably influenced by the anti-German sentiment of the time, the commander of the French expedition to Casablanca, General d'Amade, had sent a signal to his government's representative at Tangier concerning a German newspaper report boasting of the desertion industry. After just one short coastal voyage, the German steamship *Riga* had disembarked fifteen Legion

LEFT: Emir Abd el-Kader, the first great Arab enemy of the Foreign Legion and leader of the Algerians for 16 years in their war against French occupation. This photograph was taken soon after his defeat in 1847, when the French sent him into exile. Later he was awarded the Légion d'Honneur for saving French lives during a massacre in Damascus.
BELOW LEFT: Abd el-Kader's cavalry in action against the 4th Foreign Legion Regiment in Algeria in 1840.
ABOVE: Final stages of the battle of Camerone, Mexico, 30 April 1863, in which just five men – survivors of a company after a day-long battle – fixed bayonets to charge 2,000 opponents. Collective death in battle – even when honourable surrender was offered – became a kind of sacrament for generations of legionnaires after Camerone. The anniversary is still the main event in the Legion's ceremonial calendar.
BELOW: François-Achille Bazaine, the Foreign Legion sergeant who became French military supremo as Marshal-of-France before the surrender to Prussia in 1871. Impeached and imprisoned, he escaped to Spain to die in poverty in 1888 aged 77.

MARSHAL BAZAINE.

LEFT: Major (later Brigadier) Paul Brundsaux, veteran of Dahomey, Madagascar, North Africa, Tonkin and the Western Front.

ABOVE: Five Legion heroes of the First World War: (centre) Lieutenant-Colonel (later General) Paul Rollet, 'Father of the Legion', with the Colour of Legion regiment on the Western Front, and a guard of legionnaires who were also Chevaliers of the Légion d'Honneur. They are (l. to r.) the German sergeant-major, Max Mader, who lost an arm fighting his countrymen for France, and Corporals Rocas, Dieta and Leva.

BELOW: A famous blockhouse built by the Legion and repeatedly attacked during the 35-year conflict in Morocco. This one, part of a chain on the edge of the desert of southern Morocco, was at Bou-Denib, and the photograph was taken soon after a prolonged assault against it in September 1908, the year Britain almost went to war with Germany in support of the French in the Casablanca deserters' affair.

A desert patrol of one of the Foreign Legion's mounted companies preparing to move out from Sidi-bel-Abbès in Algeria in about 1910. Each mule was accompanied by two soldiers, one riding for an hour while the other marched. Such teams, with food and ammunition, covered up to 40 miles a day in deadly heat. The men shared their water with the mule when necessary and – *in extremis* – ate the animal if that proved necessary for survival.

Rollet, at Sidi-bel-Abbès soon after the First World War, inspects recruits about to go on guard duty. After the First World War, the Legion rank-and-file included men who had been officers up to the rank of general in armies elsewhere. (Rollet, incidentally, never wore a shirt but – as here – used false cuffs and collar.)

LEFT: One of the first of the many: on Boxing Day 1914 Bruno Garibaldi, a descendant of the Italian revolutionary hero, led a Legion assault on a German trench at Bolante Plâteau (Argonne) on the Western Front and was killed. Here, the wounded Lieutenant Baccarelli escorts the body back.

BELOW: Colonel Duriez (centre), commander of the Foreign Legion Marching Regiment (an amalgam of all other decimated Legion units in France), in a front-line trench with his men shortly before his death near the Marne on 17 April 1917. He was one of a long list of Commanding Officers of the Legion who died in action.

ABOVE: Bearded and bemedalled pioneers of the Legion, with axes in place of rifles, march in a Bastille Day parade, as ceremonial bodyguard. In the early 1930s the Legion was the most decorated fighting unit in the French army.

BELOW: A more poignant occasion: the Bastille Day parade in Paris in 1939. By now the Legion included a high proportion of Germans and German-speaking Austrians and Czechs. Less than a year later, after the French surrender, the Germans demanded the repatriation of such men. The French obliged, even though these were enemies of Hitler who had fought for France. On Goebbels's orders they were organised into a sacrificial regiment, 2,000-strong, to fight with the Afrika Korps in the Western Desert.

OPPOSITE: During the long siege of Free French forces, virtually encircled by Rommel's Afrika Korps at Bir Hakeim, Libya, in the spring of 1942, the Bren Gun Carrier – open-topped, fast-moving tracked vehicles manned by legionnaires – launched one surprise counter-attack after another against German armour, artillery and supply columns. One of the leaders of these raids, Captain Pierre Messmer, later became a French Prime Minister. In 1986 he was still an MP.

RIGHT: General Pierre Koenig, the legionnaire who led the breakout from Bir Hakeim, perched on the roof of his American shooting brake, a staff car which looked like a Bonnie and Clyde wreck after the escape.

BELOW: Koenig's driver was Susan Travers, a young Englishwoman later admitted as the only woman to serve with the Legion, as a legionnaire. At Bir Hakeim she won a Croix de Guerre after driving through a minefield and three concentric rings of enemy machine-gun fire. Her only anxiety: that the car would break down and she would be blamed.

LEFT: A bird's-eye view of the opening stages of the tragic battle of Dien Bien Phu, a vast area of interconnected strongpoints with an integral airfield. In the autumn of 1953, although it was dependent upon air supply across hostile territory, it seemed impregnable. Once General Giap, the Viet-Minh leader, brought heavy artillery to bear from jungle-clad hills overlooking the airfield, the air bridge was cut and the position doomed. With it, France's 70-year domination of Indo-China ended.

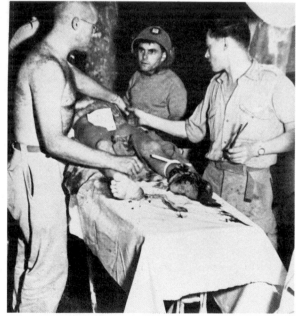

LEFT: On the ground the war was more intimate. Here a Vietnamese soldier who came face to face with a French reconnaissance patrol is taken prisoner. Soon he will face the captors' interrogation. And within a few weeks, those captors still alive in their turn will become prisoners.

ABOVE: Towards the end of the siege of Dien Bien Phu, casualties could not be evacuated. With the doctors they lived in a muddy underground earth bunker, being shelled incessantly. In this famous photograph of the operating theatre, the surgeon, Major Grauwin (left), prepares to amputate a foot.

deserters at Tangier on 16 August. The total number of German deserters between 1 January and 12 September, the date of the signal, was forty-seven, eighteen of them escaping in the month up to 15 August. But since the operation to secure the Chaouia hinterland beyond Casablanca, d'Amade conceded, there had been several hundred desertions including Spaniards and Austrians. He added dolefully, 'It is the natural and logical consequence of France's employment of foreign mercenaries in place of her own nationals.'

D'Amade was wrong. He should have known, even if the Hague International Tribunal did not, that desertion was an endemic problem throughout the French army at that time. The Combes government's anti-Catholic witch-hunts to 'republican-ize' Church and State institutions alike (see p. 116) were having a greater impact upon army morale in France than among the robust, swashbuckling colonial soldiers. As Alistair Horne re-minds us, in 1907 no less than 36 per cent of territorials failed to respond to their routine military service call-up notices. 'Between 1907 and 1909 the numbers of desertions multiplied from 5,000 to 17,000; while between 1906 and 1911 the number of disci-plinary courts martial doubled.'

Anyone enterprising enough to create an agency whose sole purpose was to facilitate desertions, as did the Casablanca Germans, was clearly promoting a growth industry which France had to stop. To make matters worse, Moroccan turbulence was capable of undoing all the diplomacy used to patch up the crises which resulted from France's desire to have an empire but not an effective professional army. So in Morocco, agreements between the two contending European powers, though full of pious intentions, did not last long.

In the aftermath of the deserters' row the two parties agreed a Moroccan Pact confirming German trading rights and French political clout. The chaos and corruption within Morocco (which France was soon to rule through locally appointed barons, or 'caids', empowered to impose taxes) reduced German ideas about profitable trade to a utopian exercise, while destabilization of the existing Moroccan government increased French control. In the same year that the Casablanca deserters were caught, the ruling Sultan of Morocco, Abd-el-Aziz, was deposed by his

brother, Moulay-Hafid, thus opening the door to French annex-
ation. French forces were already at hand, if without a formal
invitation. Zouaves, Chasseurs and legionnaires had landed the
previous year, 1907, in a policing operation to stop Moroccan
tribal raids into Algeria.

The new Moroccan monarch was not popular and within three
years he was expiring under pressure of a siege around him at Fès.
He appealed for help to France. In May 1911 a French relief
column, in which the Legion figured prominently, marched to his
aid. Legionnaire Christian, stopping almost single-handed an
enemy attempt to penetrate the column's supply line, enjoyed the
unusual honour for a private soldier of having a local village
renamed after him. At Alouana on 15 May, meanwhile, a
company of 6th Battalion of 1 RE was massacred in an ambush in
the disputed southern borderland between Algeria and Morocco.
Two legionnaires, cut off and dying of their wounds, removed the
bolts from their highly accurate Lebel rifles so that the weapons
would be useless to an enemy. When a relief column turned the
bodies over, the bolts were still concealed under them.

With the disintegration of Morocco into a series of tribal areas
each seeking independence from the other, events now followed a
predictable political course. By March 1912 Moulay-Hafid had
placed his country formally under French protection. Morocco
was now another French colony. General Hubert Lyautey, an
enlightened soldier who believed that one doctor was worth a
battalion of infantry, became Resident of Morocco, but he
commanded 38,000 soldiers rather than medical men. The
Moroccans made their displeasure vividly obvious and rose in
angry protest all over the country.

German anger was also aroused by France's apparent betrayal
of the status quo. In 1911 the German gunboat *Panther* appeared
in the Moroccan port of Agadir. The vessel was ostensibly
there to safeguard German citizens at risk in French-controlled
Morocco. The whole world knew otherwise: the Germans were
piqued by France's failure to make German trade rights a reality.
So this crisis rumbled on also, like a summer thunderstorm, until
Germany grudgingly backed down in November in exchange
for an enlargement of its Central African territories. The quarrel
was another milestone on the road to Armageddon. Germany

had now given way twice during disputes in which, in the spirit of the age, what counted among the great powers was public machismo. It was also clear that the next time there was a quarrel in Europe, Germany would not be the one to play the role of the great powers' good neighbour, and back away from confrontation.

The year of the *Panther*, 1911, was just three years away from the quarrel to end them all, which awaited only the starting gun at Sarajevo. Only now, at the last moment, did French opinion about its soldiers take another U-turn. With a clear and present danger of armed conflict in Europe, everyone loved a soldier.

When at last war broke out in August 1914, Lyautey was obliged to provide France with forty major units of battalion size. Only three months before Sarajevo two French army groups, one marching east from Fès, the other coming west from the Algerian borderlands at Guercif, had linked up at Taza after prolonged hill fighting. This link did little more than define the opposition and contain it within the Atlas mountains. But with the beginning of the European war, the Zouaves, Spahis (and their horses), Algerian infantry, the bad lads of the Joyeux, Senegalese riflemen, some newly-composed Moroccan regiments and several battalions of the Legion were all shipped off to northern France.

Lyautey ignored a suggestion that he should withdraw to the Moroccan territories occupied by France prior to 1907. He determined to hold what had been won, with fewer troops. The only Europeans left to fight for France in Morocco were two battalions of legionnaires. They were all German or Austrian nationals who had exercised their right not to fight against their own countrymen on the Western Front.

Whether in Morocco or France, they were becoming, in Lyautey's eyes, 'my most cherished soldiers . . . my supreme force'. Times had changed rapidly since Lyautey's predecessor in Morocco, d'Amade, had written his jaundiced report in 1908 about 'these foreign mercenaries'. Lyautey's 'supreme force' was all he had left.

CHAPTER 8
A Rendezvous with Death
(1914–18)

In the offensive . . . let us even go to excess . . .
What the enemy intends . . . is of no
consequence.

– Colonel de Grandmaison, GSO (Ops), 1913.

I have a rendezvous with Death
At some disputed barricade.

– Legionnaire Alan Seeger, 1916

There is a brief moment at the beginning of any major armed conflict when novelty blends with a frisson of anarchy and euphoria to produce a cause for otherwise unfocused lives. It is in that spirit that men sign on to be soldiers without thinking too much about what this can imply. The gesture is somewhat like casting dice with only one certain outcome: that life will never be the same again. So they came to the recruiting offices everywhere in Europe in August 1914, patriots and romantics, every man a village Hercules grateful for the excuse to break the mould of a boring, repetitive life. In England during the first four months of conflict, 1,250,000 men volunteered.

Nowhere was enthusiasm for the war greater than in Paris. Many volunteers for service with the Legion were foreigners past the first blush of youth: forty- and fifty-year-olds whose knowledge of warfare derived from music-hall soliloquies and Victorian ballads. They came, the engineers who had thrown up profitable lives in South America, fugitives from holy orders, barbers, at least one distinguished surgeon, art students, journalists, and illiterates staking everything to prove they were as good as the next man, accomplished writers such as Blaise Cendrars,

Alan Seeger, Ernst Jünger, and briefly, songwriter Cole Porter, as well as Americans fearing they might miss the action. In all, 44,000 men from fifty-one nations other than France joined the Foreign Legion during the Great War – 20,000 in Paris alone – and most of them came during the first month or so of the conflict. By comparison, the Legion's total manpower in 1913 was 10,521.

Yet the 44,000 were a fraction of the bodies supplied by the Armée d'Afrique as a whole. Just before the war, in the spring of 1914, Algeria alone had 33,000 Muslims in French uniform, a number which grew rapidly to 170,000 with the declaration of war. To those were added thousands more from Tunisia, Morocco, Senegal and – in the case of the Joyeux – soldiers of no specific provenance. At the beginning of the war they still wore red trousers, thought to be good for morale. Sighted down the barrels of German machine-guns across open ground they made soft, ready targets.

The Legion handled the growth precipitated by the 'duration only' volunteers by creating three *régiments de marche* which were lumped into the Moroccan Division alongside the Zouaves, Tirailleurs, Spahis, Joyeux and the rest. The first two of these new regiments comprised three rookie battalions and one battalion of veterans drawn from the 'real' Legion in North Africa. These regiments of origin, 1 and 2 RE based respectively at Sidi-bel-Abbès and Saïda, also provided some necessary stiffening of experienced NCOs. Throughout the terrible war to come, the Legion's 3,314 NCOs remained the regimental backbone in the campaign against the Turks as well as on the Western Front. The percentages by nationality and language of these non-commissioned leaders provide a very different picture of the Legion's composition than is suggested by the amateurs of fifty-one nationalities who signed up after August 1914. A total of 40.5 per cent were French (or 44.4 per cent if Alsace and Lorraine are included) but many of these were drawn from the military 'nursery' at Rambouillet, and most of the 3rd *Régiment de Marche* of 1 RE were drawn from the Paris fire brigade. (This is not as eccentric as it seems: the Paris fire service was, historically, a military unit subject to military law. For this reason many of its members who remained in Paris on station during the 1871

Commune, out of a sense of duty to the city, were treated as deserters and were among the 20,000 executed for 'crimes' against their country.)

Of 32,000 foreigners joining the French army between 21 August 1914 and 1 April 1915 (including men from the lost provinces of Alsace-Lorraine) almost 5,000 were Italian. There were also 3,393 Russians, 1,462 Belgians, 1,369 Czechs, 1,467 Swiss, 595 Turks, 541 Luxembourgers, 379 British citizens, 300 Greeks, 200 Americans (including South Americans) and 1,072 Germans. In spite of a deliberate policy decision after 1871 to enhance the number of Francophone NCOs in the Legion, the percentage of German corporals, sergeants and warrant-officers serving on the Western Front throughout the Great War represented 8.4 (or almost 280) while 3.1 per cent (102 men) were nationals of another enemy, Austria-Hungary. Had they been taken prisoner and their nationalities discovered they would have died before firing squads. At the beginning of the war some units still depended upon an embarrassingly large percentage of Germans, notably the 2nd Mounted Company of 1 RE with 70 per cent of its NCOs, including an RSM, originating from one of the German states. The other NCO nationalities between 1914 and 1918 were: Italian (10 per cent), American (6.6 per cent), Swiss (5.6 per cent), Belgian (4.1 per cent), Russian (3.2 per cent), others (14.1 per cent).

There was no problem about posting men from hostile nations who did not wish to kill their fellow-countrymen. After a regimental reorganization in 1915 the number of Legion battalions serving on the Western Front diminished from an initial sixteen to three. In addition there were five in Morocco, one in the Middle East (fighting the Turks), three in Indo-China and two in Algeria.

While the Legion's 'duration only' rookies were receiving some hasty basic training at Lyons, Avignon, Tours and Reims, the French high command was demonstrating the scale of the incompetence so fastidiously cultivated in its ranks by the civilian politicians of the *belle époque*. A total of 800,000 soldiers were launched into an unco-ordinated offensive to recover the lost territories of Alsace and Lorraine without regard for enemy tactics. The Germans unsportingly declined to play to

French rules, ignored Belgian neutrality, and swept round the northern flank and on towards Paris in a 'Battle of the Frontiers' which lasted a mere two weeks. In that time the French army, headed by Marshal Joseph Joffre, lost 300,000 men and nearly 5,000 officers, about one-tenth of the total officer strength.

With German scouts within sight of the Eiffel Tower, the civil government of Raymond Poincaré stealthily slipped away to the good life at Bordeaux. The front was finally stabilized only after a desperate stand on the heights overlooking the river Marne and the Saint-Gond Marsh to the east of Paris (at a cost of 100,000 officers and men) with reinforcements brought to the front from the capital by taxi. Both sides now dug in for four years of trench warfare. Of 103 officers fighting with the Moroccan Division on the left of this battle from 5 September, forty-six were dead when it ended twelve days later, while only 700 men remained alive out of 5,000 men sent to the front line on 1 September. It was, and would continue to be, the price of a mindless French military doctrine known as '*l'offensif à outrance*': in theory, offensive warfare to *excess* irrespective of the opposition but in practice collective suicide serving no useful military purpose. Such intrinsically sacrificial tactics were not aided by French reliance upon light, mobile 75 mm field guns (maximum range, 7,400 yards) as their main artillery, a gun entirely out-classed by the enemy's bigger and more plentiful 21 cm Skoda howitzers (maximum range, 10,280 yards).

On Christmas night 1914, an additional Legion *régiment de marche* – the 4/1st composed largely of Italians and led by Lieutenant Colonel Giuseppe Garibaldi, grandson of the revolutionary leader – moved in bitterly cold conditions against the Germans through woods on the Argonne near Verdun. At its inception the unit included four other members of the same family and was known, not surprisingly, as the 'Garibaldi Brigade'. By the spring, the regiment's 429 dead included two of its Garibaldis, the first of whom, Captain Bruno, died in the first attempt on the German trenches on 26 December. In May 1915, with Italy's entry into the war, the remnants of this regiment were transferred with honour to the Italian army. So far the remaining Legion units – loosely linked together as 1st Foreign Legion

Brigade under Colonel Theodore Pein – had occupied quiet, if freezing, sectors of a front which stretched almost 500 miles from the Swiss frontier to the Belgian coast. One of the *régiments de marche*, the 3/1st, was disbanded in March following a break-down of discipline near Santerre. Most of those serving in its three battalions – Russians, Italians and Belgians – were nation-als of France's allies and were promptly shipped back to their own armies.

It was May 1915 before the majority of legionnaires at last faced the Germans together with a mixed regiment of Algerian-European Zouaves and Algerian (largely Berber) infantry. Their objective, about three miles across rising ground north of Arras, was an elaborate German fortification on Vimy Ridge known from the disturbed chalk soil around it on Hill 140 as the 'White Works'. To prepare for this first great concerted attempt to pierce the hardening German line on a thirteen-mile front, French artillery had maintained a continuous barrage of ineffective shrapnel shells for five hours. At 9.58 a.m. on 9 May the guns abruptly stopped. In the eerie two-minute silence which fol-lowed, the officers – some dressed in Number One uniform with white gloves – studied their watches. At exactly 10 a.m. they nodded to the buglers to sound the advance, and clambered over the parapet into no man's land.

Today, the site is a few hundred yards from the motorway linking Paris to Calais. But on that brisk summer's morning unbroken countryside ran north-east towards the great green-backed whale of Vimy Ridge as veterans and rookies, chins on chests, churned forward under the weight of grenades and ammunition, slithering in mud already churned up by the guns. After perhaps 1,000 yards they hit the first line of German wire. This was intact and as the troops arrived and the wire-cutters began their laborious work, the enemy machine-guns chattered to a deadly tap-dance rhythm which veterans of the Western Front would never forget. Men were falling, their eyes registering surprise as the life went out of them. The advance continued more hastily as artillery shells exploded among them, tearing living men apart to leave no trace but a helmet or a boot, the wearer's foot still inside it. The survivors kept moving, the rookies touched increasingly by the unreality of this laborious march to death, as if they were spectators rather than participants. Veterans braced themselves for the inevitable. Another line of wire; another hailstorm of death. Since there seemed to be no alternative, they advanced even faster. When they reached their objective the Germans were retreating. There were not many officers left to rally them and give orders. But with the remaining NCOs they now grouped together, hurled grenades pre-emptively into the trenches as they occupied them and then moved on through the German position into the cool, solid blockhouses. So far the attack had been costly but successful. The most adventurous legionnaires even slipped into the villages of Vimy and Givenchy. Then the shells started to fall upon them with remarkable accuracy. French shells, fired by French guns, from somewhere behind them.

The men took cover in the excellent German dugouts and licked their wounds while they waited all night for the relieving follow-through force to arrive. By next morning, they had a shrewd idea of the terrible losses they had suffered. In the afternoon they were hit by the German counter-attack they could not hold, for they were the only ones to have advanced so far and were about to be outflanked. They slipped and slithered down the south-west face of the ridge, three miles back to where they had started the previous day.

Neither the legionnaires nor the Algerians could blame their own officers, of whom there were precious few left anyway. The Legion lost fifty officers including its Commanding Officer, Colonel Theodore Pein and all three battalion commanders, majors Mullet, Gambert and Noire. With them went 1,889 NCOs and legionnaires. The Algerian troops alongside them in the Moroccan Division had suffered as harshly. Colonel Cros of the Zouaves and many of his men were among the dead, somewhere out there among the mud and bloodstained barbed wire.

Pein's death was news throughout the division, for he was one of the most charismatic soldiers to emerge from the Armée d'Afrique. The son of one of the 1830 conquerors of Algiers and a first generation settler, or *Pied Noir*, he was totally unafraid of the Sahara and more at ease with a team of desert irregulars known as 'goums' than among his brother-officers from France. He was blamed more often than he was praised for his conquest of the oases of southern Algeria and was probably the only man to accuse Lyautey of lacking nerve in his occupation of Morocco. Pein had swept out of Lyautey's headquarters, waxed moustache bristling, and set off in 1909 to prove that he could cross the Sahara with just one batman on a motorcycle. (The machine became bogged down after several days and the two men almost died of thirst.) The historian Douglas Porch, describing the effect of the attack on Hill 140 as 'a massacre', writes:

> The shrapnel shells had hardly dented the German trenches. Pein could not contain himself: he leaped out of his command post and joined the second attack wave. Incredibly, his men managed to seize Hill 140 but at colossal cost. As the survivors arranged themselves in the trenches to await the inevitable counter-attack, Pein went forward personally to reconnoitre the ground to his front. A sniper brought him down with a bullet that entered his side and penetrated his chest. He crawled into a shell hole, where two legionnaires found him. Pein was transported to the rear, but died soon after. He was buried in the cemetery of the small village of Acq, just behind the lines, his head appropriately pointing toward the enemy lines. That afternoon, a German counter-attack drove Pein's brigade from Hill 140.

A week later, on orders of the high command, the operation was repeated with much the same result. Further east, in the Champagne area, later that year another of the Legion's newly-formed *régiments de marche* (the 2/2nd) led the division into battle at a German strongpoint known as Navarin Farm. In two days – 27–28 September – this unit of 1,600 men lost more than 50 per cent of its manpower to gain a few yards of territory.

One of those severely wounded in that battle was an Englishman whose courage the French recognized the following year with a Médaille Militaire and Croix de Guerre. As a result, the way was now open for Legionnaire John Ford Elkington to be rehabilitated in his own army. A year before his wound, he had come to France as Lieutenant-Colonel Elkington, commanding the 1st Royal Warwickshire Battalion. From the first battle of Mons the British Expeditionary Force had been hurled back to Le Cateau where Elkington and his men were part of a day-long action on a scale which the British army had not fought since

Waterloo. The total British casualties were 8,077 men dead or wounded.

The survivors fell back on St Quentin. There, Elkington sought the assistance of the Mayor. His soldiers were hungry and exhausted. They needed, he explained, some food and somewhere to rest. What happened next is described by Arthur Osburn in *Unwilling Passenger*. The Mayor – like his predecessors around Orléans in 1870 and his successors of 1940 – refused the request for food and shelter. Under pressure from Elkington, the Mayor relented. But, to ensure that St Quentin was preserved as a combat-free zone, would the English colonel sign a document agreeing to surrender to the German army, if it should arrive? Elkington unwisely agreed to this condition and signed. The Germans advanced in another direction, but the surrender document, listing the forces under Elkington's command, was already on its way to the enemy with a polite note from the Mayor.

Major Tom Bridges of the 4th Royal Irish Dragoon Guards told the Mayor that he had no business 'as a loyal Frenchman' to assist Allied troops to surrender, particularly since the Germans had not actually arrived at St Quentin. According to Osburn the Mayor replied:

> Monsieur le Majeur, I do not want our peaceful town unnecessarily destroyed because it happens to be full of English troops. I have asked your colonels and their men to go and fight outside St Quentin but they say, 'No, we cannot fight! We have lost nearly all our officers. Our Staff have gone away by train and we have no artillery. Most of us have no rifles or ammunition and we are all very, very tired!' Then M'sieur, I say to them, 'If you will not fight please go right away and presently the Germans will enter St Quentin peacefully; so the inhabitants will be glad to be tranquil and not killed and all our good shops not burned.' But they reply to me, 'No, we cannot go away. We are terribly, terribly tired and we have had no proper food nor rest for many days. Yesterday we fought a great battle. We have not got any maps and we don't know where to go, so we will stay in St Quentin and have a little rest.' Then I say to them, 'Since you will neither fight nor go away, then please surrender to the German commander and now all is properly arranged.'

The leaking of Elkington's surrender document even before the town came under serious threat finished his career as a regimental officer. He was court-martialled and cashiered. But two years later, the decorations awarded to Legionnaire Elkington were gazetted in Paris, and the coincidence of name noted in the War Office. King George V took the initiative in rehabilitating the former colonel, whose British commission and rank were restored. In recognition of his bravery as Legionnaire Elkington, he was also awarded the DSO, a unique honour in the circumstances.

Only a few months' experience of '*l'offensif à outrance*', combined with lack of proper artillery support, was required to reduce the Foreign Legion Brigade to the elements of one regiment of three battalions. In November 1915 they were combined into a single unit named the *Régiment de Marche de la Légion Étrangère*, or RMLE, commanded by Colonel Cot.

Meanwhile, in an effort to break the deadlock on the Western Front in 1915 and to relieve pressures on the Russians in the east, an Anglo-French force moved against Turkey in a disastrous series of naval and land battles which ended with the evacuation of the survivors of Gallipoli in January 1916. Among the French units taking part in this affair, as part of a newly-created Armée d'Orient, was the *Régiment de Marche d'Afrique* (RMA), comprising four battalions of Zouaves from Algeria and Tunisia and a single Legion battalion. After punishing battles in the first week of May 1915 only one captain survived among the RMA officers to lead a few hundred men. Of the Legion battalion only an NCO and a ragged company were still alive. Subsequently the RMA was part of a French-led, multi-national force which painfully fought its way across Salonika and into what is now Yugoslavia and Hungary. In November 1916 as part of a drive to assist a new ally, Rumania, the Legion battalion occupied Monastir (Bitolj). King Alexander of Serbia, with the quarrelsome French General Sarrail, fêted the troops but the advance northward was then stalled until the last months of the war. By then, worn down by losses, the Legion battalion was dissolved, its survivors shipped to France for the last year of the war.

On the Western Front, the battle honours of 1916 still echo with peculiar sadness in the consciousness of the nations which were there. For France, this was the year of Verdun; for Britain, the year of the Somme. By an odd turn of events and probably because of its own reputation as a regiment still full of fight, the RMLE found itself on the Somme rather than at the exclusively French abattoir of Verdun, further east. Joffre, the French commander, had originally intended his 'big push' across the Somme to be a day of glory for French arms but the German General von Falkenhayn beat him to the punch in February with an offensive to the east at Verdun which he knew the French would do anything to arrest. By enticing them into such a battle, von Falkenhayn declared, 'We shall bleed the French Army white.' He almost succeeded. The French army lost 542,000 men in ten months, many from the twenty regiments drawn from the Armée d'Afrique other than the Legion. But almost as much German blood was shed: a total of 434,000 men lost. The hero of Verdun was 'Firepower' Pétain but his pyrrhic victory cost Joffre and von Falkenhayn their jobs.

Verdun had started amid the hacking frost and short winter days of February. A drum roll of artillery announcing the Somme battle began on midsummer's day, 24 June, across a forty-mile front and continued for five days. During the preceding four months, thousands of French soldiers had been replaced on this line by British volunteers fresh from training camps. The British would have preferred to fight at a time and in a manner of their own choosing, but they were committed by Joffre's initial, disastrous decisions. The original plan required an attack by sixty French divisions across a thirty-mile front. In the event the French contribution was eleven divisions including the Moroccan, across a front of six miles just south of the river Somme itself. The British now provided eighteen divisions. When they went over the top on 1 July, they had been in the line for ten months; the Germans, for almost two years.

Where the British and French sectors met, the Commanding Officers of the King's Liverpool Regiment and the 3/153rd *Régiment d'Infanterie* moved across no man's land together at 7.30 a.m. The French officer, Major Le Petit, and his British counterpart, Colonel Fairfax, led the advance arm in arm.

A total of 100,000 men went over in the first wave, the morning sun burning off the mist that shrouded them. The

RMLE, in reserve for a change, watched as men of the Colonial Infantry moved off ahead of them, up the slope, going north-east towards their first objective, the little hamlet of Assevillers. At 9.30, after heavy fighting, the 'Porpoises' as these former Marines were known, relayed news that they had succeeded. Now it was the legionnaires' turn. They were to move up the line to relieve young Breton reservists of the 39th Regiment (that same regiment which had made good the Legion's losses of 1870) as well as the Porpoises. At Assevillers, the RMLE dug in and waited. It was three days before they were given further orders. By then, with 57,450 of the British force killed or wounded on the first day, the shine had gone off this offensive. Any further projected advance would take on the appearance of yet another suicide mission. That is just what the Legion was now invited by General Bourdoulat to pursue.

The village of Belloy-en-Santerre, as the hinge of the local German defensive network, was an almost impenetrable burrow of tunnels and gunports flanked by dense lines of medium machine-guns. In front of the village there was an open, regular forward slope. The RMLE assembled in the early morning darkness for an assault at dawn on 5 July. The Americans in a battalion commanded by the New Zealand legionnaire Major James Waddell were making bad jokes about cold turkey left over from their national holiday the day before. First the bugler sounded 'Le Boudin' (the regimental march), then the more rapid notes of the Charge.

Loaded down with 60lb of equipment which included wire-cutters and grenades (their British neighbours carried even more, including baskets of messenger-pigeons) the legionnaires moved on to the battlefield in open order towards an objective which was an enticing half-mile away. The Germans, unable to believe that they were being offered such ready targets, held their fire until the legionnaires were a mere 300 yards away. Then in a matter of seconds the 11th Company on the right of the line was swept away by a weight of flying, hot metal. The survivors charged, rallied by a Swiss baron, Captain de Tscharner with the cry, '*Vive la France!*'

As they seized the sewerage ditch on the southern edge of the village the second wave of legionnaires came under yet more intense fire. The Egyptian legionnaire Rif Baer glanced to his side, confirmed that his American friend, the poet Alan Seeger, was still intact and waved to him. Seeger, a tall, gangling, moustached figure grinned back cheerily and charged on. Then he, too, was down, screaming with pain as he rolled out of sight into a shell-hole. Later they heard him cry for water, and his mother. Harvard graduate, Paris poet, Legionnaire No. 19522, Seeger had met his rendezvous with death, and it was neither dulce nor decorum.

Those legionnaires who survived the deadly open ground now had to fight a house-to-house battle for the village. When grenades did not produce the desired result they used the bayonet. By nightfall, the regimental bugler was sounding 'Le Boudin' from the centre of a now-derelict village and the first of many German counter-attacks was being prepared. That day the regiment lost 844 men and twenty-five officers, one-third of its total strength. A few days later on the night of 7 July the RMLE was handed another hard target at Chancelier. There another 400 men became casualties. In the disastrous week since 4 July more than half the regiment had gone, dead or seriously wounded. On the Somme this was about par for the course. The three armies would lose a combined total of 1,265,000 men before this battle was finished.

By the time the Legion was in serious front-line action again, momentous changes had taken place in the upper echelons of France's military leadership. Philippe Pétain, the hero of Verdun, was not allowed to succeed Joffre probably because Pétain made no secret of his contempt for politicians. General Robert Nivelle was chosen instead. Nivelle, an attacking general as well as a sound republican, set in train an offensive of which the Legion was part in the spring of 1917. It led directly to the darkest and most discreditable hour of the war for the French army. The Legion's courage was untainted by what was happening on neighbouring sectors. Not the least piquant element in this was that the regiment's most spectacular and successful act of individual heroism was the work of a German legionnaire fighting against his own countrymen. It was a performance in striking contrast with the mutinies and firing squads to be found among other French units.

In mid-April, soon after taking over, Nivelle put 800,000 men into an offensive across a fifty-mile front on the river Suippes in Champagne country east of Paris between Soissons and Reims. A long artillery bombardment preceding the assault failed to suppress deep-dug German defences. By 9 May, the attack was visibly gaining no ground. French casualties totalled 130,000 and German losses some 163,000 including 30,000 taken prisoner.

The impact of yet another pyrrhic victory as well as the example of the Russian Revolution caused a widespread mutiny in the French army during which some divisions openly planned to march on Paris. Pétain was now hastily appointed to command the Western Front in succession to Nivelle. Not only did Pétain quell the mutiny, he seems to have done so without the knowledge of the Germans. Of 23,385 men convicted of offences connected with the revolt, Pétain approved the execution of only fifty-five, a very modest number by the standards of, say, 1871. But Pétain knew what the French tommies – the '*poilus*' – had been obliged to suffer. His role as the 'Army Doctor' was his best contribution to his country. Pétain was appointed on 15 May. There were five mutinies in July, three in August and one in September.

The Legion's objective in Nivelle's grand plan was the strong-point of Auberive, on the edge of a ragged wood where the remnants of silver birch were still discernible. Though they had never seen it before, for most legionnaires it had certain familiar features. Like so many other of RMLE's targets it commanded a salient (this one known as the 'gulf') and was perched on high ground above a flat, level killing ground known as the 'billiard table'. It was also – of course – overlooked by well-sited machine-guns as well as a vital position on the extreme right flank of the French advance. The security of such an operation would only be as good as the hinge on which it turned. The Legion's task was to secure the hinge.

The men went over the top in pouring rain and near-freezing temperatures at 4.50 a.m. on 17 April. One of the first to buckle and die in the mud was the Commanding Officer, Lieutenant-Colonel Duriez, an avuncular, paunchy man who had been photographed only a day or so before in a front-line trench with three of his men alongside a rudimentary signpost announcing 'Auberive'.

The legionnaires advanced in teams of no more than a dozen and when it was necessary to crawl forward in order to stay alive, that is what they did. By dusk they had occupied the south side of the 'gulf' salient and a corner of the silver birch wood. It was little to show for a close-quarter battle involving bayonet and grenades, of which 50,000 were to be used – about ten per man per day – during a five-day battle. In the early hours of the second day, snow replaced rain and the RMLE was ordered to withdraw and regroup.

Of the various company tasks allocated for the next attempt, Captain Fernand Maire – the son of an earlier Legion hero – was ordered to wipe out opposition in the 'gulf' salient. He had calculated that the German response would follow soon after French artillery fire was lifted, a sure signal to everyone that the French infantry was about to move forward. By timing his attack ahead of the official start time he was across no man's land and into the temporarily vacated German front-line trenches before either side was fully aware of what he was doing. Others were less fortunate. One company of 275 men was reduced to nineteen by the end of the day. As well as the Commanding Officer, the RMLE had now lost two valuable and experienced captains, Germann and de Lannurien. Yet they had also seized a five-mile corridor driven through mud and blood into the enemy position.

News from the rest of the front was not so good. A total of 150 French tanks had been wrecked by German guns before they could be brought into the battle to support the infantry. True, the Germans had withdrawn from the ridge known as Chemin des Dames, to the left of the hinge occupied by the Legion, but this was a ruse. The German generals knew that the French were about to move the 10th Army into a gap in the line, so they would convert the ridge into one vast chopping block.

The day after that shambles, 21 April, the men of RMLE's 6th Company were catching up on their sleep in Trench 67. That it was wet, almost freezing cold, and that the dead and sleeping bodies lay indifferently side by side made no difference to men who had now been fighting without relief for four days.

One man was not asleep. Sergeant-Major Max-Emmanuel Mader, a former German soldier and a legionnaire since long before 1914, decided to see what this long, well-built trench had to offer apart from corpses. It ran north, directly towards the enemy positions. At its furthest extremity he had a clear view into a valley on his right, overlooked by a German machine-gun position no more than a few yards away. While he was studying this, one of his own young sentries nudged his elbow. Legionnaire Bangerter (barely eighteen years old and only just promoted to Legionnaire 1st Class) was pointing down the valley to a bunch of *poilus* of the 168th Regiment. Led by a lieutenant, they marched with weapons slung on one shoulder, heads and eyes on their boots, military lambs to the slaughter. Legionnaire Bangerter wanted to fire off a warning flare but Mader stopped him.

Ten of the dormant legionnaires were shaken awake, told to equip themselves with grenades and to form up for a patrol with the Sergeant-Major. He briefed them and then set off over the rough ground outside the trench at a point where the German gunners were unsighted. Following a fold in the ground he contoured round the slope. The enemy's attention was riveted on the prey obligingly marching up the path towards them until Mader gave the order and grenades rained into the German position, scattering those men who could still move. The patrol from 168th was only a few yards away now. Mader sprinted down to this team across open ground and snapped at the lieutenant leading it, 'No time to waste. Follow us.'

His own men were holding the position they had just taken, content not to push their luck further. Mader charged through them. His prey had retreated down a long trench at the end of which, in a deep gunpit, was a battery of 150mm artillery pieces. Mader, noting that some of the enemy had gone to ground in a bunker, signalled to the men behind him and pressed on. The gun crews, in their emplacements under camouflage netting, had heard the noise of battle nearby but Mader – a tall figure in French uniform hurling bombs and ordering them in colloquial German to surrender – still took them by surprise. The survivors were not disposed to argue. As well as the prisoners, Mader's team took possession of an entire battery of big field guns, a detail not overlooked in the citation signed personally by Pétain for Mader's Légion d'honneur.

Though it did not seem much like it at the time, that bitterly cold spring of 1917 was the turning point of the war for an increasingly demoralized French army. In April the United States entered the conflict on the Allied side and from now on the side with the biggest bloodbank was the side which would ultimately win. But Britain's support for its allies' armies – including payment to neutral America – was all but exhausted. In May, Nivelle was sacked and replaced by Pétain and that, in 1917, was good news for the *poilus*. The British armaments industry, like its army, was proving far more potent than the Germans had calculated in replacing losses.

Within the RMLE, however, none of these important developments mattered half so much as the arrival on Camerone Day, 30 April, of the new Commanding Officer, Colonel Paul Rollet. A soldier's son, Rollet had been a Legion officer since 1899. He was small, flamboyant, richly-bearded and eccentric. Like Pein he had attacked the Sahara on a motor cycle. He also shared his predecessor's lack of respect for senior officers in an army where blind obedience was encouraged. Support of the men serving under him against his superiors – a policy of 'My men, right or wrong' – as well as his sense of theatre aroused a loyalty which blended awe and idolatry. In the past he had led his mounted company across a desert on foot, shod in rope-soled sandals, marching twice the distance of his legionnaires. (They, after all, took turns to ride the mule.) The sandals earned him his nickname, 'Capitaine Espadrilles', but they were not his only sartorial eccentricity: he wore a steel helmet only once, and that was for the Bastille Day parade in Paris in 1919. Otherwise, he favoured a battered kepi worn over a light, tropical uniform without a shirt, irrespective of weather conditions. He carried an umbrella in preference to a personal weapon and was usually accompanied by a dog. All these tokens informed his soldiers that he had the '*baraka*', the gift of seeing the right road and remaining unimpaired in spite of regular battle wounds. His soldiers, who were not untouched by superstition, revered him for it.

In 1917, the fusion of Rollet's charismatic confidence and his legionnaires' fighting spirit set the regiment on a uniquely hard road for which its new-found élan – in an army which was short of élan – made it uniquely suited. In August Pétain selected RMLE to spearhead a breakthrough near Verdun across a network of trenches near Cumières Wood. Waddell's men, watched by Pétain and the American General Pershing, went into action singing a popular song of the day. A few hours later, well in advance of the official timetable, the regiment had taken 2,000 yards and 680 prisoners including twenty officers from an élite German unit. As the three Legion battalions swarmed through the enemy defences like angry termites, Rollet drafted a waspish reply to a signal from above which seemed, however obliquely, to counsel less haste: 'You have given the Legion too limited an objective. It has assigned itself to others.'

In December 1917, a peace agreement between Germany and Russia released fifty German divisions for service against the British army on the Somme, a move anticipated by Field-Marshal Sir Douglas Haig who had hurled 324 tanks into the gallant failure of Cambrai to break the German line before it was too late. In January 1918, the RMLE was fighting in Lorraine but was then withdrawn briefly, to be sent back up the line to help hold the massive enemy offensive now bending the Allied line back as far as Soissons on the main road to Paris near Compiègne. The Santerre battleground should have been familiar, for it adjoined the site of its sacrificial battle at Belloy in 1916. Yet again, the Legion was to save the day, but at daunting cost.

On 4 April the Germans made a final, fanatical effort to break the Allied link near Hangard, about fifteen miles south of Amiens. Another, equally important, enemy objective was the Calais-Paris railway. On 26 April, four days before Camerone Day, the RMLE was hurled into an assault backed up by British tanks at Hangard Wood, still saturated by German mustard gas, against the German 19th Division.

The first Legion battalion pitched into the fight was reduced in short time by machine-gun fire to one officer and 187 men. In one company only an experienced legionnaire survived to take command. While the tanks laid down covering fire the other two battalions went in to take their revenge in hand-to-hand fighting. The objective was seized and the French line held intact just two miles from the vital railway, but at a cost to the regiment of 833 men and eighteen officers dead or wounded. Rollet was not among them. At the end of this first Ludendorff offensive of 1918 (there would be another four) the total Allied losses were 160,000 dead or wounded, 70,000 taken prisoner and 1,100 guns lost. Enemy casualties were on the same scale.

The RMLE had not been brought up to strength again before it was committed to another desperate counter-attack dangerously close to Paris at Soissons. At 4.45 a.m. on 18 July, in a second Marne battle, the legionnaires moved forward through Villers-Cotterets forest behind a creeping barrage and a screen of French tanks to storm a series of fortified positions and take 450 prisoners in two hours. By the time this German offensive collapsed, the regiment had suffered 1,400 casualties including the seemingly indestructible Sergeant-Major Mader. With his right arm and shoulder blown away, Mader was taken to a base hospital to die. He regained consciousness as the last rites were being performed, and survived to old age.

In September 1918, a last great hammer blow against the Hindenberg Line was needed to end the war. North of Soissons, at the beginning of the month, the RMLE was at the forefront of this assault. A battalion led by Major (later Colonel) Maire took a key position held by 500 enemy. The regiment was then committed to thirteen days in the line, days and nights of almost continuous fighting during which the only food they received was bread and water. One of the last actions was fought in the darkness of a long tunnel into which a jaunty Rollet led his men with every appearance of confidence in the outcome.

The end of the war found the regiment at Château-Salins, a town which had been in German hands since 1870. To the sound of 'Le Boudin', the RMLE staged its own victory parade there on 17 November, six days after the last shots of the war had brought Europe's most ruinous conflict to an end. The regimental colour was the second most decorated of the entire French army. Only one unit – the Moroccan Colonial Infantry Regiment – had received one more citation for its collective bravery. Among the twenty-one other regiments which had distinguished themselves with multiple citations, nine belonged to the Armée d'Afrique.

If France's best fighting troops were not strictly French, aside from the officers leading them, then those who became French through blood shed rather than blood received at birth, were numerous indeed. Of the 42,883 Legion volunteers who had fought on the Western Front, more than 30,000 were killed or seriously wounded. McLeave estimates that of the 8,000 Legion professionals sent to France in 1914, fewer than fifty survived the war.

The Legion contributed more than blood. In this war, in a very special way, the regiment salvaged France's military honour. The five-day battle for Auberive in April 1917, which ended inconclusively after the loss of a commanding officer (Duriez) and hundreds of men, was not a direct *military* necessity. We have the authority of the Armée d'Afrique historian Colonel Jean de Pradel de Lamaze (see General R. Huré, et al.) for the proposition that 'the RMLE attacked in Champagne on 17 April during a limited offensive at Malmaison *designed to restore morale* . . . Lieutenant-Colonel Duriez . . . fell at the head of his troops . . . "Marvellous regiment," said a fifth citation.'

The French government understood what was happening. One of Rollet's first tasks when he succeeded Duriez as the RMLE's Commanding Officer in 1917 was to lead a colour party to Paris (bearing the regimental ensign) for the 14 July parade where the regiment was decorated with the Médaille Militaire in tacit recognition of the fact that during the mutinies of 1917 the RMLE had remained unshaken.

As the exhausted survivors of the war celebrated the armistice in November 1918, one group of Allied soldiers was still fighting, unaware that the conflict had ended. These were the men of a multi-national expeditionary force which had left Kings Cross Station, London, bound for northern Russia a few months earlier.

In March 1917 the Tsarist regime – an ally of Britain and France – was overthrown. Russian troops promptly walked away from the war in their tens of thousands. A minority travelled to France to join the Foreign Legion. Their separate battalion was known as 'the Russian Legion'. In Russia itself, meanwhile, the Bolsheviks, having supplanted Kerensky's parliamentary government, made peace with Germany. Potentially this released about 500,000 enemy soldiers for service on the Western Front at the end of 1917. To reduce this threat the Allies, including the Americans, set out to organize renewed attacks against the Germans in Russia with the aim of tying down enemy divisions still in the east. By the time the German onslaughts of spring and summer 1918 had unexpectedly collapsed (and with them Germany itself), the force sent to northern Russia was locked in physically by winter ice and politically by support for a divided Russian force now fighting against the Bolshevik Red Army.

Among many novel military formations created after the Allied landing at Archangel was a Slavo-British Legion of former Bolsheviks (and others) specially released from prison. Dressed in British uniforms and taught to cheer – in English – 'God Save the King!', they were led by British officers and NCOs, nine of whom were soon murdered during a mutiny at the front. Alongside this force there emerged a unit described by the overall Allied commander, General (later Lord) Ironside, as 'a Russian Company of the Foreign Legion'. E. M. Halliday, an American historian who studied the expedition, concluded in *The Ignorant Armies* that the French had hastily matched the creation of a Slavo-British Legion by setting up a Foreign Legion recruiting office of their own. The French seem to have avoided the most fatal British mistake: their locally-recruited legionnaires were almost all White Russians rather than Bolsheviks. The volunteers even included the disillusioned Chief of Staff of the local anti-Bolshevik army, General Samarine. His overnight debut as Legionnaire Samarine was not a unique experience for the Legion, but it did little to add to the credibility of indigenous anti-Red forces. In a situation which Ironside himself described as Gilbertian, Samarine was hastily promoted to captain.

The new force was now taken in hand by one Captain Barbateau, said to be a French-Canadian and assuredly a French army reserve officer. Like today's Canadian Arctic troops – unique among NATO forces – Barbateau had much faith in snow-shoes. He named his company after a famous seventeenth-century team of north Canadian scouts, '*Les Coureurs de Bois*', the Forest Racers, or perhaps, Rangers. Unfortunately, the Canadian snow-shoes he ordered went to the wrong unit and the type his men received from England were unsuitable for fine, dry, powder snow created by 85 degrees of frost. Still, for the southern offensive towards Moscow from Archangel during Christmas 1918, Ironside and the anti-Bolshevik leader Chaikovsky looked for great things from Barbateau's team.

The temporary legionnaires were one of two main prongs in a pincer attack on the neighbouring settlements of Kodish and Plesetskaya on the Emtsa river. In the event, the only Allied unit to arrive for the party was a mixed Canadian-US force (Canadian artillery and two companies of the US 339th Regiment) totalling 450 men. In spite of the absence of their Legion allies, they dislodged 2,000 Soviet Red Army soldiers from Kodish.

What went wrong? Most of Barbateau's men blamed the snow-shoes. Instead of running across the snow, as legend said they should, they sank into it to their thighs and rapidly became exhausted. Ironside had another theory. He observed that on a subsequent operation, the *Coureurs de Bois* had in fact surrounded the Bolshevik position allocated to them at Avda, the next village on the road south beyond Kodish, but that they had returned after four hours' skirmishing, reporting that the enemy was too strongly entrenched to be attacked. In *Archangel, 1918–19*, Ironside added: 'I was not surprised when I was told that it was my old friend Samarine, now a captain in the Legion, who had been in command of the raid.'

If the French were not performing well, the British were even less impressive. An English colonel in charge of the machine-gun company required to give fire support to the Americans took no part in the fight because, as Ironside put it, 'He had succumbed to the festivities of the season.' (The colonel was relieved of his command.) The third missing ally, the White Russian 1st Archangel Regiment, determined at the last moment to wait 'for the right kind of day'.

By the time the long Russian winter was drawing to an end, most of the Allied interventionist forces (led by the French navy at Odessa) had experienced mutinies among men who did not understand what they were doing in Russia now that the war against Germany was over. Behind a screen of despairing White Russians, most of the expeditionary force withdrew from the north in the summer of 1919; as the White Sea ice melted to unlock the harbours the Americans departed, followed by the French and the British Royal Marines. By September none of the interventionist forces remained in that part of Russia.

Most of the 'Russian Company' of the Foreign Legion remained with the doomed anti-Red army which finally surrendered on 19 February 1920. According to the Legion historian Pierre Sergent, this specially raised *'bataillon de marche'* participated in the defence of Archangel in July 1919 and was then dissolved. Many of the legionnaires rejoined the White Russian army of General Yudenitch and took part in the attack on Petrograd (Leningrad) strongly defended by Trotsky.

The attack crumbled and took with it the last traces of the north-western anti-Bolshevik army, which included Finns, Letts and White Russians with French advisers. It might be doubted whether the curious hybrid that passed as a unit of the Foreign Legion was any more like the real thing than, say, the Breton-dominated battalion which helped to destroy the Paris Commune in 1871. However, one advantage offered by *some* special forces is that, when expedient, they can be more readily disbanded than an established regiment of the line. There are times when the concept of a *'bataillon de marche'* seems to have served the same purpose, to the long-term detriment of the Foreign Legion proper.

CHAPTER 9
Desert Warlords
(1918–40)

Colonel Paul Rollet: 'What did you do in
civilian life?'

– Recruit at Sidi-bel-Abbès, c. 1920:
'I was a general, *mon colonel*.'

The French, a people of etiquette, imagine that
the Legion is full of criminals and barefoot
savages.

– Colonel Fernand Maire, in a letter
from his deathbed, 1951

The army which returned to pick up the unfinished business of colonial warfare after 1918 was critically different from its predecessor. Rollet, in charge of the Legion depot at Sidi-bel-Abbès, asked a new recruit, 'What did you do in civilian life?' 'I was a general, *mon colonel*,' the man replied. Probably he had served, like Legionnaire Samarine, in the Tsarist or White Russian armies. The Legion would soon be able to create a whole new regiment composed largely of ex-counts and minor princelings, for Europe in the early 1920s contained thousands of displaced Russians, Germans, Austrians, Serbs, Bulgars, Turks and Irishmen (some of whom had left German prison camps to change sides after 1916 and fight the English); men whose only trade was now soldiering, and whose nationality had gone along with their possessions.

Their recruitment to the post-war French army helped to offset the grievous loss of manpower on the Western Front where almost 30 per cent of all French males aged between eighteen and twenty-seven had perished. The boom in Legion recruitment in the early twenties was part of a very grim equation indeed. In

1920, for example, 72 per cent of men serving in the 1st Foreign Legion Infantry Regiment (REI; one of several new formations) came from one or other of France's recent Great War enemies, in spite of the fears of Foch and others that it was only a matter of time before Germany invaded France again. In 1922, a battalion of the 4th REI included 79 per cent of Central Europeans of whom 46 per cent were German. Only 7 per cent of the battalion were French. Because of renewed anxiety that this would lead to German domination of the NCO ranks, or even 'Germanization' of the Legion as a whole, strenuous efforts were made to find NCOs among the non-Germans. It was not easy; France had squandered too much blood and talent on the Western Front. The men chosen were often too young and indisciplined.

There was another, less easily defined way in which the post-war army was different. This had to do with the psychology of the survivors of 1914–18. Some, including many NCOs at the depot regiment at Sidi-bel-Abbès, 1 REI, rushed into domesticity and marriage as soon as they could obtain permission. But there were others, including some of the best of the officers, who had been living on dangerously borrowed time for so long that they did not care for civilians. There was a wildness and a strangeness about them that merited the nickname 'the Musketeers', with all the tempestuousness of Gascony that reference to Alexandre Dumas implies. Here, for example, is the Breton Colonel Fernand Maire as recalled in *Historia* magazine by a former comrade-in-arms, Jean-Pierre Dorian:

> At Meknès – in Morocco – in the basement of the Maroc-Hotel, a bar packed with people every night, a mass of twits [civilians] and the uproar, increased tenfold by the heat, created a stinking atmosphere.
> 'I'm going to shut them up.'
> Having chosen a particularly lively horse, he mounted it and charged down the steps like a Centaur, at a gallop into the middle of the throng, which broke up and ran screaming out of the place.
> When someone – one of his superiors, perhaps – disagreed with him, he would rise courteously from his seat and then in went the dagger: 'Those who don't approve of me will always find a place between my chair and me!'

Maire had limped away from the Western Front in defiance of all natural laws, along with his friends Rollet and Captain ('Five

Hundred Corpses') Corta. One night he had played an unwilling fourth at bridge in a dugout in northern France, fingering his small ivory crucifix, fighting the rising terror at picking up the 'dead man's hand'. The game ended at dawn and the four bridge players shook hands, gravely. At 5.35, in the attack that followed, he was hit in the left thigh by a bullet and carted away to a field hospital. His fellow bridge players were already dead.

'Don't trust any legionnaire who tells you he has no fear,' was one of his aphorisms. Another, 'Fear is coloured blue.' And again, 'The French, a people of etiquette, imagine that the Legion is full of criminals and barefoot savages.'

He was not the only one to acquire an ironic and even malicious view of the world about him. The Danish Prince Aage, who joined the Legion when his bank went broke in the great crash of 1922, readily assented when a journalist from Copenhagen asked to entertain to dinner a group of Danish legionnaires then in the punishment cells, to prove that they were all nice boys at heart. The dinner ended with the journalist, a woman, in tears and much of her clothing forcibly removed. It was as if, after what they had endured, they were hoisting warning signals to proclaim: 'Beware! This cage contains a dangerous animal – Man.'

In France's second campaign to subdue the Moroccans, battalion commanders like Aage and Maire had god-like power over their men and the local inhabitants. They were known as 'caids', – in this context, slang for 'warlords' – and this was their golden age, serving under the great caid, Marshal Lyautey, whose faith in the Legion was such that two of its soldiers were his permanent bodyguard. Yet, because of the unfortunate history of desertion from the Legion via Morocco, some of the commanders felt obliged, during a particularly dirty war, to take a firm line about this problem. Early in the 1920s, after Maire had lost 106 men in a body down the freedom road to Spanish Morocco, he offered local Berber tribesmen a twenty-franc bounty if they brought a deserter back. If they delivered just the man's head, the bounty increased to 100 francs. An alternative punishment was a term – in practice of indeterminate length – with the 'disciplinary' battalion at Colomb-Bechar, where one of the less severe punishments was to make by hand 1,000 bricks a day in desert summer temperatures, failing which the prisoner received no food.

Lyautey had held on to most of the land conquered before 1914, but only just, during the years of the Great War. In the embittered Bou Denib area in 1916 he could do so only by creating a mixed battalion of legionnaires and Joyeux. Under the inexorable pressure of Arab and Berber opposition, a force of legionnaires, now reduced to only six fighting companies (although on paper they represented four battalions), was obliged to give up some of its fortified hill posts. Even to evacuate these was a risky business. In July 1918 the regiment lost fifty dead during a retreat from Gaouz.

Meanwhile in Paris, the RMLE led the first Bastille Day parade since the end of hostilities in Europe. Out in front, uncharacteristically wearing a steel helmet, Rollet carried a much-decorated regimental colour. The Legion's long, slow stride provoked the usual problems for the orthodox infantry following them. In the brief euphoria which followed the war, the Legion was briefly 'in', and the regimental band was sent on a concert tour of the United States.

It was November 1919 before the heroes of the Western Front returned to Sidi-bel-Abbès where the regiment was dissolved and reorganized as the Third Foreign Legion Infantry Regiment (3 REI). Instead of the Champs Élysées the legionnaires found themselves endeavouring to occupy a rugged part of the Middle Atlas mountains known — because of its obdurate opposition to French rule as well as the colour required to illustrate its bleak contours on the map — as the 'Taza Stain'.

Over the next two or three years a regular pattern of operations was established. In the spring the fighting columns would move a little further into the enemy heartland, fighting and building blockhouses as they went. The offensive continued through the heat of summer and cool of autumn. Then, stocked with food and ammunition for six months, a small party of legionnaires would be left to survive the North African winter as best it could. Since some of the peaks were over 6,000 feet, snow and driving rain were normal winter conditions. Whenever the men moved out of their tiny forts to repair a telegraph wire, draw water from a stream or build more road, they were exposed to ambush. Partly

as a result of this bush warfare after the stirring events of the
Great War, morale within the Armée d'Afrique, including the
Legion, was not good. The stylish Rollet, commanding 3 REI but
also emerging as the Father of the Legion, feared that the
combination of static defence and low morale would soon have
the inevitable result: a siege, after which the defenders would
have nothing left intact but their honour. As late as 1929 the
effects of lost élan were still disastrously visible. At Djihani, in the
lonely wastes of south Morocco, Lieutenant Fiore allowed himself through tactical ignorance – and what one Legion historian
describes as 'lassitude' – to be drawn into a pitched battle in open
countryside against superior numbers. Forty-one legionnaires
died. The anniversary of this event became a holiday among the
nomadic tribes from the edge of the Grand Erg – a sand sea 100
miles deep by 400 miles from west to east – to the Mauritanian
border.

In France, the shock of this event led to the re-equipment of
many Legion regiments with automatic weapons to increase their
firepower and their chances of survival. Rollet was less concerned
with hardware than men. He demanded more stringent selection
of Legion recruits, backed up by more efficient methods of
administering basic items such as pay. At the time of Rollet's
complaint, in the early 1920s, the depot at Sidi-bel-Abbès was
creaming off the best men for garrison duty in a comparatively
pacific Algeria. Yet his suggestions were shot down by a barrage
of bureaucratic objections from a grey man at Sidi-bel-Abbès
named Major Riet. Paris – faithful to its instinctive love of
hierarchy – gave its backing to the 'Mother House' and found
against Rollet although 73 per cent of the Legion's fighting
strength was now concentrated in Morocco. It was the first of
several spectacular misjudgements by the Defence Ministry in
Paris in overruling the views of soldiers on the spot in Morocco,
some of whom would soon become the scapegoats for the
Ministry's failure to respond.

In some measure these misjudgements were the result of a
re-emergence in France itself of a phobia about the army. With
the recovery of Alsace-Lorraine in 1918 and the satisfaction of
national self-esteem, France – led by the political Left but all too
ready to follow a poor lead – overturned the 'Union Sacrée'

which had enabled a left-wing president, 'Tiger' Clemenceau, and a hard-nosed soldier, Marshal Foch, to work as effective partners in spite of their frequent public quarrels. Soon army officers in France were learning not to appear in public in uniform, except when the duty required it. At a time when a major was paid a mere £4 per week, many of them were so hard up that they could only meet their bills by moonlighting as cab drivers and waiters. This situation coincided with the emergence of the most brilliant and successful North African general to oppose France since the initial conquest of Algiers in 1830.

Abd el-Krim, a well-travelled, well-educated Moroccan, first made war against another occupying power, Spain, whose enclave on the north Moroccan coast offered some tempting fruit. It is thought that from the beginning he was astute enough to recruit Legion deserters as his expert advisers rather than torturing them to death. Whatever the reason, he scored the most spectacular victory of any indigenous African leader over a regular European army when he wiped out General Sylvestre's Spanish army at Anual in July 1921. At least 12,000 Spanish soldiers were killed. Equally important, all their arms and ammunition, including a substantial quantity of artillery, military vehicles and field telephones, were carefully harvested and placed on the rebel inventory. In French Morocco Lyautey took note, alerted Paris, and asked for prompt reinforcements. He was refused, except in one particular for which permission had been granted anyway. This was the creation of a new type of force within the Legion, the *Régiment Étranger de Cavalerie* (REC). The regiment would be a genuine cavalry force, riding horses. Initially, the military high command had seriously considered a Foreign Legion brigade (an echo of Bernelle's all-arms concept of the 1830s) which would include artillery and sappers, but for reasons of cost, only the cavalry – an anachronism in an age of tanks, armoured cars, self-propelled guns and military aircraft, but an inexpensive one – survived. True, one of the infantry's famous mule companies was soon to be mechanized but the new cavalry recruits despised the wheel.

As it happened, there was no shortage of cavalrymen. Two White Russian armies commanded by Wrangel and Dennikin, well furnished with Cossacks, had just emerged from defeat at the hands of the Reds. There were also some Hungarians and German Uhlans who had not forgotten how to ride a horse and wield a sabre at the same time; French officers and NCOs from the Chasseurs d'Afrique, the Spahis and some French mainland regiments. Many, if not most, of the officers were from the minor nobility. It was no coincidence that the officially titled 1 REC was immediately and unofficially renamed the *Royale Étranger*. (A subsequent unit, mainly mechanized, named itself the '*Dauphin Étranger*'.) In 1921, it was a diverting military prospect that, in Morocco, France was marching – or, rather, cantering – purposefully into the nineteenth century while a rebel Berber warrior was acquiring as much twentieth-century technology as he could, but this interesting exchange of roles never properly materialized since the new – probably the last – horse-mounted cavalry unit to be raised by a European country soon found itself fighting in a theatre of war far removed from Morocco, described later in this chapter. Thus, the creation of 1 REC – important as it was for the long-term evolution of the Legion – did nothing to relieve Lyautey's anxiety about Abd el-Krim's intentions.

These became even more apparent in April 1924 when the Beni-Uriaghel tribe made an experimental *razzia* (the energetic collection of other people's goods) against tribes which had submitted to French rule. Lyautey pushed his line of blockhouses and mini-forts nearer the Moroccan frontier. These garrisons were manned by Turcos (Algerian infantrymen) and Senegalese in preference to the Legion because of fears of desertion. But it was too late to close the stable door on some of the regiment's bolting horses. Prince Aage of Denmark, at the outpost of Tadout in 1923, inspected the guard – a Russian, a Spanish-Moroccan, a German legionnaire and a German corporal as guard commander – and saw them march off to an isolated tower. Once inside they hoisted the ladder up after them and settled down for a night of boredom. Next morning they did not parade for inspection. Aage and six armed legionnaires discovered the ladder abandoned in the desert and some time later, still at the top of the tower, the corporal – quite dead, his throat cut – and the Russian in a state of gibbering hysteria, crouching in a dark corner of the tower. The other two members of the guard had vanished and were never seen again.

The most famous deserter of them all was Sergeant Joseph Klems from Dusseldorf who had joined the Legion in 1920 and served with the Mounted Company of the 2me *Régiment Étranger d'Infanterie*, one of four such regiments in the expanded, post-war organization. He was ambitious, efficient and ruthless and by 1922 was promoted to sergeant, a spectacular progress. Then, because of an unspecified 'moral fault', he was reduced to the ranks again. This would not have troubled a more experienced NCO, or someone better versed in Legion history, or someone less isolated (by his brutality as an NCO) from his fellow legionnaires. Kunassec, for example, one of the rare survivors of Camerone, still serving thirty-six years later in 1899, had been made up to sergeant six times, and 'busted' five times. The system was a self-reinforcing and ultimately democratic process, for the corporal or sergeant who broke the unwritten rules about junior leadership (which are immutable and cannot be learned from books) would pay dearly, like a policeman detected in crime, when he was reduced to the ranks. These were facts which ex-sergeant Klems either did not know or chose to ignore. Back in the ranks, he could not ride the hard time which followed and he deserted, taking his weapon with him, in 1923. Initially he took refuge with tribesmen in the Middle Atlas who helped him. From there he made his way to the Rif mountains, where he introduced himself as 'the German Pilgrim' – that is, convert – to Mecca, or 'Hadji-Aliman'. El-Krim was more concerned with Klems's technical knowledge and his soldiering ability than with the condition of his soul. Here, Klems was on home ground. The artillery pieces and machine-guns taken from the Spanish required some servicing and their crews needed training. All these things the renegade legionnaire could supply. Klems became el-Krim's chief of staff and right-hand man, advising on tactics as well as weapons. Above all, he gave the guerrilla Berber army a sense of panache and self-confidence in fighting the French, who were a tougher nut to crack than the Spaniards.

In the spring of 1925, with an army of 30,000 warriors, el-Krim crossed into French Morocco and steamrollered his way across the country. On Klems's advice, mountain forts which could not be induced to surrender were surrounded and invested by a besieging force while the rest of the invading army, claiming to represent a 'Republic of the Rif', marched on its triumphant way. Within a few weeks thirty French border outposts were hastily evacuated and nine captured, out of a total of sixty-six. Paris now panicked and started to send the reinforcements Lyautey should have had before, but it was too late. French Morocco, it seemed, was doomed as more and more tribes, pacified at great cost before World War I, joined the rebellion.

The forts which resisted this invasion produced stories of desperate, if ill-fated, courage. Lieutenant Pol Lapeyre, after holding a fort for seven weeks in total isolation, blew the place up, along with himself and thirty of his soldiers as enemy tribesmen swarmed through the broken gates. At Mediouna, a volunteer assault force of sixty legionnaires and four officers tried to infiltrate a deep Berber cordon surrounding another fort whose defenders were also preparing to immolate themselves. The break-out attempt, under cover of darkness, ended with the deaths of all but three of the Legion's rescue party.

On 25 April 1925, just ten days after the initial attack upon French Morocco, el-Krim's main force was almost at the gates of the capital, Fès. By now no prisoners were being taken by either side and most French troops, particularly the legionnaires, kept the traditional last bullet for themselves. And yet, inexplicably, el-Krim hesitated. Some argue that he could not come to terms with the situation he had created, or believe in his own success. Conceivably he suspected an elaborate French trap: no one had yet expelled the French from any major centre they had garrisoned, though there had been some near-misses. Whatever the reason, el-Krim's temporary loss of nerve gave the French time to draw breath and regroup. No fewer than fifty battalions were withdrawn from France's Rhineland army of occupation for a counter-offensive led not by the Armée d'Afrique's most famous hero, Governor-General Lyautey, but Marshal Pétain, who had never served outside metropolitan France. Pétain was a safe political bet with the folks back home, while Lyautey, selected as the latest military scapegoat, returned to a country which treated his homecoming, as it had responded to Bazaine's return from Mexico, with contemptuous silence. Convinced of the venality of French politicians, Lyautey resigned from the army only to re-emerge in less lustrous circumstances shortly before his death in 1934 as an organizer of a right-wing coup attempt in Paris, an attempt which itself was a reaction to France's failure to rearm in face of Hitlerism.

Pétain was an efficient – if cautious – defensively-minded technician, provided he had superiority of numbers and fire-power. This could not be said of all his contemporaries. As well as the extra manpower he had the advantage of more artillery, armoured vehicles (where there were roads on which they could be driven) and even aircraft for reconnaissance and ground support. Like the British General Montgomery, he took over with advantages denied to his predecessors. In spite of that, his counter-offensive was almost a year in preparation (a year in which isolated Legion units repeatedly had to fight for their lives) but when it was unleashed on 8 May 1926, it rolled back el-Krim's guerrilla army as rapidly as that army had advanced the year before. By 23 May, the Moroccan leader was making his 'last stand of honour', surrounded by French forces, and by 26 May was signing a surrender document.

The border country between Algeria and Morocco did not require an el-Krim to teach it the ways of guerrilla warfare. It would be another seven years, the summer of 1933, before the last tribal redoubt surrendered. For the Legion the fighting of those years was punctuated by gradual but steady moderniz-ation. In March 1930, for instance, the first of the Legion's motorized companies was created when a team from 2/2me RFI under Lieutenant Gambiez handed over its mules and started to discover the sweet mysteries of four Berliet armoured cars at Meknès. Elsewhere, as part of their permanent occupation of the Atlas mountains as well as the oases beyond, the regiment created at such places as Ksar és Souk a vast white barracks across whose gleaming parade grounds entire battalions could march in re-view. On the new road from Marrakech to Ouarzazate, straight across the Grand Atlas, legionnaires started carving a tunnel seventy yards long and ten feet high. Afterwards, resembling the powerful pick-and-shovel coalminers of the same era, they were photographed beneath a plaque which told the world: 'The mountain barred our road. The order came, all the same, to go through it. The Legion executed that order.'

It was all part of a process of spreading French rule until it engulfed the whole territory. The fighting also continued. On 23 May 1930 a Legion mounted company from Algeria was surrounded on the southern border area near Wadi Guir by 750 enemy and rescued by the 3rd Mounted Company of 2 RE and a Saharan cavalry squadron. On 29 August 1930 at Tadighoust another mounted company – the 1st of 2 RE – lost twenty-one dead in a bitterly fought action for which the French President Gaston Doumergue, visiting Fès, decorated the regimental colour with a collective Croix de Guerre.

One of the last peaks to be conquered for France was Bou-Gafer, a sheer, needle-shaped spine of rock known as the 'Cathedral', which legionnaires took at bayonet point in 1933, climbing uphill. The operation cost the regiment another fifty lives and ended not in surrender but with the disappearance into caves and potholes of an elusive, tenacious enemy.

Another tribal stronghold, Jebel Baddou, in the heart of the Grand Atlas, surrendered after a siege lasting almost three months. Approximately 3,000 tribesmen and their families, as well as hundreds of 'irreconcilables' from other parts of the country, and 15,000 sheep were surrounded. Whenever they emerged from caves to draw water they were targets for either machine-gun fire or aerial bombing. Thirst finally brought about their submission to a mixed Armée d'Afrique team including the Legion, some of whose climbers had been pitched over a sheer 3,000-foot drop by desperate Berbers who dived off with the express intention of taking an enemy soldier to eternity with them.

The tribesmen's surrender followed a well-established ritual known as the 'targuiba'. It was not a ceremony calculated to promote reconciliation. A full twenty-four hours after the last gunshot, the guerrillas assembled and handed over their rifles, symbol of their manhood. Then a bull and several sheep were sacrificed to provide a feast for the victors. Finally, with their wives, they were the spectators of a military parade staged by the French force which had just defeated them.

Not all of France's enemies surrendered in this elaborate fashion. Sergeant 'Hadji-Aliman' Klems, on whose head a price was fixed after the surrender of Abd el-Krim, was betrayed by one of his native wives. The cave in which he was hiding was surrounded by legionnaires. He chose surrender rather than a heroic last stand and went on to face a court martial which sentenced him to death. But the wheels of justice grind more slowly than the chariots of war and by the time sentence was passed early in 1927 he had become an international celebrity around whom the operetta *The Desert Song* was woven. German diplomats, enthusiastically supported by Parisian communists whose war-cry was 'Better shoot a French general than a foreign soldier', persuaded the government to commute the sentence to life imprisonment on Devil's Island. In 1934, under pressure from the Nazi regime in Germany, at a time when France was again on the brink of civil war, Klems was repatriated. He died by his own hand in prison, in Berlin, in 1939 while serving a sentence for a minor crime.

If the Armée d'Afrique thought it had encountered a hard enemy in Morocco, it had a lesson to learn about fanaticism as well as courage from another embittered mountain tribe at the other end of the Mediterranean. In May 1916, the secret Anglo-French agreement signed by Sir Mark Sykes (Britain) and Georges Picot (France) to divide Turkey's empire between their countries was the first step towards Western domination of the Middle East and the betrayal of the anti-Turkish Arab rebellion led by T. E. Lawrence. In 1917, when a British force under General Allenby was also making war against the Turks in the region, a 'French Detachment of Palestine-Syria' was attached to it to stake France's claims to the spoils of war. This comprised a *régiment de marche* blending Algerians and Frenchmen from the 115th, artillery, a mixed African cavalry unit, an air squadron and what was described as '*la Légion d'Orient*', comprising Syrians and Armenians under French officers. The detachment achieved some remarkable coups, notably at Nablus, north of Jerusalem, where eighteen cavalrymen charged against a position defended by several thousand Turks who panicked and broke, bringing about the surrender of the entire town.

Faithful to Sykes-Picot after the war, the League of Nations placed the whole of Syria under French mandate, or protection, in 1921. Ostensibly this was to help the Syrians ultimately to stand alone. In fact, as Lord Balfour confessed in a secret Cabinet memorandum: 'Do we mean in the case of the "independent nation of Syria", to consult principally the wishes of the inhabitants? We mean nothing of the kind.' (See Hirst, bibliography.) France's answer to the same rhetorical question was to expel from Damascus the victorious King Feisal, who had been the first of the Allies to enter the Syrian capital on the heels of the retreating Turks. (His offence: an attempt to found an Arab kingdom. The British found him a throne in Iraq.)

Within a few months of the Mandate taking effect, two battalions of the 4th Foreign Legion Infantry Regiment (4 REI) were on their way supported by a squadron of the newly-founded *1re Régiment Étranger de Cavalerie* (1 REC) to conduct what were described as 'police duties'. In fact, what was needed to make the Mandate stick was armed conquest of a country of mountain and desert in which anarchy reigned. The ruling Turks had been defeated. There was no agreement about who was to succeed them. A series of ambushes and pitched battles resulted, in which French colonial forces – Senegalese as well as North African and Legion troops – suffered substantial losses. A hundred Saharan camel corps soldiers and their three French officers were annihilated. After the battle the French troops were chopped up and fed to the dogs. The officers' heads were transported to a town just inside the Turkish border to be displayed on a butcher's stall.

By 1925 it seemed that Syria was at last becoming reconciled to the French presence but then the Druze, a Muslim minority group, staged their own spectacular revolt which had nothing to do with the Bedouin grievance about the Sykes-Picot betrayal. In July 1925 a delegation of five Druze chieftains arrived at French headquarters in Damascus to enquire about the successor to their recent, and popular, French 'district commissioner' figure. This officer, Captain Carbillet, was typical of the best French colonialists, an Arabist who really cared about the people he governed in the name of France. In two years, Carbillet had pressured his masters to provide funds for schools, roads and – most important of all – water wells, where none had existed before. The man whom the Druze delegation saw about this fairly mundane affair was General Sarrail, the so-called 'Red Republican' officer who, far from agreeing to a replacement of the popular captain, locked up the Druze delegation. The scene was now set for bloodshed and the nearest victims, as it happened, included legionnaires drawn from the new 1 REC as well as the 4th Foreign Legion Infantry Regiment.

Young Captain Landriau was on honeymoon in France when he was summoned to move his 166 officers and men, plus 165 horses and fifteen mules of 4th Squadron, 1 REC, from Sousse in Tunisia to reinforce French forces in Syria. All the officers and several of the senior NCOs were French, including the Squadron Sergeant-Major Gazeaux. The rest were a mix of Cossacks, White Russians, Germans, Yugoslavs, Bulgars, Greeks, Danes, Swedes and Englishmen. Some had spurned infantry commissions in the Legion rather than pass up the honour of belonging to the Legion's first mounted soldiers. One such was Legionnaire Odintzoff, whose official military age of forty was an underestimate of at least ten years. A former Tsarist colonel who had defied the famous cavalry motto 'Any huzzar who's not dead at thirty is a blackguard', Odintzoff was a contented and effective trooper. By contrast, young Lieutenant Dupetit, the squadron's 'Benjamin', had only just left military academy, and it showed.

Almost as soon as they came ashore in August 1925, their horses slung two-by-two in nets from the foredeck of the troopship *Porthos* down to the Beirut quayside, the squadron was under pressure to get to where the action was – inland to Damascus and then forty-five miles south, towards the Druze mountains, where 200 Frenchmen were besieged. Landriau noted in his campaign diary on the way south his contentment with his unit's blend of Cossack veterans, who had seen it all, and German discipline. For additional firepower he had with him the machine-gun company of 4 REI.

His orders were to rendezvous with 5 Battalion, 4 REI, at the little market town of Messifré until a sufficient force could be assembled there to march on beleaguered Soueida with some chance of relieving it. Already there had been one disastrous false start. A column sent by General Sarrail a few weeks earlier had lost 1,000 men.

There was little comfort for Landriau when he reached the rendezvous unscathed: only the bleak message, relayed by heliograph from the besieged town nearby, to a French aircraft: '3,000 men on Messifré.' Yet by dusk on 16 September, a full twenty-four hours later, there was no sign of trouble. The waiting legionnaires commanded a defensive wall on one side of the town, overlooked only by the elegant dome of a shrine commemorating a local holy man (marabout). Inside, the horses and mules were tethered guarded by two platoons commanded by Lieutenant Robert and Squadron Sergeant-Major Gazeaux. So stealthy was the assault by thousands of Druzes at 2 a.m. that it was not detected by the outposts held by the legionnaires of 4 REI on a three-kilometre perimeter until the enemy were on top of some of them. Things rapidly became noisier after that.

The screams of horses as they were butchered told the defenders that the Druze were inside the defences, probably with the complicity of the townspeople. The sentries guarding the animals died with them. The survivors, including Robert and Gazeaux, retreated towards the perimeter wall where Landriau's main force was concentrated, calling on their comrades not to fire upon them. By way of reply, the men on the wall unloosed a flare which hung, like stage lighting, over the forty or so Druzes who were keeping close to the legionnaires they were still stalking. The infiltrators were cut down in a swathe of gunfire.

From the dome of the marabout shrine a dozen more of the enemy used the light of the flare to shoot at the legionnaires. Landriau sent for another lieutenant, Castaing, to remove the nuisance. Castaing nominated Sergeant-Major Serval to lead the assault, and arranged for a 37mm machine-gun to provide covering fire. This did not help another senior NCO, Maréchal de Logis Schelmann, who was killed the instant he put his head over the wall at the beginning of the assault. But the machine-gun did blast an enormous hole in the dome and killed most of the enemy snipers occupying it.

Robbed of their tactical observation post, the Druzes kept coming. In fact, they started to come even more recklessly, attacking in waves on foot and on horseback as if to roll over the defenders by sheer body weight. They ran instead into intensive rifle and machine-gun fire and, when that did not suffice, into the points of the cavalrymen's sabres. From the most exposed position, the northern corner of the town, the unit's young subaltern,

Dupetit, scuttled to Landriau's command post, seeking permission to fall back with his platoon. Even as this was being given to him, a bullet in the brain killed him outright.

By 5.30 a.m. a conference of troop commanders convened by Landriau during a temporary lull concluded that if they could hold on until daylight, then French air power would be a critical factor to favour their survival. It was now clear to Landriau that the Druzes were prepared to face virtually any threat short of aerial bombardment in their efforts to overrun the town. This assessment was entirely correct. At six o'clock there was another onslaught and then, at first light, the Druzes eased themselves out of the beaten, bloody town of Messifré, taking with them those wounded and dead not actually lying under the French guns. With daylight, the air power did not return, but nor did the Druzes in any number. Landriau, fearing the worst, kept his men in a state of alert. Towards the end of that day, a column of Turcos – a battalion of 16th Algerian Tirailleurs commanded by Colonel Daumont – came to the rescue of its Armée d'Afrique colleagues. The *Royale Étranger* had had its baptism of fire. It had lost twenty-five dead including the youngest officer, as well as twenty-four wounded out of a total of 165 men. A subsequent Druze statement admitted that the guerrilla casualties included 500 dead.

The relief of Messifré was not big news in turbulent Syria that year. Damascus itself was frequently besieged or, as a variant, the French in Damascus were besieged by the angry inhabitants. In November, reduced to 100 men, Landriau's team was stationed in a hill fort at Rachaya on the Lebanese side of Mount Hermon, alongside a squadron of Tunisian Spahi cavalry. On 19 November, a reconnaissance patrol under Lieutenant Gardy came under fire on the southern side of the town and was brutally parted from the security of the fort as thousands of Druze moved into the area from the surrounding mountains. Leaving his wounded hidden in the care of Maronite Christians, Gardy contrived to find a back way into his base early next morning. There was not much he could do about three men who had been carried off when their horses, alarmed by the gunfire, had bolted beneath them.

By the time he returned, the fort – an ancient Turkish installation nestling comfortably, if not so securely, within a huddle of houses in the town – was all but sealed off and communication to the outside world depended upon six carrier pigeons. The Spahi officer commanding the garrison, Captain Grancher, had been ordered to hold it at all costs. The French High Command feared that if Rachaya went, it would provoke a domino effect which would lead, all too swiftly, to France's complete expulsion from Syria. That afternoon, the shooting began as an estimated 4,000 enemy probed for a weak spot. At the end of that first day the garrison had lost four dead and fifteen wounded and the Druzes, attacking well-sited machine-gun and grenade-throwing positions, somewhat more.

From dawn next day, the position came under heavy sniper fire from adjoining buildings. Grancher, visiting one of his forward observation posts to see the attack on the south side for himself, was shot through the temple and the command passed to another Spahi officer serving alongside Landriau, the Legion commander. That evening, enemy soldiers armed with German grenades taken from Turkish stores crept close enough to hurl them on to the roof. A French military aircraft dropped a more encouraging message attached to a stone. This promised a French attack on the Druze rear two days later.

Next morning, as Druze chieftains gathered with new reinforcements to witness – they hoped – the spectacle of French deaths, it became clear that during the night one of their assault teams had made the first big breach in the fort's defences by tunnelling into a cellar below a tower dominating the south side of the fort. For the next twenty-four hours the French garrison fought a nightmarish, close-quarter battle during which they were forced to retreat to a strongpoint on the northern third of the citadel. During that withdrawal, a German legionnaire, Kapf, hurled back a grenade thrown along a tunnel by the Druzes and then, in spite of his wounds, used a sabre taken from a dead enemy to lead a charge of six legionnaires to retake the same tunnel. Sergeant-Major Gazeaux was the last of four men defending the main west gate and its tower to die after holding the place with grenades and swords against overwhelmingly greater numbers. The garrison's horses were slaughtered, as they had been at Messifré, and the last pigeon released bearing the Spahi commander's message: 'Situation very critical. I cannot hold after tomorrow morning for want of ammunition. Send at least a battalion as a matter of extreme urgency. Everyone has done his duty.'

A Legion bayonet charge led by Lieutenant Gardy during the last few hours of the siege averted total annihilation: by the time a relief column marched over the horizon from the Bekaa valley the survivors had virtually no ordnance left and were preparing to 'do a Camerone' by charging the enemy with bayonets fixed, to sell their lives as dearly as possible. As it was, the siege had cost the squadron fifteen lives and forty wounded. None died a cavalryman's death, on horseback.

The *Royale Étranger* mourned some of its most experienced soldiers including Popoff, an enormous Cossack who had lived as a colonel in the Tsarist army before dying as an NCO for the French. Alone in a room in a dusty desert fort, paralysed from the waist down by a grenade fragment in the back, he tried in vain to crawl towards a trap-door that was the only way out.

It was another five months before the French were able to recapture the besieged town of Soueida in the foothills of Jebel Druze, the relief of which had signalled the start of this guerrilla war. The legionnaires led an assault on one side of the town, and the Tunisians took the other. Of 6,000 enemy found there, 500 were killed. The French losses were eighty dead (six officers) and 300 wounded.

Minor skirmishes continued until 1927, but there were no new major battles in the area before World War II. The Legion garrison in Syria – four infantry battalions and a mounted company – was first given the title the Regiment of the Legion in the Near East, or RLPO, echoing the name of that ad hoc group of Syrian and Armenian refugees recruited in Palestine as '*la Légion d'Orient*' of 1918.

In October 1939, during the 'phoney war', the RLPO was redesignated 6th *Régiment Étranger d'Infanterie* (6 REI). Once the phoney war became real, 6 REI would fight on behalf of Vichy France and the Axis powers, including Nazi Germany while other, equally valid Legion regiments would emerge as the backbone of de Gaulle's Free French, or even remain neutral. Such divisions were the splintered mirror-image of France herself in World War II. Not all the Armée d'Afrique could paper over the cracks when the Maginot Line fell.

CHAPTER 10
Honour Betrayed, Honour Restored
(1940–45)

We demand the return of our people from the
French Foreign Legion. They will be formed
into units for Africa. They can rehabilitate
themselves there.

– Dr Josef Goebbels, 8 March 1941

Their leader asked us, in perfect German, if we
wanted 'a better life' than sitting in a prison
camp. We could get this, he promised, by
joining the Foreign Legion.

– Ex-Prisoner of War Rudolfo Biallas, Wehrmacht veteran,
recalling his confinement in a French camp, May-June 1945

Armistice Day 1940 was not the most auspicious time to volunteer for the Foreign Legion. Not only was it the occasion for France to surrender to the Nazis; it was also the day the French empire – upon which the Armée d'Afrique, including the Foreign Legion, depended for its existence – began a dramatic decline. Even worse, drastic cuts imposed on the French army by German armistice terms inspired yet another proposal to dissolve the Legion in spite – perhaps because of – its bravery during the brief French resistance to invasion during that first spring of World War II.

None of this deterred Arthur Koestler, in 1940 already a prominent Anglo-Hungarian writer. He had seen a film some years before in which the actor Jean Gabin, hunted by the police, had walked into a recruiting office to disappear by joining the nameless ones, *les morts vivants*, of the képi blanc. Koestler, a Jewish socialist as well as a naturalized subject of the only nation still at war with Nazi Germany, was also a man on the run the day Marshal Pétain (aged eighty-four) succeeded Paul Reynaud as

Prime Minister of France, and promptly surrendered to Hitler. So Koestler presented himself at the army recruiting office in Limoges, telling them that he was Albert Dubert, a cab driver from Berne in Switzerland.

The Legion sergeant and his clerks, pausing in their discussion about how long it would be before the Germans arrived at the barracks, were sceptical about this new recruit. With some understanding of the regiment as well as France, Koestler explained that he really wished to join the 'Old Legion', not one of the *régiments de marche* which had been thrown together for the duration only (and in some cases already annihilated). The sergeant shrugged, handed him four printed forms to sign, arranged a quick medical check and despatched him on his way. Koestler, after being sent unescorted to a series of military camps around a country in chaos, reached Marseilles on 11 August. By now the German armistice terms were beginning to bite, so, along with four Spaniards, a Turk and a Rumanian, Koestler was killing time while awaiting demobilization. His military service could be counted in days, and yet in that time France had been divided into an Occupied and an Unoccupied Zone.

The Unoccupied Zone remained that way only so long as the new French government, based at Vichy, co-operated with the Germans in apprehending people on the run whom they wanted to interview. High on the list were German nationals whose loyalty to the Nazis was not particularly noticeable. Many were now in Vichy territory. By chance, in Marseilles, Legionnaire Koestler bumped into two former ministers in the pre-Nazi Weimar Republic government. Like him they were trying to escape. They had visas to enter the United States but the French would not grant them permits to leave the country. Six months later, along with twenty other prominent political refugees, they were handed over by Vichy to the Nazis. So were 76,000 Jews handed over, a third of them French by birth of whom fewer than 2,000 survived. Those subsequently murdered included 8,000 children.

Koestler was more fortunate. In the refectory at Fort Saint Jean barracks he took his place at a mess table. Nearby four surly individuals in civilian clothes glowered at him. Then one said, in English, 'There's no bloody salt in the bloody soup.' With these

British soldiers, on the run like himself, Koestler discharged himself from the Foreign Legion and made his way by public ferry from Marseilles to Oran. As he would later admit: 'I was only a phoney sort of Legionnaire, when in urgent need of a – temporary – false identity. To claim ex-Legionnaire status would be another imposture.'

At Oran, with the help of the American consulate, Koestler and his companions came under the care of an exotic underground operator calling himself 'Ellerman', who smuggled them to neutral Lisbon, where the British embassy was delighted to see them. According to Iain Hamilton, Koestler's biographer, Ellerman was really Baron Rudiger von Etzdorf. The Baron had fought the British at Jutland. He was also one of the first prominent Germans actively to work against the Nazis.

Koestler was merely one of hundreds of transients to be accommodated by the Legion on orders from Paris at this time. Miroslav Liskutin was one of about fifty Czechoslovak pilots who were put into Legion uniform and sent to Sidi-bel-Abbès after volunteering to fly for France in 1939. Their own country had been overrun by a Nazi invasion in March that year. In the event, the only enemy Legionnaire No. 84202 Liskutin encountered were bed bugs in a barracks at Oran. Liskutin was finally transferred to the French air force just before the surrender of May 1940. At Merignac air base near Bordeaux, as he recalled later, local French servicemen seemed overjoyed about the armistice. In his unpublished memoir *Stormy Skies – Reminiscences of an Aviator*, he wrote: 'All the aircraft at Bordeaux were sabotaged as the Germans approached – probably by French airmen.' This should not have come as a surprise to a refugee from Central Europe. As Paul Johnson has observed:

> The French ... knew that to enter an all-out war with Hitlerite Germany might mean a repetition of 1870, and it took them fifty-six hours of agonized hesitation to respond to the German assault on Poland, which had been their sworn ally since 1921. The military protocol which General Gamelin had signed in May 1939 with the Polish War Minister, Kasprzycki, pledged that the French air force would take immediate offensive action against Germany as soon as Poland was invaded, and that a French army invasion of Germany would follow within sixteen days. Neither promise was fulfilled.

Liskutin escaped to England to join the RAF. When he eventually retired it was as Squadron-Leader Liskutin DFC, AFC.

If Koestler escaped Nazi scrutiny of the Legion after the French surrender, others did not. Ever since 1870 the presence of large numbers of Germans in its ranks had been of concern to the French, usually for the wrong reasons. The issue had aroused German anxiety during the Casablanca deserters affair of 1908. Now in 1940, it was again Germany's turn to put pressure on those of its nationals who had chosen to fight under the French tricolour. The issue was raised repeatedly during meetings between the German and French armistice commissions from the moment France surrendered. The official record [see bibliography] is meagre but it reveals, for example, that at a series of joint meetings between 17 and 20 August 1940,

The German sub-commission has demanded a swift reply to its questions about the 220 legionnaires of the Reich who, having finished their engagements, are returning to Germany; about all the Germans serving in the French Foreign Legion who have been demobilised since the Armistice (nominal rolls; personal details; date of joining the Legion; re-engagement and length of engagement); about the approximate number of Germans serving in the Legion classed according to where they are in mainland France or overseas including Indo-China.

During the next round of talks from 6 to 9 September the request was repeated. Later that month there were complaints that German officers had been refused access to camps where German nationals were thought to be living. At Camp de Fuveau in armistice region XV (probably near Châlons-sur-Saône) a team of Luftwaffe officers found 'forty German nationals, ex-Legionnaires, whom they took to the base at Marignane', near Marseilles. This little coup repeated an earlier success of 27 August when fifty former legionnaires were handed over at the same camp to the same sub-commission.

The precise status of these people remains ambiguous. The president of the German commission, General von Stulpnagel, in a note to a colleague of 16 October 1940 expressed concern that

German refugees were being held against their will in the Unoccupied Zone because of earlier pro-German activities, as well as ex-legionnaires who actively wanted to return to Germany. So many such people were contacting the German control commission offices in France that he suggested the German Red Cross organization should be asked to help them.

The day after this odd observation, Colonel Vignol, a French member of the commission, noted that the legionnaires concerned had been transported to Camp de Fuveau. However, the 'numerous desertions' about which Colonel Vignol expressed his anxiety did not square with the German belief that their ex-legionnaires were ardent to go home. A week later a German telephone message, reproduced as part of the official record, noted that the French delegates had just been told that a German commission charged with organizing the repatriation of German ex-legionnaires would arrive on 31 October by car at Arbois, south of Besançon. Evidently, the number of legionnaires to be removed was substantial: the convoy sent to escort them was said to contain sixteen people. This 'special German Control Commission' charged with repatriating former legionnaires from the Unoccupied Zone makes another appearance in a French progress report for the period 21 to 27 October. This says:

> The commission cannot handle the Legion units stationed overseas. The commission asks the names not only of the legionnaires who admit they are German, but also those who describe themselves as Austrians, Czechs and Poles who have become German and those who, it is supposed, could be German.

Precisely how many German legionnaires were betrayed to the Nazis by Vichy, after fighting for France against Germany in 1940, and how many were fifth columnists who positively sought repatriation to fight for Hitler at that time, remains a mystery. The issue vanishes from the official French record of the armistice commission's deliberations after October 1940. But clearly the disappearing trick employed by 'Legionnaire Dubert', alias Arthur Koestler, rapidly became a wasting asset. Expert French contributors to a recent history of the Armée d'Afrique blamed the legionnaires concerned. The history comments:

The continuation of the Foreign Legion was a hard struggle. Germany started by demanding the repatriation of all Germans. Then it was Italy's turn to claim her own. Yet inviolable cover had been assured to those who wanted to hang on to the identity which they had gained under the French flag. Then, under the pressure of negotiation, it was agreed that such repatriation required a written request from the interested party [i.e., the legionnaire concerned]. The only ones to benefit from this breach of the soldier's contract were a few hundred Germans and Italians badly integrated into the Legion who went off to join the Axis and perhaps, later on, the frozen plains of Russia. [General R. Huré, et al.]

As things turned out, France would later discover a sufficient number of home-grown volunteers to fight against communism to form an entire French division of the SS, serving in SS uniform on the Eastern Front. There is no evidence that the Foreign Legion, or former legionnaires, were involved in that episode. So what *did* Germany do with those legionnaires it was able to claim back? On 8 March 1941 Hitler's propaganda genius, Dr Goebbels, noted in his personal diary: 'We demand the return of our people from the French Foreign Legion. They will be formed into units for Africa. They can rehabilitate themselves there.'

In fact, about 2,000 German legionnaires were siphoned off for service with Infantry Regiment Afrika 361 which fought against the Eighth Army as part of the Afrika Korps 90th Light Division. This division was a key unit in the Wehrmacht assault on the Legion at Bir Hakeim in 1942, though the written record suggests that 361 Regiment did not join the 90th until just before Alamein, a few weeks after Bir Hakeim. If former legionnaires were obliged to join combat against their old comrades in the Western Desert, it would be unusual but not impossible. In Syria in 1941, the year before the great Western Desert, it would be unusual but not impossible. In Syria in 1941, the year before the great Western Desert battles, Free French troops including legionnaires fought against those of Vichy France, if without much conviction. In his *African Trilogy*, Alan Moorehead recorded what the Vichy soldiers told their allied captors:

Why shouldn't we fight? We're professional soldiers obeying orders and you came here on a deliberate aggression. You think it would have been easy for us just quietly to submit: but what about our friends and relatives imprisoned by Germany? The Boches keep threatening us. They say they will take reprisals and they mean it. We've got to fight.

If such were the sentiments of *French* soldiers fighting for Germany against the Allies, then they illustrate with incidental, but terrible, clarity the pressure which was almost certainly brought to bear upon Germans whose cover was blown by Vichy after the surrender of France in 1940. Not all of these 'renegades' were unwilling volunteers for the Wehrmacht. Some – see Appendix II – regarded it as a natural extension of their Legion service. So did Vichy.

As well as those individuals who were turned round by Germany and Italy, some entire Legion units were openly used by the Axis powers as useful additional pieces on the big strategic chessboard of World War II. The American historian Robert O. Paxton commented:

> The German Armistice Commission was more interested in the defence of French West Africa [from Allied invasion] than of French North Africa. For example, the 1st Foreign Legion Regiment was transferred from North Africa in the summer of 1941 when movement of US troops into Iceland had heightened fears for Dakar. It took another six months (for the French) to fill the North African gaps. [Robert O. Paxton, *Parades and Politics at Vichy*]

Some elements of the Foreign Legion survived the political and military ambiguity of their situation by reason of sheer remoteness from the main action, whether in the southern reaches of the Sahara or – as in the case of 5 Foreign Legion Infantry Regiment – in Indo-China where (loyal to Vichy policy) they permitted Japanese occupation of the territory without opposition.

In the summer of 1940, some unknown but heroic staff officer, living dangerously, saw to it that 5 REI was reinforced by between eighty and 100 legionnaires who were in the Nazis' 'most wanted' categories. They included German Jews and socialists, some of whom had joined the Legion in search of political asylum. The Legion went to extraordinary lengths to conceal these men a full twelve months after France's surrender and three months after Goebbels's announced intention to hunt them down. In June 1941, escorted by a famous legionnaire,

Second Lieutenant Chenel and his detachment, the men – dressed in civilian clothes and officially designated 'No. 1 European Workers' Detachment' – were carried in three heavy trucks from Aïn Sefra, deep in the interior of Algeria, to Colomb-Bechar in southern Morocco. From there, in a journey more readily imagined than described, they continued in high summer across 1,250 miles of Sahara Desert track to Bourém, on the river Niger. After further adventures they reached Camp Kati, west of Bamako in what is now Mali. There a train was waiting to carry them to Louga, one day's ride from the coast of Senegal. At Louga they were joined by a second 'European Workers' Detachment' in the care of Captain Winter who immediately handed them over to Chenel and left. Three special railway coaches were attached to the routine train from Louga to Dakar, where the clandestine legionnaires were now concealed in a quayside warehouse. At this point they still had no idea of what their true destination was. Chenel was able to reveal to them at Dakar – which was loyal to Vichy – that they were being embarked for Tonkin to join 5 REI. Then they were loaded stealthily, after dark, aboard the transport *Cap-Padaran* bound for Indo-China by way of the long haul round the Cape. They were the last reinforcement to reach 5 REI before its long isolation from the rest of the Legion.

Elsewhere around the defeated French empire, yet other regiments merged with one another to satisfy the terms of the armistice, or disguised themselves as quasi-military organizations such as border police. Only one major unit of the Legion, The Syrian garrison's 6th *Régiment Étranger d'Infanterie*, became a convincing servant of Vichy under the influence of General Dentz, commanding the Army of the Levant. But, in general, the Nazis could be well satisfied with the performance of their French ally in the spring and summer of 1941. As Goebbels noted on 16 May that year, shortly before the Allied invasion of Syria: 'For the most part the French are doing us great service at the moment.'

With the wisdom of hindsight it is easy enough to condemn all pro-Vichy officers and men as unheroic collaborators. This would be an over-simplification. General Auguste Nogues, commanding 120,000 men in North Africa, was ready and willing to continue the fight after the armistice, but Vichy warned him that he would receive no supplies and was certain to lose. Under the terms of an armistice agreement with Italy on 24 June 1940 France's colonies formally became neutral. With the fall of France that month, the advice of senior French officers to their government was that Britain would not survive long and the war would soon end. With memories of 1871 still sharp, many old soldiers feared a new Paris Commune or a repeat of the Russian experience of 1917. General Weygand (aged seventy-three) openly expressed a greater distaste for Stalin than Hitler. Others followed the more discreet but equally right-wing leadership of the hero Pétain. Robert Paxton wrote:

> Service to Vichy came naturally to most professional officers . . . All but a handful accepted Marshal Pétain's counsels of patience . . . With the Marshal as Chief of State they embarked enthusiastically on a new domestic mission of national re-education and redirection . . . French officers believed that the campaigns of 1941/42 were a stalemate and that to plunge back into the conflict would invite another war of attrition on French soil followed by almost certain social revolution at home and loss of empire abroad . . . By default they left the major part of the war of liberation to amateurs.

And he might have added, to foreigners also. It is a paradox that Pétain, the defensive strategist of Verdun whose only first-hand experience of war outside his own country was one brief campaign in Morocco, should have destroyed French credibility throughout its empire as a result of his surrender in Europe, a capitulation aimed at preserving everything French including the empire. The salvation of French honour and credibility was left in the hands of an officer whom Pétain described as 'that viper I have nourished in my bosom', with a tiny minority of regular French officers willing to follow his Cross of Lorraine into exile abroad, and disgrace at home. In 1940 and for long afterwards, the prognosis for a sound or even a gallant and honourable military career behind General Charles de Gaulle was such that no prudent professional soldier would have followed him. But a luminous portion of the eccentric minority who did so – and whose heroism has been better recorded since the Allied victory of 1945 than the deeds of the great majority who stayed loyal to Vichy – were the men of the 13th Demi-Brigade of the Foreign Legion, or 13 DBLE.

The DBLE found itself in Scandinavia in 1940 as a result of a series of historical accidents. According to Colonel Marcel Blanc (in Col. Villaume, et al., *Revue Historique des Armées*) the unit should have gone to fight the Russians in Armenia, presumably to defend French interests in northern Syria. However, this operation was cancelled and the unit was supplied with documents and maps relating to Finland rather than to Asia Minor. Finland had been invaded by the Soviet Red Army on 30 November 1939, Russian confidence boosted by a mutual non-aggression pact agreed with Nazi Germany on 22 August. Britain and France, in spite of their problems with Germany, prepared to fight alongside the Finns in Operation Petsamo. The Legion unit, around 2,000 men, was exercising Arctic warfare skills in the Alps when Finland surrendered on 13 March 1940. However, on 2 April, the Nazis attacked neutral Norway. Thus the Legion group, commanded by Lieutenant-Colonel Magrin-Vernerey (*nom de guerre* 'Monclar') joined a Franco-Polish force to fight the Germans in Scandinavia instead of the Russians in the Caucasus. Some authorities regard such operations as a useless form of displacement activity on the part of the French to avoid the real issue, the direct confrontation with Germany on the French border. Paul Johnson, for example, writes:

As the minutes of the Anglo-French staff discussions show, it was the British who pressed for action on the main German front, and the French who wished to do nothing there, while planning diversionary schemes in Scandinavia, the Caucasus, Salonica, Finland and elsewhere . . . French passivity on the Franco-German border combined with largely meaningless activity elsewhere played straight into Hitler's hands.

Unaware of the extent to which they were pawns in a campaign to give the appearance of military activity while in fact keeping hostilities away from French soil, the legionnaires landed on 13 May at two modest fishing harbours, Bjervik and Meby, about seven miles north of the major Arctic port and city of Narvik, under covering fire from the Royal Navy. After a week of skirmishing, the Germans still held Narvik. Faced with a deteriorating situation in France itself (hit in a lightning offensive through Belgium and Holland by 45 Wehrmacht divisions under von Rundstedt), the British commander in Norway was ordered on 24 May to withdraw. The French general, Bethouart, did not accept this. Certainly he wanted to have one last shot at defeating the Germans holding Narvik.

Put ashore north of the city under naval covering fire at midnight on 26 May (which did not help much in the Arctic in summer), the legionnaires had to climb from the shore of the fjord to a railway line under constant German fire. It was their second opposed landing in two weeks. The permanent way, following a crooked shore, snaked into a series of tunnels bored through the mountain before reaching Narvik at the end of a long peninsula. The railway was the only practicable route into the city and the Germans saw to it that their guns were lined up on the tunnel exits. Another two days' hard fighting and much naval gunnery practice were necessary before the city was seized and its vital port installations destroyed along with ten aircraft on the ground. Ironically, the ultimate beneficiary of the action was Soviet Russia, an ally of the West and a potential victim of German air power only after Hitler's treachery in attacking his Soviet friends in 1941. For the French forces, the Narvik victory was a modest but valuable morale booster. The Legion had advanced to within a few miles of the Swedish frontier at a cost of seven officers and sixty other ranks. But elsewhere on 7 June, as the Legion rearguard finally withdrew behind a convincing row of military dummies, things were going from bad to worse. Italy had just joined the war on Germany's side, creating a maritime threat in the Mediterranean for which British naval units were needed instantly. From France each new day brought news of fresh disasters.

With the invasion of France, the Maginot Line (a political alibi for military inaction between the wars) did not impede the Wehrmacht. The defending army included six new Foreign Legion units whose nominal rolls listed 6,000 aliens, many of them German anti-Nazis, several thousand young Frenchmen and a sprinkling of real legionnaires under French officers. The 21st and 22nd *Régiments de Marche de Volontiers Étrangers* (RMVE; Marching Regiments of Foreign Volunteers) came into being in 1939 followed in May 1940 by 23 RMVE. However, they bore little relation to the Legion proper and their standards of discipline, equipment and leadership were poor.

The other units were the 97 Divisional Reconnaissance Group, an armoured unit with 7th North African Division; plus two mainly French units, the 11 REI (initially commanded by the redoubtable, if eccentric, Colonel Maire) and 12 REI. From mid-May the 97 Reconnaissance was in continuous action on the Somme for three weeks and sacrificed half of its strength between 9 and 22 June. The 11 REI lost three men out of four in defending Inor Wood and Saint-Germain between the rivers Meuse and Chiers during the same lethal fortnight. While formations all around them surrendered the survivors stole back to French-held territory. At Soissons on 6 June, 12 REI, reduced to just 300 men and fighting a way out of encirclement, ceased to be a coherent unit. On 10 June, 21 RMVE collapsed and dispersed in the Ardennes forest battle, while 22 RMVE was cut down to half its original strength after just three days' combat. The most successful of the new scratch teams of foreign volunteers was 23 RMVE, which defied Panzers and Luftwaffe dive-bombers for two days. This regiment withdrew from the front line on 17 June, the day the French government started publicly to withdraw from the war.

The 13 DBLE, meanwhile, had returned from Norway to France just three days earlier on 14 June, the same day that General Dentz (later to command Vichy troops in Syria) had accepted a German occupation of an unscarred Paris. There was some brief talk of fighting on in Brittany and since the demi-brigade had landed at Brest, it was earmarked for that operation. But the legionnaires barely had time to smoke their first packet of Gauloises before Pétain (who took office on 16 June) signalled his intention to surrender. So 13 DBLE promptly got back on board a boat and returned to England. Like the survivors of 11 REI, who weaved their way back to North Africa in small, discrete groups, the veterans of Norway knew there would be no medals for having given the Germans a bloody nose only to end up on the losing side immediately afterwards. Who next might the new French regime, in collaboration with Dr Goebbels, seek to 'rehabilitate'?

Even as the Pétain armistice deal was taking shape, de Gaulle in

London (having smuggled his family to safety in advance) made a famous speech to rally the fighting French to Britain, and Churchill proposed a joint Anglo-French nation. The demi-brigade landed in England on 19 June, the day after de Gaulle's broadcast and just three days before the French capitulation document was signed in the famous railway coach at Rethondes.

Not everyone joined de Gaulle. After some thought only half of the 13 DBLE volunteered to fight for an apparently lost cause. True, the Legion's colonel, 'Monclar', was with the Fighting French. Yet General Bethouart, overall French commander in Norway, was not, in spite of a ringing declaration addressed to his Norwegian opposite number on 7 June: 'We will continue the battle that we have pursued in France until final victory delivers your country, like our own.'

In the event, only half of 13 DBLE threw in their lot with de Gaulle as volunteers. There were fewer than a thousand of them. They nevertheless comprised more than half of the nucleus of the French forces still prepared to continue the fight alongside an isolated Britain after France had surrendered. The number of true-born French volunteers could be counted on the fingers of one badly mutilated hand. The legionnaires who did not join the Free French returned under the command of Major Boyer-Resses to Morocco. There, so far as Vichy was concerned, the unit known as 13 DBLE was formally disbanded and ceased to exist. The battle of Bir Hakeim would prove otherwise.

As a political frost settled over France, de Gaulle led his tiny force in an armed convoy from Britain and around the Cape of Good Hope to Somalia. It was one of the more bizarre crusades of our time: an ex-armoured warfare specialist with a random, polyglot collection of French-speaking soldiers behind him, making ritual visits to as much of French Africa as they could reach from the sea. Cameroon came over to him and so did Gabon. But the Free French were not universally welcomed. At Dakar, Senegal, far from rallying to de Gaulle, the garrison shot at its would-be saviours. But it required the Syrian adventure to throw into grim relief the extent of France's alienation from what de Gaulle was trying to achieve.

Like French North Africa, Syria had had its chance to ignore the Pétain armistice in 1940. The difference between the two colonies was that Syria had immediate access to British help. Not only was there a British liaison team in Syria in 1940; the British were able to welcome allies into the armed camp of British-controlled Palestine adjoining Syria. As in North Africa, there were senior officers in Syria ready to lead their men over. They included several battalion commanders of the 6th *Régiment Étranger d'Infanterie* (6 REI). Their legionnaires were ready to follow them and they, in turn, were prepared to follow into exile a highly regarded staff officer, Colonel de Larminat. De Larminat's circular to the French Army of the Levant, confirming France's surrender, proposed: 'Soldiers, French and non-French alike who . . . accept the risks of rebellion will be welcomed into the British Army in Egypt as a French volunteer corps to pursue the struggle against the enemy.' The circular then suggested that volunteers should make preparations to depart. One of the first units to hurl its kepis into the air at this news was 6 REI. It was ready to move when it learned that de Larminat was already in prison on the outskirts of the Syrian capital, Damascus. Then came rumours of de Larminat's impending execution. With the help of a Legion commando team de Larminat was spirited out of captivity after dark on 30 June 1940. Next morning he was taking a swim in the Sea of Galilee, before breakfasting with his first British hosts, the Warwickshire Yeomanry.

Almost a year passed before the British moved against the French in Lebanon and Syria. The delay resulted from the diplomatic fiction, sometimes useful to both sides, that Britain and Vichy France were not at war. Only when the Germans started using Vichy bases in Syria from which to mount their campaign against the British in neighbouring Iraq did the British have a sufficiently plausible reason for invading France's territories in the Levant. By then, in a separate incident which hardened French opinion against Britain, the Royal Navy had attacked and sunk a large part of the French Mediterranean fleet with the loss of many French lives.

From the beginning of the war in the Levant it was clear that the campaign was not going to be one fought for appearances' sake by two stage armies. A Scottish Commando supported by Royal Navy guns offshore suffered severely when it tried to cross the Litani river in Lebanon as men of 6 REI and two Algerian battalions picked them off from the commanding heights over-looking the crossing. When the crossing was at last accomplished an Australian column was repeatedly charged by tanks of the 6th Chasseurs d'Afrique.

Initially, the column attacking Syria enjoyed better luck. Led by the 5th Indian Infantry Brigade it invaded on the night of 8 June 1941, and within two days a combined task force, including 13 DBLE, was astride the Damascus road. It was a droll place for one of Britain's allies to suffer a conversion, but Monclar, the officer commanding the Free French legionnaires, resigned on the eve of the push to Damascus itself. In Norway against the Germans, and later in Eritrea against the Italians during the long pilgrimage to Palestine by way of the Cape, Monclar and his men had fought bravely, but in Syria his resolve crumbled. In *Our Enemies the French*, Tony Mockler comments:

> Monclar respected the unwritten rule that the Legion should never fight the Legion . . . The effect of the resignation on Free French morale was inevitably severe. It was felt most in 13 DBLE which . . . took little or no part in any subsequent fighting . . . Fortunately for the Free French, Monclar's chief of staff Colonel Marie-Pierre Koenig, also an officer of the Legion . . . did not follow his commander; nor did any other officers.

During the crucial weeks which followed, 13 DBLE reorga-nized under Lieutenant-Colonel Dimitri Amilakvari ('Amilak'), an elegant White Russian prince aged thirty-six who never exchanged his kepi for a steel helmet. Meanwhile there seems to have been a liberal flow of intelligence between the two Legion camps and they never had to face each other directly in battle.

But if 13 DBLE was involved in this campaign only selectively, 6 REI was less inhibited. One of its officers is believed to have hanged a messenger sent to him in disguise from the Free French, an execution carried out on the orders of a Vichy general. As the Allied force – Australians, Indians, British and Free French – thought they had Damascus ripe for capture on 14 June so the Vichy commander, de Verdilhac, struck at his enemy's rear. Australians and men of the Royal Scots Greys fled from Mard-jayoun, pursued by the armour of the Chasseurs d'Afrique and a

Legion battalion under Colonel Robitaille. The same armoured force secured the surrender of the 1st Royal Fusiliers at Kuneitra. At Mezze the Indian Infantry Brigade was annihilated in a four-day action against the tanks of Colonel Lecoulteux. By 21 June, a British estimate of the Free French morale was that de Gaulle's men were extremely tired and reluctant to go on killing their countrymen.

After a series of confused night battles on the night of 20 June, Damascus fell to the Allies. In Syria the war now moved north to the eerily beautiful ruined Roman city of Palmyra. In 1941 it was held by a 500-strong garrison, half of which comprised the 15th company of 6 REI's 4th battalion under Captain Collot. His little team was thinly spread across several locations. These included an ancient fort on Yellow Ridge, a height overlooking the city; Fort Weygand camp just outside it; and concrete blockhouses within two barbed wire compounds known as T2 and T3. Just eleven legionnaires held T2; only twenty-two (three French NCOs, nineteen legionnaires) its twin. In successive waves the opposition included the RAF Regiment, Household Cavalry, Yeomanry regiments from Warwickshire and Wiltshire, the Essex Regiment and Glubb Pasha's Arab Legion from Jordan.

T2 surrendered to the Household Cavalry after a token exchange of fire. Successive attempts to dislodge T3 broke under French air attack. It was almost a week before the fort on Yellow Ridge was taken after dark, on 28 June, when an Essex Regiment patrol under Lieutenant Grimby found it occupied by only six legionnaires. Fort Weygand did not surrender until 3 July. T3 held out until the next day and negotiated a local ceasefire, its negotiators accompanied by three Wiltshire Yeomanry prisoners to remind the English that, in Syria at least, Vichy France should be taken seriously. The worst battle of all, for the English, had been an action against Vichy snipers lurking among the fallen columns of Roman Palmyra. Only after the non-Legion element of the Vichy garrison, who were Bedouin Arab levees, deserted *en masse* did the odds change in favour of the attackers. A total of 165 Vichy prisoners included six French officers, eighty-seven legionnaires (most of them Russian or German), twenty-four Arab soldiers and forty-eight airmen.

Syria was now all but occupied by Allied forces. In Lebanon the war continued. There, 1, 2 and 3 battalions of 6 REI were punishing the Australians as well as the British. A doleful Cheshire Yeomanry officer noted on 21 June: 'Prisoners captured from the Foreign Legion include many Spaniards. They say they are fed up and say this is general of French troops. They seem to fight very well all the same' (quoted in Anthony Mockler).

Early on 6 July the Australians advanced against the exposed, crumbling hills below Damour after a four-hour artillery barrage. From deep slit trenches the defending French rolled hand grenades down the slope at them and the attack faltered. Next the entire 2nd Australian Infantry Brigade was sent on a long march to outflank the French stronghold. The three-day battle which followed left both sides red-eyed with fatigue. The Legion had now been reinforced by Algerian and Senegalese riflemen and real Frenchmen of the 24th Infantry. The Australians tried another approach, through orchards and olive groves. These were densely infested with sniper positions and other local strongpoints. The attackers gained some ground only to be hurled back down the mountain before a furious Algerian counter-attack. The Australians went in again at midnight, astonished to discover that the enemy had left.

The Allies moved on towards the main objective, Beirut. By now the Vichy General Dentz had opened negotiations for a local armistice. The fighting was not quite finished. A battalion of Free Czechs overran a Legion outpost and was in turn pushed back by a counter-attack just before the ceasefire took effect on 12 July.

In this thirty-four-day conflict each side had lost more than 1,000 men. At the end of it, soldiers of the defeated Army of the Levant were permitted to retain personal weapons and claim repatriation aboard French ships. Before embarking, every French soldier passed through a marquee in which a British officer, sitting at a table alongside a Free French interpreter, invited the man to join de Gaulle. In all, 692 legionnaires and 962 North Africans accepted the invitation. With other volunteers including ninety-nine officers and 328 NCOs, this additional strength – 4,500 – almost doubled de Gaulle's manpower. Yet it was thin gruel when compared with the number who chose to go home to France. The Vichy loyalists exceeded 32,000. None expected de Gaulle to be on the winning side of this war. The majority of those supporting him were Foreign Legionnaires or colonial troops from Africa and elsewhere, rather than France.

From Syria, the action moved to the deserts of Egypt and Libya. At the epic battle of Bir Hakeim the men of the 13 DBLE dramatically retrieved their own reputations – tarnished in Allied if not French eyes – as well as that of France. More immediately, they made de Gaulle a serious political figure for the first time since his flight to England. In 1942 the Legion restored de Gaulle's credibility by doing what it did best: fighting an unwinnable action against impossible odds while snatching the real honours of an essentially sacrificial battle. In fighting as it did, 13 DBLE also set the style for the rest of the Free French Brigade to emulate. Only later would President de Gaulle threaten the Legion with dissolution. His ruthlessness in 1962 could not diminish the significance of Bir Hakeim for France and the Desert War as a whole. For this reason, Chapter 11 is dedicated to that action, viewed largely through the eyes of one of its more remarkable veterans. Bir Hakeim exhausted the 1st Free French Brigade and it was followed soon afterward by another catastrophe, the death in action during the run-up to Alamein of the Georgian Prince Amilakvari, commander of 13 DBLE. For five months the two battalions of 13 DBLE (one commanded by Amilakvari's successor, Major Bablon, the other led by the Bir Hakeim veteran Captain de Sairigné) rested, re-equipped and retrained in Tripolitania under Koenig's command. In April 1943 when the unit rejoined the fighting strength of the Eighth Army for the final conquest of North Africa by the Allies, it emerged into a world politically changed beyond recognition.

The preceding year, 1942, was not only the year of Bir Hakeim and El Alamein; it was also the year that the US became a full participant in the war, the year when the Allies invaded French-controlled North Africa, the year German troops seized control of Unoccupied France. Knocked from its uneasy perch of neutrality – a perch weighted in favour of Germany – France changed sides for the second time in two years after some hard-fought actions against the Allied invaders in North Africa as well as Syria. With France, most of her foreign legionnaires also found themselves engaged in a political turnaround against the Third

Reich. The men of 13 DBLE (known to the rest of the French army as the 1st and 2nd battalions, Foreign Legion, of the 1st Free French Brigade) remained with de Gaulle as part of the British Eighth Army. They were tainted by one of the worst heresies known to the French official mind: that of being out of line and being proved right by events.

When the combined US–British task force landed a total of 107,000 men at Casablanca, Oran and Algiers as Operation Torch on 8 November, confusion among the French High Command was total. General Alphonse Juin surrendered Algiers to US General Charles Ryder the same day. At Casablanca the Allies lost seven ships, three submarines and 1,000 men, and General Auguste Nogues fought on for three days. The French historian Raoul Girardet recorded a typical junior officer's dilemma and his reaction to it:

> I stopped believing in the virtue of obedience the day when, on a Moroccan beach, I received two contradictory orders at ten minutes' interval; one from my major, to rally with my section to the disembarking American troops; the other from my colonel, to resist to the bitter end.

Confusion, also, as the Germans entered unoccupied Vichy France on 11 November, the day after Admiral Jean Darlan surrendered to the Allies in North Africa. The armistice army ceased to exist with the end of Vichy France, yet only one senior officer, Jean de Lattre de Tassigny, rebelled and escaped to join the Gaullists. The core of the regular French army of the future was now the Armée d'Afrique of whom only 10 per cent supported de Gaulle. In the immediate aftermath of Operation Torch, this was of less importance to the French than the risk of leaving the liberation of French North Africa to an exclusively Anglo-American army. French credibility demanded French participation in the process of expelling the Germans though, in the longer term, the consequences of four years of division between pro-Vichy and Free French forces would expand beyond the confines of World War II.

In its hasty *volte-face* the Armée d'Afrique conjured up its best, most reliable troops from distant shores, its legionnaires. These included survivors of the Battle of France against the Wehrmacht in June 1940 and veterans of 6 REI who had mauled the Allies in Syria. About 30 per cent of them were Spaniards who had fought against Franco's pro-fascist army in the Spanish Civil War. One of the first units to be retrieved from French West Africa was the 1re *Régiment Étranger d'Infanterie* (1 REI). There followed much regimental reorganization to create those battle-worthy but politically neutral and peculiarly French organisms, the *bataillons de marche*. Thus 1/1 REI was under 'autonomous command' on the Bou Arada front, opposing von Arnim's men from December 1942 until it linked up in April 1943 at Jebel Mansour with two battalions of the 4th demi-brigade (also brought from West Africa) to create the 1re *Régiment Étranger d'Infanterie de Marche*, or 1 REI(M). Another *régiment de marche*, 3 REI(M) was raised in Morocco from elements of 2 and 3 REI. By January 1943, after suffering heavy casualties at Kasserine, it was reduced to six companies before being reinvigorated with a transfusion of manpower from 2/1 REI's bloodbank at Sidi-bel-Abbès. Other such units included 1 REI(M) and two squadrons of 1 REC acting as an autonomous cavalry reconnaissance group.

At the beginning of 1943, some 15,000 Axis soldiers – many brought from Italy and Sicily – were being squeezed by a gigantic pincer. One claw was the Eighth Army including 13 DBLE, approaching from the east; the other, the Anglo-US army which had landed two months earlier in the west. Between December 1942 and the end of the campaign in May 1943, the Legion's six Armée d'Afrique battalions were caught up in a stubborn, miserable mountain war of fighting patrols, of retreat and counter-attack on the southern flank of the main action. The first two months at least were also a time of bitter cold combined with driving rain.

On 19 January the Germans used the mighty Tiger Tanks of 10th Panzer Division for the first time combined with the heavyweight punch of 88mm guns, in a desperate effort to break out of Allied encirclement. They were opposed by one of 1 REC's lightly armed cavalry reconnaissance squadrons equipped with armoured cars discarded by the Americans in 1921.

Leading this team was a certain Lieutenant de Nedde, real

name, Zur Nedden, originally a German engineer and a legionnaire since 1925. De Nedde felt no serious inhibition about
fighting the Wehrmacht: he had fought with the French corps in
Poland and in the Baltic States against the Third Reich. De Nedde
later told a friend:

> The Colonel offered me the chance to opt out of operations in Tunisia
> (as was the case with all legionnaires of German origin). But this offer
> was a shock. For more than fifteen years I owed everything to France.
> For me this was the time to give back what France had given me.
> [Col. Villaume, et al.]

De Nedde's out-gunned squadron, together with Legion infantrymen, used the irregular terrain to close to within 200 yards to
hit German armour and infantry follow-up forces with 60mm
mortars and 47mm weapons captured from the Italians, as well
as their own well-worn long-barrelled 75mm anti-tank guns. The
advance by 10th Panzer's Tigers on the key Mausoleum cross
roads could not be halted but it was impeded long enough for an
American counter-thrust to be launched.

During the same onslaught three days later, on Jebel Serdouk
most of 1/3 REI under Major Lappara, together with a squadron
of REC, were surrounded by 10th Panzer and the Wehrmacht's
334 Mountain Division. At 11.30 a.m. on 22 January the legionnaires began a concerted break-out. The war diary of the 2nd
Company of 1/3 REI recorded the moment:

> We jumped over a ridge and saw our first Germans about 55 yards
> away. We were greeted by a violent burst of automatic fire. After a
> brief stop our Captain, Valentin, shouted 'Forward!' We came over a
> second ridge. The shooting became very violent but we continued in
> the same fashion, as if this were an exercise. Everyone was absolutely
> cool.

Two German companies dissolved under an intense barrage of
French automatic fire as the break-out swept away with it
prisoners and captured weapons. One enemy officer, a veteran of
the Russian front, was taken prisoner at 2 p.m. and promptly told
his captors he had experienced nothing like it before. But while
the centre of this French thrust advanced almost three miles in the

first hour, the flanks were being punished. The battle continued until dusk at 4 p.m. Concealed in the gathering darkness, 700 legionnaires were still cut off, tantalizingly close to the friendly sanctuary of ground held by an Algerian division. Lappara rounded up those who could be mustered around his temporary command post and stealthily edged away. Of the 700 he brought 220 out with him. Later that night Second Lieutenant Labruyère rounded up fifty survivors of the Legion's armoured car squadron and led them out also. But some invaluable veterans had been left where they fell that grim day. As Valentin's company diary would recollect:

> At the third ridge we had to dive to the ground as we were caught by a German machine gun on our flank. Colour-Sergeant Bucereau fell as well as Sergeant Christ, Corporal Byricnter, Legionnaires Marty, Alonzo, Gilson . . . In spite of that, we kept going.

After this action, 3 REI was reduced to a mere six companies out of sixteen. It was augmented by the Gombeaud battalion, originally part of 6 REI in Syria, and placed on the southern flank of General Patton's GIs. Thus Major Gombeaud's Spaniards, having fought the British, Indians and Australians in the Levant, were now allies of the Americans in attacking the Germans and Italians. In May, in preparation for the final Allied push, 1 REI(M) was also augmented. It acquired men who had fought in France in 1940 and veterans of Norway who had opted not to follow de Gaulle. There was also a battalion which, according to a cryptic official report, 'directed to Syria in 1941, had been held in Yugoslavia'.

Both this unit and 3 REI, with the Moroccan *Division de Marche*, were in the forefront of the final efforts to destroy the Axis forces in Africa. When the end came, it was with surprising speed. On 7 May Tunis was captured. On 11 May, after days of bitter fighting, 3 REI's commander, Colonel Lambert, negotiated the surrender of 10,000 German and Italian soldiers at Zaghouan. On the same day, men of 1 REI, 'electrified' by the experience of gaining ten miles of the Depienne Plain, captured 132 enemy officers and 2,750 soldiers at Jebel Koumima north of Sainte-Marie du Zif, in the German rear. On Jebel Garci Koenig's

Free French legionnaires were still fighting on Ridge 245, suffering severe casualties, up to the final twenty-four hours of German resistance preceding General von Arnim's surrender on 13 May.

It was appropriate that the minority who had followed de Gaulle into exile should be the last French soldiers in action on African soil in this war. They had been there from the beginning. They did not need to look askance at either the Americans or the British as the tide turned in favour of the Allies. France owed her credibility, such as it was, to their 'rebellion'.

After the Allied victory in North Africa both elements of the Foreign Legion – the 13 DBLE of the Free French Corps and the ex-Pétainist battalions from North Africa – paused to re-equip with an avalanche of American equipment, ranging from boots and gaiters to infantry-carrying armoured half-track vehicles. The 13 DBLE was the first to re-enter the war. On 13 April 1944 it rejoined the Corps commanded by General Alphonse Juin in Italy. While Kesselring's tenacious army fought to hold a series of defensive lines stretching from one Italian coast to another, so the Allies painfully chipped away between November 1943 and May 1944 to demolish them at Monte Cassino and on the Anzio beachhead. This was a campaign for mountain troops, a speciality of the 13th which it had not been able to practise much in the desert. But at Radicofani, north of Rome, a Legion subaltern and six men climbed an enemy-held mountain so as to be able to attack a castle from above and behind with grenades. The nine survivors left by this surprise onslaught surrendered.

After just four months in Italy, the Free French legionnaires were withdrawn in order to land in southern France. Eight weeks earlier an Anglo-American army had successfully disembarked to begin the battle for Normandy. Now the Americans and French Gaullist forces hastily tried to hit Occupied France from the south also. So urgent was the Legion's need of new recruits that it composed a third battalion of 13 DBLE from Ukrainians who had fought with the Wehrmacht before surrendering or escaping to join the Maquis. Other volunteers came from non-French members of the Resistance movement. Thus reinforced, the unit prepared to fight a hard winter campaign in Alsace and Lorraine, over some of the same ground it had fought in 1870. And there at last it was joined, towards the end of 1944, by its comrades of the

Moroccan Division. In Tunisia, there had been just enough available legionnaires to create two *régiments de marche*. After the punishing series of actions against the Afrika Korps and 10th Panzer, there were sufficient survivors to make up one *Régiment de Marche de la Légion Étrangère*, or RMLE. The pattern as well as the nomenclature of World War I was being repeated.

The regiment trained for nine months in North Africa with its American gear (new drivers were needed for seventeen half-tracks per company) before joining 5th Armoured Division as mechanized infantry. There were three battalions in this regiment also, though in the new European campaign battalion-size units rapidly ceased to mean much. The real fighting organism typically blended a section or two of infantry in their armoured half-tracks, a squadron or troop of tanks and a battery of light, fast-moving artillery.

In spite of Vichy's betrayal of 1940–41, the RMLE still contained some superb German soldiers who had been kept out of sight during the Goebbels witch-hunt. Now that France had changed sides, France needed her Germans more than ever.

One of the most cunning of the German legionnaires was Sergeant-Major Moulin, alias Porshmann, who, during the advance into Germany itself, issued orders by telephone to Wehrmacht units in villages not yet occupied by the Allies. He told the men where and when to assemble, without saying why. Every time, the men paraded only to find themselves surrounded, their war ending on a note of bathos. Until then, the Legion's road to Germany via Belfort and Colmar had been anything but playful in spite of the *poilus*' bad jokes about winter sports as ice filled up the metal treads of half-tracks designed for desert warfare. In 1870 these same hills had echoed to the sound of underclad legionnaires' coughing their lungs out in temperatures below minus 20 degrees Centigrade. In 1944, in similar temperatures, a warmer uniform included white camouflage but the cold was still paralysing. In spite of that, General Schlesser ordered an RMLE combat group to assault a Colmar suburb at 1 a.m. The order came as the men prepared to eat. The food was abandoned and the men prepared to move out. The general was present, watch in hand, to see them cross the start line on time.

The other realities of war were as grim as ever down the road at

Jebsheim. The 3rd RMLE's 9th Company found itself in a three-day battle there in which 500 enemy soldiers died and 300 surrendered, but only after they had mauled the French in a series of small, personal duels between German snipers and the legionnaires. Further north, as the Wehrmacht offensive rolled over the Ardennes in December 1944, Himmler arrived on the scene exhorting his men to recapture Strasbourg, which was defended by the Legion. The Germans tried hard for four days, but failed.

It was February before Colmar was liberated; April before the Legion crossed the Rhine and Sergeant-Major Porshmann was able to use his wits to save the lives of fellow-legionnaires and his own erstwhile countrymen. By the end of the month a reconstituted French High Command was ordering the 2nd RMLE to advance no further. At the sharp end of a combat group which had already rattled across the Danube and Lake Constance, the Legion's point team turned its radio off and kept going. The men halted at last at Arlberg in Austria on 6 May. They had restored radio contact in time to learn that French forces were to stop shooting.

In 1945, as the days of Louis-Philippe, France wasted no time in seeking foreign volunteers for the next bloodbath. Between October and December of that year, a staggering total of 12,000 new legionnaires was recruited and trained.

One day soon after the war ended in May 1945, a team of German-speaking French officers, smartly dressed in their Number Ones, arrived at a prisoner of war camp near Compiègne. Each billet was roused and the inmates paraded outside in a scene reminiscent of the sheep-and-goats exercise after the Syrian conflict of 1941. Ex-Lance-corporal Rudolfo Biallas, a Wehrmacht soldier and former member of the Hitler Youth movement, told the present author:

> Their leader addressed us in perfect German. He asked us if we wanted 'a better life' than sitting in a prison camp. We could get this, he promised us, by joining the Foreign Legion. No one from our hut volunteered. Most of us had had enough of war. Out of the 5,000 men in the camp only about fifty or sixty accepted. These were mostly SS men or 'DPs' – Displaced Persons – from Eastern Germany or

somewhere else under Russian control. Those people could not go back home. There was nothing for them there. They were the ones who joined the Foreign Legion.

Herr Biallas believes that the 'Commission', as the recruitment team described itself, visited other prison camps in France at that time. If true, it was a characteristic tit-for-tat gesture. In 1940 the Third Reich had recruited Wehrmacht soldiers from the Legion, abetted by Vichy. In 1945 France made a point of recruiting Germans in captivity. In the backwash of Germany's defeat there was no shortage of genuine German volunteers for Legion service. But this was not sufficient to staunch the wound to French credibility throughout much of her vast empire, a wound inflicted as much by France itself as by its adversaries, who had included Germany, Italy, Britain, Australia, India and the United States in approximately that order. The only serious protagonist with whom France had not been at war was Japan. But in March 1945, France became engulfed in conflict in South-East Asia also. Although it was not obvious at the time, a new age of colonial warfare was about to begin.

De Gaulle, it is true, had achieved a greater historical consistency than most of his compatriots. Like Churchill, he had defied Hitler from the beginning. But even de Gaulle's credibility depended in the first instance on what a small group of non-French soldiers, including foreign legionnaires and one young Englishwoman, did at Bir Hakeim in 1942.

CHAPTER 11
The Extraordinary Miss Travers
(Bir Hakeim, 1942)

Of course we could have tiptoed away from Bir
Hakeim. But I would be obliged to leave among
the wounded those German, Italian and
Spanish legionnaires who had served with
honour and fidelity . . . I could not expose
them, as an officer of the Legion, to such a
dishonourable solution.

– General Pierre Koenig, Commander,
1st Free French Brigade

In her dugout in the Western Desert, the young Englishwoman
checked the condition of her .38 Webley revolver, pondering
whether she would have the resolve to use it to kill any German
soldier who entered the place. The daughter of a Royal Navy
captain who had retired comfortably on his pension to the Côte
d'Azur, she had attended a finishing school in Florence and
played junior championship tennis at Wimbledon and Budapest.
She was twenty-nine when the war started, and someone later
described her as 'a very good-looking girl, tall, slim, but perhaps
rather aloof and fastidious'.

She did not like the idea of being totally vulnerable; nor did she
want to depend upon some man to take care of her. To her
comrades of the Legion she was 'Miss Travers', or sometimes,
simply 'Miss'. It was a sort of nickname, most affectionately
rendered into franglais as 'La Miss'. It was well known that La
Miss took care of herself as well as others. With characteristic
timing, she had acquired the revolver as part of a deal. On her
way to this war, she had picked up a .303 rifle while crocodile-
hunting in the Congo. A French naval officer had taken a fancy to
this weapon and her price was his service revolver.

Now the time was coming when she was to prove her courage in ways which required her to risk her life to save others. To be sure, the revolver was a derisory enough object when set against the artillery shells, high explosive bombs dropped from howling Stuka dive-bombers and heavy calibre machine-gun bullets raining upon the patch of desert in which she was living. Yet it was a useful morale booster in the present battle, a battle in which, almost by accident, France might just recover the military honour it had lost in 1940. The small French force involved had travelled from northern Norway to Britain, to Dahomey and round the Cape to fight the Italians in Eritrea and at last, via Syria, to a desolate spot on the vulnerable end of the Allied line in Libya.

Bir Hakeim might not be the most glamorous place to die but in the summer of 1942 it was of pivotal importance to the Allied cause. The previous January, the port of Benghazi – full of supplies for the attack on Tripolitania – had fallen to Rommel. This was a disaster for the Eighth Army, whose generals needed a sheet anchor in the dangerous, shifting shoals of desert warfare to protect the only other port in the area, that of Tobruk. Alan Moorehead has described how from Gazala, on the Mediterranean coast,

> They decided to define their position with a solid minefield stretching about thirty-five miles from the sea southward into the desert but they did not man the minefield. Instead they sealed up their troops in or behind the minefield in a series of isolated forts or 'boxes'. These boxes faced four-square, ready to meet attack from any direction. It was the old idea of the British square at Waterloo adapted to modern, fast armoured fighting. Each box was completely surrounded with a ring of landmines and barbed wire.

At the end of the line, the fulcrum for this system was Bir Hakeim. It was evident that the German General Rommel would have to roll up this modest garrison so as to prevent its becoming a nuisance to his rear as he swept the British and Commonwealth Eighth Army into the sea at Tobruk to the north. That in turn would give him a clear run to the Suez Canal 500 miles to the east. The rest of North Africa would then be ripe for the picking. With this big picture in mind, he briefed the first troops attacking Bir Hakeim that they could crush it in fifteen minutes. In the event, using his best troops, guns, tanks and aircraft, and with a ten-to-one advantage in manpower, he required fifteen days to do the job. But initially he believed he could be generous to the enemy he was about to defeat, by offering decent surrender terms.

The French commander, General Pierre Koenig, saw it all rather differently. The easy option was to get out fast, without even becoming a prisoner of war. As he put it in *Ce Jour-là: Bir Hakeim*:

> Of course we could have tiptoed away from Bir Hakeim. We would have had to abandon our wounded, our guns and those vehicles still intact. It would have been against my conception of military honour to do so ... In 1940 I was at Namsos in Norway, where we re-embarked with our arms but not the rest of our material, a humiliating memory. A few weeks later, in Brittany ... we suffered the indignity of seeing troops alongside us, our troops, using their vehicles to take flight. We were the Free French. We couldn't do that. In any case, if I adopted such a solution, I would be obliged to leave among the wounded those German, Italian and Spanish legionnaires who had served since the beginning of the war with honour and fidelity. I could not expose them as an act of deliberate policy to the reception awaiting them as prisoners. My reflexes as an officer of the Legion could not allow me to tolerate such a dishonourable solution.

The phrase 'honour and fidelity' is inscribed on discharge papers to describe the service of every faithful legionnaire. Koenig was about to demonstrate that the arrangement cut both ways and bound both parties. Susan Travers, as Koenig's driver, was to participate in the deadly serious business of 'honour and fidelity' to a degree which she could not have imagined when, skirting round an order extracting all female personnel from the battleground, she found a plausible pretext to return. She had been Koenig's chauffeur for less than a year. Her predecessor, a man, had been killed driving over a mine. Given the chance to replace him, she said, 'I was delighted.'

The Legion was represented at Bir Hakeim by 500 men of the 13th DBLE. As well as the Legion, the 1st Free French Brigade included a bewildering variety of fighting (and some brave but emphatically non-fighting) men, a polyglot force which was a microcosm of France and its empire. There were tough Bretons of the naval gunnery squad, the Fusiliers Marins, manning anti-aircraft Bofors; Tahitians of the Pacific Battalion; Arab sharp-shooters from Algeria and Morocco; Lebanese sappers; orderlies from Cambodia and Vietnam; gunners from Mauritius and Madagascar; even Africans of Chad's Oubangui-Chari tribe whose ad-hoc provisional *bataillon de marche* counted witch-doctors among its number. More orthodox medicine was pro-vided by the English nurses and American Quakers who were conscientious objectors. The Legion respected them for their courage. (One of them, James Worden, was later made a Companion of the Liberation.)

When the assault began, the 3,723 men and one woman had been encamped in their barren, stony wilderness since February, three months before and non-combatants, including female nurses, evacuated. A crude defensive box of barbed wire, ditches and trenches ten miles in circumference, Bir Hakeim was note-worthy for only one nugget of defensively useful high ground. This conveniently faced the enemy on the north-east corner and was called Point 186 or, since it was used to spot for the artillery, the Observatory. Around it looped a broken circle of sand and rubble built over old water-storage tanks.

At the southern exit of the box was the remains of an ancient fort. Outside the wire there were more formidable defences: two vast minefields forming a V which ran around the garrison, north-south, on both sides of the wire. One arm of the V ran in a continuous belt of lethal explosive all the way to the coast in front of a position held by the South African division. Every sort of mine, from anti-tank to anti-personnel, was buried there and during the long, hot wait the sun or the driving wind had been sufficient to detonate some of this ordnance, sending rocks flying and causing random casualties within the wire. The minefield was to prove a mixed blessing.

The period before the siege had been made tolerable by forays outside the wire in vehicles, usually under cover of darkness, for reconnaissance purposes and, occasionally, as fighting patrols which kept enemy heads down. Koenig, an old Legion hand who led from the front, was in charge of some of these 'Jock Columns' himself, with Miss Travers as his driver.

When, finally, the enemy came looking for a way into the

fragile box, it was 26 May. This was no surprise, and by now all female personnel, including Miss Travers, had been politely evacuated to a rear echelon area around El Adem. She put it laconically: 'We left in a hurry because we were told the Germans were coming.' She drove an ambulance back. At two o'clock that afternoon, the southern approaches to Bir Hakeim were hit by a furious artillery barrage which was clearly the overture to a full-scale assault. The units assigned to this were two élite Italian divisions, the Ariete Armoured and the Trieste Motorized. They were merely part of a more ambitious strategy aimed at hitting the Allied defenders from the rear after a ride through the desert, south, round the base of the V at Bir Hakeim and then pell-mell into the British and their Commonwealth comrades further north at 'Knightsbridge'. While the Italians were hitting the French, the German 15 and 21 Panzer brigades would strike north. Meanwhile, the 90th Light Division – a German motorized infantry and armoured car unit which included ex-legionnaires – sought to crush the Allied reserves further east at El Adem.

The first men to come under fire were members of an Anglo-Indian screening force who were on the enemy side of the minefield and outside the wire. Part of the famous 7th Armoured Division accompanied by the 3rd Indian Brigade, under British command, they fought a holding action through the afternoon until night fell. With darkness came the throbbing sound of engines outside the compound and the tell-tale squeak of tank tracks. An aircraft flew over the garrison, dropping flares which briefly shed a sick and unnatural light. More flares were fired from the ground, somewhere south and then south-east. Dawn brought a clear sky that was not characteristic of the weather during the rest of the battle, and with it a radio in Koenig's headquarters at the centre of the defended area crackled into life. It was a British voice – from 7th Armoured – announcing in clipped, urgent tones that Bir Hakeim should pull down the shutters and mine the established entrances. Then came the sound of battle and another message from the British force, that it was about to counter-attack. After which there was no further radio contact.

Koenig was not a man to sit and wait for something to happen.

His marauding Legion patrols, riding in open-topped Bren-gun Carriers roared out into the desert, traversing secret safe routes through the minefield. They flashed back ominous news. German tanks were to the east of Bir Hakeim, back in the direction of the garrison's supply base and, ultimately, its only source of water. Bir Hakeim had been outflanked.

At 9 a.m. next day, 27 May, the defenders spotted a tell-tale dust-cloud approaching from the south-east. At about 1,700 yards, through binoculars, the legionnaires identified the source: the ubiquitous Panzer MkIV tank with which Hitler had overrun Europe. With a 75mm gun and top speed of twenty-five miles per hour it was formidable as well as familiar.

The tanks came in two waves, first fifty, then another twenty. At 1,500 yards both sides roared opening salvoes at one another. On the left of the tank column the first of the Panzers bucked and lurched under the impact of the mines, then stopped. From the French side, eleven long-barrelled anti-tank guns – also 75mm – concentrated their fire in one broadside. The foot soldiers accompanying the tanks were the next target. They clambered into lorries and turned back but the tank crews showed more courage. Six of the MkIVs charged into the garrison. It was not their lucky day. The position they attacked was held by Legion gunners who calmly held their fire until the last moment. The tanks were within 20 yards of the Legion's forward command post – whose captain was obliged to burn his flag and code-books in anticipation of being overrun – when the guns opened up with devastating effect. Then, as the surviving enemy swung round and fled, the legionnaires went after them with grenades and small arms.

The élite Italian Ariete Armoured Division lost thirty-three tanks in less than an hour. The leader, a dashing cavalry colonel named Prestissimo, was in his third tank when he was captured. The others had been shot to pieces around him. He was now in a lamentable state, wounded, burned and almost naked. The Legion's padre, Abbé Mellec, dressed him in pyjamas just before General Koenig arrived.

'We were told we could crush you in fifteen minutes,' the Italian told him. 'You know, in the First World War I fought alongside the French. But this conflict is fratricide. We were told your position was only lightly defended and that the mines had been removed.'

In fact, the French had spent many weeks of preparation burrowing into the rock below them to create a series of strongpoints which would withstand even a direct hit. And the minefield had been sown as assiduously as a field of French barley. Prestissimo was one of ninety-one prisoners from that first engagement, which Koenig now followed up by sending out more fighting patrols.

This initiative reaped a rapid reward. An enemy supply column, spotted among the mirages and the growing sandstorm, was taken to replenish Bir Hakeim's larder. With it came the first German prisoners of war taken by French forces since 1940. In another encounter that day, five captured British vehicles and two German trucks came upon a Bren-gun Carrier apparently occupied by dead legionnaires. At very short range indeed, the legionnaires came to life again and opened fire. Four of the enemy vehicles were still in working order after this episode and were taken back to Bir Hakeim with two prisoners. By the end of the day, Koenig's men had acquired an enemy tanker carrying 1,000 litres of drinking water, 154 Italians and 125 Germans. An added bonus was the release of 654 British and Indian soldiers taken prisoner during the preliminary battle outside the wire.

Its supply line cut by the raiders emerging from Bir Hakeim, the main German tank force skirting the southern edge of Bir Hakeim turned back, only to come under fire from more of Koenig's marauding patrols which destroyed seven armoured cars and several trucks.

So far, so good. But the increase in the garrison by the equivalent of a battalion of men – the released Indians who had not eaten for two days and were now desperate for water – created its own problems, one of which was that some of the men were emptying the radiators of the French vehicles.

Elsewhere on the Allied front events had taken a disastrous turn. While the 1st Free French Brigade were holding their ground so tenaciously, the British 150 Infantry Brigade from Yorkshire and Durham, less than ten miles to the north, was unexpectedly defeated. Rommel's forces there had been trapped in a minefield, most of their fuel and ammunition expended, without hope of resupply and under constant air assault. In an almost suicidal gamble, Rommel ordered his beleaguered men to attack. In a battle which raged through 31 May the British force was broken with a loss of 3,000 prisoners and 123 guns.

Until that disaster the Eighth Army high command had confidently prepared for its own counter-attack, and as part of that plan had ordered some of Koenig's men to move almost fifty miles west to hold a key position at a small hill known as Rotunda Segnali, until the British got there. Koenig sent a team of Tahitians. In the same mood of confidence the Legion had spent the two or three preceding days attacking the Germans wherever they could be found in the desert around Bir Hakeim. Young Captain Pierre Messmer — later to become Prime Minister in post-war France — shot up fifteen German tanks with cannon at 1,500 metres and then went on to create havoc in an Italian convoy. At the same time, a French convoy set off from the rear echelon area of El Adem with another week's supply of water, food and ammunition for Bir Hakeim. On the return journey it removed the released Indians, fifty-four French wounded, and prisoners of war.

By the time the significance of the British defeat had started to sink in, Koenig's Tahitians were far away to the west, under punishing air attack from the Luftwaffe awaiting a British relief column which would never come . . . and Susan Travers was on her way back to Bir Hakeim from the rear area to the east. Her own explanation of how that happened is characteristically prosaic. A long way from the front line, on the road to Alexandria, she had collected a new staff car for Koenig's chief of staff, Colonel Masson, from a base workshop.

I took it and went back along the road until I got to our brigade workshop, which was a bit further along towards the enemy. A convoy was going up to the rear echelon area and I joined it. They were not very pleased, really, that I had returned. Then I managed to get a word with a convoy going into Bir Hakeim itself. I sent a note to General Koenig saying, 'Here I am back at the rear echelon with the new staff car. Can I come?'

He said, 'Yes you can.' The Germans seemed to have left. The Eighth Army was taking the offensive and was going to chase them, you see.

By the time she was bumping along the road between the rear echelon and the front all other traffic, including the supply column, was rolling in the opposite direction. Rommel was at large again, his supply line restored as a result of his victory over the British and Bir Hakeim was about to be cut off for good.

She got back in time for a resumption of German air raids which were to be part of the daily life and death of Bir Hakeim for two agonizing weeks. From noon on 1 June there were five raids of between twelve and twenty-four big Junker bombers unloading 500lb bombs on the position. Before the battle was over, the Luftwaffe would make 1,400 sorties against the French to drop 1,500 tons of high explosive.

Susan Travers had already organized a pit in the stony desert for her precious staff car about 200 yards from Koenig's staff headquarters. On the parapet around it were piled the usual sandbags. Her personal quarters were in a bunker deep enough for her to stand upright and furnished with two items she had acquired in London soon after the fall of France when she had joined de Gaulle's forces. These were a folding bed and a collapsible bath for tropical use. With strict water rationing in force, the bath was not overused. There were also the supply boxes. As she later explained:

> I did not suffer much from thirst because I was not having to make any physical effort. On the contrary, I had a stock of corned beef and I had bought my own supplies, a case full of tinned sardines and asparagus. I used to say to myself, 'It would be a pity to leave this lot to the Germans,' so I ate it religiously for lunch every day. Every day, a tin of asparagus. That wasn't bad.

It was often stiflingly hot in the hole, but better than being caught out in the open by the Luftwaffe. More than forty years later, she recalled,

> There were a lot of bombardments from the air by Stuka dive bombers. They were very unnerving. First of all, we heard them coming. We knew they were coming for us. Then they made a lot of noise when they dive-bombed. It was a frightening noise and no one liked them. They attacked at any time of day, but not, thankfully, at night. In our quartier-general there was an elderly Chinese orderly

known as 'Trompette' because he had a trumpet and he would stand up and blow it as an air-raid warning.

To hit back at the Stukas we had Bofors [fast-firing, multi-barrelled cannon] but there were lots of complaints about the absence of the English aeroplanes. When they arrived, the Germans were never there. It was as if the Germans were hiding behind a cloud or something. Nobody went out to watch the raids. They were too frightening. The hospital was not very far away. A bomb fell on the men there and killed them.

(The RAF in fact flew 200 sorties in support of Bir Hakeim in one day, but the withdrawal of a vital radar hampered them.)

The effect of these raids on Susan Travers was to make her hungry. Just after dusk, as the incoming fire eased off, she would emerge from her shelter and make her way to the field kitchen to collect a mess tin of heated corned beef and some gossip. So did others. 'When the bombardments stopped in the evenings,' she said, 'people popped out of their holes like rabbits.' When she had eaten, she found it easy to sleep. Koenig's observation of her demeanour at the time was that 'she was always calm'.

The Legion was not deterred from its marauding habits by the bad news from the north nor by the renewed air attacks on the base. During the first two days of bad news elsewhere, the legion's commander, Lieutenant-Colonel Amilakvari took to the desert with four guns to look for a German workshop. He found several tanks and destroyed them. Later, in a chaotic action fought among bewildering mirages, Captain Gabriel de Sairigné, commanding the unit's heavy weapons company, opened fire on German and British tanks impartially in a chaotic running battle in which friend and foe came, it seemed, from every direction. Next morning, 2 June, it was evident that the enemy was determined to stop such attacks. At breakfast time, two divisions – tanks, armoured cars and trucks – lumbered towards Bir Hakeim from the west and north and the Legion patrols were recalled to the base. The Legion gunners promptly shot at them, setting one on fire. Then, around 10 a.m., Koenig took a call on his field telephone from Major Babonneau, commanding the front-line 2nd Foreign Legion Battalion.

'A vehicle with a white flag is approaching us,' said Babonneau.

'It could be a trick,' Koenig suggested.

'The vehicle has stopped and two negotiators have got out carrying a white flag. They are walking towards us.'

'Right. Blindfold them and bring them to my HQ.'

The tall, bearded de Sairigné loomed over the two Italian officers, covered their eyes, then drove them on a bumpy, disorienting circuit on the back of a pick-up for fifteen minutes before taking them to Koenig. They spoke no French and the French officers relied upon school Latin to understand. But the Italians' meaning was clear enough for all that: '*Rommel . . . italiani . . . circumdati . . . Bir Hakeim capitulare . . . Rommel exterminare.*'

Koenig cut the monologue short. Slowly and with great emphasis he said: '*Je regrette vivement, messieurs. Allez dire à votre général que nous ne sommes pas ici pour nous rendre.*'

The Italians saluted, murmured '*Grandi soldati*' in a tone which suggested 'Great but dead soldiers', and were escorted out. By the time de Sairigné had conveyed them back to the perimeter their driver, intimidated perhaps by the presence of legionnaires who had once been Italians themselves, had taken off in panic. The first Italian 105mm shell hit Bir Hakeim about thirty minutes after the officers returned to their own lines, on foot.

There were more serious problems that day. The Tahitians signalled that they were making a fighting retreat from their forward position with the help of a rescue convoy of ambulances and supplies despatched from the beleaguered base. Six ambulances crammed with wounded men lurched across the desert track back towards the sanctuary of Bir Hakeim. The valuable supply column was seized by a grateful enemy and two ambulances simply disappeared. Then the area was struck by a sandstorm.

Even without the added nuisance of war, a sandstorm is an unpleasant experience. Fine grains of dirt find their way into ears, down the neck and armpits, mixing with sweat to make an abrasive porridge. The temperature rises rapidly and tempers shorten. This one was no different. As an official account of Bir Hakeim records, 'The heat became insufferable . . . The absence of water meant we could not satisfy our thirst.'

In such a situation, the only sensible reaction is to remain stationary, under shelter, conserving moisture, and that is what Susan Travers was doing. She had one book, an ancient tome called *Said the Fisherman* purloined from a Cairo library and this she read, slowly and not without pleasure, in her dugout.

By 3 June, it was obvious to both sides that Bir Hakeim was a key piece on the desert chessboard. Rommel could not safely pursue the rest of his strategy without taking it. Likewise, the British needed time to reorganize their defences which only a delaying action at Bir Hakeim could buy for them. The Luftwaffe came in bright and early at 6 a.m. to make the first of the day's twelve raids, during which they lost eight aircraft. At 9 a.m., Major Babonneau's legionnaires were confronted by another peace party, two men in British uniform waving a white flag as they walked uncertainly towards the French position. Suspecting a trick, the men of 2 Legion Battalion (2 BLE) fired at them.

The men came on, and were identified as British prisoners of war released by the Germans to act as messengers to the French. One of the men was driver to a Captain Tomkins, British liaison officer to Koenig, who had been taken prisoner during the period of false optimism the previous day. The emissaries carried a note, personally signed by the German commander, which said, 'Prolonged resistance on your part will generate unnecessary bloodshed – You'll suffer the same fate as the two English brigades which were destroyed the day before yesterday . . . Hoist white flags and come out without your weapons.'

The French General Koenig was furious, not least because Rommel had disregarded military protocol in addressing his message to the troops of Bir Hakeim, rather than their commander. Furthermore, Koenig complained, Rommel's syntax – his imperative use of '*Ihr*' rather than '*Sie*' as a form of address – suggested that Rommel already commanded the French garrison. Such discourtesy, Koenig commented, indicated that they were not living in the same world and he made a note to take the matter up with Rommel personally after the war. His immediate answer was an artillery barrage from the French guns and an order of the day to his troops along the lines, 'This day France expects . . .' The artillery duel rolled on all day. The late afternoon was enlivened by the arrival of a South African Spitfire which had lost its way and was now running out of fuel. It landed safely and –

thanks to a crude runway created overnight by Babonneau's men – took off safely, and refuelled, at dawn next day.

June 4 began with the customary dawn chorus of a dozen Stuka dive-bombers and incoming artillery shells, ended with unsuccessful probes by enemy tanks, a sandstorm at dusk, and a new form of nocturnal warfare between enemy pioneers trying to dig a path through the minefield, and legionnaires trying to stop them. It was a dangerous, intimate form of warfare in which only the distinctive shape of a helmet proclaimed who was friend and who foe; a war fought silently with knives and sometimes less silently with grenades. During the day, Koenig sent the Legion commander, Amilakvari, to report on the state of 2 BLE, holding the sensitive eastern flank of the position. The prince donned his kepi, saluted, and was about to leave when Koenig told him, 'Put your helmet on, Amilak.'

'Bah!' snorted Amilakvari. 'With or without helmet, death knows when it is your turn.'

From Koenig's headquarters, the general and his chief of staff watched through binoculars as Amilakvari, marching as if on parade and the only living thing in sight, strode towards Babonneau's command post. Then a cloud of dust caused by the latest explosion obscured the figure; and cleared again. There was no sign of Amilakvari, until a telephone call, and a familiar voice which said, 'Everything is fine here. I am staying for dinner.'

(A few months later, on the edge of the El Alamein battle, Amilakvari was killed by a shell splinter through the head. At the Legion's museum near Marseilles, they still preserve the headgear he was wearing at the time: a colonel's black kepi ornately decorated with braid on top and a small, jagged hole through each temple.)

Susan Travers had just one task to perform. This was to keep the staff car ready to move. During one of the early air raids a bomb splinter had punched a hole in the radiator. She persuaded a Vietnamese driver to unhitch the damaged radiator. Then they both carried it to Bir Hakeim's own spartan field workshop, where mechanics welded solder over the hole. As the siege tightened, she made only one other foray from her dugout – to the hospital to see if help was needed there. It was not. By the time she set out on the return journey, the desert wind, the *Khamsin*, was blowing hard again and 'it was like a fog'. She groped her way to the headquarters compound, sweating with the effort, relieved at last to be back in her hole in the ground. Her nose and eyes were clogged with sand, but at least she was home.

At 4.30 the following morning, 5 June, Koenig was woken by another call from Babonneau. A car with full headlights on had driven up to a Legion position. Three German officers wanted to speak to the commander. Koenig curtly replied that he would not receive them. Rommel's logic about needless bloodshed might seem impeccable, but in 1940 Frenchmen had been too logical by half and France had lost its name. Koenig told Babonneau that the German visitors had just five minutes to get out.

On their way out, the two officers had driven only a few yards when their vehicle hit a mine and blew up. They rolled out of it, shaken but unscathed, and had to walk home. The legionnaires, meanwhile, searched the vehicle for booty. One trinket which they sent up to their headquarters was an Iron Cross. Meanwhile in the pre-dawn darkness to the north, they could hear the rumble of gunfire. Another big battle was in progress out there.

The bad news filtered through after daybreak. The Eighth Army's Operation Aberdeen, aimed at breaking the 15th and 21st Panzer divisions, had stalled in an intensive combat later known as the battle of the Cauldron. At dusk the night before, Rommel had unexpectedly counter-attacked, and had won. The British had lost 6,000 men dead, wounded and missing, as well as 150 tanks. As the mist cleared at around 9 a.m., new and markedly heavier artillery of up to 210mm slammed shells into the French position from east and west. Yet each time the attacking infantry tried to move forward, they were stopped by the half-buried, almost invisible French guns. De Sairigné's diary for that day, with a proper sense of priorities, commented: 'At 12.35 it rained (not much, but it's extraordinary). The attack has been stopped without difficulty by a good barrage of 75s.'

Rommel now paused in his advance through the British sector, left 21 Panzer to lay siege to Tobruk and gave his undivided attention to Bir Hakeim. Having taken personal command of the assault on the Free French, he did not do things by halves. Four divisions – two Italian and two German – backed by the Luftwaffe's entire Libyan air force of 500 aircraft and twenty-one artillery groups took up positions around and above Koenig's box. A total of 3,700 men inside the wire were now to hold off attacks by 37,000 outside it. In the first move, two infantry battalions supported by tanks struck from the south at a junction of positions shared by the Tahitians and 2 BLE. From 500 metres twenty-four French 75mm guns, collectively firing 192 rounds a minute, tore the attack apart. The scattered individuals who came on – and many did – were picked off by rifle fire. Soon, German ambulances were out with white flags, retrieving the dead and the dying. Two more ground attacks that day also failed.

Rommel convened a conference of his senior commanders, an 'O Group', to tell them that he would lead the next assault himself. 'I need Bir Hakeim,' he told them. 'The break-out of our forces depends on it.'

As a necessary preliminary, his combat engineers cleared a route through the minefield. Under cover of early morning fog, the French replaced the mines the Germans had removed. Later that day Rommel's superior, Kesselring, flew in from Berlin to reproach Rommel. According to the German historian Paul Carell he told the Afrika Korps commander, 'Drop this tactic of small, economic groups for your assault. Attack this dirty little hole with large numbers of ground troops.' So Rommel now tried to overrun the garrison with simultaneous attacks from the south, the west and the north, preceded by raids from heavy Junker bombers. The ground attacks were led in the north by an élite force of SS soldiers and heavy tanks of the Brandenberg Regiment collectively known as 'The Flak'. Rommel had chosen his time well. The fog which had covered Koenig's mine-laying teams also screened the German 88mm guns until they were well within range of the French position. The 88, like the Panzer tank, was a weapon which the Allies never quite matched during World War II. Firing horizontally down open sights at the French position a few hundred yards distant, it pounded the high point known as the Observatory to dust. In reply, says an official account, 'Everyone fired back at the same time.' But it was no longer enough. The French gunners, foxed by mirages, could not properly identify the real targets. The German assault broke only as a result of a timely intervention by RAF aircraft.

After a pause brief enough to be almost imperceptible, the German shelling and a raid by sixty Junkers resumed. Several French vehicles were on fire by now and the wounded lay unattended where they had fallen. Those who might have assisted them were themselves trapped by delayed-action bombs as well as new incoming fire. Yet another enemy advance was stopped, this time during a fierce action between enemy tanks and Koenig's outgunned Bren-gun Carriers.

At noon Koenig issued new orders, the essence of which was that the Legion battalions with their Bren-gun Carriers and 75mm anti-tank guns were to play a mobile role to plug any gaps which appeared in the defences. Messmer's company was in action without respite for forty-eight hours. When, eventually, they fought their way out only sixteen of them, including Messmer, were left.

As the RAF and 7th Armoured Division made renewed, but unsuccessful efforts to take the pressure off Bir Hakeim, Rommel plunged into the battle in person and crossed the minefield to urge his men forward in German and Italian. On the exposed southern approach to the base, the defenders came under a combined onslaught from thirty-five Junker bombers, artillery and tanks. By the end of the day, fires were everywhere within the compound. The most spectacular and costly pyre burned over what had been Koenig's ammunition dump. Yet the line held firm. Rommel noted in his war diary, 'In spite of our punch, the attack was halted . . . It was a remarkable feat by the defenders.'

That night, and the next – 8 June – more convoys ran the gauntlet of fire in and out of the garrison under cover of darkness, escorted by British armoured cars. During the last few kilometres of this deadly journey they were met and defended by Messmer's men. The convoys gave an unexpected lease of life to France's chances of fighting any longer.

Meanwhile, Rommel varied his tactics. He tried tanks without infantry, infantry without tanks, and the two together. He dedicated the whole of the Afrika Korps assault engineers to the task of clearing a path through the minefield. The French forces – backs to the wall and, as Koenig himself admitted at this time, 'prisoners of our own gesture' – fought on, sometimes doggedly and sometimes like men drugged by the exhilaration of battle.

None now rated his chances of survival very highly. This desperation produced remarkable results. When it seemed that the northern perimeter was about to be engulfed on 8 June, Captain Wagner – a Czech who had joined de Gaulle's forces in London and subsequently transferred to the Legion – led a charge by the Bren-gun Carriers of 2 BLE outside the defended area. His beard flying in the wind, he took his little force into the enemy's rear to seize twenty-five prisoners and stop the momentum of the German assault.

Shortly before dusk, Koenig had moved the 75mm anti-tank guns of the Legion's 9th heavy weapons support company into the battered northern sector and arranged for distribution of the remaining supplies, including one gallon of water per man. An attempt to air-drop material into Bir Hakeim had failed and the wounded, untended, remained in the front line. At 6 p.m. on 8 June, the Observatory – whose African defenders were half-dead through thirst and exhaustion – fell to the Germans.

As the morning mist of 9 June cleared, four 88mm guns, six 50mm heavy machine-guns and five groups of 20mm opened up in concert on the Legion company holding elevated ground nearest the OP. Enemy infantry, Koenig noted, made no attempt to follow through. At 8.30 a.m. the position was bombed by forty Stukas, but their own mounting losses infuriated the Luftwaffe's higher command, who regarded Bir Hakeim as a sideshow. Finally, in the afternoon, after another raid on the northern face by forty-two Junker heavy bombers, the infantry moved forward in close formation, only to be halted and broken by a counter-charge of Bren-gun Carriers. This time the leader was Lieutenant Jean Deve, who served under the name of 'Dewey'.

Dewey was a French veteran of World War I from which he held a Croix de Guerre. Between the wars he became a railway-man and a left-wing militant. After the fall of France in 1940 – 'La Débâcle' – he was thunderstruck by the reluctance of erst-while political allies to continue the fight. A man of obstinate, Breton stock who never foreswore his socialism, he travelled to Britain and joined the Legion. In this action, one of the last in the defence of Bir Hakeim, a 105mm shell scored a direct hit on one of Dewey's vehicles, killing the three legionnaires on board. On the southern perimeter, meanwhile, although all the French anti-tank weapons in the sector were destroyed, the enemy's 90th Light Reconnaissance Tank regiment was so badly mauled by the Tahitians that it withdrew leaving 250 dead.

The Legion also had a price to pay. The enemy guns were now engaged in a careful effort to pinpoint the key French firing positions as accurately as possible. When an ammunition store serving one of the guns was hit, detonating 100 shells in a single, shattering explosion, it left only one of the crew, Sergeant Nicolas, without serious injury. Nicolas put a rudimentary tourniquet on the arm of one of his men and they opened fire on German tanks about to overrun their exposed position. The tanks stopped, fearing a trap as Nicolas rounded off the performance by escaping with his injured Legion comrade slung across his shoulders.

As the battle moved with a dramatic and terrible logic towards its climax, some of the legionnaires were seized by a sort of battle madness, a euphoria which could have only one outcome. One such legionnaire was Sergeant Hascoet of 3 BLE, whose accurate gunnery knocked out in quick succession two enemy mortars and a 77mm gun. General Koenig sent his congratulations to the sergeant and a crate of beer to the team. Greatly refreshed, Hascoet now spotted a German 50mm machine-gun and knocked it out with his first shot. He then climbed on to the parapet around his gun, shouted 'Hurrah' as he performed a war dance – then instantly fell back upon his own gun, mortally wounded.

Towards the end of the day that Hascoet died, a day in which the battle see-sawed back and forth on the crumbling northern perimeter, Koenig received a short, but momentous message from Eighth Army HQ. Further resistance by the Free French Brigade was no longer necessary 'for the progress of the battle'. The other Allies were now satisfied that they would be able to handle whatever else Rommel had to use against them. The RAF flew a supply drop and delivered 170 litres of water which was immediately earmarked for the wounded. Canned food was distributed more generally, but after living on tea during the past days, many men had little appetite for corned beef, biscuits or tinned herring. Ammunition was more important. The gunners were down to their last few rounds. With a little food, a cup of water if they were lucky, and a basic supply of ordnance, the brigade now knew it had to hold on just a little longer.

Koenig was as unwilling as ever to consider surrender. He was going to fight his way out of encirclement taking his wounded and his weapons with him. That meant a night operation, for which he would need twenty-four hours' preparation. They would leave on the night of 10 June, if they survived that long.

The day before the battle ended, Koenig confided to Susan Travers that they were going to attempt the break-out. She was to say nothing to anyone. She packed her gear and checked the vehicle yet again. Later, as the word of the planned escape spread discreetly, one of the men told her to break the windscreen because it would shatter under the impact of a bullet. 'Anyway,' he added, 'you can't see through it at night.'

During the night of 9 June, the noose around Bir Hakeim had tightened, so much so that enemy bombers flew over the area without endeavouring to make an attack. The two sides were now too close together to make it certain on a misty morning that a bomb destined for the French would not kill Germans and Italians. Performing a regular morning chore, the signallers repaired field telephone lines wrecked the day before. The morning fog cleared at around 9 a.m. and Captain Wagner's company of 2 BLE started the day in a spirited fashion by taking on an entire Italian battalion in a close-quarter battle in which the legionnaires' principal weapon was the hand grenade.

Then, after regular but wild shelling, Rommel made yet another attempt to crush the garrison in a single, bold *coup de main*. The new attack, launched around 1 p.m., was preceded by a raid of 130 aircraft, which must have required most of the desert Luftwaffe's serviceable machines. This assault was dedicated exclusively to the battered northern front. The air raid was followed by a heavy artillery barrage under which ten enemy tanks crept forward, fragments of shrapnel from their own artillery bouncing off the hulls as they advanced.

Bearing the brunt of all this was the support element of the Legion's 9th Company. To back them up, Koenig again sent in his mobile reserve of open-topped Bren-gun Carriers. A call for help to the RAF produced Spitfires which made low-level runs over the enemy, machine-gunning as they passed. Further north, out in the open desert, the 7th Armoured Division struck at the enemy rear. The battle raged on until failing light at about 7 p.m. robbed the enemy of air support. With the setting sun, an eerie silence settled over the battleground and the garrison's artillery pieces started to cool at last. The gunners – black Africans and 100 attached British soldiers as well as legionnaires – had stood up fearlessly throughout this day of fire to provide the most effective local support of all. In total, the twenty-four 75mm guns had fired 42,000 shells since the siege began – a daily average of 700 shells per gun – and the 25-pounders 3,000. Most of them were now unserviceable.

Bir Hakeim presented a sorry spectacle, even after dark. From every corner, fires burned. The stench of death was becoming apparent. The watchful legionnaires, still unsure of what was to come, noticed their officers were using their last water supplies to shave. They were also changing into clean uniforms. More than any written order, it was a signal to the men that they were moving out. The men insisted on following the Legion tradition, presenting arms to salute the dead. Later that night, more formal instructions were given. The wounded, the vehicles which were still mobile, the weapons were all loaded up in orderly fashion and the Lebanese sappers cleared a way through the mine-field. Anything which could be of use to the enemy was blown up.

Koenig had chosen a characteristically audacious route out of encirclement, through a gate on the south-western flank of Bir Hakeim, apparently towards enemy territory. Its value was that it was an unguarded corridor through an over-extended enemy line, towards open desert. The plan was that men of 3 BLE would move out on foot to guard the flanks of the escape corridor while the battalion's Bren-gun Carriers led by the veteran socialist, Dewey, would form a vanguard for the convoy proper headed by Koenig's staff car driven by Susan Travers. Behind the staff cars – that of Amilakvari following Koenig's – would flow a long line of guns, trucks and ambulances carrying 200 of the most seriously wounded. Fighting men who could still march, would march.

These included one of the Legion's fighting Germans, Colour Sergeant Eckstein of 3 BLE who had fought on during this long last day after losing an arm, and now insisted he was not a stretcher case. About eight miles to the south a British force already waited at a desert cairn, a beacon known as B837. This was marked by three red lamps which – to reduce accidental discovery – pointed south, away from Bir Hakeim.

In midnight darkness, the first Bren started up its engine and moved off into the murk of fog descending on the desert. It carried as pathfinder Lieutenant Bellec, who was aged twenty, and a former student priest who had developed a taste for soldiering. He had also become an accomplished desert navigator. This time, however, he had not travelled more than 100 yards when his carrier hit a mine and blew up. Instantly, enemy machine-gunners – equipped with the new, fast-firing MG42 – turned their attention to the direction from which the sound came. Behind Bellec in a second Bren-gun Carrier, Colour Sergeant Boufflack became the next victim. Doggedly, Bellec took over a third carrier and was blown up yet again. The convoy halted once more and everyone except the drivers dismounted to reduce the weight applied to any more mines there might be. Something had gone tragically wrong with the escape plan. They were now in darkness, at risk from enemy fire as well as their own mines.

The drivers, including Susan Travers, were instructed to turn about and return the way they had come. Behind her, Amilakvari's vehicle edged round. She in her turn hauled her vehicle round 180 degrees.

'Then the vehicles really started to blow up,' she recalled. 'The staff car now in front of mine was one of the first. The wheels were hit. I gingerly went round Amilakvari's disabled vehicle and drove back a bit.' To do so, she was obliged to drive over a minefield in total darkness amid the sound of other vehicles exploding into flame, illuminating the column for the German machine-guns which opened up with tracer. Dewey's escorting Bren-gun Carrier charged the nearest machine-gun – a 50mm – crushing and killing its crew. The column came under fire again and he repeated the performance. When he went in a third time, to hit yet another machine-gun, he succeeded as he himself died of the bullet wounds his victims inflicted on him. (Next day, exhausted and unlucky legionnaires among 500 men taken prisoner during the break-out noticed one particularly gruesome monument to Dewey's courage: his severed head dangled over the edge of his vehicle.)

For a time the confusion was almost total. The main part of the convoy, alerted to a disastrous navigational error, had now foraged a way to the correct route. But awaiting orders, it stood stationary as German tracer bullets cut the darkness. The patterns they sliced across the night sky revealed that the escape column would have to run the gauntlet not once but three times through hostile guns of increasing calibre.

Koenig and Amilakvari both climbed into Koenig's staff car. Amilakvari, with a Thompson sub-machine-gun across his knees, sat in the front with Susan Travers to act as her navigator while Koenig occupied the rear seat. She recalled:

> The General said, 'There is nothing for it, we have to get in front. If we go, the rest will follow us.' We drove past the others very gingerly, up the side of the convoy and through the tracer bullets which hit the car, but not us, and straight on. It is a delightful feeling, going as fast as you can in the dark. My main concern was that the engine would stall and that the General would be taken prisoner and that would be my fault. The engine did cut out sometimes but not that night. We went away in the dark. It seemed to me that I drove into every hole there was. It was a matter of visibility, really. When, much later on, Koenig himself drove for a time, he did no better.

As they charged through the last enemy line they were peppered with rounds from a 13.2mm Breda which sent sparks flying from the top of their Ford Utility.

Desert driving in normal conditions is a tricky business in which, if the vehicle doesn't hit a slope at the right angle and speed, it will turn over or dig itself into the sand and stop. In the darkness, her foot hard down on the accelerator, Susan Travers seems to have caused even the redoubtable Koenig some misgivings.

> The General kept saying, 'You are going to break the car to pieces.' I remember at one point during the escape I was certain that the vehicle had been hit by something heavy. We had been, by another staff car following and which drove into us.

The fact of the matter was that sitting behind the driving wheel, Susan Travers could not see as clearly as she needed to. She was also trying to absorb instructions from Amilakvari, who was navigating by the stars, about the route they should follow. Now that they were away from Bir Hakeim, Koenig was standing, head and shoulders exposed through a porthole cut in the roof, to observe the route and to spot enemy vehicles. Behind them, inevitable confusion. As de Sairigné noted: 'After 2 a.m. it was every man for himself. Smashed vehicles blocked the escape routes. Many others blew up in the minefield.'

No one seems clear about how long they drove before they stopped to check their position. Navigation in the desert is usually done by dead-reckoning, as at sea, by sticking to a given compass bearing and checking the distance run on that bearing by reference to the milometer. During the helter-skelter escape from Bir Hakeim the process had been approximate, to put it mildly. They stopped but Susan Travers did not turn off the ignition. This was prudent, as it turned out. Compass in hand, Amilakvari got slowly out of the vehicle, one foot on the running board beside the door. Then as Koenig started saying something to him, Amilakvari put a hand over the General's mouth and whispered close to his ear, 'There is someone there.' The voices were German. It dawned upon Koenig and his team that they were about to drive straight into an enemy tank laager. Navigation forgotten for the time being, Amilakvari jumped back into the car and said, 'Go!' From the darkness, a voice challenged them in German, '*Halt! Wer da? Halt!*'

Bullets followed them as they raced westward, zig-zagging into the mist. One armoured car, its headlights full on, tried to follow them. They curved down into dead ground, went up again the other side and behind a bank and lost it. Gradually, they turned south-west, then south away from the coast, the battle, and further into the desert. The light changed and with a misty dawn came the realization that they had survived to fight another day. After the intense nearness of death during the preceding weeks, the fact of being still alive and unwounded was hard to comprehend. They were also quite alone in an unfamiliar and deafening silence.

Susan Travers handed over some of the driving to Koenig and

noticed that she had a headache. Then, her senses dulled by
fatigue, she slowly realized why: she was still wearing the steel
helmet she had rammed on her head when the convoy had formed
up the previous night. Through the haze, they saw three vehicles
moving along in good order. In an account derived from notes left
by Koenig he recalled:

> I suggested to Amilakvari that we should join them, but he counselled
> me to do nothing of the sort. He thought they were probably enemy
> and he wanted nothing less in this world than to be taken prisoner.
> He was correct. I had less right than anyone to become a Nazi
> propaganda pawn.

At about 8 a.m. the mist cleared and the sun shone from a
cloudless sky. They reckoned that they were still only about
twelve miles from Bir Hakeim, but sufficiently far south to be out
of harm's way. They at last swung east, towards Allied lines,
driving fast and confident now, bounding over the desert.
Another ninety minutes and they turned north again in an effort
to find the Eighth Army's rear echelon. Koenig's account records:
'We stopped twice, the first time because we realized we were
thirsty and drank what was left of the water; the second time
when we saw a New Zealand cemetery, entirely silent in the sunshine . . . We saluted our dead comrades.'

Surprisingly, it was only now that Koenig's morale appears to
have slumped. Having failed to find the rendezvous with the
British force, he and Amilakvari were deeply troubled by their
further failure to sight any vehicles or other remnant of the
garrison they had commanded. They were reasonably certain that
the British were not far away. They found it intolerable that they,
the two top commanders, should be the only ones to survive the
inferno. In part their perception was shaped by simple exhaustion, but a sense of military honour and loyalty to their troops
was also prominent in leading them to a breathtaking conclusion.
Susan Travers described it: 'They were going to leave "La Miss"
with the 2nd Free French Brigade, which was not far away, then
go back to Bir Hakeim and give themselves up as prisoners of
war.' There they would have the bitter satisfaction, perhaps, of
leading their men in captivity.

Koenig's notes said:

We were convinced that the column of vehicles behind us at Bir Hakeim had not been able to follow; that most of them did not have the firepower to break through the enemy lines. We concluded that we had had miraculous luck. As for the soldiers on foot, we imagined how difficult it would be to expect a significant number to have penetrated three lines of encirclement. At one point I proposed to Amilakvari that we should return to Bir Hakeim. We could not return alone to our own side, I thought. He did not have much trouble in persuading me that there was nothing going for this idea, but he did share my evaluation that the episode was looking like a disaster.

With Susan Travers back at the wheel, they drove on. After the pounding she had given the vehicle during the escape, at least one shock absorber had collapsed and soon the brakes were to fail also. Then there was the matter of at least eleven bullet holes in her precious car. One round seemed to have passed between Amilakvari and Koenig. The Ford was now more like a souvenir of Bonnie and Clyde's adventures than a General's staff car.

At about 10.30 a.m., they made contact with a British armoured regiment's field workshop. Susan Travers, sang-froid still intact, gave no sign to her countrymen that she was British. From this unit, Koenig sent a signal to the Eighth Army, relating his escape and his intention to go to the rear echelon. 'I acknowledged that on my advice, the departure of the force had resulted in considerable losses and that the 1st Free French Brigade was no longer combat-ready.' At about noon, the party arrived at 2nd Free French Brigade HQ where, it seemed, their worst fears were confirmed. A staff officer there was despondent about the fate of the garrison. He could only tell them that his general, de Larminat, had left at 5.30 a.m. with two trucks and six ambulances for the rendezvous with the British. Unable to eat, they sat and waited. With characteristic practicality, Susan Travers took her vehicle to the unit's workshop and asked its team to repair the shock absorber. When that job was done she returned to the staff headquarters, parked the vehicle, stretched in the shade beneath it and slept.

It was several hours before Koenig started to receive signals telling a different story. 'A miracle, the impossible had happened and in spite of the pain caused by the loss of several friends, an immense joy entered my heart,' wrote Koenig. In the early evening, a tattered, proud column of men started to arrive in ambulances and trucks. The sound of engines and men's voices, expressing the rare sound of laughter, aroused Koenig's driver. She told the present author: 'I woke up and saw all these ambulances with the wounded, and then everyone. It was a great victory! This was my best memory, this moment when I saw everyone arriving after Bir Hakeim, and I was there, waking up under my vehicle.'

By 7 p.m., some 2,500 men were accounted for, but it was another ninety minutes before the last vehicles out of Bir Hakeim arrived. Indeed, some survivors were still walking in from the desert three days later, among them the remnants of the Oubangui-Chari. But many did not come back. During the siege, losses had been remarkably low but the six final hours of combat, the period of the break-out, cost the Free French Brigade seventy-two dead, 763 missing and twenty-one wounded. Not surprisingly, given their 'stay-behind' role in guarding the flanks of the escape route, the Legion suffered severe losses. The majors leading both battalions were taken prisoner. Puchois, heading 3 BLE, was surrounded by twenty Germans, rifles trained on him as their officer said in perfect French: '*Vous pouvez vous rendre, monsieur. Votre conduite a été admirable.*'

The compliment, though well meant, enraged Puchois – a tall, monocled figure with a head bandage – at least as much as the fact that he had no ammunition left. His reply was to throw his pistol at his captors. With him into the bag went the burly Babonneau, chief of 2 BLE, who gave his interrogators a false name. Months later, both men outsmarted their captors by addressing family postcards, via the Red Cross, to a certain 'Uncle' Koenig. Colour Sergeant Eckstein, last seen during the break-out resting quietly to eat a hunk of bread because 'this damned arm' – the amputation of a few hours before – 'has made me a little tired', also became a prisoner and lived to fight another day.

Messmer and a certain Captain Lalande (who, as a colonel in 1954, commanded the 'Isabelle' strongpoint at Dien Bien Phu) lay like corpses to evade detection a few yards from German troops. Lalande spoke good German. Unable to resist a joke even in this situation, Messmer suggested Lalande resurrect himself and say something to them. Some time later, two escaping Legion Bren-gun Carriers came past, scattering the enemy. The two officers jumped on board, took charge, and shot up a German command vehicle on the way back to sanctuary.

Captain (later General) Jean Simon of the Legion's heavy weapons company was in a vehicle which crashed into a trench full of German infantry. He and his two companions escaped in the confusion which followed the novel use of their truck. Some men, when they reached the rendezvous, could not believe their luck. Legionnaire Alberto Rachef recalled that when he crept towards it 'dead from thirst and fatigue, intoxicated by the noise of battle and the stench of blood, unshaven, finding myself outside a mass grave without knowing how or why, I lay up near the sentries and at last heard the word "Yes". Never have I loved the English as at that moment.'

At the beginning of the siege, the defenders of Bir Hakeim were expected to hold their ground for five days, which became seven, and finally – at most – ten days. It would be pleasant to record that the magnificent fifteen days won by the 1st Free French Brigade transformed the Allied position; that they laid the foundations for the great counter-attack that began later in the year with the battle of El Alamein. In fact, the day after the break-out the British armour at Knightsbridge suffered the greatest defeat in its history and lost 250 tanks out of 300. In the 'Gazala Gallop' which ensued, what was left of the Eighth Army fled to the security of the Egyptian border. Another two days later, the 2nd South African Division surrendered at Tobruk. Such sudden defeats were in total contrast with the glittering courage of the Free French.

A year after the battle, Susan Travers returned to Bir Hakeim on a commemorative visit with Koenig and others. Mines still made it a dangerous place and, as she put it:

> Koenig had been grumbling at a lot of people because they were driving carelessly over them. On this occasion he was driving, with me as his passenger. He drove straight over a mine and the vehicle was blown up. I was severely bruised. It was the only time I became a casualty. I was sent off to hospital with strict instructions to say

ABOVE: Algeria, 1960: a troop-carrying helicopter known as a 'Banana' puts down a team of Legion paras in the hostile Berber mountains of Lower Kabyle. On some operations, such search parties were shot to pieces before the helicopter had left. This photograph was taken by a British legionnaire, Chief-Corporal Jim Worden, a former RAF pilot.

BELOW: When Legion patrols achieved surprise, they could hit targets at long distance with terrifying accuracy, using such weapons as this 57mm recoilless rifle.

ABOVE: If the 'contact' with enemy troops was big enough, the French army employed air strikes and artillery to support the infantry in Algeria. Here, a team from the Legion's First Paras (1 REP) march nonchalantly into action behind a barrage of napalm.

LEFT: The enemy were equipped with a range of modern weapons including land mines. In this mine-clearing operation on the border with Tunisia at Bec de Canard ('Duck's Beak') in 1959–60, men of 2 REP use electronic mine detectors to identify the presence of mines. The hazardous task of lifting them, however, still begins with the probe of a fighting knife blade into the soil. Will the mine explode? Does it have a simple anti-handling device, such as a grenade, attached to it? The courage required for this task is cold, clinical.

ABOVE: The 'stop' team in a rare patch of marsh in low ground near Orléansville wait while another group from 2 REP act as beaters. At any second the waiting marksmen might come face to face with a frightened, armed and dangerous enemy.

RIGHT: After the long, agonising wait, death came swiftly in the Algerian war. The three bodies in this photograph included that of an Algerian National Liberation Army colonel, 'Amirouche', much respected by his Legion opponents.

LEFT: With fresh eggs and bread and reconstituted soup on the menu, a sergeant-chef of 2 REP handles the field cooking in Algeria while 'his boys' murmur encouragement.

BELOW: More often food was insufficient in a fast-moving, big-scale guerrilla war. Legionnaires, including officers, fought and marched beyond the threshold of exhaustion. In this famous study of 1 REP on the Tunisian border, the unit's usually dynamic commander, Lieutenant-Colonel Pierre Jeanpierre, slumps unconscious, back against a rock. When someone suggested his men were tired he replied: 'Why complain? I'm giving you glory, aren't I?'

ABOVE LEFT: The English Legion sergeant Tony Hunter-Choat, circa 1960. He was one of the postwar trail-blazers from Britain and one of a tiny minority. Today 15 per cent of the existing Legion para unit, 2 REP, are British.

ABOVE RIGHT: An Anglo-German section of legionnaires of 1 REP with captured Algerian enemy flag in the Sahara, early 1958. The group includes the former Dulwich College student, Hunter-Choat (second from left, standing) and Corporal Ray Palin from Liverpool, extreme right.

RIGHT: The boy they called 'Ouled': 1 REP's mascot and human ferret, regularly put into mountain potholes to sniff out Algerian fugitives. His innocence was skin-deep. In action he was deadly.

BELOW: Sergeant 'Boby' Dovecar, the Yugoslav who deserted from 1 REP after the putsch against de Gaulle failed. He joined the clandestine terror group, the OAS, with other legionnaires and was executed by a French firing squad on 2 June 1962. His last words were 'Vive la Légion!'

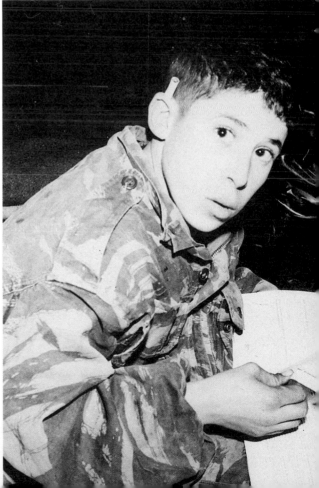

ABOVE: Legionnaires explore the charms of urban Djibouti during the March 1967 referendum on remaining in the French Union. In 1985, thanks to the Legion's presence, Djibouti was a refuge for Europeans obliged to flee from nearby Aden, many aboard the royal yacht *Britannia*.

RIGHT: In the wilderness of Djibouti in 1975 a legionnaire discovers an abandoned piano: former Royal Artillery officer Bob Craigie Wilson, a brawny Scot, in action with 2 REP. The piano was later taken to Legion HQ and converted into a bar.

BELOW: A training jump more dangerous than many operations: men of 2 REP hurl themselves from a heli-copter into the sea, without a parachute. One jumper can be seen leaving the aircraft from the front starboard door. The technique was subsequently abandoned.

LEFT: A more formal desert occasion: a colour party of the 4th 'Compagnie Portée' – Saharan patrol specialists, in distinctive baggy trousers – presents arms. Ritual is important to the Legion. At times the tattered survivors of a long siege have greeted their relief column with just such a gesture.

BELOW: In October 1962, obliged by Algerian independence to leave the home it had built for itself at Sidi-bel-Abbès, the Legion brought to its new base in France its most precious relic: the artificial wooden hand of Jean Danjou, hero of Camerone.

BELOW: The modern Legion: paras of 2 REP training at Calvi, Corsica (many Britons among them), parade with equipment before drawing parachutes. These legionnaires, however, are now also an organic part of a largely non-Legion unit, 11th Para Division.

ABOVE: Dress informal but practical to intercept dust and other unhealthy particles to be encountered in Chad: Operation Manta, 1984.
BELOW: A new form of soldiering and not one which any professional relishes much: the art of 'peacekeeping' (or how to act as a target without striking back and provoking an international incident). Here a team of legionnaires await transport out of Beirut in September 1983.

nothing about what had happened, but somehow, the word got around. The next time I encountered some Legion officers they pointed, laughed and rubbed their backsides as if in pain. They knew all right.

Susan Travers remained attached to the Legion as a driver for the rest of their war in Italy, southern France and a bitter winter campaign on the Franco-German border. Sometimes she drove an ambulance, sometimes a truck and occasionally, a self-propelled anti-tank gun. With the end of the war, she applied for formal membership of the Legion. No woman had ever been admitted to the regiment and, not surprisingly, the request was refused. But she was different. As Koenig had put it, explaining why he had evacuated the few women under his command from Bir Hakeim:

> We were not misogynists yet we did not want to be burdened with women during a battle. But Miss Travers was known, respected and loved by everyone in the division. She had been there with us from the beginning . . . She had been adopted by the Legion as an exception-ally dedicated person . . . A '*garçon manqué*' who could demonstrate a unique self-discipline. She was used to the punishing life we led and her presence presented no problem of any sort.

So, not for the first time, the French high command made an exception, though in her case, on paper, a certain fudging of genders was deemed necessary: it was as *Monsieur* Travers that she was formally appointed to the regiment with which she had served for five years of warfare, as an Adjutant-Chef or Sergeant-Major.

In other times, five years would constitute a full term of service with the Legion. Regimental purists might argue – some do – that she never wore the white kepi of the fighting legionnaire, but at Bir Hakeim and after that seemed to make no difference.

She went with her regiment to Vietnam and there ran the 'foyer', a club for the rank-and-file. In 1947 she married a veteran of eleven years' Legion service, Nicolas Schlegelmilch, who had fought with 6 REI in Syria as well as at Bir Hakeim with 13 DBLE. When Susan Travers left the service, she suffered none of the re-entry problems encountered by other war veterans: 'I was

married. I had a child. Nicolas was still in the Army. We went to
Morocco. I had another child. Nicolas left the Army and worked
for Elf Petroleum for eighteen years. It was a good job. It was time
to settle down.'

She and Nicolas still share a contented life together in a small,
sleepy town in a sun-dappled valley a few miles north of Paris.
Her decorations include the Croix de Guerre awarded after Bir
Hakeim, as well as the Médaille Militaire, Colonial War Medal
and several campaign medals. Her two sons have done well. She
has no regrets.

CHAPTER 12
Road to Dien Bien Phu
(Indo-China, 1945–54)

The case of Indo-China is perfectly clear.
France has milked it for one hundred years. The
people of Indo-China are entitled to something
better than that.

– US President Franklin D. Roosevelt, 24 January 1944

The French Under-Secretary of State . . .
suggested that the US could commit naval
aircraft to the battle of Dien Bien Phu . . . by
placing such aircraft, painted with French
insignia and construed as part of the French
Foreign Legion, under a nominal French
command for . . . air strikes lasting two or
three days.

– Official US report of events in Paris, 23 April 1954

France's war in Vietnam from 1945 to 1954 was aptly described
by the French themselves as the 'Dirty War'. It was fought largely
by non-Frenchmen (for French conscripts were excluded from
such hostilities) to sustain French pride and the privileges of a
corrupt minority of pro-Japanese collaborators in Indo-China, as
well as by soldiers passionately determined to arrest the spread of
communism. Unfortunately for the soldiers, including 10,000
legionnaires still buried in Vietnam, France's political credentials
for fighting on behalf of anything in Vietnam were not of the best.

After the French surrender to the Third Reich in June 1940,
France's political collaboration with the Axis powers grew more
blatant in direct ratio to the collaborators' distance from Europe
In France, for example, there were around 190,000 identified
collaborators opposed by about 170,000 patriots active in the

Resistance movement. The activities of both groups were usually covert. However, in Syria in 1941 the entire Army of the Levant had employed the excuse for systematic and public collaboration that it was repelling an invasion of neutral French territory when it shot at Allied troops. In the Far East, long before Pearl Harbor, Vichy's representatives went further. In August 1940. Vichy France agreed to allow the Japanese General Nishiara free use of three airfields in northern Indo-China; the right to put 5,000 soldiers north of the Red River valley; to traverse Tonkin to make war against nationalist China, one of the Allies; and to evacuate a division fighting in China by way of Tonkin. The Japanese, once they were ashore, effectively occupied the whole country, brushing aside isolated resistance by French units including elements of the Legion. Subsequently, Vichy endorsed a treaty for the common 'Franco-Japanese defence' of Indo-China. As recorded by the historians who compiled *The Pentagon Papers*, the American Acting Secretary of State, Sumner Welles, announced in August 1941:

> This government is impelled to question whether the French Government in Vichy in fact proposes to maintain its declared policy to preserve for the French people the territories both at home and abroad which have long been under French sovereignty.

President Roosevelt was more blunt. He swore that the French would never be allowed to profit from their 'sell-out' and pronounced: 'The case of Indo-China is perfectly clear. France has milked it for one hundred years. The people of Indo-China are entitled to something better than that.'

While too many Frenchmen were earning notoriety as Japan's political consorts, a group of Indo-Chinese nationalists plotted in May 1941 to raise a secret guerrilla army to throw out all foreigners. Their leader was a man who had been a founder-member of the French Communist Party in Paris and was already in 1939 a respected figure within the tiny political élite leading the Comintern. His name was Nguyen Hai Quoc which he changed to Ho Chi Minh ('He Who Lights The Way'). In the event it was more than two years before the new guerrilla force – the Viet Nam Doc Lap Dong Minh (League for the Independence of

Vietnam, or Viet Minh for short) – could put on a token show of resistance in September 1943. By then Ho Chi Minh had been imprisoned by the nationalist Chinese government of Chiang Kai-shek. The Viet Minh, meanwhile, like similar groups of partisans in Malaya and Burma, was receiving a small but valuable flow of weapons, training and moral support from an Allied source: in this case, the OSS, America's counterpart to Britain's Special Operations Executive (SOE). When Indo-China started its long slide towards anarchy in the spring of 1945, the Viet Minh was ready.

The year 1945 was one in which things moved fast in Indo-China, particularly in those provinces which constitute the modern state of Vietnam. In March of that year, when it was obvious that the Allies would soon win the European war and turn their undivided attention to the East, the Japanese concluded that the French could be relied upon no longer. Japanese troops seized key points, overturned the French regime and induced the nominal head of state, Emperor Bao Dai, to declare Vietnam independent of France under Japanese protection. Briefly in 1945, Bao Dai was Japan's puppet-ruler. The day would come when – like the Vicar of Bray – he would serve the same purpose for France.

This did not seem so likely in the spring of 1945 when French soldiers, particularly the Legion regiment whose garrisons had faithfully paraded before the tricolour every morning during the twilight years of the alliance with Japan, were ordered to lay down their arms and submit to internment. Those who demurred received the same brutal treatment already familiar to the British and Australian prisoners in Japanese death camps.

The Japanese had not forgotten that the only serious exchange of fire with the French in 1940 – at Lang Son on the Chinese border – had involved the 5th *Régiment Étranger d'Infanterie* (5 REI). (In fact, that clash had occurred immediately after Catroux's deal with the Japanese and resulted from French nit-picking over the small print of the agreement. It was not defiance of Japanese occupation as such.)

Throughout the region in 1945, isolated groups of legionnaires and other colonial troops showing signs of resistance were rounded up and bayoneted to death in attacks as treacherous as that on Pearl Harbor. At Lang Son in 1945, the French civil and military commanders accepted an invitation to dine with the Japanese and were promptly taken prisoner. They refused to order their people to comply with Japanese orders. The local garrison, including a company of legionnaires, put up a spirited defence of two fortified barracks. One of the defenders was Sergeant Muller, a German who had fled from the Nazis in 1939. Gas was used to overrun the second fort, where sixty men of 5 REI died. The survivors were put against a wall and machine-gunned as they sang, defiantly, the Marseillaise. Afterwards, Japanese guards bayoneted anyone showing signs of life. Re-markably, three people survived this massacre, including the Greek legionnaire Tsakiropolous. He limped away in the dark-ness to take refuge at the home of his wife, and was betrayed almost immediately. A few days later, on 12 March 1945, along with the French Political Resident and General Lemonnier, the local commander, Legionnaire Tsakiropolous was ceremonially decapitated.

From other parts of Indo-China, the 3,000 survivors of 5 REI gathered on the Black River to begin an epic march to freedom: more than 500 miles through the jungle first to Thailand, then to China, still a nationalist state and one of the Allied 'Big Four'. During the fifty-two days of the Legion's long march, the column was repeatedly ambushed, usually by the Japanese. Each time it fought its way out of entrapment and formed up with fewer men than before. Three battalions had left Vietnam in March. The equivalent of just one such unit, about 1,000 men, crossed into the sanctuary of China. The regiment had become a lost legion. By the time it marched back, after the Japanese surrender in August, France had written off the unit. As a Vichy regiment, it was disbanded immediately on its return to Indo-China in 1946 and not rebuilt until three years later.

During the first year after Japan's defeat, reminders of the Japanese occupation and the consequences for France's political image in the region were intensely embarrassing. Such was the political schizophrenia that some officers were ordered to appear before a 'purification commission' in Paris, to answer for their conduct prior to the Japanese attacks of March 1945, while simultaneously receiving decorations which acknowledged their resistance to the Japanese after that date. They had obeyed impossible orders and could not understand why they were treated as pariahs for doing so.

It was a grim end to one of the Legion's more benign traditions, that a posting to 5 REI was a posting to paradise reserved for men with impeccable disciplinary records and more than ten years' Legion service. During the years since the siege of Tuyen Quang in 1885, the legionnaires and the Indo-Chinese had gradually adjusted to one another fairly comfortably. No one forbade a legionnaire to marry a local woman, nor were the soldiers going to lean too heavily on their in-laws. In some parts of the country it was an unintended, but highly successful, hearts-and-minds operation – a political as well as a domestic marriage whose credibility was smashed by French collaboration with the invader. Some people would dispute that there had been a paradise to lose, whatever 5 REI's experience. Under French rule, there had been nearly 700 summary executions in one average year, 1930.

France's problem in 1945 was to find a way back into Indo-China other than by invading the country and thus trampling publicly on the human rights for which, ostensibly, World War II had been fought. A return was to be accomplished in spite of the fact that France's legitimate, constitutional links with Indo-China had been broken repeatedly since 1939: by the Allied and German renunciation of Vichy; by the fact of Japanese conquest; by Bao Dai's repeated disavowal of French protection; and, finally, by the creation of a popular, locally-controlled republic. After six years, France was about to restore the status quo, though this meant riding over Ho Chi Minh who had genuine popular support in the country, as events would demonstrate. An official US study (*The Pentagon Papers*, compiled – not for publication – from confidential government sources by a team of thirty-six professional historians between 1967 and 1969) compared Ho Chi Minh to Yugoslavia's Tito, and noted:

Ho built the Viet Minh into the only Vietnam-wide political organization capable of effective resistance to either the Japanese or the French. He was the only Vietnamese wartime leader with a national following, and he assured himself wider fealty among the Vietnamese people when in August–September 1945 he overthrew the Japanese, obtained the abdication of Emperor Bao Dai, established the Democratic Republic of Vietnam, and staged receptions for in-coming Allied occupation forces – in which the DRV acted as the incumbent Vietnamese government. For a few weeks in September 1945, Vietnam was – for the first and only time in its modern history – free of foreign domination and united from north to south under Ho Chi Minh.

French restoration was achieved with the indispensable aid of the British, who were themselves suspicious of American anticolonialism. The British were also anxious for the future of the Commonwealth, even if they were more ready than the French to recognize that the days of imperial colonialism were past. The British reduced their embarrassment by helping the French in practice, while pretending to be surprised by the result of such help. In 1944, President Roosevelt had made clear his opposition to a French return to Indo-China but, after his death in April 1945, his successors were not going to encourage anyone to transfer power in Vietnam to a veteran communist. Trapped by conflicting policies, the Americans froze into immobility, avoiding aid to France (such as the provision of troopships to move men to the region) while ignoring Ho's repeated pleas that Washington make human rights stick in Vietnam.

At Potsdam in July 1945 it was left to the Allied military commanders, the Chiefs of Staff, to create spheres of influence within which the Japanese forces could make an orderly surrender in the region. North of the Sixteenth Parallel, the Joint Chiefs assigned the responsibility to Chiang's China; south of it, to Lord Mountbatten's South-East Asia Command. This was dominated by the British, whose Fourteenth Army had liberated much of the region including Burma and Malaya with the help of guerrilla groups similar to the Viet Minh. The line effectively divided Vietnam into two nations. In the north, the centre of gravity was Hanoi, Ho's power base. The Chinese recognized Ho, whose underground army seized power on 19 August, rather as a cat might recognize a mouse as its potential dinner.

In what seems to have been a covert race to capture control of the region, the Royal Air Force parachuted a Free French team into the Tay Ninh region of South Vietnam on 22 August, only a week after the Japanese surrender and less than a week after Ho's coup. By contrast, the British – the official Allied presence – did not land their own representatives until 2 September, and did so by more orthodox means. The clandestine French paras were led by an enigmatic representative of the Free French called Colonel Jean Cédile, a colonial administrator. It was 12 September before the British – the official Allied representatives – set up shop in Saigon. By then, Cédile was hard at work, taking soundings among the still large French community. The country was calm but potentially in a state of chaos that made it ripe for opportunists. There were still around 70,000 armed Japanese in Indo-China (who would be used by the British and French to maintain public order before being sent home); thousands more unarmed French and other soldiers in prison camps; freebooting Vietnamese gangs – criminal, political and religious – all armed; and an angry, fearful population of 20,000 French civilian *colons* in Saigon alone. As *The Pentagon Papers* relates:

> The British landed a Gurkha battalion and a company of Free French soldiers in Saigon. The British commander regarded the Vietnamese government with disdain because of its lack of authority from the French and because of its inability to quell civil disorder in South Vietnam. Saigon police clashed with Trotskyites, and in the rural areas, fighting broke out between Viet Minh troops and those of (rival nationalist groups) Cao Dai and Hoa Hoa.
>
> Spreading violence . . . prompted the French to importune the British commander to permit them to step in to restore order. On the morning of 23 September, French troops overthrew the Vietnamese government after a tenure of only three weeks. The official British account termed the French method of executing the *coup d'état* 'unfortunate' in that they 'absolutely ensured that countermeasures would be taken by the Vietnamese'. Vietnamese retaliation was quick and violent: over one hundred Westerners were slain in the first few days, and others kidnapped; on 26 September, the US commander of the OSS in Saigon was killed.
>
> Thus, the first Indochina War began in Cochinchina in late September, 1945, and American blood was shed in its opening hours . . . The French *coup d'état* thrust conflict upon the Vietnamese of Cochinchina. The question before the communists was how to respond; the . . . leadership determined . . . that to maintain leadership of the nationalist movement in South Vietnam they had to make the Viet Minh the most unbending foe of compromise with the French.

What that account omits is that the leader of the French coup, was the enigmatic Colonel Cédile, apparently operating independently of every military organization, covert or otherwise. For manpower he created an instant commando of 1,400 ex-war prisoners who were specially released from detention at a Colonial Infantry barracks. Cédile's team armed them with the aid of the British, who beat a hasty retreat from the scene after handing over control publicly to France on 9 October. By then, the unquestionably legitimate General Jacques Leclerc was present with a force of Free French regulars.

Over the following months, heeding American warnings about the futility of a collision, both French and Vietnamese sought some sort of settlement as guerrilla warfare gradually consumed the countryside. In March 1946, as a French task force prepared to make an opposed amphibious landing at Haiphong, there was a breakthrough in negotiations between French diplomats and Ho, whose efforts to internationalize the crisis had failed. Under a so-called 'Accord' of 6 March, France recognized the Vietnamese Republic and the Vietnamese agreed to respect French interests. There were some who criticized Ho Chi Minh for this deal. He snarled back:

> You fools! . . . Don't you remember your history? The last time the Chinese came, they stayed one thousand years. The French are foreigners. They are weak. Colonialism is dying out . . . They may stay for a while, but they will have to go because the white man is finished in Asia. But if the Chinese stay now, they will never leave. As for me, I prefer to smell French shit for five years, rather than Chinese shit for the rest of my life.

Extremist criticism of Ho on the Vietnamese side was matched by extremism on the part of influential Frenchmen, notably socialists serving in the latest government-of-passage in Paris, playing the ever-popular nationalist card. Their extremism contrasted strongly with the moderation of the soldier sent to investigate on the spot. Leclerc, the Free French veteran who had led an epic march from Chad to join the Allies during World War II, visited Ho, then wrote: 'In 1947 France will no longer put down by force a grouping of 24 million inhabitants which is assuming unity . . . The capital problem from now on is political.' He and other senior officers knew that when the chips were down, France did not have a sufficiently large army to dominate the vast jungles of Vietnam. Later events would demonstrate that such a task was beyond the resources of even the United States. From 1885, bluff and friendship combined had kept the tricolour flying over Indo-China but these were no longer enough: friendship had been dissipated and military bluff would be tested. This did not inhibit France's High Commissioner in Saigon, the powerful Admiral d'Argenlieu, from denouncing the Accord. He registered his amazement 'that France has such a fine expeditionary corps in Indochina and yet its leaders prefer to negotiate rather than fight'. The force which landed in Saigon just a month before the 6 March Accord included thousands of legionnaires: 2 REI on 6 February followed by 13 DBLE, then 3 REI (formerly the RMLE).

Under the terms of the Accord, France also acquired the right to base troops in North Vietnam. They landed unopposed in Haiphong, but they were sitting on a powder-keg. As the Pentagon study explains:

The return of the French to Tonkin (North Vietnam) in March 1946 created an explosive situation. North Vietnam, a traditionally rice-deficit area, had experienced an extraordinarily bad harvest in 1945. Severe famine was scarcely helped by the concentration of armies in the Red River Delta – Vietnamese irregular forces, the most numerous belonging to the Viet Minh; some 150,000 Chinese; and then the French Expeditionary Corps. The people were not only hungry, but politically restive; the popular appetite for national independence had been thoroughly whetted by the Viet Minh . . . While feeling against all foreign occupiers ran high, the French remained the primary target of enmity.

The Chinese were only slightly more unlovable, in Vietnamese eyes:

In famine-wracked North Vietnam, Chinese hordes under booty-minded warlords descended on the Democratic Republic, supplanting its local government with committees of their own sponsoring and systematically looting. Ho vainly sought aid abroad; not even the Soviet Union proved helpful.

The uneasy peace between the French and the Viet Minh held tackily together until November, when brawls involving the two sides led to shootings and assassinations. There is no agreement about who started these 'incidents'. In mid-December, Ho sent a telegram to French premier Léon Blum warning him of the sensitivity of the situation. By the time it was delivered on 26 December, the two sides were at war.

In Hanoi on 19 December, amid rapidly rising tension, Viet Minh troops cut off the city's water and electricity supplies, then hit French positions with artillery fire, mortar and small arms. Ho and his colleagues disappeared into their jungle hides. But even at this eleventh hour, Ho and Leclerc sought to avert a final show-down. In January 1947 Leclerc warned Paris: 'Anti-communism will be a useless tool so long as the problem of nationalism remains unsolved.' The following month Ho received a French 'offer' which was, in effect, an invitation to surrender. He replied:

> In the French Union there is no place for cowards. If I accepted the French conditions I should be one . . . The Vietnamese people desire only unity and independence in the French Union and we pledge ourselves to respect French economic and cultural interests.

The West never resolved the issue of Ho's nationalism until it was too late. Was the man primarily a Vietnamese patriot or a communist ideologue prepared – like so many of his erstwhile comrades in Europe at that time – to sell his country's freedom down the nearest Red river? Only after the United States' defeat in 1975 did it become unambiguously clear to Vietnamese non-communist patriots such as the Vietcong Minister of Justice, Truong Nhu Tang, that the great anti-colonial crusade was not to promote true Vietnamese nationalism but narrow, North Vietnamese communist domination. (Ironically, Tang was one of the first refugee 'boat people' – destination California – after a lifetime of opposition to France and the US in his homeland.) For the French in the late 1940s there was an alternative and doomed strategy to a deal with Ho Chi Minh. This was the campaign promoted by Admiral d'Argenlieu to bring back Bao Dai. As the Admiral said: 'The return of the Emperor would probably reassure all those who, having opposed the Viet Minh, fear they will be accused of treason' (quoted in *The Pentagon Papers*).

In view of the recent treason of Bao Dai and that of Vichy itself it was a curious definition of political legitimacy, yet it found favour in Paris. The bargaining would jog along for several years because no one could take it seriously: even Bao Dai himself was sceptical. In the Paris of the unstable Fourth Republic, governments came and went. The French Expeditionary Force was soon paying a heavy price for their collective unreality. If the dirty war made no great impact on popular opinion in France it was because the number of French lives at risk was a small proportion of the armies defending French policies in Indo-China. The composition of the expeditionary force in April 1953, for instance, was approximately as follows:

French:	51,000
Foreign Legion:	20,000 to 30,000
North African:	30,000
Black African:	17,000
Indo-Chinese Auxiliaries:	55,000

Even this total of 173,000 men under arms was but a fraction of the French Union's ultimate tally of anti-Viet Minh forces. The regular armies and auxiliaries of the whole Indo-Chinese region, all combatants for France in this war, provided another 300,000 men. As General Hubert de Seguins-Pazziz would point out, on the thirtieth anniversary of the conflict: 'Neither our governments nor public opinion wanted to recognize the war for what it was. It never acquired a "national" character. It was an affair left to professional soldiers.'

'Rapid penetration' was Leclerc's watchword during France's first year of paradise regained. In practice what occurred was a form of military coitus interruptus. Using every scrap of transport available, including 800 American-built Lease-Lend jeeps and trucks bequeathed by the British, the Legion deployed tiny groups of men to isolated forts throughout the country from Tonkin in the north to the deep south of Cochin China. It was an optimistic replay of North African colonization as practised in a vanished age of superior European firepower. Most of these garrisons had to be supplied by road. The convoys which supported them were promptly ambushed on tortuous jungle roads. The convoys became slow-moving targets; the forts, sitting ducks. One of the first VIP victims of the convoy war was 13 DBLE's distinguished veteran de Sairigné, now a colonel and the demi-brigade's commander. He was escorting a column of ambulances when he died.

To meet the changing conditions, new units evolved. 1 REC acquired amphibious, go-anywhere vehicles known as 'Crabes' for use in the flooded paddy fields and swamps of Cochin China. Open-topped and entirely vulnerable, they were quickly replaced by the closed, hull-down Alligator. Elsewhere the Legion's first two para battalions were created from a core of volunteers belonging to the 3rd company of 3 REI under Captain Morin. 1 BEP (*Bataillon Étranger de Parachutistes*) landed at Haiphong in the autumn of 1948: 2 BEP at Saigon the following February. A grizzled sergeant-major was not impressed by this innovation. He believed that to allow legionnaires to jump out of aircraft willy-nilly was an incitement to desertion, even if the drop was invariably on a beleaguered fortress in hostile jungle.

There was, in truth, nowhere for the legionnaire to desert to except the grave in a country where everyone, including locally recruited kitchen staff, was the enemy. At Trung Chan in Cochin China a company of 2/13 DBLE was poisoned by hallucinogenic soup of great potency made from a local cabbage called '*datura*'. After dinner, some men moved about on all fours, barking. The captain in command wandered 'like a ghost', naked on the parade square. Only one soldier, dieting because of illness, was unaffected and able to summon help from headquarters. A relief column reached the company just ahead of the Viet Minh.

Already in 1948 it was becoming clear that whole areas of Vietnam would have to be conceded. The most unstable region was Tonkin on the Chinese border. Once it had been the legionnaire's preferred home-from-home: now it was his abattoir. On the night of 25 July the fort at Phu Tong Hoa astride the strategically sensitive road linking Hanoi and the Chinese border came under accurate mortar attack which breached the perimeter fence. Inside, a company of 3 REI, heavily out-numbered, fought on even after more than half their base was overrun, until they were relieved three days later. By then, twenty-one legionnaires, including the two most senior officers, were dead. The forty survivors, wearing their best Number Ones, presented arms as reinforcements drove through the gate. They included the remarkable Corporal Horst Murati, an expert in fine art history and former U-boat commander Oberleutnant von Murati.

Meanwhile, in another part of the forest, the French were taking a political initiative whose centrepiece was the discredited Bao Dai. In June 1949, the French High Command and Bao exchanged letters in Saigon formalizing Vietnamese independence under the Emperor's rule. Recent experience of Japanese occupation had taught the Vietnamese what that meant. This time the ugly realities behind the Elysée's clichés were less convincing than usual. One of Bao Dai's early recruits to his new Vietnamese National Army was a certain Le Van Bay Vien, chief of the secret society of Black Flag brigands and pirates known as the 'Bin Xuyen'. Bay Vien had also collaborated with Japan and was the leader of attacks against the French in Saigon in September 1945. Nevertheless, Bay Vien was appointed the first Colonel of the new force although (or perhaps because) his concerns were as much criminal as military. According to Pentagon research, Bay Vien was briefly an ally of the Viet Minh, which decided to assassinate him. He then threw in his lot with the French and afterwards paid Bao Dai what Colonel Lansdale (an American observer) termed 'a staggering sum' for control of gambling and prostitution in Cholon, and of the Saigon-Cholon police.

> The French accepted the arrangement because Bay Vien offset the Viet Minh threat to Saigon. By 1954, Vien was operating 'Grande Monde', a gambling slum in Cholon; 'Cloche d'Or', Saigon's pre-eminent gambling establishment; the 'Nouveautés Catinat', Saigon's best department store; a hundred smaller shops; a fleet of river boats; and a brothel, spectacular even by Asian standards, known as the Hall of Mirrors . . . He ruled Saigon absolutely; not even Viet Minh terrorists were able to operate there.

Bay Vien was recruited in the year that the great evacuation of the Chinese border area began, slowly at first, with the sacrifice of Bac Khan and Nguyen Binh. At Nguyen Binh, locally recruited tribesmen-turned-partisans, fighting alongside the Legion against the Viet Minh, were discreetly disarmed on orders from French headquarters. The legionnaires quietly removed the men's weapons from their armoury while they were paraded elsewhere. After the Legion withdrew, the departed partisans were hunted by the Viet Minh with great thoroughness, tortured with equal care, and then executed. None of these events impinged much on popular opinion in France. In February 1950 the French National Assembly formally anointed Bao Dai as their puppet-ruler in Vietnam, unworried by the amount of arms now starting to flow into Tonkin from China. But a few months later something *did* penetrate Parisian indifference. At a place known as Cao Bang, seven entire French battalions were swallowed up in the jungle as effortlessly as if by some enormous Chinese dragon. Nothing had happened to the French army in the colonies on such a scale. Its true significance did not sink in until three years later. Cao Bang was the shape of things to come at Dien Bien Phu. But even in the short run it was very bad news.

By the summer of 1950 Cao Bang, at the junction of North Vietnam's two principal highways, the RC3 and RC4, was an isolated community of civilians opposed to the Viet Minh, defended by 1,000 legionnaires of 3 REI and 600 Moroccans. Back in Saigon, General Carpentier devised a plan according to which this force would be withdrawn in several phases. The first stage was a fifteen-mile march along a main road to a minor fort named Dong Khe. There it would be met by a 5,000-strong escort of Moroccan soldiers, and the Legion's paras of 1 BEP.

Viet Minh intelligence about this plan was first-class and might have been the result of espionage in Paris as some soldiers suspect. On 16 September, two companies of 3 REI holding the rendezvous post at Dong Khe were overrun after a two-day siege. By now the Cao Bang column, still accompanied by its civilians, was already on the move, like a vulnerable and naked hermit crab moving house. In an effort to retrieve the situation, 1 BEP was parachuted into the area. It endeavoured to recapture the lost rendezvous and was repulsed. As the remainder of the Moroccan escort column arrived on the scene, the jungle around this relief force erupted into a forest of hostility. No one knows exactly how many enemy soldiers had been prepared by the cunning General

V. Nguyen Giap for his enormous ambush. Some expert estimates suggest as many as 30,000 guerrillas.

The agony of Cao Bang continued until 8 October. The 1 BEP was repeatedly given the task of defending an increasingly jumpy Moroccan force. In one grisly episode the paras were ordered to make their way down a narrow, precipitous mountain path held by the Viet Minh, in pitch darkness. Legionnaires were snatched individually in the darkness by well-organized teams of guerrillas, dragged away and butchered by groups of men wielding knives. The nocturnal descent cost 100 Legion lives. Next day, the BEP was selected to lead everyone out of the valley at the other end. The order to march came too late for a surprise attack to be mounted, and too early for French air cover. The Legion vanguard was shot to pieces by enemy machine-guns at short range. A handful of men got through with the aid of hand grenades and freakish good luck. They were followed by a stampede of panicking Moroccans.

Approaching the scene in the opposite direction on foot through the jungle was the column from Cao Bang, moving in good order, though it could hear the sounds of battle coming from the fatal Coc Xa valley. In good order, that is, until Moroccans fleeing from that battle reached the column and spread panic among their fellow-countrymen. In the shambles that followed, the two French forces lost about 7,000 men dead or taken prisoner. The 1 BEP was virtually annihilated: only a dozen survivors led by the remarkable adjutant, Captain Pierre Jeanpierre, aided by Lieutenant Roger Faulques (later a mercenary in Africa) reached the reception area prepared for the breakout, several miles south of the battle. Others, such as Colonel Charton – a Legion officer since 1928 and leader of the Cao Bang column – were prisoners of the Viet Minh for forty-six months. The catastrophe confirmed what even the bravest soldiers knew well, that the Tonkin border with a now-communist neighbour was no longer French Indo-China. It was part of the Democratic Republic of Vietnam.

The reaction of the government and people of France was insensitive even by Parisian standards. As recorded by the Armée d'Afrique historian General H. de la Barre de Nanteuil, a new law was approved to ensure that young Frenchmen called up for military service could not be sent in peacetime to areas where military operations were taking place, or participate in them.

No less damaging for the morale of the expeditionary force was a decision that none of the casualties from Indochina could be taken across Paris because of possible left-wing demonstrations, or the decision when blood was being donated, to specify that it would not be used for the casualties of Indochina. [General R. Huré, et al.]

This action, more than any, threw an entirely new light on France's perception of those foreigners whose sacrifice of life itself qualified them, they had thought, as Frenchmen *'par le sang versé'*. Such gestures were a gift to Viet Minh propagandists who now worked vigorously on the North Africans in Indo-China, particularly those who had become their prisoners. In North Africa itself, the cause of separatism from France was gaining ground. It would gain more when the prisoners returned home.

In the backwash of the Cao Bang defeat, the French government renewed its determination to try to win the war in Indo-China after all, apparently unaware that it was now pursuing two mutually contradictory policies; pacific at home, warlike overseas. It sent a new commander who combined (like Sir Gerald Templer in Malaya) the top civil post of High Commissioner with that of military Commander-in-Chief: the formidable Jean de Lattre de Tassigny, the only senior Vichy officer to join de Gaulle. Throughout 1951, he wrought the miracle of making a French victory seem plausible. The bait he employed, with remarkable success against such a shrewd tactician as Giap, was the instant, fortified camp erected at speed on hostile territory before the enemy could respond. For the Viet Minh to retain credibility such places had to be attacked, with consequent casualties. To sustain such operations de Tassigny needed more troops from France but only a fraction of the number he required was sent. He therefore withdrew three out of four battalions serving with 13 DBLE in the south of the country to meet the more serious enemy, General Giap, in Tonkin.

Giap responded to de Tassigny's strategy by accepting heavy losses, and then disrupted the French rear in the coastal delta with guerrilla and terrorist attacks. The French were then obliged to make a fighting retreat from the new base to defend their own backyard. Throughout 1952, the struggle for control of Tonkin repeated the pattern over and again. The war was going nowhere. It was a virtual stalemate. And as the bill increased at home, the French were again restless for settlement of the affair. In May 1953, a new French commander, Henri Navarre, took office with the task of 'creating military conditions favourable to a resolution of the conflict'.

Far from being resolved, as had seemed possible towards the end of 1951 when every major Viet Minh offensive had been squashed, new disaster threatened the French in November 1953. Giap's men were poised to engulf a large and characteristically isolated French base between Viet Minh territory and French-controlled Laos. Navarre's response was to gamble with virtually his entire army in North Vietnam, a total of 15,000 men in thirteen battalions, by placing them at another frontier location of which few people had heard until then. The site, a sprawling ten miles by five of undulating countryside crossed by a river, already contained an airstrip capable of launching military transport aircraft. True, it was in low ground 125 miles from Hanoi, and surrounded by jungle-clad hills, but General Navarre and his artillery advisers calculated that they could wipe out any artillery that the opposition might place on the high ground surrounding the site. The French, after all, enjoyed air superiority and could interdict any attempt by the Vietnamese to bring up such weapons. Perhaps that is why the senior French gunner on the spot dug in his own meagre collection of 105mm guns only to protect the crews from mortar attack.

When the area was seized initially in November by four para battalions, it was called Dien Bien Phu. Its low hills acquired more seductive names, to identify eight massive underground strongpoints covered by tons of logs and earth: Anne-Marie, Gabrielle, Beatrice, Dominique, Eliane, Claudine, Huguette and Isabelle. Its elaborateness resembled that of the Maginot Line. The subterranean hospital, to take one example, had more than forty beds, operating theatres, X-ray room, dental surgery, resuscitation ward and all the other paraphernalia of modern medicine. As well as the airfield, the base area included Thai civilian villages and a main road.

For the next four months, Giap kept the new fortress sufficiently engaged to encourage the French to remain on a site which might have been designed as a death trap by Giap himself. At the same time, 75,000 Viet Minh pioneers sweated round the clock in jungle trails, invisible to air photography beneath the jungle canopy and moving by night when such cover did not suffice, to haul two hundred 105s into position. These guns were dug in with great care and then ranged, equally carefully, on the French command posts. Alongside them the Viet Minh created a thicket of heavy anti-aircraft cannon with which to snap the air bridge upon which Dien Bien Phu ultimately depended. Hundreds of tons of ordnance were concealed in deep bunkers. The guns were accompanied by four infantry divisions – about 40,000 men – trained and equipped in Mao's Red China, though it was the artillery that was to cause 75 per cent of French casualties. Yet when the first few artillery rounds dropped on the French in February, the garrison did not take the matter so seriously. The air traffic officer displayed in his dugout a piece of wood containing fragments of the first shellburst as a souvenir. Soon, he would collect more souvenirs in his chest.

On 13 March, the real battle of Dien Bien Phu began with a barrage of pitiless accuracy that slammed into strongpoint Beatrice, held by the Legion's 3/13 DBLE, which lost thirty-six men dead, wounded or missing. French counter-batteries failed to halt the hailstorm of incoming fire. A few days later the garrison's artillery chief, Colonel Charles Piroth, unable to live with his error in underestimating the Viet Minh, killed himself. He had already lost one arm in an earlier battle, yet chose a two-handed weapon, a hand-grenade, with which to end his own life.

The little army that was left to fight on was soon outnumbered by four to one and was overwhelmingly non-French: nine units out of thirteen (or 70 per cent) were from the Armée d'Afrique and of these five were Legion battalions. The remainder were Thais (two battalions), Senegalese, Vietnamese paras and French paras. The Legion was represented by elements of 13 DBLE, 3 and 5 REI on Beatrice, on isolated Isabelle three miles south of the main position, and on Claudine. The Legion's paras were part of the encampment's mobile reserve.

The garrison was crushed with steady, relentless pressure as the world watched, fascinated, during preparations for a conference involving the two sides in Geneva. Beatrice was overrun by Vietnamese infantry two days after the initial barrage, with a loss of 326 men. A shudder passed through Dien Bien Phu. If the Legion could not hold this strongpoint, they were all doomed. Gabrielle, defended by Algerian infantry, was abandoned the same day. Another two days and it was the turn of Anne-Marie, defended by the Thais. The Viet Minh had suffered so many casualties that no further ground assault was possible for almost two weeks. But the artillery fire continued relentlessly. After seven days the air strip was no longer usable by day. After ten days the main road of Dien Bien Phu, its logistical backbone, was also closed. Another eight days' shelling and the air strip was out of action for good. The last aircraft had been shot to pieces before it could get away. No casualties could be evacuated. Commerce with the outside world was now a one-way trip by parachute. There was no shortage of volunteers for that fatal journey, particularly among the legionnaires. The men of 2 BEP jumped in to join their comrades of 1 BEP, who had been present as the garrison's mobile defensive reserve from the beginning. More remarkable were the hundreds of soldiers of 3 and 5 REI as well as other regiments who joined the action from early April without parachute training. As one officer said of the First Colonial Paras: 'You know how it is with the paras. They like to win or get wiped out together.'

Through the long agony French air cover, far from suppressing the Viet Minh even with the aid of napalm, was itself suppressed by a halo of hot metal each time an aircraft approached. As the perimeter shrank, parachute supplies became less accurate. Hostile shellfire, by contrast, concentrated on a diminishing killing zone with increasing power. Nothing stayed alive above ground. Beneath the earth, the field hospital commanded by Dr Paul Grauwin – an honorary legionnaire served by risk-defying legionnaires of 13 DBLE to drive his ambulances – degenerated into a glutinous hole of collective, perspiring flesh; amputated limbs; living stumps upon which white grubs grazed; oozing mud; discarded dressings; faeces; dead bodies; exuberant fungi. Round the clock, shells fell once every second, drumming on the roof creating casualties similar to those of the Western Front in 1916, but with one difference: there was no rear echelon, no way out of Dien Bien Phu. Even Grauwin, who had seen almost everything since his days in the wartime French Resistance, was impressed by the legionnaires he met now, 'astonishing men, with their courage and air of mystery'. They included Corporal Heinz of 2 BEP, wounded three times, patched up and returned to battle. The fourth time they brought him in, terribly wounded during a counter-attack on Huguette, he was near death. Grauwin records in *Doctor at Dien Bien Phu* that when they finished operating, without much hope:

> Heinz was nothing but a trunk with one leg sticking out of it . . . [Yet] he became the life and soul of his shelter, commenting wittily on every item of news brought to him, imitating the flight of a plane with his two poor stumps. Every morning he nearly broke my heart by saluting me with his right stump.

By the end of April many men wounded in the early stages of the battle were – in some cases miraculously – on the road to recovery. As new casualties flooded in, these half-recovered cases were returned to the fighting. Grauwin wrote:

> So they returned to the spot where they had been wounded some weeks before, to find those of their comrades who were still whole and fit. They did not like to hang about doing nothing . . . The moment would come when they got up and said: 'Let me have that machine-gun. I've only got one leg . . . give me a box to sit on and then you'll see what I can still do with my hands.'
>
> 'I've still got one arm left and I've not forgotten how to throw a grenade.'
>
> 'I've still got one eye. Let me have that tommy-gun. I won't have to close the other eye, so it will be easier for me.'
>
> So I had to send back to their fighting positions hundreds of wounded who were well on the way to being cured – abdominal cases, amputations, limbs in plaster, muscular wounds, thorax wounds and those who had lost an eye. Nearly all these were wounded a second time, and I am sure that a third of them were killed in the blockhouses in the course of the final week.

On 23 April, 2 BEP attempted a counter-attack. It failed. Soon after, a few hundred survivors of 2 BEP, 8th Assault Regiment and 6th Colonial Paras combined to recover the patch of hill known as Eliane 2. Hundreds of lives were lost. Twenty minutes later the Viet Minh charged back, into their own mortar barrage as it fell on the position, and recovered it. It was a replay of another recent loss, that of Claudine, about which a legionnaire of 13 DBLE said: 'Hundreds and hundreds of them . . . We killed masses but always more came on, jumping over the bodies of the others.'

The reinforced Viet Minh army, which had been grinding down Dien Bien Phu since 31 March by tunnelling and gradual encroachment when it was not engaged on massive frontal assaults, launched its final ground attack on 6 May. Tens of thousands of fresh soldiers roared down from the hills, across the low-lying French wasteland. That night, only a forlorn patch at the centre of the area, plus the isolated Legion outpost of Isabelle, remained unconquered. Next day, the central headquarters area was taken and the remnants of 3/3 REI attempted to fight their way out of Isabelle. A handful succeeded and somehow insinuated their way into the jungle. Fewer than a hundred reached French lines.

Dien Bien Phu surrendered on 8 May. The defeat was to bring about the fall of the government of the day in Paris and deal a blow to the constitution of the Fourth Republic – France's first post-war attempt to run a democracy – from which it finally expired four years later in 1958. One French general compared it to Waterloo. It certainly tolled the bell for most of the empire that France had acquired since 1830.

There was one other side-effect which concerned wider interests than those of France about which the world did not learn until years later. The battle raised an 'extreme risk' (to use Churchill's contemporary description) of nuclear warfare between the West and communist powers including Soviet Russia.

By 23 April 1954, as 2 BEP was hurling itself into a final, despairing counter-attack, the government of Premier Laniel was becoming desperate. In Paris on that day, according to the Pentagon record:

The French Under-Secretary of State, André Bougenot, in the presence of Premier Laniel, suggested to Douglas MacArthur II, Counsellor of the Department of State, that the United States could commit its naval aircraft to the battle of Dien Bien Phu without risking American prestige or committing an act of belligerency by placing such aircraft, painted with French insignia and construed as part of the French Foreign Legion, under nominal French command for an isolated action consisting of air strikes lasting two or three days.

Such a course, had the Americans assented to it (and some including Secretary of State John Foster Dulles were ready to approve such an attack, under the code-name 'Vulture'), might well have provoked a Chinese counter-stroke. In that event, Dulles believed, the use of nuclear weapons would be necessary to make the Chinese pause. In Washington, in fact, an Anglo-American military planning team was soon to agree in principle that if war with China resulted from Chinese aggression in South-East Asia, then an air attack should be launched immediately at military targets in China. A secret policy document made public in Britain thirty years later, in 1984, quotes the planners as follows: 'To achieve a maximum and lasting effect nuclear as well as conventional weapons should be used from the outset.'

Interestingly, the US Army Chief of Staff General Matthew Ridgway was arguing at about the same time that 'the use of atomic weapons in Indochina would not reduce the number of ground forces [needed] to achieve a victory in Indochina'.

Congressional leaders in Washington put a brake on US participation in a bombing run over Dien Bien Phu, using airmen disguised as legionnaires, by insisting that Britain must be party to such action, and that France must guarantee Indo-China real independence. Neither of these conditions could be fulfilled. Prime Minister Sir Winston Churchill noted that the Americans had just tested their first thermonuclear (hydrogen) warhead. He suspected that they wished to demonstrate the strategic edge they now had over Russia. Churchill's private papers reveal his thinking:

The British people would not be easily influenced by what happened in the distant jungles of South-East Asia: but they did know that there was a powerful American base in East Anglia and that war with China, who would invoke the Sino-Russian Pact, might mean an assault by hydrogen bombs on these islands.

For the British, therefore, Dien Bien Phu was too close to home for comfort. The French had no such bases and the Americans were probably out of reach of realistic reprisal. As Churchill saw it, the risk of total war was extreme, 'and of all the nations involved, the United States would suffer least'. Yet he did not need to worry unduly for there was no chance that France – while inviting American forces to join the battle for the French empire – would allow Indo-China to become a matter for international control. Even the agony of Dien Bien Phu was more acceptable than the loss of face such an arrangement might imply. France would either win on her own narrowly nationalistic terms, or walk off the pitch completely in South-East Asia. As General Navarre, French supremo in Indo-China, put it in a message to his Foreign Minister, Georges Bidault (later paraphrased by the Pentagon):

The only alternatives were (1) Operation Vulture ('*Vautour*'), massive B-29 bombing (which Secretary Dulles understood would be a United States operation from bases outside Indo-China) or (2) a French Union request for a ceasefire (which Secretary Dulles assumed would be at Dien Bien Phu only, but which General Navarre, as it turned out, meant should apply to all of Indochina).

In accepting the second option the French government sacrificed its empire in Indo-China, broke many promises to its supporters there, and lost office. The Legion lost 1,500 dead and 4,000 wounded at Dien Bien Phu alone.

Riding the white water on the edge of these momentous events with the single-mindedness of a surfboard champion crossing a big, unstable roller, one legionnaire was engaged in a private war. This he would bring to a more satisfactory conclusion than the French government at Geneva during the brief interval between the defeat of Dien Bien Phu and France's ceasefire in July. According to Legion folklore Legionnaire Eliahu Itzkowitz, from Rumania, had volunteered to wear the white kepi for only one reason: he wanted to kill another legionnaire.

Itzkowitz was a Jew. With the rest of his family he was one of thousands rounded up at Chisinau in Rumania in July 1941 by

Nazi extermination squads drawn from Germany and Rumania itself. He was then aged ten. When the war ended he was the only one of his family still alive and the city of Chisinau, occupied by the Red Army, had been renamed Kishinev, capital of Soviet Moldavia. Itzkowitz's family were among 53,000 Jews slaughtered in and around Chisinau during the Nazi occupation. Of these 10,000 were massacred in one day alone in 1941. Nevertheless he blamed a single Rumanian Nazi guard named Stanescu for what had happened. Shortly before the liberation of the area in 1945, Stanescu disappeared. Itzkowitz dedicated himself to finding the man. Within a year he had found not Stanescu, but his quarry's son. No matter: Itzkowitz stabbed him with a butcher's knife and served five years for the attack in a Rumanian prison.

On his release the angry young Jew, harder than ever, emigrated to Israel, became a soldier and joined the Israeli paras. He met Jews from every quarter of Europe. All had stories to tell about the holocaust and the people implicated in it. From a Frenchman he learned that in 1945 an enigmatic Rumanian whose description matched that of Stanescu had joined the Foreign Legion at Offenburg in the French zone of Occupied Germany. Itzkowitz applied for a posting to the Israeli navy. Soon afterwards, during shore leave at Genoa, he made his way by train, in civilian clothes, to Marseilles. Within days he was on his way to the Legion's training camp at Saida.

In June 1954, on a routine road patrol between Bac-Ninh and Seven Pagodas, a patrol of 3 REI came under fire. Itzkowitz took cover and was joined by his corporal. The two men stretched on the ground together, seeking a field of fire. The Jewish legionnaire rolled carefully on to one elbow, scrutinising the corporal.

'Aren't you Stanescu?' he asked softly in Rumanian.

It is not often that a legionnaire's *nom-de-guerre* is punctured so blandly, particularly when he is in combat. Disconcerted, the corporal replied, 'Yes . . . Who are you?'

'Stanescu. I'm one of the Jews from Chisinau.'

The safety catch was off his sub-machine-gun, the muzzle steady, inches from the corporal's shirt.

'This is for the others!'

It was almost the last long burst fired by the Legion in this particular campaign, one in which the regiment lost more men than at any time since World War I. It was certainly the last automatic fire of World War II. Yet Corporal Stanescu's death was dismissed at the time as another routine loss to add to the other 10,000. Only after Itzkowitz had completed his service, and obtained an honourable Legion discharge, did the French authorities comprehend why the close-quarter fire which killed Stanescu was from a French weapon.

CHAPTER 13
'The War for Nothing'
(Algeria, 1954–58)

You must realize that every time a bomb
explodes in Algiers we are taken more seriously
here at the United Nations.

– Spokesman of Algerian National Liberation Front (FNL)
to journalist Edward Behr, *c.* 1956

Following unwritten but perfectly clear rules
. . . on the orders of the . . . socialist
government . . . intelligence officers used
two methods of questioning . . . electric
shock and water.

– Jean-Claude Goudeau, Director-General, *Minute*, in
1985, recalling Algiers, 1957

The foreign legionnaire is bound to France not by patriotism but
by necessity and his sworn oath. Desertion counts not as betrayal
of country (and is therefore not treasonable) but as repudiation
of a contract. For the legionnaire the sanctity of the contract he
has made with the regiment and his comrades is the core of a
new-found identity. Not surprisingly then, the Legion treats
solemn promises, even those handed down by politicians, with
greater seriousness than other, more worldly organizations.

To understand this passion for loyalty to a pledge is to
comprehend why the Algerian War of Independence, fought
between 1954 and 1962, became in the eyes of thousands of men
who had fought for France 'the war for nothing'. The sacrifices
exacted by this war ultimately provoked a unique mutiny on the
part of a uniquely disciplined fighting machine. The reasons are
buried deep in French history. It is a complicated story, at the
heart of which is a paradox. How could it be that men who

carried out their orders – to stop a revolutionary war in its tracks – could be converted into rebels themselves within two years of their victory? More perplexing, how could men who had served time in the death camps of Nazi Germany in their defence of freedom, bring themselves to oppose a legitimate government and adopt terrorism in defence of Algeria's white settlers who had, for the most part, sided with Hitler?

The key mutineers of 1 REP were the very opposite of the fascist parody drawn by their political enemies in France and elsewhere. But they did belong to a very special generation of men who had seen France dishonour herself with the surrender of 1940 (itself entirely comprehensible in the light of 316,000 dead at Verdun a mere twenty-four years before) and, repeatedly, thereafter. Algeria was one betrayal too many. The hard-bitten veterans of the Legion were under no illusion about the unlovable nature of the settlers ('*Pieds Noirs*') but they were passionately concerned for their own honour and that of France. That above all else was supreme.

And what of the settlers? As the writer Edward Behr has pointed out, their presence in Algeria was

> the outcome of more than a century of haphazard and unregulated colonization, tempered less by French policy changes than by political and economic vicissitudes in France – and later in Europe – which forced an increasing number of Europeans to seek their fortunes in Algeria . . . As early as 1832 some 400 Frenchmen, refugees from the banks of the Rhine, embarked at Le Havre bound, as they thought, for the United States. After they had been at sea for several days they discovered that a dishonest shipping agent was taking them to Algeria instead.

By 1945, their descendants dominated the economic and political life of Algeria and influenced much that happened in metropolitan France also.

The men on the other side of this war, the Armée de Libération Nationale (ALN), were equally the prisoners of their own history. At first they were a dissident splinter group of Algerian nationalism, disowned by the acknowledged leaders. But, having triggered off a rebellion at the wrong time for the wrong reasons (to head off deepening splits within their own movement) they faced the choice of death on the battlefield or a lifetime of imprisonment. For them it was imperative to polarize opinion as rapidly and as effectively as possible so as to provoke a 'real' war, one which would make them politically respectable.

The catalyst of their strategy, therefore, had to be an act, or acts, which would outrage the settlers and provoke them into blind, counter-productive violence. So, if this was a war for nothing, it was also – given the elements at work in the political cauldron of Algeria during the decade after the German defeat of 1945 – inevitable.

One of those elements had been Algerian gallantry on the battlefields of World War II, on the side of the Allies. Ben Bella, a leader of the revolt, ended his first war as a sergeant-major fighting for Free France. When that war ended the people of Alsace, for example, handed flowers to their heroes, men of the 7 Régiment de Tirailleurs Algériens, for whom the short sea journey back to collaborationist Algeria was a time-capsule back to nineteenth-century servitude.

The founders of the ALN – six mystery men with no established reputation in Algerian nationalist politics – had to look no farther back than 1945 to discover a model detonator for their revolution in 1954. The trick was to provoke settler intolerance. All over Europe, 5 May 1945 was a day of public euphoria. It was VE Day, when civilians could at long last sleep without the risk of being bombed and buried alive in the night; when the soldier's life-expectancy suddenly stretched beyond 'the next op'. For those who had fought the whole six years since 1939, convinced they were now living on borrowed time, the end of the war was like a last-minute reprieve from the gallows.

Not surprisingly, the day was celebrated in most places with feasting and dancing in the streets. In the little Algerian market town of Sétif some young tearaways hijacked the celebratory parade, waving nationalist banners, and chanting demands for home rule. The local police responded to this bravado by shooting several demonstrators. The first victim was a young man carrying the subversive slogan: 'Long live the Allied victory!'

The Algerians, in their turn, cut loose and started to murder random Europeans. Women were raped, homes despoiled and looted. The French authorities responded with a combined operation involving naval bombardment and aerial attack as well as ground assault. When this bizarre VE-Day 'party' was over, the European dead numbered 104. Estimates of the number of Algerians killed ranged from about 1,500 to Cairo Radio's exaggerated guestimate of 50,000. The French military commander, General Duval, was satisfied three weeks later that order, of a sort, had been restored. But he warned the settlers, 'I have given you ten years of peace. Don't throw them away. Everything must change in Algeria.'

During the next nine years and six months nothing did change, much, except French governments. From 1954 to 1958 – the first four years of the Algerian war – there were six administrations until, with military backing, de Gaulle was elected on an implicit understanding that Algeria would remain part of France.

It was clear from the beginning that this was going to be a particularly dirty war. On the morning of 1 November 1954, a battered green-and-yellow bus groaned up a mountain road, gears crashing at every hairpin bend. In these wild, beautiful and often deadly Aures mountains, local tribesmen deodorized their way of life under the phrase, '*Bandits d'honneur*'. At the back of the bus, admiring the scenery, a newly-married French couple, Guy Monnerot and his wife, enjoyed their first break since coming here. They were both teachers and had chosen to put their socialist ideals into practice in one of Algeria's poorest provinces. They were chatting to an elderly, dignified Arab *caid*, a French-appointed official.

Ten miles from the nearest town, the bus driver was confronted by a row of boulders across the road. He jammed on the brakes, aware of what was to come. A squawk of children and chickens behind him was stilled by the entry of a tall tribesman carrying a Mauser pistol. The man took just three hostages: Mr and Mrs Monnerot and the *caid*, Hadj Sadok. The bus had stopped at a point 6,000 feet above sea level and in spite of unseasonably warm weather, a keen wind made the passengers shudder slightly as the hostages left the shelter of the vehicle. The *caid* was shaking with anger.

'Call yourself a man?' he asked their captor. 'How can you pick on a woman and an unarmed civilian who has come here to teach our children?'

His protests were cut short by a long burst of machine-gun fire from behind the boulders which dropped all three hostages like fairground dummies. The *caid*'s body was then dumped back in the bus with instructions that it be delivered *pour encourager les autres*, to the local administration in the town of Arris. The bus drove off and the 'soldiers' of the ALN disappeared into the countryside. Guy Monnerot, a bullet in the chest, lay gasping for breath alongside his wife. The only shelter from the wind was afforded by a milestone that reminded them that Arris, the nearest town, was ten miles away. Young Madame Monnerot, wounded in the hip, clung to Guy and prayed for his survival. Her prayers were not answered. By the time help arrived, she was a widow.

Apologists for the ALN assert that Monnerot died by accident. According to their version, the local ALN commander, carrying a drawn Mauser and covered by a machine-gun crew, thought his prisoner, the *caid*, in gesturing towards his robes, was reaching for a concealed gun. The guerrillas' machine-gunner responded to this gesture, hitting the teachers in the same burst. Furthermore, it is asserted, the guerrillas had specific orders not to attack French civilians. The hard facts remain that the terrorist in charge of the murder squad was very near the top of the ALN hierarchy and that Guy Monnerot was left to expire on the roadside alongside his gravely wounded wife. Monnerot could have been carried to emergency treatment on the same bus that conveyed the body of the *caid* as a symbol that hostilities had started.

There were numerous other attacks that day on more orthodox military targets around Algeria, most of them combining incompetence with nervousness. None had the emotional impact of the Monnerot murder. An accident? Certainly French influence of all kinds in nationalist mountain areas was proscribed by the self-appointed leaders of the revolt. During the next few weeks entire communities were terrorized into joining in. The pattern of public torture and execution of dissenters was one which was followed by other 'liberation' campaigns of the same period: scenes of horror in remote mountains in French North Africa were replicated from the rubber plantations of British Malaya to the bush villages of Kenya. After their experience of

Indo-China as well as their observation of events elsewhere, French officers believed that the real enemy was international communism rather than Algerian nationalism.

Any doubts about the style of warfare to be waged by the ALN were removed by the movement's five basic rules of engagement, issued three months before hostilities began, which permitted all forms of conflict and concluded: 'Never make a frontal assault.' The attack groups launching Algeria's bloodbath were described by their own leaders as 'terrorist commandos'.

When the shooting started the French authorities had 37,000 sharp-end troops in Algeria, just enough to mount static guard on key-points but not enough to regain the initiative and destroy rebel credibility. Yet, in spite of the shortage of military muscle in those early days, Paris was not anxious to hurl into the conflict the veterans of Indo-China. Dien Bien Phu had fallen six months earlier on 7 May 1954, missing the VE-Day anniversary by hours. With that heroic defence finally extinguished, the hard timber of what would later emerge as 1er REP went into Vietnamese prison camps. The French government formally acknowledged defeat in Indo-China on 31 July and promised internal autonomy to the Tunisians the same day. Such dramatic withdrawals from a crumbling empire helped to convince the ALN that only a modest push was now required to liberate Algeria also.

In fact, this three-sided war (French Army, ALN, *Pieds Noirs*) would last nearly eight years and cost around 60,000 lives. It would be fought to virtually no rules, with all three camps responsible for atrocities of one sort or another. Yet when the rebellion began Paris instructed the local administration in Algiers that it could not expect any of the Indo-Chinese veterans to join the fray before Easter 1955. The decision had little to do with humanitarian considerations. It was a matter of – to use officialdom's word – 'disintoxication', and a 'cure' of the malaise of Indo-China.

The veterans concerned, men such as Lieutenant Antoine Ysquierdo, a Legion officer whose first battles were against Rommel's Afrika Korps, could have put their names to any one of a dozen such ailments, some lead-induced, others acquired in bed. During combat in Indo-China, he wrote, 'We were not there to become introspective . . . A little fighting here, a little concubine there . . . Here's to you, Laslo! Let's have a can of beer and piss-and-forget.' (Laslo – surname Tasnady – was Ysquierdo's platoon sergeant, a Hungarian who had joined the Legion in 1946, and an authentic hero who would die in action in Algeria. Ysquierdo would survive long enough to end up among the bemedalled officers put before a court martial.)

On their return to Algeria in 1955, the veterans of Indo-China were clapped into barracks under guard, ostensibly because of an unspecified epidemic. Then they were briefed. Ysquierdo's definition of the word 'briefing' reflected the regiment's deep scepticism about the Algerian campaign from the beginning: 'A briefing is a routine meeting of senior planners before every shambles.'

The briefing officer's opening burst was along the lines that, 'You must understand, gentlemen, that this is not the Far East. First of all, we are in close geographical proximity to metropolitan France, in an ex-colony which is now an integral part of our national territory.' There was nothing special about this. French schoolchildren were taught that since 1834, Algeria had been as much a 'part of France' as Brittany (1491) or Savoy (1860). Only a few months before, in the full glare of the National Assembly, the Minister of the Interior, a certain François Mitterrand, had formally confirmed what every French schoolboy was being taught. Their scepticism only partly subdued, the soldiers of 1er REP went to work, if not to war as they knew it. They despised their first big operational task as *un boulot du flic* ('a civvy cop's job'), rather than real soldiering.

In 1956 the ALN started an urban terror campaign which, predictably, begat counter-terror among the more extreme settlers. This, in turn, involved elements of the gendarmerie in terrorism. As a destabilizing mechanism, the bombings had been effective enough, yet the nationalists still lacked a convincing political fulcrum with which to lever the French out of power. That instrument, one which would involve the entire Arab population of Algiers itself, was unveiled in January 1957. In an awesome display of its power, the ALN prepared an unlimited general strike which was to paralyse the city. It was to be passive protest on a scale which had not been seen since Gandhi's campaign of civil disobedience in India.

What happened as a result of that threat was still making front-page news throughout France in 1985 as the reputations of the former soldiers – some of them now prominent in public life – were reappraised by an unforgiving younger generation of Parisian journalists. In spite of legal amnesties now covering the period, the wounds inflicted during what would become, in effect, a civil war had still not healed after twenty-eight years.

On 7 January 1957, General Jacques Massu, commanding the 10th Parachute Division including 1er REP, was ordered by the French Governor-General Robert Lacoste to take control of Algiers and restore order 'by every means possible'. The key element in these orders was delivered verbally. The main participants agree that their effect was to give *carte blanche* to the paras.

The ALN strike was set to begin twenty-one days later. Two days before that deadline, on 26 January, three ALN bombs exploded in a busy shopping area of Algiers killing twenty people and mutilating many others, including students and some small children, for life. Like 'Bloody Friday' in Belfast many years later, the indiscriminate nature of the assault as well as its effects ranked it as an atrocity which remained in the public conscience longer than the predictable crop of headlines. Amid the hysteria around them, the paras now derived a grim satisfaction from the job they were about to do. It was tangible and clear, which made a change from trying to confront an enemy who preferred to shoot in the dark, from the back, and then run. It was also dirty work. As Captain Estoup, one of 1er REP's officers explained at his trial five years later,

> At Saint-Cyr Military College I was never taught to organize the supply of fruit and vegetables for a city such as Algiers. In January, 1957, I was ordered to do just that. I was never taught at St Cyr to exercise the functions of a local police chief, but I was ordered to do so in Algiers. I was never taught how to organize a voting booth, to open schools, markets . . .

In the event, matching the ruthlessness of the ALN, the paras mounted the most successful military strike-busting operation of the century. Businesses which were closed were opened, by force if necessary, the key staff pursued to their homes as if they were guerrillas hiding in the mountains. Those who could not be found were to discover on their return that the shop or office was still 'open' days later, no locks on the doors, and the stock gone. The buses were brought out of the garages and the drivers ordered to drive them. The children were then taken to school, with a para sitting at the back of the class to ensure that the teacher got on with the job of teaching them.

In one episode described by Ysquierdo,

> The job of bringing a particularly densely-populated working class area to life was in the hands of a young captain who was not short of imagination. At 4 a.m. on the second day of the strike the unit's bugles sounded 'Reveille', on the streets. Then the doors were vigorously shaken. The 'hard men' dressed in a hurry, picked up their papers and came out to stand where they always stood in the morning for the bus to work, with military cordons in place to make sure they didn't miss it.

The strike failed after three days but for 1er REP this was only the beginning of the Battle of Algiers. The Kasbah, a honeycomb of alleyways, cellars, sewers and tunnels comprising the old Arab quarter, was invested for nine months while the local leaders of the ALN were hunted down. Three men were prominent on the wanted list: Larbi Ben M'Hidi, one of the original six founders of the ALN; Yacef Sa'adi, and the assassin Ali la Pointe.

Less than a month after the ALN's urban offensive had started and eight days after the organization's latest bomb outrage (eleven dead and fifty-six wounded) M'Hidi was captured. He committed suicide in prison soon afterwards. The ALN's other key men in Algiers then came under crushing pressure.

Sa'adi surrendered to 1er REP on 23 September after hurling a grenade at the first two legionnaires to burst into his hideout at 3 rue Caton. These were the regiment's Commanding Officer, Colonel Pierre Jeanpierre, leading from the front as usual, and Sergeant-Major Tasnady. Jeanpierre was slightly wounded and Sa'adi was taken alive.

Soon afterward, Ali la Pointe was discovered in a chamber hidden behind false walls at 5 rue des Abderames. He refused to give himself up. It was clear that he and his companions were armed. This time, the first man into the hideout might not be as lucky as Jeanpierre had been a few days' earlier in the capture of Sa'adi. The CO himself agreed that the guerrilla hideout should be blown up. Adjoining houses were evacuated as a team of four entered the building: Lieutenant Simonot, a Vietnam veteran; the small, aggressive Corporal Ray Palin from Liverpool; Legionnaires Flores and Protegma, both German. Palin and one other had cleared the upper floors of the building after spending the night there and at 6 a.m. had an explosive charge set against the dummy wall they had identified concealing the hide. Simonot's Vietnam experience had given him an instinct for the next ambush. This time he was certain that death awaited the first legionnaire to go through the hole they were about to make in the wall. He ordered the team to retire a pace or two. Leaning over an upper balcony, weapon cocked, Palin watched the point at which the blast would occur. Neither he nor his Lieutenant could have known that the point they had chosen for their charge was immediately opposite Ali la Pointe's own high-explosive store, separated from it only by a few centimetres of plaster. The explosion not only gave access to Ali's grotto. It demolished most of the building. Palin lost his left eye and suffered a severe wound to the hand. Years later, at a Camerone Day anniversary, he cheerfully blamed himself: 'When I lost that eye, I was peering down to see what was going on. I was being nosy, as usual.'

In October 1984, thirty years after the start of the Algerian war, the left-wing Paris newspaper *Libération* decided to commemorate the anniversary by looking for a war crime and chose to pursue an increasingly successful right-wing French politician named Jean Marie Le Pen. Le Pen had served as a reserve lieutenant with 1er REP for three months during the first Battle of Algiers in 1957. *Libération* accused Le Pen of being involved in the torture of terrorist suspects during that brief period of service, although he was already a Member of Parliament and a prominent public figure. Le Pen sued for defamation. In the ensuing lawsuit, *Libération* won the first round and Le Pen won the second at an appeal hearing. He was thus cleared of carrying out any act of torture himself. The litigation had now run its course. But independently of Le Pen's personal history, the case had general importance. It reignited throughout France a passionate debate about the role of the army in suppressing terrorism and the use of torture by both sides in Algeria. Undiluted by the passage of almost thirty years, the question of torture – and whether it could be justified in any circumstances – suddenly re-emerged as a quarrel which had power to demonstrate how bitterly divided France remains about the role of the army when it is left to resolve a political problem.

One of Le Pen's journalistic allies, writing for the 'counter-attack' issue of *Minute* in February 1985, was remarkably candid about what had to be done in Algeria. In 1957, Jean-Claude Goudeau, later to become *Minute*'s director general, was a young press officer attached to Massu's staff. He recalled:

> I saw how intelligence officers obtained information from terrorist prisoners which enabled them to prevent attacks and neutralize the bomb-carriers . . . The officers were not content to put polite questions to the FLN killers. Following unwritten but perfectly clear rules by the military high command on the orders of the civil power – that's to say, a socialist government of which François Mitterrand was part – they used two methods of questioning because these were very effective and produced no after-effect. These were electric shock and water.
>
> It was not, of course, the intelligence officers who were doing the job themselves. They used people whom we had turned round. These were former guerrillas who had themselves suffered this disagreeable experience and had cracked.

Monsieur Goudeau's testimony that torture *was* practised by the paras in smashing the Algiers terrorist network is backed up by too many other responsible people to be dismissed as eccentric. General Paris de Bollardière, a distinguished fighting soldier who asked to be recalled from Algeria in 1957 because of this issue, told *Agence France-Presse* in 1985, 'The debate about torture is about a real event and the latest debate shows that the Algerian drama has not burned out.'

A British authority, Alistair Horne, concludes that:

> The Battle of Algiers could probably not have been won without resort to institutionalized torture – freely admitted by Massu – on a large scale. The long-term result of this was that, although it may have won the battle, it lost the war for France through the violent and persistent reaction which it aroused . . . As one distinguished French

soldier, General Pierre Billotte, remarked of it in Algeria, 'Whatever its form and whatever its purpose, it is unacceptable, inadmissible, condemnable; it soils the honour of the army and the country.'

The issue could not be dealt with in isolation from the immediate political background. The use of paratroopers as policemen can be defended in a worsening terrorist situation, but Governor-General Robert Lacoste's decision to hand over total responsibility to the army can not. As Edward Behr, an eye-witness of the Battle of Algiers, has put it:

> By doing so, Lacoste himself avoided dealing with the moral problem of justifying torture as a means of obtaining information. As army officers were quick to point out, the problem was not Lacoste's but theirs, and detailed instructions from the French government on what was, and what was not, permissible did not come in time. The result was the 'Battle of Algiers' became, for the paratroopers who fought it, and for France itself, a pyrrhic victory.

Scapegoatism is not a novel experience for the Legion. However, the most thoughtful and articulate veterans of the 1957 campaign do not accept that the effect of torture was to unify the Arabs, transcending differences of class, culture and tribe, leading to military victory. They argue that Algeria was not another Indo-China, but that de Gaulle ceded power to a defeated ALN because of his pursuit of an altogether different goal from victory in this latest prolonged colonial war. What need of colonies – this argument runs – if nuclear superpower status gave new expression to French grandeur? Indeed, the Algerians were the more plausible victims of a pyrrhic victory. Once independence was achieved, they promptly started cutting each other's throats. The only founding father of the revolution to survive the war against the French, Krim Belackem, was assassinated after taking refuge from his comrades of post-colonial Algeria in Germany.

At the time that torture was being used by the French, no one was in a more exposed moral position than the Roman Catholic padre of 1er REP, Father Delarue. He produced for Massu's 10 Para Division a guidance document entitled 'Reflections of a Priest on Urban Terrorism'. This argued a classic doctrine derived from Christian (e.g., Aquinas) and pre-Christian (e.g.,

Aristotle) sources of choosing when it is necessary – and soldiers *have* to make choices – the lesser of two, or least of several, evils as a temporary expedient in an imperfect world. Delarue wrote:

> One has the right to interrogate efficaciously someone we know is not a killer, but who knows those responsible, who has witnessed a crime, who has provided shelter for some bandit. Such a person is culpable, in complicity with the killers, and responsible for the death of innocents.

At the time the words were written, there were innocent victims in abundance of the bombs planted by Yacef Sa'adi's terrorists, including children who lost one or more limbs. No appeal to humanity would have deterred the ALN (or its political arm, the FLN). A prominent French sociologist, Germaine Tillon, tried bravely in a dramatic underground confrontation with one of the leaders and evinced only a sickening demonstration of crocodile tears from the mastermind behind the outrages. ('Ah, you are right!' he told Madame Tillon. 'We *are* all murderers.' And continued killing.)

At that time the Algerian nationalists sensed – wrongly – that they were about to score a quick, easy victory. France had just been defeated in Indo-China and had precipitately withdrawn from Tunisia. All the auguries favoured a hard line. Edward Behr – no friend of the French paras – later recalled, 'Cold-bloodedly, an FLN spokesman at the United Nations [in New York] once replied when I questioned the efficacy of such methods: "You must realize that every time a bomb explodes in Algiers we are taken more seriously here."'

It is that knowledge which moved Massu to turn on the *Libération* inquisitors, twenty-eight years after the event, with the comment,

> But there is torture and torture. They [ALN witnesses against Le Pen] have not been terribly tortured since they seem to be in very good shape twenty-eight years after. If they had been badly tortured they would not be in such shape. If we had engaged them in orthodox warfare and hit them with machine-gun rounds or cannon shells, or if they had been deported, they would not have had such effrontery. Don't talk to me about your 'torture': it's a great word.

It would, perhaps, have gratified the cynical veterans of 1er REP who stepped ashore in Algeria in 1955 questioning the moral basis of their latest campaign, to learn that among the first people to absolve the army as well as themselves from *Libération*'s accusations were the civilian politicians of a socialist administration who were running the show when the torture started. Even in the absence of any written orders about interrogation there was no ambiguity about the handover of police power and administrative control of the city of Algiers to General Massu's paras in January 1957 by Governor-General Lacoste. Massu's recollection, in February 1985, was that the orders were to stop the terrorism by whatever methods were necessary. It was a job neither he nor his soldiers wanted: 'a shitty job' was his description to fellow-officers at the time.

In 1985, the Defence Minister at the relevant period, Maurice Bourges-Manoury, and Max Lejeune, then Secretary of State for the Armed Forces, joined with Lacoste in asserting that the whole government, with Prime Minister Guy Mollet presiding, had agreed to give the army authority to stop terrorism.

> The then Minister of Justice, Monsieur Mitterrand and the prosecutors working for him had accepted the army's role in the judicial process . . . If the ministers ordered vigorous action in the struggle against terrorism, they did not at any time envisage and assuredly did not order the use of torture. In these circumstances they denounce the campaigns against the army, which accomplished its mission in extremely difficult conditions.

Mitterand did not contribute to that statement perhaps because, by the time it was drafted, he was President of France. As head of state, he might be expected to avoid such controversy. In other circumstances, however, it is reasonable to conclude that he, too, would have exonerated the administration of which he had been a member, of any knowledge of torture.

Libération now extended the debate beyond the military past or political future of one man. Introducing the *leitmotif* of the Guilty Older Generation, it suggested that concealed knowledge of torture was a dirty memory carried by 2,400,000 conscripts who lived through that time. Those people are now the backbone of the over-forty generation, 'who, electorally speaking, carry a lot of weight today'. Suddenly, it seemed, the soldiers of 1er REP were now a mere handful among France's 2.4 million 'guilty men'.

For the paras the first Battle of Algiers was drudgery and they were glad when it was over and they were turned loose into more open spaces. In the event they went from one extreme to the other, from the claustrophobia of the Kasbah to the vast wilderness of the Sahara. It was a curious interlude, prompted by the civil authority's fear that the first oil to flow from the Algerian Sahara along a pipeline to the coast would be sabotaged by the ALN. Urged on by their Colonel, Jeanpierre, the men of 1er REP broke through the silence of the Bedouin communities, a silence maintained, for the sake of a soft life, with the complicity of the local French military. The paras soon struck a rich vein of information which led to stake-outs, confrontations and manhunts. One of these ended when a legionnaire on the receiving end of a burst of fire captured and then strangled his Arab opponent. Another close-quarter engagement was concluded when a German legionnaire used his entrenching tool (a small shovel) as a weapon with which to decapitate his enemy.

Peremptorily, the pipeline operation was called off and the regiment despatched to a mountain wilderness on the border with Tunisia. Here, during a short, vivid four months of continuous combat, Jeanpierre's style of leadership would make him and the men who followed him the stuff of which legends are made. He would live long enough to create a full measure of glory only to die in almost the last battle of the frontier. He was the only soldier lost by the regiment that day and the manner of his death was strangely theatrical, performed in something like slow motion before an audience of his own soldiers. Such a death, in the Legion, is a sacramental act.

Statistics help to put into context a series of murderous engagements led by Jeanpierre immediately after the Sahara operation, in the spring of 1958. These were spread over a wide area and were collectively known as the Battle of the Frontier. They were small beer when set against the great set-piece battles of Stalingrad or El Alamein or even Dien Bien Phu. But in the modern world, where the deaths of eighteen British soldiers at Warrenpoint, Northern Ireland, in 1979 and the deaths of 200 US Marines in Beirut in 1983 make headlines, the mini-war on the border between Algeria and Tunisia was impressive. The 1er REP killed or captured 2,000 guerrillas. These were not bogus, Vietnam-style body-counts inflated by the corpses of murdered civilians, but real soldiers. The regiment's own losses are the best evidence that the paras were not simply hitting unarmed bystanders. Total 1 REP casualties were 123 dead and 350 wounded out of a combat strength of 850: a 50 per cent loss of manpower within twelve weeks and this among supremely fit young soldiers whose basic training lasted a rigorous seven months. Such losses were not a new experience. Since its foundation as 1er *Bataillon Étranger de Parachutistes* in 1948, the unit had twice been written off as a coherent military organization by the weight of its casualties in Indo-China.

The Algerian frontier was no slaughter of innocents on either side. If the Legion had a favourable casualty ratio throughout the war it was because it had superior fire-power (including artillery, napalm and chlorine gas), mobility (including helicopters) and communications. Theoretically the fact that the legionnaires were fighting a territorially defensive battle should also have given them a potential advantage in any exchange but this was not a textbook conflict. For a start, no one was seeking to hold ground in an orthodox military sense. The campaign was, rather, a deadly game of hide-and-seek among deep ravines cut into high mountains, ravines whose undergrowth concealed bomb-proof caves, natural tunnels and – for the unwary intruder – instant death. The ravines were transit camps for ALN soldiers infiltrating from the haven of Tunisia to the interior of Algeria. The 1er REP intercepted these parties, joined battle with them, hunted the survivors until they surrendered or died. The regiment did this job without rancour, certainly without the bigoted passions of the settlers.

From the outset, two very different men started to impose their personalities on 1er REP's Algerian war. First, there was the Commanding Officer, Jeanpierre, a complex, obsessive man who lived for and through his soldiers. His father, an infantry captain, had died in battle in 1916 when Jeanpierre was aged four. The boy grew up determined to follow the father he never knew, and joined the army as a private soldier when he was eighteen, rising through the ranks to take a commission with the Legion in 1937. With the surrender of France in 1940 (still serving in North Africa) he was one of many honourable soldiers who initially

served under the legal – if not legitimate – government of World
War I hero Marshal Pétain. Posted from Algeria, Jeanpierre
fought with 6 REI in Syria, against the Allies, returned to France,
left the army and joined the Resistance. He was finally arrested
and sent to Mauthausen concentration camp in 1944.

After the war, back in the army, he rejoined the Legion and
spent two hard-fighting tours in Indo-China. On the day the
Algerian war started, 1 November 1954, Jeanpierre took over
command of his own regiment at last. He was now aged forty-
two, a man not given to sharing confidences with anyone, and
driven by a sort of crusading zeal to fashion out of his job-lot of
veterans and rookies an élite among the élite soldiers of 10 Para
Division commanded by the powerful and charismatic General
Jacques Massu. The competing 'firms' included Bigeard's Colonial Paras. Jeanpierre was to make his men march faster, carry
more, shoot straighter and die harder than anyone. Furthermore,
he would show them how to do it, by example. He was a lateral
thinker who would discard precedent when it no longer made
military sense. Typically, he tackled an apparently impossible
mission – to halt the ceaseless, silent movement of guerrillas
through the barrier of wire and sensors – with a series of
innovations. First, he put his men to work after dark at a time
when only the Algerians ran night operations. Second, he used
the unique, god-like platform of the helicopter to control the
battle like a chess master, a familiar technique in later years, but
not in 1958. Finally, he created the 'rouleau compresseur', or
steamroller.

The steamroller was let loose when Jeanpierre knew that he
had a sizeable party of rebels bottled up in one of the ravines.
Other commanders would not wittingly put their men into the
hornets' nest such a double-edged opportunity presented. They
preferred prudently to wait until the artillery or the air force
could be brought into the action. Such commanders usually lost
their quarry as a result, or – by giving the opposition time to
organize a coherent defence – suffered unnecessary casualties (as
did the Americans in Vietnam, for similar reasons).

Jeanpierre, by contrast, travelled light and struck instantly. He
discouraged his men from carrying food. That they would have
to forage from the enemy, when they had killed him. Some days

they ate, some days they did not. Like primitive animals, they were even more dangerous, as well as fleet-footed, when hungry. The men were loaded with additional ordnance instead. Used intelligently, his soldiers would then provide their own short-range artillery, and this they called the 'steamroller'. Sections moving in line abreast halted at a given signal. Then each lobbed a grenade into bushes. This was followed up with concerted bursts of automatic fire into the same target area. The technique was not infallible. Some spectacularly cool individuals could survive this treatment and still come out fighting, taking a legionnaire before dying themselves in a venomous, close-quarter shoot-out. But for the most part it worked. The first time it was tried, 1er REP killed ninety-two out of a party of 100 guerrillas before breakfast, took five prisoners and eighty-six firearms. Furthermore, it was perfectly suited to the corporate legionnaire personality; the marching and singing together, day and night, expressed themselves naturally in this ballet of death. It broke with precedent in avoiding an unnecessary waste of Legion manpower.

The second man whose personality imposed itself on the regiment's history at this time was the Hungarian Sergeant-Major, Laslo Tasnady, a performer who emerged from the corps-de-ballet to become one of the superstars of 1er REP. In 1946 he had come from Budapest to join the Legion sixteen months after VE-Day. Off the battlefield, like an actor off-stage, he was not an impressive figure: a man of less than medium height and of stocky build, with a round, characterless peasant's face and a surprisingly soft voice. He was never short of courage, but his personality had undergone a change as a result of something that happened in Vietnam. Until then, he had been happy-go-lucky.

In 1949 Tasnady was with a convoy overrun by Vietnamese troops and their women. He dived into the undergrowth and remained there, quite still, while the women stripped the wounded French soldiers, decapitated them and then emasculated them also. For the only survivor, it was a brutal initiation into the business of war which all professional soldiers encounter eventually, a loss of innocence about human nature. And it was this reborn Tasnady who was waiting, alert and catlike and predatory, the day a group of six prisoners – wrongly believing that they were about to be summarily executed – slipped their escort in Algeria and unwisely ran down a wooded valley towards him.

As Tasnady's company commander, Antoine Ysquierdo tells it: 'Laslo aimed his carbine . . . six shots, regularly spaced, rang out and each fugitive was "pinned" by one round, like picking off rabbits.' The internal row was immediate, for the prisoners had only just been handed over by 1er REP for interrogation by Intelligence, who could not be convinced that this was a series of accidents compounded by Tasnady's deadly marksmanship. Those who served with Tasnady found the story all too credible. It seemed that he was fated to be pursued by adventures. The extraordinary tended to become the norm when he arrived on the scene and the more bizarre the adventure, the more calm, relaxed even, Tasnady became. It was a characteristic he shared with other warriors of a very special kind, including the SAS VC Anders Lassen.

It was Tasnady, also, who was to blow his way into an apparently impregnable rebel mountain hideout (during a fierce gun battle) by hanging, head down, on a rope lowered from a precipice above the entrance before placing, very calmly, a satchel loaded with grenades and other explosive material, with one grenade from which the pin had been removed. Tasnady had just the time left on the fuse – between four and seven seconds – to be hauled clear before an almighty explosion tore the cave apart. The acrobatics, it should be said, began only after other, more orthodox means had failed.

Then there was the operation which started with a piece of discarded tomato. One calm afternoon a corporal serving with Tasnady – a former professional poacher and smuggler who could read the countryside like a book, even if he could read no books – spotted a freshly discarded tomato skin under a pine tree. This led him to a bush, beneath which were uneaten stores and, nearby, a cave. The corporal could smell the enemy inside it and so could Tasnady. The Sergeant-Major summoned his latest 'recruit', an Arab boy aged about twelve who had become his section's mascot. The boy, known as 'Ouled', was given a torch and sent down the hole. He knew the drill: if he spotted someone he shouted that there was no one there. The trick had worked before. Fifteen minutes passed before they got the signal: 'No one here. Only an old blanket.'

The boy re-emerged, four fingers held up in a silent, pre-emptive body-count.

'We know you are in there,' Tasnady called down. 'Come out or we will gas you! You've got five minutes.'

The five minutes passed and Tasnady nodded. The cave entrance was blocked and a chlorine gas grenade hurled inside. During the next ten minutes traces of the yellow gas could be seen drifting out of fissures in the rock. These were promptly blocked up. ('Just like badger-hunting,' said Ysquierdo later.)

The first man to stagger out of the underground gallery choked, vomited and still managed to gasp an answer to Tasnady's instant question, 'How many are you?' 'Seven . . . Excuse me . . . *Vive la France!*'

Only one man did not surrender immediately. One of the NCOs went back into the hole, leading before him the first prisoner to surrender, a rope binding his hands behind him and looped about his neck. The Legion escort carried a torch in his left hand and, in the right, in addition to the prisoner's bond, a pistol. For gasmasks the men wore motor-cycle goggles and rags soaked in water. They had not gone far when their quarry, surviving in some pocket of uncontaminated air, spotted them and opened fire at point-blank range, killing the hostage. The Legion corporal, dragging the now-dead hostage as a shield in front of him, retreated, shooting back as he did so. In the confines of the cave, the shots were deafening and the stench of cordite joined that of the gas. When the man re-emerged, more gas grenades were hurled in and the air holes re-sealed.

By now the other prisoners, who had surrendered, were persuaded that co-operation was the better part of valour and were helping to pinpoint other, similar underground hideouts. Ysquierdo called for the regiment's special cave-hunting team but they were too busy elsewhere, he was told. Finally some gasmasks were supplied, together with one bullet-proof vest and some smoke-bombs. In the event, only the masks were needed as an aid in recovering the last body.

In the last of the big frontier battles – at Guelma on 18 and 19

March 1958 – the regiment killed 192 guerrillas and took eight prisoners. The only anomaly in that statement, given the nature of the event, is that any prisoners were taken. Colonel Jeanpierre, as we have noted, was pushing his men to greater and greater efforts, and achieving military miracles. The morale of any fighting unit improves when it is fighting, and is at its best when it is fighting and winning. But Jeanpierre's appetite for action was imposing its own stress even on the fighting machine he had created. He was now a man alternately high on the adrenalin of battle and deep in a trough of fatigue: a famous Legion photograph reveals him exhausted, slumped asleep against a rock, beret tipped over his eyes, boots still firmly laced. When his veteran company commanders suggested that the regiment needed a break, that it was tired (and for 'tired', read 'exhausted') he simply shrugged it off as if it was his own fatigue which was the issue.

'What are you complaining about?' he asked blandly. 'I'm creating glory for you.'

This was the Jeanpierre who would tell a newly decorated young NCO, Sergeant 'Boby' Dovecar, after the next battle:

> The goal of a Legionnaire is the supreme adventure of combat at the end of which is either victory or death. What matters is the action, the combat which places you on a different plane from the rest of the herd. Camerone, 1863, was like that: victory or death.

On April 30 that year, 1958, the regiment celebrated Camerone Day on the battlefield, though it sorely needed the rest of which the company commanders had spoken to Jeanpierre. The ALN, certain that the Legion would be drinking hard, chose to launch its well-advertised spring offensive on the 30 April anniversary, unaware that Jeanpierre, still spoiling for a fight, had moved his men overnight by truck and helicopter into another regiment's sector to meet a particularly large ALN incursion.

The men went into action with shouts of 'Camerone!' and Jeanpierre's steamroller swung destructively forward to the music, sung in unison, of the Legion's song 'Le Boudin'. Captain Pierre Sergent, in his vivid account of this battle, notes that men did not trouble to take cover, but fought as if drugged or drunk. Fighting knives were drawn and the legionnaires hacked their enemy to death in the most sanguinary celebration – for that is what this was – of Camerone Day since Camerone itself. The slaughter went on in a series of adjoining wadis for most of an entire day. At the end of it, in addition to the enemy dead and the meagre eight prisoners, the regiment picked up their weapons: six machine-guns, six automatic rifles, thirty-seven sub-machine-guns and seventy-five rifles. Soon after that battle, near Souk Ahras, the frontier zone was calm at last, for the good reason that the ALN had concluded that infiltration from Tunisia was a waste of life. But one or two pockets of resistance remained and before he finally quit the area, the Colonel could not resist a last shoot. He found his quarry in a remote valley high in the Djebel Mermera almost a month after Camerone Day.

He and his regiment had now been engaged in continuous military operations for nine months. What should have been a mopping-up task unexpectedly turned into a siege when a force of ALN guerrillas was encountered in a rocky position from which all approaches could be covered by the defenders' fire. On one side, a sheer cliff overlooked the paras, on another, a smooth slope that was a natural killing ground. Artillery fire was called down and, accurate though it was, it barely scratched the surface of the mountain. When it was over the enemy emerged and resumed his target practice. The Legion Captain whose company was bearing the brunt of this, Ysquierdo, proposed an air attack with napalm bombs. Jeanpierre, aboard his Alouette helicopter, decided to take a look for himself. He came in at tree-top height, swooping over friend and foe alike, map on knees, green beret held in place by earphones and therefore unable to hear the long bursts of automatic fire that accompanied each pass. On the ground, however, his legionnaires could hear and see that this time – whether he realized it or not – the CO was pushing his luck to its extreme. He did not want to summon an air strike for this was clearly an infantry affair, a textbook problem for the Legion as well as a question of pride. And then it happened. One enemy round cut the Alouette's fuel supply and the engine stopped. The pilot was too low to salvage a crash-landing. In perhaps three or four seconds the machine was out of sight . . . Then the sound of the crash in an adjoining wood. The first Legion section to get there, led by Lieutenant Simonot, arrived in time to open fire on the guerrillas who were about to loot the wreck. Inside, Jeanpierre rested against the pilot. Ysquierdo, the company commander, arrived seconds later with his medic but only to confirm what they all knew. Eight years earlier, in October 1950, Ysquierdo had rescued Jeanpierre and twenty-three other survivors of the Legion's 1st Para Battalion in Vietnam. The rest of the battalion had been wiped out. This time, Jeanpierre's luck had also run its course.

The death of the CO in action hurts every man in the unit, for he is the man everyone, however hard-boiled, depends upon and identifies with. The 1er REP took no prisoners after the death of Jeanpierre. His loss, however, reverberated for longer than a single day. He had moved the regiment into a momentum which at times seemed almost out of control. Now, at a stroke, it all stopped. The impact of that change was disorienting, the silence deafening. At the funeral soon afterward, conducted among the Mediterranean rose gardens of Zeralda of which Jeanpierre had been the architect, some of his men swore an oath over his coffin. The oath they took was to preserve Algérie Française.

CHAPTER 14
The Centurions' Revolt (Algeria, 1959–60)

You are the Army of France. You do not exist
outside it . . . I must be obeyed for France to live
. . . Vive la France!

– President de Gaulle, with 1 REP, Algeria, September 1959

While 1 REP was fighting its war on the Tunisian frontier, momentous political events were taking place in Algiers and Paris which would have a greater impact on 1er REP than anything – even the death of its beloved Commanding Officer – of which the enemy was capable. Chronologically, Jeanpierre's death was a pivotal event marking the shift between the old order – a traditional Legion battalion fighting with great courage and no political sense – and (the day after Jeanpierre died) the innovation of de Gaulle, the Fifth Republic, the politicization of the regiment and final disgrace. None of these developments was actually sought by 1er REP. But if Tasnady's initiation in Indo-China into the sometimes dehumanizing effects of combat was the loss of one sort of virginity, then the next phase in the regiment's history could only be described by an idiom from the intelligence world: to be 'rubber dicked', that is, to be tricked in darkness into believing that one is experiencing real love-making instead of a counterfeit.

By the spring of 1958, French governments were surviving for a matter of weeks, and their evident weakness left a dangerous political vacuum. The latest administration, that of Prime Minister Gaillard, expired on 16 April leaving no effective government in Paris (for the third time within a year) as the frontier battles blazed away. Then on 9 May came news that the ALN had executed three French soldiers illegally held prisoner in

Tunisia, a reprisal for the lawful executions of an Algiers bomb-maker and two other urban terrorists. The executions, like the reprisal-murders in captivity of the British sergeants taken by the Zionist terrorist movement, Irgun, in Palestine in 1947, generated blistering anger, particularly among the *Pieds Noirs*. There was no government in Paris to receive their protests so the settlers did the next best thing and – on 13 May – they occupied the main government building in Algiers.

The pressure was now on to demolish the whole sordid mess of unstable, Fourth Republic government, forcing President Coty to resign also. Some senior soldiers, none directly linked with 1er REP, had already made secret contact with de Gaulle, who was then living in that strange, twilight world of political has-beens and rulers-in-waiting. In response to the paras' invitation to run for President, he didn't say yes, but he didn't say no, either. What, in fact, were the kingmakers seeking? Their faith in orthodox politicians was now entirely destroyed, yet they knew that an attempt to extend military rule from Algiers to France would inevitably lead to civil war. Somehow, France had to be 'saved' as they saw it. The only answer was to create as head of state the soldier-statesman le 'Grand Charles' de Gaulle.

De Gaulle, they believed, was 'sound' on Algeria. By now, Algérie Française mattered to them because it was a symbol of past pledges and future national honour. They did not love the settlers: they knew them too well. As for de Gaulle, he had provided them with a series of texts, uttered with that oracular certainty that made the world listen when he spoke, to reassure them. In February 1945, when head of state for the first time, had he not refused to meet Roosevelt in Algeria because Roosevelt had proposed it as a convenient *neutral* venue to discuss the Yalta agreement? De Gaulle came dangerously close to making a political joke out of the embarrassment it caused. He said: 'For Roosevelt Algeria was perhaps not France. All the more reason for reminding him. How can an American President invite the President of France to visit him – in France?' Or again, in 1947: 'Algeria is our domain . . . Whatever happens, France will not abandon Algeria.'

Unfortunately, like more antique oracles, de Gaulle could be fickle, even inconsistent. Since the wartime days he had spoken about the desirability of independence in *Africa*. He was all things to all men, and was compared to a man who has promised marriage to several women. What he scrupulously avoided was a commitment which would reduce his chances of regaining power. The political generals, led by Salan, either did not know this, or chose to ignore it in the belief that they could manage him. If so, they were wrong.

They had an impeccable alibi. They were not living in some calm ivory tower or a university department of political science at Nanterre, or a fashionable Left Bank café, they were fighting a war on three fronts: a guerrilla campaign on the Tunisian frontier; terrorism in the cities and direct political action by the *Pieds Noirs* which came close to being a political counter-revolution. General Paul Ely explained their dilemma very neatly. 'The army,' he propounded, 'has become the only unifying factor between a rebellious Algeria and a leaderless France.'

Thus it was that on 12 May 1958 as Algiers came to boiling point in its anger over the execution of the three French prisoners, Salan sent a secret signal offering 'units to be at the disposal of the general staff to maintain public order in Paris'. It was the first signal to metropolitan France that 'Operation Resurrection', the plan to mount a parachute assault on the French capital, was a hard reality. By now another government of random nonentities was in being in Paris.

In Algiers next day, as the settlers' leaders occupied the main government building they created what they called a Committee of Public Security. With a vast mob already assembled on the square outside, the commander of 10 Para Division, General Jacques Massu, was invited to join this new body and did so, it appears, in an effort to ride out the political storm rather than be crushed by it. After all, he had already been legally responsible for the security and administration of Algiers since the beginning of the war on urban terrorism in the city in January 1957. Massu made a snap decision to join the *Pieds Noirs*' Committee and emerged on to the balcony to be announced as its chairman. The announcement was received rapturously. Another long stride towards politicizing all the troops under Massu (including 1er REP) had now been taken, but even more surprising events were to happen during that anarchic week.

For the first three days of the settlers' backlash, the government in Paris could hold on to the conviction that the *Pieds Noirs* were an unscrupulous, unrepresentative one-ninth of the population. Then the Muslim population joined the protest. Some writers were later to assert that Arabs who joined hands with the protesting *Pieds Noirs* were bought, pressurized, or both. If so, there were hundreds of them, ordinary people who had had enough of terrorism. They wanted not fascism but stable government and they wanted the warriors of both sides out of their homes and off their streets.

During the last weeks of May, as the front-line soldiers at last sealed off the ALN's supply line – and thereby consigned the organization to a lingering death – the military king-makers in Algiers were able to assure de Gaulle's return to the presidency. It was, it seemed, game, set and match to the army.

The process was flawed. More and more local Committees of Public Safety were set up around the country with full army participation. At the top of the heap, Massu was making promises about Algérie Française which he and others assumed, with good reason, reflected the views of de Gaulle. As Pierre Sergent described it, Assu's aide – then Major Saint-Marc – was acting as public relations officer and privately expressed his misgivings to Massu about running the communities. Massu retorted, says Sergent, by 'brandishing' the legal directive provided by Governor-General Lacoste eighteen months earlier, at the beginning of the first Battle of Algiers. This had handed over administrative and security control of the city to Massu, to cleanse it of terrorism. Effectively it was a declaration of local martial law which had never been rescinded. Massu would follow that up with the holy writ of de Gaulle's past speeches. And what was good enough for General Massu was good enough for his paras, including 1er REP.

It was yet another example of the French army moving into a moral and political vacuum as a result of a sense of duty to a France whose sense of duty was inferior to that of its army. Whatever the soldiers did in the service of such a regime would be, in the perfect world of journalists and historians, the wrong thing. The soldiers were not fools. They knew this and were angry about the bad press they received, however well-authenticated a given story might be.

The 1er REP, still disoriented by the loss of Jeanpierre as well as the sudden halt to the momentum of the operations he had generated, was posted in July to Algiers where, under the friendly, avuncular direction of General Massu, it would take its second lesson in street politics. The regiment was not unwilling to learn from Massu. Although not a legionnaire he was a good fighting soldier, a charismatic para general who had such a high regard for 1er REP that he accepted an invitation to become one of the regiment's honorary corporals. In the consequent ritual of military brotherhood, Lieutenant Degueldre handed 'Corporal' Massu the quarter-litre draught of rough, red wine to drink. Other ceremonies were under the control of Sergeant Dovecar.

In that strange, bitter-sweet summer of 1958, the mere threat of 'Operation Resurrection' had done the trick in spite of a demonstration against the army by 200,000 Parisians. (Interestingly, the units earmarked to take part did not include any from the Foreign Legion. Those guiding 'Resurrection' had determined that it should be an exclusively French affair. It was one in which even the gendarmerie and Riot Police known as 'CRS' controlling Paris were ready to participate.) The latest government, led by Pierre Pflimlin, resigned after holding office for just twenty days. An exhausted, seventy-six-year-old President Coty followed this example, inviting de Gaulle to succeed him.

De Gaulle had not dissociated himself from the army's more or less public arm-twisting of the *ancien régime* on his behalf, a silence which the generals interpreted as an eloquent endorsement of Algérie Française and, more important, of their political function in choosing him as their caesar. In Algeria itself, through the Public Safety Committees, the army now enjoyed the novelty of participating in local government but – while it was true that, for the most part, the buses *did* run on time – it was all less abrasive than in the days of the ALN's sponsored strike of 1957. Reconciliation was in fashion. Ysquierdo recorded the piquant experience which followed the release on amnesty of hundreds of ALN men, when the soldiers of 1er REP were running the infrastructure of civilian life (which is a posh way to describe, for example, the movement of melons to market). The newly released prisoners, he said,

> called on us, their former 'torturers', for backing in their search for work . . . Many examples could be given of the reciprocal goodwill which existed between the paras, who were hard but not insensitive men, and the majority of Muslims who wanted security, justice and understanding.

In the autumn, a referendum partly organized by the army produced an overwhelming vote in favour of complete integration of Algeria with metropolitan France. De Gaulle himself, on his first triumphal trip to Algeria, had stoked up the euphoria with the vague but avuncular pronouncement to a 100,000-strong crowd: 'I have understood you . . . The route you have opened in Algeria is one of renovation and fraternity . . . Throughout Algeria there is only one sort of citizenship and it is French through and through.'

In fact, the new President of France – as he admitted, much later – had decided already that Algeria's only viable future was as an independent state. By the time he started to hint publicly about this change of line, 1er REP was out of the city, exploring a new environment. But according to Ysquierdo's comrade, Captain Pierre Sergent, as it left Algiers for the Saida sector in Oran on 11 October 1958 it was 'by no means the same regiment as that which had fought at Guelma a few months earlier. On orders of its chiefs, it had made a political gesture which would bind its future.'

In good faith, the officers and men of 1er REP had given their word – in some cases over Jeanpierre's coffin – to be true to an ideal which they thought their government shared. In this they were mistaken. Three days after 1er REP quit Algiers all military men were ordered by Paris to withdraw from the Public Safety Committees and any other political activity. General Raoul Salan, aka 'The Mandarin', French supremo in Algeria and Leclerc's chief negotiator with the Viet Minh in 1945, was posted to a harmless sinecure in Paris. Massu was the next to be moved on. From now on 1er REP would be fighting militarily in the countryside and politically in Paris and Algiers. The political battle was to prove the more deadly.

An honourable 'Peace of the Brave' was on offer to the guerrillas from de Gaulle in October 1958 but the paras, under their new supremo, Air Force General Challe, kept up the pressure. A series of 'Challe offensives' concentrated French muscle on specific mountain areas – hitherto untamed – day and night, until the ALN was eliminated. It was working nicely. Discreet surrender, with weapons discovered later by accident and no questions asked, was now an accepted and winning formula. As part of this offensive 1er REP was given the novel task of winning hearts and minds in the mountains around Orléansville. This meant opening village schools whether there were teachers available or not. The Legion paras took on this job with characteristic gusto with the result that the infants of mountain villages in Algiers were learning to speak French with accents imported from Bavaria, Hungary, Italy and elsewhere. But, unlike the first teacher victims of the Algerian war, Guy Monnerot and his wife, these teachers were not soft targets. By night they were soldiers again, predators in search of the few remaining armed men who never appeared near the villages except after dark to collect food. On those occasions it was business, and ambush, as usual. The English legionnaire Simon Murray, who joined 1er REP's brother regiment, the 2nd Legion Paras, a year or so later, described the process:

> Just after midnight . . . They were coming towards me. The beginnings of panic set in – I thought my breathing was far too heavy and I put my handkerchief in my mouth. Visibility was nil . . . When you are about to shoot five people coming around the corner you tend to sweat a little . . . The thought of your gun jamming is too horrible to dwell on and the thought of not killing them all before your magazine is empty brings on an unendurable thirst. The only compensation is the fact that it is dark and you will be aiming at their backs. The form is to let them go past you and then give it to them from behind. To shoot them from the front is unnecessarily sporting and could lead to a charge . . . of attempted suicide.

The 1er REP's dual role was to lead to a barbed exchange in September 1959 between de Gaulle and the regiment's Commanding Officer, Colonel Henri Dufour, at the regiment's latest HQ, a mountain schoolroom. Dufour presented his standard VIP briefing on the local situation. Then, staring hard at the President, he went on:

> Every morning in every village we hoist the colours. The local people are not obliged to attend this ceremony but they are always there. Then the officer or NCO will deliver a little pep-talk on the way things are going. He must always conclude with a form of words which I have made obligatory. This is, 'I remind you, in the name of General de Gaulle, President of the Republic that you are entirely a part of France.'

De Gaulle did not need to be reminded of the source of the quotation. It was from his own memorable Algiers speech a year earlier. By now, however, the President was using weasel words in his public statements and scores of army officers whose political profiles were judged too high were being posted out of the country. De Gaulle coolly thanked the Colonel and his regiment for the good work they were doing, then addressed the assembled officers in his turn. 'You are the Army of France. You do not exist outside it, it is your *raison d'être* . . . Given the person I am, at my level, I must be obeyed for France to live. I am sure you will [obey] and I thank you for it. *Vive la France!*'

It was in that summer of 1959 that many of the fighting men began to wonder what exactly they were fighting for, other than maintaining a vow of absolute obedience unilaterally exacted by a caesar whom they had – they thought – invented in the first place A few weeks before, 1er REP had suffered its most cruel loss since the death of Jeanpierre. On 14 May, Sergeant-Major Tasnady's section hit a well-concealed and fiercely defended ALN hospital, whose entrance was a hole high on a chalk cliff, concealed by a bush, on one side of a long valley. It was in attacking this that the Hungarian performed his famous rope trick and swung the satchel of fizzling explosives into the hole. Seven dead were recovered, though none of the remains were identifiable.

The team broke for lunch and marched on. It was hot, and the sun shone. The only sound, aside from the quiet tread of para-boots, was the chirrup of crickets. Up ahead the leading section had just signalled that it had reached the end of the valley and the rendezvous where the pick-up trucks were waiting. Then a burst of fire, and Tasnady was down. Death from a bullet wound in the back of the neck was instantaneous. Tasnady's captain, Ysquierdo, was on the scene in seconds and has put on record that Tasnady was hit not by a bullet but a shotgun pellet. Worse, within a week, Tasnady was only one of three Hungarian veterans, all Sergeant-Majors not yet aged thirty, killed in the service of the Foreign Legion. The others were Istvan Szuts (3rd Infantry) and Janos Valko (5th Infantry). All three lay in state at the same time, like medieval knights at the Legion's depot, Sidi-bel-Abbès.

It had seemed to many, including the depot commander Colonel Brothier, that Tasnady was indestructible. That spell was now broken. What had started as an adventure, a crusade even, was turning sour. All the signs were that the conflict was winnable, in time; the sealed frontiers and the internal 'Challe offensives' made victory on the battlefield as certain as the contemporaneous British feat of arms in Malaya.

And then, on 16 September, de Gaulle scored the greatest and most decisive own-goal of the shooting war. He made a broadcast floating three political models which all Algerians could choose by referendum. These were complete independence (which he did not advise); absorption into an enlarged France, which would then extend 'from Dunkirk to Tamanrasset' (known to legionnaires as 'Fort Laperrine'); or a government of Algerians remaining in close relationship with France. About three months later, the President released 7,000 ALN prisoners, 58 per cent of the rebels taken in combat. 'Most of them rejoined the rebellion,' drily recorded Colonel Henri Le Mire in his *Histoire Militaire de la Guerre d'Algérie.*

Worse than the unconditional release of hostile prisoners, de Gaulle had let the genie of independence – and a possible ALN victory – out of the bottle a mere three weeks after his latest ringing public declaration to the effect that as long as he was alive, 'the ALN flag will never fly over Algeria!' After hearing the U-turn of 16 September, Saint-Marc – veteran of Buchenwald and the Legion's battles – felt that something precious had been smashed. His feeling of betrayal was widespread and given expression by General Massu in an interview with a German newspaper a few weeks later. The newspaper betrayed the conditions Massu imposed on the interview. A verbatim account, harvested by a tape-recorder concealed by the reporter and

unambiguously attributed to Massu was published, criticizing de
Gaulle.

De Gaulle promptly summoned the popular commander of 10
Para Division to Paris and sacked him. The *Pieds Noirs* of Algiers
exploded with anger and set up barricades which they held for a
week in January 1960. Unwisely, the gendermerie was ordered by
Paris take a hard line also. Fourteen of its members and eight
civilians were shot dead in the ensuing confrontation. 1 REP,
boots still caked with dirt from the latest operation in the field,
was hauled out of Zeralda at 4 a.m. and sent to the capital to
restore order. The paras cooled the situation on the streets but
raised political temperatures in Paris by fraternizing with the
demonstrators. Common cause was discreetly established that
week between some of the regiment's officers, notably Degueldre, and the most extreme settlers.

What was all right by these officers, was OK by the men they
led. As a veteran of the Sidi-bel-Abbès depot, Colonel Brothier,
put it at Sergeant Dovecar's subsequent trial:

> One of the exceptional characteristics of the Legion is the dog-like
> devotion of the men to their officers. It is from them that they find the
> structure and the balance that civilian life did not give them. Thus,
> they transfer all their attachments and affection to their officers,
> for they have no critical sense. In their officers they will forgive
> everything, even the most extravagant actions.

It is the Legion's great source of strength, and its historic
weakness.

The officers concerned, who were later court-marialled or
forced to become fugitives in their own country, were described
by de Gaulle as '*les paras perdus*' (the Lost Paras) but, from where
they stood, it was the politicians who had lost their way in
Algeria. This became bloodily evident to them later that year.

Early in November, while politicians of both sides sparred at
long distance about the terms on which they might talk, the
regiment was sent to the Aures mountains to hunt down an ALN
'*Katiba*', or company, thought to comprise 125 guerrillas. The
precise location was misunderstood and Lieutenant Godot, a tall,
blond Adonis, leading the assault chose as the helicopter landing

zone an exposed hill position surrounded by concealed enemy marksmen. During the next two hours, until a merciful darkness enabled them to evacuate, Godot's men were sitting targets. His own presence of mind in calling down covering fire from helicopter gunships, which could not see what they were shooting at, reduced the casualties. Even so, the regiment lost eleven dead including a sergeant-major and a sergeant and six wounded.

The funeral of these men took place at Zeralda a few days later. By now, any pretension by Paris to an Algérie Française had become political compost. Jeanpierre's successor, Colonel Dufour, followed Legion tradition in delivering the funeral oration. With evident emotion, he declared over the ten coffins, 'It is not possible that your sacrifice will be wasted. It is not possible that our countrymen in metropolitan France will not hear us.'

Dufour was followed by the regimental padre, Father Delarue, who said: 'You have come from every country of Europe where people still love liberty, to bring freedom to this country. Yet you have fallen at a moment when, if we can believe our ears, we no longer know what we are dying for.'

The politicians' response to this episode was not intelligent. Colonel Dufour's tour of duty as CO of 1er REP was arbitrarily ended and he was ordered back to France. Before he could leave, Lieutenant Roger Degueldre passed him a message sent by several hundred prominent settlers. It said, simply, 'Don't leave us . . . at least not before de Gaulle's impending visit.' Dufour then went into hiding and the regimental standard, without which a new Commanding Officer could not be formally installed, mysteriously vanished.

De Gaulle was due in Algeria on 9 December. According to some accounts, Dufour invited other Legion commanders at Sidi-bel-Abbès to join him in kidnapping the President as he visited an isolated spot named Aïn Témouchent. There were no takers for that scheme but, elsewhere, no shortage of anti-Gaullist plots among men who had given a lifetime to serving France. In Paris they even held one of their meetings at Napoleon's old school, the École Militaire, in the shadow of the Eiffel Tower. The commanding officers of three other parachute battalions indicated to a leading plotter, the Algerian-born

General Edmond Jouhaud, now in Paris, that they were ready to seize key points as part of an overall revolt against the rumoured plans for independence. Dufour, having taken soundings in Algeria, was gloomily satisfied that the plots lacked conviction. He was right. He gave himself (and the flag) up and was posted to Germany.

By now, 1er REP was on operations again in the Constantine area. But in their handling of the paras, the authorities now proceeded to score another unnecessary 'own-goal' by approving a scheme to allow the ALN flag to fly over Algiers during yet another referendum. When the officers of 1er REP heard that, they decided that enough was enough and ordered their men to remain in camp.

The regiment was now on strike in the best French tradition. Bureaucratic assertion of power had produced – as it always does in France – an obstinate refusal to fall into line. It could have passed off, as these things do, with gestures and a lot of noise. Instead, the men flying desks in Paris and enemy flags over Algiers reacted by posting virtually every officer of 1er REP as far from the Legion and Algeria and one another as possible.

> This was the real beginning of the 'Revolt of the Centurions' [wrote Pierre Sergent later in *Historia*]. One by one the young officers refused to leave Algeria. Lieutenants Michel de la Bigne and Roger Degueldre of 1er REP went underground . . . Captain Jean-René Souetre, a commando, created his own maquis in January 1961, near Oran, along with three of his sergeants.

Other of 1er REP's officers bided their time, went quietly to new postings in France and then, alerted by coded messages, took some sick leave, citing old wounds as the cause. A lot of old wounds started to cause trouble among the Legion's veterans and all of the victims, by an odd coincidence, decided that the best cure was Algerian sunshine. None of their new superiors was aware of this until it was too late.

CHAPTER 15
Enter the Firing Squad
(Algeria, 1960–62)

Good heavens! One never knows what is going
on inside the head of a very sick person.

– Lieutenant Roger Degueldre, from the condemned cell,
Fort d'Ivry, Paris, July 1962

By December 1960, the scene was set for all-out mutiny, led by
the paras, yet it was another four months before the inevitable
happened. The French government, in forcing some of its best
fighting men to desert their consciences or desert from the army,
had created an underground resistance movement and all but
incited rebellion. Throughout that deadly spring of 1961, it was
business as usual on the surface, with 1er REP operating in the
Ouarsenis mountains. Reports on the plots seem to have flowed
back regularly to the various Intelligence services monitoring
events. But neither side knew, until it was too late, exactly when
the Algiers coup would happen and who would join it.

The last man of any consequence to come in was Major Élie
Denoix de Saint-Marc. He was the antithesis of de Gaulle: an
emotionally secure aristocrat who despised politicians and
admired fighting soldiers. He had rejoined the army shortly
before out of simple patriotism (he needed neither the salary nor a
reputation) because of his concern for the diminishing fortunes of
a regiment he had left only a few months earlier.

Massu's successor in charge of 10 Para Division, Saint-Hillier,
appointed Saint-Marc as a sound second-in-command of 1er
REP shortly before the regiment's latest and ailing CO, Maurice
Guiraud – Dufour's replacement – disappeared on real sick leave.
For 1er REP's mutiny to have some sort of legitimacy, Saint-
Marc's participation was now imperative. Without it, without

1er REP as a whole – rather than a random selection of Legion paras – the rebellion would lack credibility even before it got started. The regiment was the star of the show, and everyone, friends and foes alike, knew it.

Saint-Marc had been discreetly invited to join the less-than-secret brotherhood of disenchanted officers and had not jumped at the opportunity. He wanted to know who was leading the movement. The Air Force General Challe would be no bad choice but there were others, more extreme, whom he would not follow at any price.

One Friday afternoon in April, Saint-Marc suddenly found himself in a villa facing Challe. Like so many others, Challe – a calm, informal, pipe-smoking individual – had been moved out of Algeria by an increasingly insecure de Gaulle. Challe, a successful supremo commanding the whole theatre until then, left the service. The night before this confrontation, he had returned from France aboard an official aircraft, disguised as a consignment of photographic equipment, to lead the resistance. Even more surprising, for Saint-Marc, was the fact that Challe was flanked by officers who had deserted from 1er REP rather than accept postings out of Algeria. These were tough young veterans who were living underground and finding new roots among the extremists of the *Pieds Noirs*. Among them, Lieutenant Degueldre, whose links with the militant settlers went back at least to the 'week of the barricades' in Algiers a year before. What the plotters would have done had Saint-Marc refused to join them is an open question. They had only hours left before they hoped to seize power. The reckless Degueldre talked in advance of imprisoning the acting CO of 1er REP.

Saint-Marc imposed conditions for his co-operation. First, this had to be a disciplined, military affair in which no settlers would have a role. He contemptuously regarded the *Pieds Noirs* as 'those assassins' and rejected attempts by some of them to join 1er REP during the putsch. His second condition was that there must be minimal bloodshed and no settling of old scores under cover of the rebellion. Challe reassured him: 'We only want to make good the promises made when de Gaulle came to power. This is not going to be a fascist *coup d'état*; nor racialist revenge. We move tonight. Are you with us? I want an immediate answer.'

As Saint-Marc saw it, there was good reason to join the mutiny. He would later tell his judges:

> I had given twenty years of my life to France; for fifteen years as an officer of the Legion, watching legionnaires die for France. Thinking of my comrades, my NCOs and my legionnaires who had died in battle, at 1330 hours on 21 April, in front of General Challe, I made my free choice. *Terminé, Monsieur le President.*

That Friday night, Saint-Marc and two of his lieutenants and their wives dined with General Saint-Hillier and members of the divisional staff. The occasion would have been a cliché of garrison life were it not for the small matter of a mutiny to be led against the host some time after dinner by some of his guests. Saint-Hillier, as a loyal Gaullist, was inevitably on the list of those who were – with every military courtesy – to be placed under comfortable arrest in the splendour of the Algiers Summer Palace.

The party atmosphere was brittle, and afterwards Saint-Marc received a telephone call in his quarter from the current supremo in Algeria, General Gambiez. The general was being plagued with rumours about an impending putsch led by 1er REP whose motor transport support group was forming up in convoy even at that moment.

'Not at all, General,' said Saint-Marc with apparent candour. 'Nothing happening. My men have been on evening leave as usual and they are coming back, as usual. No operations are planned this weekend. We are standing down.'

Around midnight, the fighting companies in Zeralda Camp were summoned to muster parade in combat gear. The roll was called, weapons and ammunition drawn to normal scales. It was familiar, everyday stuff. Then from the shadows stepped the 'lost' officers to resume command of men who had not seen them for three months. The regiment's novices had never seen them before. The men were told, 'General Challe is assuming command in Algeria and we are acting in support. We move off in a few minutes.'

The targets assigned to 1er REP were the principal military headquarters (Army Corps HQ at Pélissier Barracks); the radio station; the civil government (Délégation-Général) HQ; the police school occupied by the CRS gendarmerie. The handful of other units publicly taking part in the mutiny, including the Legion's armoured Cavalry Regiment, brought the number of forces available to the rebellion to 3,000. In spite of excellent staff work for the first, critical phase of the takeover, key points *not* seized included the telephone exchange. From the outset, the loyalists could inform Paris of what was happening. Most army units, while toasting the rebel emissaries who visited them with champagne, were careful to stay on the sidelines.

The air force, ignoring its old boss General Challe, flew transport aircraft back to France. Fighter pilots there made it known that they would shoot down any transports trying to drop the paras on the Champs Élysées in a re-run of 'Operation Resurrection'. The navy was entirely out of sympathy with the mutiny: one of its cruisers lay a mile or so offshore, its 16-inch guns ranged on the Legion's vulnerable coastal base. Since all the urban centres of Algeria were on or near the coast, it was evident from the beginning that in the navy de Gaulle held the trump card. The rebels were outgunned.

There were other reasons why, from before the beginning, the rebellion was a lost cause if only because everyone except the Foreign Legion (most particularly the thousands of conscripts from metropolitan France) had homes to go to when the party was over, politically as well as domestically, and those homes were not in Algeria. True, the *Pieds Noirs* – for whom Algeria *was* home – had a powerful motive to back the rebellion. But only a few hundred Legion rebels were fighting, like those stateless Frenchmen of a preceding generation at Bir Hakeim, for such intangible, unprofitable substances as 'honour' and 'fidelity'. Like Bir Hakeim, it was an unworldly ambition and, because the real world of French politics was still a cynical one, it was guaranteed to fail. This did not worry the clear-thinking leaders of 1er REP. They had an aphorism to cover the situation: 'to do a Camerone', fighting to the death as a matter of identity as well as principle. In the Legion's view, such an opportunity does not come often and is an honour to be seized gratefully.

To begin with, 1er REP succeeded astonishingly well. There was no element of surprise and the twenty-mile road between

Zeralda and Algiers city was blocked at four places by gendarmes. Yet the big convoy of lorries with Captain Pierre Sergent
up front bluffed and bullied its way through all the barbed-wire
chicanes set up to stop them and drove on to Pélissier Barracks.
Most of the office lights were on and a suspicious guard had
bolted the front door. Sergent talked his way alone into the
building, still wearing his green beret. He reached the office of
General Vezinet before being suspected and darted out again
pursued by shouts of 'Stop that man!' The paras then found a way
in through the back of the headquarters, over garage roofs.
Following another distraction at the front, they poured into the
main entrance as well. Only a handful of legionnaires, in fact,
were required to subdue the headquarters.

There was a farcical struggle when Vezinet tried to draw his
pistol on Lieutenant Godot. Godot it was who had led the fatal
pre-Christmas mountain assault during which eleven of his men
had died, an event which, indirectly, had triggered the regiment's resistance to de Gaulle. Vezinet's attempted resistance was
promptly squashed by Godot's escort, Sergeant Bobby Dovecar.

Panting angrily, the General told Godot, 'In my day, lieutenants did not arrest generals.'

'In your day, generals didn't betray their men,' Godot replied.

Elsewhere, meanwhile, the Commander-in-Chief, General
Gambiez, made a brave effort to halt the rest of the runaway
Legion single-handed. The lieutenant in the vehicle he stopped
waved him aside with 'Yes, I know who you are and you are no
longer important.'

The Hussein-Dey police school, replete with sleeping CRS
specialist riot-control police, went quietly when a 1er REP team
arrived. Indeed, only one man – an infantry sergeant charged
with guarding the radio station – offered real resistance to a team
led by Captain Estoup and was shot dead.

Algiers was *en fête* for most of the weekend. But the rebellion
had not won support in Constantine, Oran, Tlemcen or Mers el
Kébir naval base. At Blida air base, Other Ranks turned on their
officers and hoisted the Red Flag. In Algiers itself, the *Pieds
Noirs'* terrorist group, the *Organisation de l'Armée Secrète*
(OAS), emptied the main police armoury and released
from prison men held on criminal charges. 'Para-phobia'

gripped Paris where the trade unions demanded 'arms for the people'.

While Challe spent most of his time on the telephone seeking support from uncommitted commanding officers, the mutiny was running out of steam. This loss of initiative was confirmed just thirty-six hours after the triumphant start when de Gaulle – using that direct appeal to individual hearts which had been his greatest weapon during World War II – made a confident broadcast which offered his opponents no quarter. The rebels, he declared, were military fanatics exploiting settler fears and they would face the full rigour of the law. 'I forbid all Frenchmen, particularly soldiers, to carry out any of the mutineers' orders even under the pretext of operations . . . Frenchmen and women, France is in peril. Frenchmen, Frenchwomen, help me!'

This broadcast sounded the death-knell for the mutiny and for Algérie Française itself. Whatever the school textbooks said, the 2.5 million conscripts from metropolitan France now knew that Algeria was a Muslim colony on the brink of independence, separated from the real France by 200 miles of sea. During the following day, a Monday, the slender support available to Challe and his fellow-generals, Salan, Jouhaud, André Zeller (a former chief of staff), evaporated. First one, then another unit ceased answering signals. An embittered Challe commented, 'I received such promises . . . I never knew there were so many bastards in the French Army.'

On Tuesday 25 April the reckoning was at hand. Offshore, the navy's big guns were turned upon Algiers and the Legion's base at Zeralda became a sitting target with no weapons sufficient to answer the threat. At 4 p.m. Challe called his top echelon together to tell them he was surrendering himself to de Gaulle.

The atmosphere within the big echoing government building the rebels used as their headquarters became infected with despair. The front page lead of that day's *Algiers Echo* mocked them with, '"I WILL GO ALL THE WAY," Says Challe.' Men cried, laughed, slept, stared moodily into space. A few were already changing into the civilian gear they just happened to have in their rucksacks. And a dedicated Pierre Sergent raged against Challe's 'treason'.

'Nothing we can do about it now,' said a colonel.

'I can go and put a bullet in his head,' Sergent snarled, drawing his revolver. He was stopped by Challe's co-conspirator, Salan. From the headquarters, Sergent went to the radio station to make an impromptu broadcast calling upon all soldiers to 'live up to their responsibilities' even if this meant disobeying senior officers. No one out there answered.

The regiment returned to Zeralda and with its acting Commanding Officer, Saint-Marc, went Challe, to rest a few hours before turning himself in for what he was convinced was a trip to the death cell. He tried to persuade Saint-Marc to flee but Saint-Marc would have none of it. He would answer for what he had done. He knew he had done nothing of which an honourable man had cause to be ashamed. Trials, punishments, were incidental to that. Such integrity de Gaulle identified as fanaticism.

The officers of 1er REP (some of them) climbed into a bus to go into detention. The men (most of them) clambered into trucks, the same trucks they had used to fight their mountain war, and moved off in convoy. The *Pieds Noirs* were out in force, strewing their road with flowers. And the men sang an Edith Piaf number which had long been a regimental favourite, '*Rien! Je ne regrette rien!*'

Camerone Day was just round the corner. The last commanding officer of 1er REP returned from leave just in time to put his signature to a document formally dissolving the regiment. The unit had bled to death in Vietnam twice before. On this occasion, it almost took the rest of the Foreign Legion with it. De Gaulle demonstrated a vindictive quality in dealing with his defeated opponents. Some Legion veterans believe he was dissuaded from dismantling the whole Legion organization – though only just – by his Defence Minister. This, as it happened, was one Pierre Messmer. With other legionnaires, Messmer had saved France's honour at Bir Hakeim. More to the point perhaps, Messmer was a living reminder that at Bir Hakeim the Legion had given de Gaulle, sitting in London as a noble figurehead but not much else, a political credibility he had lacked until then.

In 1961 de Gaulle, a smart politician, allowed discretion to be the better part of revenge and this was, maybe, just as well. It would be only seven years before left-wing students and other practitioners of chic revolution struck at the heart of Paris itself.

De Gaulle, wobbling under the hammer blows of a workforce chanting 'Re-sign, de-Gaulle!' fled to Germany at the height of the crisis to seek reassurance that the French garrison there would not let him down. The officer in charge was Massu, former commander of 10 Para Division and still an honorary corporal of 1er REP. The President's appeal did not go unheeded. De Gaulle survived 1968 and received a lesson in loyalty along the way.

At a conservative estimate, at the time of his peaceful arrest on 7 April 1962 in a police station by a patient, calm gendarme who was relying on old photographs for an identification, Lieutenant Roger Degueldre, aged thirty-six, Algeria's most wanted man, was responsible for 300 premature deaths not authorized by any government, in one month (February 1962) alone.

Degueldre was much more than a renegade Legion officer who had joined an underground army. He was head of the Delta Force, a chillingly efficient assassination machine which enabled the OAS extremists among the *Pieds Noirs* to conduct a reign of terror in the European ghetto of Bab-el-Oued and for a time, throughout most of Algiers and beyond.

Delta Force never numbered more than about a hundred men, mostly German ex-legionnaires. It was tiny when set against the French National Front volunteers (which alone supplied 2,000 men), Fascist Party members and the other elements of the OAS including even a loyal ring of French monarchists. Delta's unique function was to discipline everyone else. It was to the OAS what the Brown Shirt enforcers were in the early days of the Nazi Party. Its fatal weakness was that the Legion rank-and-file were motivated only by the regiment's traditional devotion to officers: that and no other conviction sustained them when they were taken prisoner and subjected to interrogation.

Delta had an apparently limitless supply of plastic explosive but it also despatched its victims with anti-tank missiles, bullets and commando knives. Mere suspicion of 'disloyalty' on the part of a *Pied Noir* living in Bab-el-Oued – and sympathy for de Gaulle or the Arabs might be enough to invoke the suspicion – generated a neatly typed instruction in military jargon. This document would authorize an '*opération ponctuelle*', a grisly euphemism for premature death. Even fervent OAS supporters came to describe Delta (though only in confidence to people they could trust) as '*une Mafia militaire*'.

The military experience Delta's force of deserters brought to the task of assassination was made even more potent by the vast knowledge of a former police chief for Algeria, Colonel Yves Godard, one of the best desk analysts to serve the Sûreté in North Africa. Other OAS members were medical consultants – often the more bloodthirsty activists – air-traffic controllers and many other things: a peerless source of information about who was whom.

Finally, the system had the covert but almost total support of the gendarmerie and much of the military structure. They felt justified in assisting the Europeans to defend their position. After all, those *Pieds Noirs* who dared to continue living on farms outside the urban areas were regular victims of sickening nationalist atrocities. For the time being, in parallel with negotiations between the two main protagonists inspired by de Gaulle, the French declared a unilateral truce in their war against the ALN. Algeria was now in a 'no peace, no war' situation tailor-made for extremism to appear credible.

When any investigator arrived from Paris to do something about Delta, within hours the OAS leaders including Degueldre would be notified. And for a long time, as the OAS hold over the European community strengthened remorselessly, teams of French security men were betrayed by their own colleagues.

Degueldre was not the only Legion officer to become a Delta celebrity (for that, in Algiers café society, is what they were). There was a brace of captains from 2 REP and a captain from the 3rd *Régiment Étranger d'Infanterie* but, unlike them, Degueldre had no familial ties with the country. He was, in fact, a mystery man from the cradle to his last letter from the condemned cell. There is some evidence that he did not know who he was. He claimed, and clearly believed, that he had fought (like so many legionnaires of his generation) with the Resistance as a hit-and-run gunman, a '*franc-tireur*'. After the liberation of France he joined the regular army but – for reasons he never explained – under a false name. Thereafter he was haunted by rumours, which his friends did not believe, that he had in fact been a Belgian who had started his military life with the fascist Rexist movement.

After the war he joined the Legion under another assumed name and claimed Belgian nationality. As a ranker, he went to Indo-China, fought with foolhardy courage at Dien Bien Phu and rescued a colonel from certain death. He became an adjudant chef – equivalent of a senior warrant officer – and then took a commission in the Legion. In Algeria, he resurrected his real name and became Lieutenant Degueldre, a man whose physical size and strength matched his courage and, as it turned out, his ambition. His brief and disastrous command of Delta provided him with all he desired, including status, on Algerian soil. Near the top of the OAS political as well as its military hierarchy was the former Legion Inspector, General Gardy, whose daughter Nicole had become Degueldre's companion.

Delta's first victim, Police Commissioner Gavoury, was kidnapped and executed in a rented flat by a team of two legionnaires and three *Pied Noir* civilians (one a police commissioner's son) on 31 May 1961. The man in charge of the team, wielding the knife, was Sergeant Bobby Dovecar, a Yugoslav who would follow Degueldre to hell and back to prove his loyalty. And that, more or less, is what Degueldre demanded. Degueldre subsequently ordered a Legion lieutenant on his team to murder his best friend, whose child was the assassin's godson, as a proof of loyalty.

The Dovecar team, with other Legion deserters, took refuge in a villa in a 'good' district, but aroused the suspicions of their nearest neighbour, a senior civil servant named Perrin. Unwisely, Perrin expressed his misgivings to the police. Soon afterwards, two men rang Perrin's doorbell and asked to speak to him. Perrin was called. The visitors shot him dead and walked away.

Dovecar and his band were now moved to an even grander house owned by the widow of one of Algeria's leading viniculturists. She accommodated them in the library which had been closed since her husband's death and preserved as his shrine. The fugitives felt uneasy in this place. It was a sticky uneasiness, telling them to go before it was too late. Dovecar set their minds at rest. He had a plan to remove them in a lorry loaded with sand that very afternoon. Next, Degueldre appeared and distributed money. Everyone relaxed, though Legionnaire Claude Tenne, and his Bavarian friend Karl, who spoke virtually no French, kept their weapons within arm's length. Tenne, according to his own memoir, was watching the window. 'Suddenly I saw a long, curved aerial belonging to a scout car. Without thinking I shouted, "Lieutenant, the cops." '

Without awaiting orders, Tenne and Karl started shooting from the window. Instantly the gendarmes in the street below fired back. Degueldre, accompanied by an unknown civilian, dashed to the garage while the rest of his team gave him covering fire. Tenne, his carbine magainzes empty, ran through a court-yard, over a wall and across fields before turning down a steep embankment which dropped into a suburban street. This was a bad mistake. True there was an alleyway into which he might disappear 100 yards off to his left, but the fugitive and his objective were separated by a small fleet of police vehicles and armed gendarmerie. Tenne had drawn his pistol now and fired it as he ran. A windscreen shattered; a cop dived for cover. Tenne zig-zagged as the bullets sang around him. He was five yards from the shelter of the alley when the first round hit him in the back, throwing him into the air . . . As he lay in the gutter, he recalled later, he was quietly certain that he was about to die. Yet it was rather comfortable, lying there in the sun. The pain, the impris-onment, the surprising recovery came later. It would be six years before he made a second, more successful and dramatic break for freedom. During those first few minutes after the gendarmes arrived, he had told himself to find a little hole in which to hide, and now 'I had found one, a black hole into which I dived with delight.'

Six other members of the group were arrested during this incident. Yet over the summer and autumn of 1961 the number of bombings, beatings and assassinations multiplied. So did the flourishing protection rackets. The Gaullist regime, which could also play dirty, now started to fund its own clandestine opera-tions among the settlers. First, with the aid of a mixed bunch of liberals in the French-Algerian community, it promoted a Move-ment for Co-operation (MPC) between the two warring com-munities which, overnight, challenged the apparent OAS monopoly of public opinion with a graffiti offensive. This encouraged some Gaullist stalwarts, including world war veterans, to come together. They were then authorized to carry firearms for self-protection. The regular police regularly stopped and searched such people and removed their arms for the paperwork to be verified. Before that lengthy procedure was complete, it sometimes happened that the unarmed Gaullist was assassinated.

The creation of MPC was only the first step. Two more undercover teams followed. The first, a mixed bag of ex-paras, civilian bodyguards and Vietnamese karate enthusiasts, was the least effective and most notorious. It became known by the name attached to it by an alert journalist: *Les Barbouzes*, or Falsebeards. It was a counter-counter-terrorist organization, which caused Algeria's public life to degenerate even further than before. They were noisy, flamboyant and careless. During their first week in action they wrote off six vehicles. They also started to bomb the homes of prominent OAS leaders and, worst of all for OAS credibility, attacked premises paying protection money. A twenty-four-man Delta team led by Degueldre in person hit the Barbouze villa on New Year's Eve 1961 with a bazooka and machine-gun attack which all but destroyed the building. The battle lasted for twenty minutes.

A month later, printing machinery ordered by the Barbouzes was delivered to their second and last headquarters. Delta had repacked the material at the airport. One of two crates was converted by Delta's chief explosives expert into a bomb containing almost 100 kilos of assorted high explosive including plastic, TNT, gomme dynamite and a substance called 'N17', together with numerous hand-grenades and metal bolts.

The driver who delivered the crates explained that they could not be opened until a Customs officer had examined them and he was on his way. The Barbouze boss, Jim Alcheik, tipped the man and waited. By 5 p.m., no one had arrived, and the Barbouzes opened the boxes. At least nineteen of them died in the huge explosion which followed. One of the survivors found himself lying on the roof of an adjoining house.

In February, the last four active Barbouzes were driving away from a hospital (where they had just deposited the latest of their wounded) when their car was shot up by an OAS team and crashed into a wall. The four were still alive, though injured. They had crashed, however, in an ardent OAS neighbourhood and were recognized as enemy. The local people, rather than Degueldre's professionals, delivered the *coup de grâce*. They prevented the injured men from leaving the vehicle, then set it on fire.

Virtually all the 'special agents' sent from Paris were buried in the same cemetery in Algiers. For security reasons, they were denied even posthumous identification. Their tombstones described each of them as 'Unknown'.

'C' (for 'Choc') Force was the official code-name attached to the second group which was sent to get Degueldre and other OAS leaders. Roger Frey, Home Secretary, appointed an experienced Resistance fighter turned policeman, Michel Hacq, to lead a force of carefully chosen French mainlanders drawn from the Gendarmerie Mobile, the national force which performs police functions from within France's armed forces. This gave them experience with, and access to, weapons of war including tanks and artillery in what was beginning to look like a civil war.

To cover the whole of Algeria, 'C' Force had just 200 men who were warned to keep their distance from the French policemen already serving there. They were, most of them, hopelessly compromised by their involvement with the OAS. Hacq felt obliged to use the *nom-de-guerre* 'Professeur Hermelin' to conceal his true identity from Degueldre. The good news was that there was one exception to the pro-OAS lobby among the indigenous civil police, a young, energetic captain called Lacoste.

Operating from its own barracks and therefore not disabled by leaks, 'C' Force started picking up OAS bombers with increasing frequency. An anonymous tip-off early in January led to a safe house concealing several of Degueldre's legionnaires. One of these, a youthful German, was happy to change sides to be attached to Lacoste as an adviser for the rest of the war.

Between early December and the end of February, 'C' Force arrested 604 OAS men including sixty-nine assassins and sixty-two bombers, picked up 642 automatic firearms, 10,000 rounds and important documents. Degueldre had not been idle, either. During the same February he was thought to be responsible for

302 out of 553 OAS killings. Within a very short time, however, two events beyond the control of either Captain Lacoste or his quarry, Lieutenant Degueldre, were to destroy the credibility of the settler case for good and with it, the OAS power base.

The first of these events was a bomb which exploded on 7 February at an apartment block in Paris. It was but the latest of many such outrages for which the OAS in metropolitan France was responsible. This one was intended to kill, or intimidate, the writer André Malraux, but it was placed on the wrong floor of the building and horribly disfigured a four-year-old girl. In theory, the man in charge of OAS operations in France was a brave, stylish and witty captain who had deserted from 1er REP when the putsch failed. This officer, Pierre Sergent, had issued an order exactly a month before, stating, 'The era of plastic [explosive] is finished.' De Gaulle foolishly prohibited the protest demonstration in Paris which followed the next day. The riots which resulted caused ten deaths among the riot-control police, eight civilian fatalities and approximately 126 wounded.

By now, the mainland French – most of whom had been, at best, lukewarm towards the cause of Algérie Française – were becoming strained by the historical fiction, broken promises and settler outrages the commitment required. But worse was to come. On behalf of the OAS its nominal leader, General Raoul Salan, declared a state of 'civil war' to exist with the Gaullist forces as well as the Arab nationalists. OAS teams in Algeria executed people working in dispensaries on the basis that they could be working for the ALN; then postmen, because they 'knew too much'. Any Arab, male or female, randomly encountered on the street in a European quarter died at the hands of roaming lynch-mobs. Finally, and most absurd, the French army was to be disarmed in any OAS-controlled area. It is to Degueldre's credit that he was against such attacks. But, like some others, he was now trapped by his own obstinate loyalty to an ideal based upon a false prospectus. And as he saw it, even serving the OAS under Salan was preferable to following a cynical de Gaulle.

Soon after dark on 22 March, a team of OAS terrorists hit a patrol of gendarmerie mobile half-tracks with anti-tank rockets as they emerged from a tunnel near Algiers University, killing eighteen gendarmes. At 8 a.m. the next day, a patrol of army conscripts gave up its weapons without a struggle. Later that day, however, it was a different story. Seven conscripts from France were shot dead in their trucks on Christopher Colombus Street, and another eleven were wounded. This was the final stroke to demolish settler hopes of winning the support of their last hope, the French man-in-the-street.

They had clearly not won the heart of de Gaulle. The assault that followed on the settler stronghold of Bab-el-Oued was a full-blooded military response including tanks and ground-attack aircraft which strafed everything. Only the artillery seem to have been forgotten in five days of punishment which matched, too close for comfort perhaps, Degueldre's long-standing dream of emulating the resistance of Budapest to the Soviet invasion. The analogy was not a fanciful one, even to more sober minds than that of Degueldre: there were many French officers who were – and are – convinced that the real enemy in Algeria was international communism. An attempt by a genuine-ly peaceful, unarmed demonstration by settlers to take the pres-sure off Bab-el-Oued merely compounded the tragedy: a bat-talion of illiterate Muslim levis, loyal to France, opened fire on a crowd which believed, erroneously, it could stroll pacifically through their lines towards Bab-el-Oued. That episode alone provoked the loss of forty-six lives and 200 other casualties. The gun-carriers, including Delta Force, slipped through the cordon in the other direction and dispersed. Those who had a bolt-hole went to it.

For the rest, there was further punishment: a last, brave and entirely hopeless expedition by most of the Delta team into the Ouarsenis mountains, was based upon the muddled idea that French units in the area would sustain them in the same way as Arab villages supplied the ALN guerrillas. Instead, the French army turned its back on the pathetic survivors of a defeated private army. The group – nine Legion officers and eighty-six men, most of them from 1er REP – were attacked on the ground by the ALN and from the air by the French air force. They straggled miserably back into Algiers and surrendered. Degueldre had not joined the party.

The gendarme Captain Lacoste now took them over. He and his men interrogated the exhausted survivors day and night. In the early hours of 7 April, the indefatigable Lacoste extracted from one of the prisoners a likely location for a Legion deserter who was said to be 'close' to the chief of Delta. Lacoste picked him up. For once, it was not someone on the run from 1er REP but from Messmer's old unit, 13th Demi-Brigade.

The new captive proved to be a goldmine of information. If anything, he recollected too much. By 3 p.m. that day he had remembered no fewer than fifteen addresses where Degueldre might be found. Every one of them was surrounded and checked out.

Degueldre, a settler colleague who had ordered the killing of chemistry dispensers and postmen, a captain from 3 REI, a captain who had deserted from the paras, an ex-police commissioner – whose 'Alpha' team of young settler rebels charged with guarding Bab-el-Oued finally pushed European Algeria over the brink with its fusillade on two lorries full of bewildered French conscripts in their harmless black berets – all of them spotted the cordon going into position around the apartment building. They held a meeting which could be compared to Hitler's last 'O' group in the Berlin bunker. Their host offered all of them space in a sort of priest-hole behind a wardrobe. The former deputy police chief, and Degueldre politely declined the offer. They had confidence in their bogus identity papers.

Degueldre had passed the first gendarmerie check in the building and was strolling towards the main door of the apartment block with studied casualness when a voice called on him to stop. The lieutenant in question had just emerged from a ground-floor flat and wanted to know more about this civilian built like a rugby forward.

'I've just been checked,' Degueldre said.

'Right,' said the lieutenant, eyeing his man. 'Let's see your papers again.'

'Esposito, that's my name there, Joseph Esposito, inspector of schools. Telephone the education department if you like. They'll confirm who I am.'

The gendarme was no fool. He sensed something about the man that was not quite right and told him to accompany him to the station.

The astonishing thing is that Degueldre does not seem to have thought of escaping. It is more than possible that he was now too tired to resist. Still, he continued to protest at police headquarters that he was due to keep a school appointment. But he did notice that the headquarters, at Hussein Dey, was the one seized by 1er REP during the putsch about a year before. And while he was so occupied, Lacoste, who had been sweating for five months to achieve just one arrest, glanced up and recognized Degueldre from photographs. After a mere token denial, Degueldre agreed that he was who he was. Perhaps he still believed he would be rescued. After all, it was only a few months since he had been the toast of European Algiers. Certainly he threatened Lacoste, in a gentlemanly way, that the gendarme captain would not leave the city alive. So they bundled Degueldre on a flight to Paris that same night and locked him up securely.

By the time he came before the special military tribunal on 28 June, his former serveant Dovecar had died before a French firing squad and the OAS supremo General Salan had been given a life sentence. Oran's university, its excellent library and much else had been destroyed by the settlers in a spiteful demonstration of scorched-earth.

Degueldre, refusing to acknowledge the legitimacy of the tribunal, sat silent throughout the hearing even when ordered to stand. Two days after the trial opened the president of the military court, General de Larminat, shot himself. The superstitious believed that Degueldre's malign, Rasputin-like reputation was responsible. Others thought it impossible that General Salan, the leader of the revolt, could evade the death sentence, while his inferior would not be reprieved. But de Gaulle made a characteristically political decision about whose head he could safely claim, without too much public outcry. Lieutenant Degueldre was ordered to be shot also. The same bureaucracy decreed that he could not receive a visit from his newly-born child, or the child's mother, during the seven short days left to him in a condemned cell near Paris.

From his death cell, Degueldre wrote a strangely disturbing testament to no one in particular, in a school exercise book.

'After a certain trial which took place last Thursday, Degueldre Roger has been transferred to his condemned cell at Fresnes.

That's what most people say. I who know D.R., and have done so for thirty-seven years, tell you that is false. D.R. is not here. The person locked up at Fresnes is called 'Jules'. (At least, that's the name I've given him.)

Jules is very different from Roger. Since his arrival, Jules has done nothing but sleep, read, drink and eat. Everyone is very kind to him. One might think he was an important person recovering from an illness which brought him close to death. He has now started to convalesce but he has to be kept under constant surveillance to avoid a relapse. It is also necessary to take care that he misses nothing, to open his door regularly and ask if he needs anything special. The nourishment he is now getting is rich and plentiful and nothing is overlooked. At night, someone has to keep an eye on poor Jules, so they put a blue light bulb on so as to be able to watch him while he sleeps but so as to avoid hurting his eyes.

In the morning, his coffee is served to him in bed, then he is allowed a little walk, always under the close and concerned gaze of one or two, even sometimes three guardians, some of them always armed. That brings me to one of the reasons why I tell you it is not R.D. who is here, for Jules takes no notice of them.

Sometimes, the director of the establishment comes to see him and brings his medicine. He has promised him this every evening until he finds it easier to go to sleep but, in fact, he has so far not brought the medicine once. Perhaps the doctor does not approve? They must have a doctor in this establishment, but Jules has not yet seen him. Instead, the padre came to see him last night. Very kind and compassionate, but Jules is very suspicious of those people. In that he has something in common with R.D.

Everybody has a sad smile full of understanding for Jules as he moves around. Jules responds with a big smile and a kind word, and he seems to hear, every time, a sigh of relief from the people who have met him.

This smile seems to say, 'Ah, he is getting better.' And Jules is entirely happy with this pleasant farce which everybody is playing. Sometimes, if rarely, cold fear strikes Jules. It is shrugged off immediately, since such fear is the business of R.D., and Jules wants none of it. That is the second reason which leads me to conclude that it is not R.D. who is here, but Jules.

Jules is detached from the world. Nothing interests him. Every day the radio goes on about a certain 'Tour de France' which would seem to be an attraction for Frenchmen everywhere. But Jules pays hardly any attention to these worthy chaps who sweat and work their way through all those kilometres when an aircraft or a car would be so much faster and relaxing.

Jules's room is all yellow, all clean and tidy, but behind the door and window are enormous bars and a grill which is permanently locked. Good heavens! One never knows what is going on inside the head of a very sick person.

Jules has got himself completely screwed up and dreams of nothing but stretching out on his bed, which is too soft for comfort, to smoke, read, eat, drink and sleep.

Every day after the walk, he is made to take a shower, always under strict surveillance. That is one of the high spots, for he can have fun asking the guardians to make the water alternatively hot and cold, and be immediately satisfied.

When Jules leaves his room, anyone who isn't a guardian goes back and hides. No one has the right to see Jules, for he is such an important person.

I think I have said everything about Jules, and about his very calm, so gentle life.

And R.D., you ask me, where is he, then? What's he doing? What does he think?

Now that is a secret which I know awfully well, but I alone know it.'

On 5 July 1962, 2,000 settlers hoping to reach the sanctuary of France, were massacred by Arabs at Oran. French soldiers, still stationed in their tens of thousands in Algeria, were instructed not to intervene. A radio ham signalled an SOS to the outside world which was picked up in Madrid and relayed to the government in Paris, which did nothing.

The next day, a French firing squad ended Degueldre's life in the grey, grim fortress of Fort d'Ivry on a windy hill south of Paris. Professional as ever, Degueldre felt obliged to instruct the nervous marksmen assigned to his execution to get on with their duty, unflinchingly. He sang the Marseillaise. Only after several incompetent attempts – arguably intended to save his life – and six *coups de grâce* by an NCO, did Degueldre finally expire.

Algeria had been formally independent for just a few days and already the victors were fighting among one another over the spoils.

The Legion remained in Algeria until 1964. But in such sordid circumstances, morale slumped. The Englishman Simon Murray, serving with 2 REP, recorded in his diary four months after Degueldre's execution:

We have had seven deserters in the last two days. There is little news about the OAS these days, although there is still a working underground recruitment operation in the regiment. I have had no further approaches . . . We have lost 136 deserters in the last four months. Discipline is on the wane, drinking is on the up. Alcoholism is a real problem now. Before, we were always on the move in the mountains and there was never time to stop and think.

[Now they were building a new camp] . . . bashing rocks, digging ditches, shovelling sand and gravel, loading and unloading bricks onto lorries, pushing wheel barrows of concrete . . . Back-breaking work. Every day is the exact replica of the one that preceded it. The prospect of doing this for another two years fills me with total despair.

In the diaspora of 1 REP which followed the putsch, there were those who, having made a gesture which they could justify morally, accepted arrest, disgrace, trial and imprisonment. At his trial in April 1962, Saint-Marc said: 'Monsieur le Président, one can ask much of a soldier, in particular that he should die: this is his métier. One cannot ask him to cheat, to go back on his word, to lie, renounce loyalty and perjure himself.' He got ten years for his cheek. There were those – a sentimental minority, no doubt – who thought this sentence unduly severe. Perhaps this was because even the public prosecutor had not dared to suggest more than five years. After all, Saint-Marc had fought with the Resistance, survived Gestapo interrogation in Occupied Paris and SS brutality in Buchenwald. When he was liberated he weighed just 90 lb, coughed blood and had trouble remembering his name. Three years later, in 1948, came the first of his three tours in Vietnam as an officer of the Foreign Legion, then the Suez operation of 1956 and the Algerian War of Independence. At the time of his court martial he had been fighting for France, more or less continuously, for twenty years. So had most of those on trial with him, almost the entire officers' mess of France's best fighting regiment.

There were also those NCOs and legionnaires who had followed their officers through the four days of mutiny, then calmly drove into a military prison camp to await whatever might follow. For some including the British legionnaire (now Sergeant) Choat there was a posting to a quick reaction company attached to 1st Foreign Legion Regiment, a posting which would ensure unremitting front-line service. In common with other soldiers who had embarrassed de Gaulle, it was noticeable that they were constantly placed in combat situations carrying a maximum of risk and minimum support from other arms (like German ex-legionnaires handed over to the Afrika Korps in 1940–41) but that, perhaps, was a coincidence. The lucky ones finished their tours, accepted honourable discharge when it fell due, and left.

Then there were those officers who followed Degueldre into the OAS and were never caught. Such men lived underground for years. Some of them had to wait until 1975, a year after the election of Giscard d'Estaing, for a complete amnesty. The most stylish of them was Pierre Sergent, a much-decorated captain of 1 REP who did not give himself up because, as he explained later, 'We did not do that in my days in the Resistance: we continued the fight.'

During his years underground, Sergent popped up like an amused, ironic sprite. One photograph shows him riding a bicycle '*en clergyman*', looking very much the local vicar. In another, taken in Milan, he is bespectacled beneath a banker's homburg, with umbrella and newspaper, the very model of an international businessman. Twice condemned to death *in absentia*, he adopted isolation as a way of life on the basis that a man on the run can trust no one but himself (and, presumably, an occasional photographer).

Sergent was amnestied after the student revolution of 1968 (and Massu's secret support of de Gaulle). He finally returned to public life as a highly successful author of Legion histories. Politically he and others like him, including Le Pen, believe they are still fighting for a restoration of what they perceive to be France's true glory, betrayed by generations of politicians. They are the true believers in a French patriotic ideal. But in 1985 – a good year – they represented just 8.9 per cent of the French electorate.

CHAPTER 16
The Legion Today:
Army of Intervention

The geographic and political situation of France
places it at the centre point . . . around which
modern international relations are articulated.

– French Defence Minister, December 1981

The tale of how a French president was taken in
by Libya's Colonel Gaddafi . . . could have been
scripted by Feydeau.

The Economist, 15 December 1984

Following the disasters of Indo-China and Algeria, the strength
of the Foreign Legion was cut from 20,000 men to 8,000. The
surviving regiments were fastidiously directed to outposts far
from metropolitan France. The Legion's formal farewell to
Africa was a defiant nocturnal parade by 1 RE at the old
depot of Sidi-bel-Abbès. There, in deference to Borelli's wishes,
the Black Flags of Tuyen Quang were ceremonially burned, and
from the flames brands were ignited and held aloft in the darkness
by all 700 legionnaires taking part in the parade.

The Legion's departure from Africa should be put in context.
The unit was in fact treated less brutally by France than many
others of the Armée d'Afrique. Between 1959 and 1964 thirty-
two regiments of Tirailleur infantry, Zouaves, Spahis and Chasseurs cavalry were disbanded. In 1962 alone, an additional
150,000 locally recruited auxiliaries were demobilized. Comparatively few of these North African soldiers were given
refuge in France and, in consequence, many thousands were
murdered by their former enemies of the National Liberation
Army. Those deaths should be added to the 15,000 mainly

Muslim soldiers who had died fighting for France in the Algerian war. The betrayal of Algerians who had believed in Algérie Française closely resembled France's earlier betrayal of her anti-Nazi-German legionnaires and her anti-communist allies in Indo-China.

The French regular army was not unscathed by de Gaulle's wrath, either. As a result of the Algiers putsch two élite para divisions – the 10th, to which 1 REP belonged and the 25th of which 2 REP was a part – were dissolved, as were individual regiments including 14 and 18 Para, Airborne Commandos and, soon after, a large swathe of the 11th Shock Regiment, until then the muscle of the Secret Service. In addition the bureaucracy instituted a witch-hunt against thousands of individual soldiers which relied upon a network of informers within the Army. As Alistair Horne puts it:

> After 1962 . . . the officer corps was extensively reshaped. The élite para and Foreign Legion regiments deeply implicated in the 1961 Putsch were broken up, their officers either purged or forced out in droves by such indirect pressures as ostentatious surveillance, frequent changes of post, forced separation from families, and passed-over promotions.

Hundreds more were sent to prison or detention camps at about the same time that de Gaulle set free 6,000 ALN prisoners. For the Legion as such there now began a diaspora symbolic of something more than geographical separation. In part it reflected a drastic change of emphasis in the role of the French army which would be necessary, irrespective of political purges, in de Gaulle's new France. Paul Johnson concludes:

> Under de Gaulle . . . France became for the first time a modern, industrialized country in the forefront of technical progress and the assimilation of new ideas. It was the very antithesis of France in the 1930s. Such a reversal of deep historical trends is very rare in history, especially for an old nation. It gives de Gaulle a claim to be considered the outstanding statesman of modern times. The transformation, of course, was not accomplished without pain, ugliness and shock; and protest. But the very consciousness of French people that their country was again a dynamic force, as under the young Louis XIV or Napoleon I, reconciled them to the destruction of traditional rural

France and, equally important, steeled them to the acceptance of co-partnership with Adenauer's Germany in the European Community.

Mutinies aside, such reforms could not have left a colonially-oriented Foreign Legion untouched even if – characteristically – de Gaulle was deserting NATO's military structure even as he was joining the European Economic Community. But equally, the diaspora of the Legion had to do with diluting the unit's rebellious spirit by blending its constituent elements (for example, the paras) with other, similar forces which were exclusively French. The dilution was carried further by the increasing number of Frenchmen serving in the Legion itself.

In 1982 Lieutenant-Colonel Patrick Turnbull, MC published in the *Journal of the Royal United Services Institute for Defence Studies*, a census of nationalities then represented in the Legion. It read as follows:

Nationality	Percentage
British	3.5
German	11.3
Belgian	2.5
Portuguese	2.5
Italian	2.12
Spanish	3.4
North African (Arab)	2.2
Black African	0.7
Middle Eastern (Arab)	2.5
Far Eastern (Vietnamese)	1.8
North American	0.9
South American	1.4
Scandinavian	1.0
Eastern Europe	5.0
Total	40.82

Turnbull observed: 'From these figures it can be seen that a good 50 per cent of those serving in the ranks at the present time are, in fact, Frenchmen, a fact capable of posing a legal problem which, if pressed, could shake the Legion's edifice to its very foundations.'

In keeping with the trend, more foreign NCOs, their first five-year contracts honourably completed, were seen to marry Frenchwomen and settle, with five-figure salaries, into married quarters. The Legion was far from tamed but it had started gradually to acquire an unfamiliarly domestic, fireside dimension which was entirely French. As Turnbull noted,

> When I first made the Legion's acquaintance in Moroccan Saharan outposts in the 1930s, prior to the outbreak of World War II, the men were built much on the pattern of the traditional 'brutal and licentious soldiery', exuding an aura of toughness born of continual active service under extremes of climate confronted by an equally tough and brutal enemy. The manning of primitive Beau Geste forts, year in year out, with no recreational facilities, was taken for granted. Few legionnaires ever took leave. There was nowhere to go, and in any case the financial situation of the average man in the ranks was such that the only amusement he could afford was a litre of pinard, cheap local red wine, on pay night or a visit to the unit-controlled brothel ... In 1900 two companies of the 2nd Regiment marched 1,250 km across open desert in mid-summer, during which time only seven casualties were reported.

The change from one tradition to another could not be wrought overnight. During the four years between the departure from Sidi-bel-Abbès and the formal opening of the new depot at Aubagne in the hills of Provence, 3 REI, for example, was sent to Madagascar (from which it was posted to Guyana ten years later); 5 REI to Polynesia; 4 REI to the French Saharan nuclear test site at Reggane, to assist with France's first atomic explosions, and then disbanded; 1 REC to Mers el Kébir; and 13 DBLE to Djibouti. It was not until 1967, a year after the basic training and administrative centre of Aubagne had been inaugurated, that a regular, fighting arm of the Legion – 1 REC's *Royale Étrangère* cavalry – was permitted to set up shop in peacetime France. It was the first time such a thing had been permitted since the foundation of the regiment 136 years earlier. With its armoured cars, 1 REC took up quarters at Orange to begin guarding Mirage nuclear bomber bases and nuclear missile silos on the Albion Plateau. The surviving para regiment, 2 REP, meanwhile, was sent off to Calvi, Corsica.

The strategy which France now pursued was tried by the British at about the same time, with the same object: that of sustaining a military presence in sensitive areas of the world without the political odium or economic penalty which now accompanied the big permanent garrisons of the 1950s, such as France's Indo-China or Britain's Suez Canal Zone. Because of the longer range and greater capacity of a new generation of transport aircraft, power projection from the home base seemed to be the best way of being in two places at the same time, invisible to potentially hostile politicians at home and angry natives on the territory to be fought over. The British tried such 'fire brigade' policies with, for example, the lacklustre Kuwait operation in July 1961 and in 1968 an exercise code-named Bersatu Padu, to reinforce east of Suez (the Malay Peninsular, in fact) from somewhere west of Southend. In the 1970s the British, facing honestly, if with occasional ill-grace, the economic impossibility of intervening almost anywhere around the globe while at the same time taking a leading role in NATO Europe *and* running a strategic nuclear deterrent, virtually abandoned power projection into the Third World.

The French did not. To resolve the conflicting demands of NATO Europe and French interests outside Europe, they hardened the long-standing difference between the professional fighting man and the amateur conscript performing his brief, twelve-month military service. The former could be sent anywhere to die for France on alien soil. The latter (unless he made a point of volunteering to serve abroad) was protected by law from involvement in any military adventure overseas. Instead, he helped to make up the numbers in Europe, where – thanks to the shield provided by France's allies still loyal to NATO – the risk of conflict was much diminished. Against this background, France set about reshaping her better professionals into a Rapid Action Force or – as it later became known in Anglo-Saxon jargon – the Rapid Deployment Force, even before the superpowers got there. It would not become obvious until France's ignominious retreat before Libya in Chad in the autumn of 1984 that her plans had omitted certain essential, but very expensive, ingredients such as long-range military transport aircraft, fast satellite communications and satellite photo-reconnaissance.

France's intervention forces effectively comprise three elements, identified by the colours of the berets they wear: red for the 11th Paras; black for the 'Seals', who are professionals of all arms who have agreed to serve overseas (hence the term 'Marine' attached to their units); green for the Legion commandos and paras. The official Rapid Action Force, including an alpine as well as a parachute division, engineers, artillery and support regiments, totals 13,500 men. The Legion paras – 2 REP – are a formal part of this organization, if a mere one-twelfth of the whole. But, elsewhere, the Legion contributes another 8,500 fighting men who have always been an intervention force in their own right. The resulting total of 22,000 troops available for military excursions outside Europe at short notice is substantially more than similar forces deployed by any other Western nation including the United States. The United Kingdom, having dismantled its last para brigade of 5,000 men in 1977, made a U-turn in policy and only began exercising its successor, 5 Airborne Brigade (again, 5,000 men) in November 1985.

So much for appearances. Several shortcomings diminish the real muscle of the French intervention force and its ability to hold together the French Community overseas. For a start, many units of the force are still spread around the world, sometimes in insufficient numbers, preserving a presence in Djibouti, Gabon, the West Indies, Senegal, Ivory Coast, New Caledonia, Tahiti, Mayotte (Indian Ocean), and French Guiana on the mainland of South America. More serious is the lack of good infrastructure to guarantee the fighting man water, food, ammunition, communications, intelligence-gathering and casualty evacuation.

Parachute operations are still at the heart of interventionist strategy outside Europe and for this the right transport aircraft are indispensable. The core of the French para capability comprises five squadrons of Transall aircraft (about seventy-five machines). These, like the C-130 Hercules, can carry around sixty-four fully-laden parachute soldiers. Unfortunately, the Transall's range is a mere 634 nautical miles with full payload compared with the Hercules' 2,100 nautical miles. An expert study of France's rapid deployment force in 1980 – when France had just three Transall squadrons flying – concluded that the

French airlift capability was between two and three battalions (say, 2,500 men) when the need to be able to resupply troops from the air was taken into account. If this assessment is correct, it means that France has no greater capacity than the United Kingdom to launch operations thousands of miles from the home base into hostile territory with any hope of success, although it has vastly greater numbers of soldiers. The truth is that both nations depend in some critical areas on the United States. When such aid is available (as it was to the Foreign Legion paras at Kolwezi in 1978 or to the British in the Falklands in 1982) the operation might work; without it, débâcles such as Chad, 1983–4 are the result.

Chad, south of the Sahara, was the target of France's first intervention operation in April 1969. The seeds of discord had been sown in 1960, when the state became independent and power passed to an élite of tribespeople from the country's cotton-growing south. Their government promptly discriminated against the Islamic, former slave-owning northerners as a revenge for ancient grievances. After two years, President N'Garta Tombalbaye stood as presidential candidate (the only one) to lead a one-party state, and was elected on a turnout of 94 per cent. The high voting figures were thought to have something to do with the enthusiasm shown by the police to induce people to cast their votes. When the French army left in 1964, the north promptly erupted into rebellion. Five years and several defeats later, President Tombalbaye invoked the defence treaty reached with de Gaulle, and four companies of 2 REP comprised the first unit to be despatched to his aid.

The legionnaires discovered that their enemies were numerous. The war was one to be fought against impure water, hepatitis, unmaintained vehicles, lack of fuel for all vehicles including aircraft, and a delinquent 'friendly' army as well as a guerrilla enemy who was usually impossible to distinguish from the civilians since both tended to be nomadic. René Backmann, reporting the campaign for *Le Nouvel Observateur*, said that French instructors attached to Tombalbaye's army had discovered an odd thing.

When the situation favours the regular soldiers, law enforcement degenerates into massacre, pillage and banditry. When the contrary applies, the troops turn tail and leave their weapons and ammunition behind for the rebels. At the beginning of 1969, the Chad army was completely demoralized.

The pickings for the Legion were meagre: a small contact here, a few weapons there, although an occasional air patrol would spot armed men in the bush — as did the Legion commander, Major de Chastenet, in October 1969; sixty-eight out of a party of a hundred resting in the bush were wiped out. A year later, a company of legionnaires descended on an airstrip near the remote north-western border town of Zouar. It was a daring air-landing which caught the opposition by surprise. The enemy, a band of Toubbou tribesmen, retreated to their native hills and took cover in familiar caves, still pursued by the paras. In the thirty-six-hour battle which followed, more than forty of the tribesmen were killed. The 2 REP lost one dead and ten wounded. In a similar action in November 1970, the Legion lost another two dead and twelve wounded in exchange for fifty Toubbous. By the time this mini-campaign came to an end in 1972, a total of fifty out of 2,500 French soldiers had lost their lives.

Tombalbaye's victory was short-lived, for instead of a united country, he now faced an irreconcilable guerrilla force in the north, backed by the Toubbous' co-religionist neighbour, Gaddafi. Gaddafi expressed his solidarity with northern Chad by claiming a strip of territory almost 1,000 miles across by 100 miles deep as his own, citing a treaty between Vichy France and fascist Italy as justification. Yet another of the chickens of 1940 had come home to roost. In 1984, Libya finally claimed the Aozou Strip as an integral part of that country's territory.

It was 1976 before France made another high profile intervention away from home. When it did so, to rescue twenty-nine French children held hostage in a school bus on the border between Djibouti and Somalia, the world applauded. Four out of five terrorists were shot dead during the rescue, as was one child. Although the operation took place only yards from an official Somali border post at Loyada, the risk of an incursion aimed at helping the terrorists to reach asylum was eliminated by a screen of 1 REC's armoured cars. The terrorists were picked off by marksmen of the French counter-terrorist gendarmerie, GIGN, flown in from Paris; the rescue proper was the work of a company of 2 REP. The perimeter group also consisted of legionnaires, drawn from the resident garrison of 13 DBLE. The rescue was a textbook example of ending a compact, single-site siege the hard way, with minimum force and a combination of military expertise.

The Legion's next rescue presented problems of a totally different order. The background to the operation was sombre, derived as it was from the satanic days of the Congo's bloody accession to independence from Belgium in 1960. With independence the tribalism endemic to black Africa led to a unilateral withdrawal by Katanga – the richest province – from the new state of Zaïre and a war in which hundreds of white hostages were butchered before they could be rescued by white mercenaries. So when, eighteen years later on 13 May 1978, a column of more than 1,000 Katangan irregulars stormed back into Zaïre from exile in Angola to seize the border mining town of Kolwezi, it seemed that a sickening chapter of African history was about to be repeated. Shops were looted, women raped, and anyone offering even passive resistance was murdered. Most at risk were 2,500 Europeans.

While Belgian para-commandos prepared their equipment in Brussels in a glare of publicity of 19 May, believing that they were taking part in a joint expedition with the French, news broke that 650 men of 2 REP had already parachuted into Kolwezi and were shooting it out with the Katangans in the streets of the town. In 1964, the Belgians had saved some hostages (though not all) at Stanleyville in a similar venture. In 1978, France was not going to wait for its ally. With thousands of lives at stake, such impatience was legitimate. Radio intercepts revealed that, in response to Belgian preparations, the Katangans were ordered to kill their leading white hostages and retreat to Angola with the remaining civilian population of Kolwezi. Events would demonstrate, however, that there was a quicker and easier way to the heart of the crisis than that selected by the French.

Among the units available, 2 REP was allotted the task because it was 11th Para Division's 'spearhead' unit, waiting at a high state of readiness. (British military observers noted – in response to government enquiries about what would happen if the hostages were British – that only one British battalion of around 500 men was fit to parachute, and that was then deployed over much of South Armagh on the border with the Irish Republic.) The Legion paras, while appearing to move at the slower preparatory pace of the Belgians, moved out of their Corsican base and flew by requisitioned civilian DC-8s to the Zaïre captial, Kinshasa.

Although France's representative on the spot, Colonel (later, General) Gras, would deny subsequently that the US had any involvement in this operation, an expert study prepared by the defence consultants DMS Market Intelligence asserted in 1980: 'For the drop on Kolwezi, an extemporised airlift had to be arranged, with the troops being flown down to Kinshasa on DC-8s and the support equipment and about 100 vehicles on United States Air Force cargo aircraft.'

In great secrecy at Kinshasa meanwhile, riggers worked round the clock to prepare five C-130s, Hercules of the Zaïre air force for the parachute lift, to augment the capacity of two troop-carrying French air force Transalls whose joint capability was a mere 128 men. (A third Transall taking part was required as an airborne command post.) Although local intelligence reports suggested that the opposition had no ground-to-air missiles to threaten the aircraft, any failure of surprise in overwhelming the Katangans would inevitably cost hostage lives. The bluff in Europe continued, meanwhile, while the real assault got under way with the former aeroclub in the town itself being chosen as the drop zone rather than some flat area of nearby bush. The men of 2 REP would be descending directly on top of positions held by the enemy. It was to be a perilous drop into the unknown which could be justified only by the urgency of the situation and the absence of some other route into the combat zone. Given the huge experience of the French in parachute operations (159 of them involving 58,167 soldiers between 1946 and 1958) the muddle at Kolwezi was spectacular.

After a flight of 4,500 miles from Corsica, the first three aircraft bringing the paras touched down at Kinshasa military airfield at 11 p.m. on 18 May. The men disembarked and went straight into a briefing at 3 a.m. It was their second sleepless night. From the outset, the airlift problems of 'Operation Leopard' were manifest. The legionnaires were to be inserted in two waves with a two-hour gap between them. The first wave would go directly to Kolwezi from Kinshasa; the second to an intermediate point 150 miles north of the drop zone at Kamina, to await the return of Zaïre's Hercules fleet. The legionnaires noted these facts, noted also that the French officer briefing them – a member of the resident French Military Mission – appeared to have come from a war zone of his own rather than the French embassy. He was decorated with debris from a road accident. He was not to blame, but his condition at that hour did not inspire confidence.

Colonel Erulin, 2 REP's commander, emerged from the briefing to learn that two out of the five troop-carrying aircraft had not yet arrived at Kinshasa; that one Transall was inoperable, and that one of the Hercules would not be fit to fly before 9 a.m. Those of his men who were on the ground drew their parachutes and started fitting them, only to discover that the American rigs were incompatible with the buckles to which French weapon-containers, etc., must be attached if the soldiers were actually to go armed to battle.

The French Military Mission in Zaïre had advised 2 REP to save the eighteen tons weight which their own parachutes would impose upon the overall airlift. Now, the legionnaires set to work to improvise fittings with pieces of wire and parachute cord, praying that they were not building malfunctions into the system. From an exit height of only 600 feet there would be no chance of recovering from a parachute foul-up. For anyone facing the stress of a para-drop, particularly one with a military operation at the other end of it, this is the stuff of which nightmares are made.

By 8.40 that morning, most of the legionnaires were settled in their jump ships, equipment of all kinds attached to their bodies, ready to go. Then a messenger handed a top priority 'Flash' signal to Colonel Gras: 'Stop Operation Leopard.' To establish contact with Paris, he was obliged to drive fifteen miles to the French embassy telephone in Kinshasa, only to be told of the next change of plan: 'Go ahead; go like the wind.' By the time Gras returned to the military airfield, Erulin had confirmed that the doubtful Hercules was not airworthy. The sixty-eight soldiers it was to carry disembarked and were redistributed among the remaining machines each of which now carried eighty men, or sixteen above the recommended maximum.

Technical hazards and problems due to human frailty were proliferating. The Transall to be used as an airborne command post was found to be still laden with ammunition destined for a Zaïre army unit near Kolwezi. Its new occupants had to hope that some stray bullet would not detonate this flying arsenal. Aircrew manning the Zaïrean C-130 Hercules had gone home at the first hint that the operation might be aborted, and had to be rounded up again. And still the problems multiplied. A Transall trooper was discovered to have a flat tyre. There was no question now of cramming further bodies into the other aircraft. Hastily, the defective tyre was reinflated and six overloaded aircraft clawed their way into the sky. The last one lifted off at 11.04, or four minutes after the time at which, according to the norms of local flying weather, no further take-offs could be accomplished safely.

The flight to the drop zone was three-and-a-half hours of overcrowded hell for the paras jammed in with their weapons and parachute rigs. The leading 'jump ship' made a navigational error and was brought back on course only after being pursued by the Transall command aircraft. It was 3.40 p.m. when the first wave of 405 men, hearts pounding, hurtled through the door, despatchers' voices screaming 'GO! . . . GO! . . . GO!', clasping equipment, buffeted by slipstream, into a void where the next second was probably the last one and, thankfully, where there was no time to think about it. Some pilots, having had trouble on the run-in, were now flying at twice the 600 feet altitude specified at the briefing. They discharged their human cargo all the same, blithely unworried that the men would now descend under slow-moving round parachutes into the path of other C-130s travelling rather faster, at the correct altitude 600 feet below. Meanwhile, just one soldier was paying for the incompatibility of the American equipment, and was hung up under the jump ship by the static line linking him to the plane. An instructor – one of a team of French experts attached to the Zaïrean army – cut him loose after ensuring that he was prepared, hand on ripcord handle, to deploy his chest-mounted reserve rig. He landed safely and went into battle with the rest.

This aerial circus, with its aborted runs followed by a drop of only approximate accuracy in high wind, had alerted the opposition on the ground. As things turned out, the Katangans had gone into hiding rather than to war. This was just as well, for some soldiers, suspended in trees and sprawled on roofs without weapons to hand, would have been easy targets. But Colonel Erulin, wiping blood from the cheek he cut in rolling on to an ants' nest, got out of his parachute harness to discover an apparently deserted town. Two companies fanned out, making friendly contact with Europeans whose eyes were wide with shock. The bodies, the wrecked homes, said it all. At last a third company, approaching the railway station, came under fire from three Katangan machine-guns. A hand-held missile hit back and destroyed two of these weapons. The third, with its gun team, vanished. The company moved on to a technical school to rescue thirty Europeans who were about to be executed. Still there was no substantial contact with the enemy.

On the edge of the Old Town of Kolwezi, shots were fired from a black township named Manika. In response, a section under Lieutenant Bourgain moved cautiously in open order across open ground separating them from the township, then smashed their way from house to house. Voices shouting for help drew them to the police station, where they freed twenty-six white and nine black hostages after storming the building and killing the Katangans guarding it. Meanwhile another section under Captain Poulet, stepping over corpses already half-eaten by dogs in the streets of the Old Town, reached the Jean XXIII School, whose cellars were found to contain at least 100 hostages. One of these directed Poulet to a convent being used as the Katangan headquarters. Behind a barrage of grenade launchers and automatic fire, the legionnaires swept into the building but found no living Katangan.

By now, the company operating near the railway station had made two interesting discoveries. One was that an ammunition train was parked there and had to be moved before it caused devastation. The other was that a road bridge rising across the railway was an invaluable commanding height overlooking much of the Old Town. The section left to guard this key point included two extremely cool customers, Corporals Morin and

Laroche. Like most of their comrades, they had had only oblique contact with the enemy so far so they were surprised, if not displeased, to observe two armoured cars emerging from the town. At that stage the Legion had no vehicles of its own, though Colonel Erulin would soon requisition those of the Belgian mining company, Gecamine. The approaching armour had to be hostile.

Morin was equipped with a hand-held anti-tank missile. To be certain of his aim as well as his identification of the enemy vehicle, he did not press the button until the target was about thirty-five yards away. Alongside him, Laroche stopped the second vehicle with a grenade launcher, also carefully aimed at ultra-short range. Drawing up behind these was a lorry, which the section hit with long bursts of automatic rifle fire before it was thrown by its driver out of sight in a skidding turn into a side street.

Colonel Erulin, meanwhile, had now set up his own headquarters at Jean XXIII School to start to take control of a confused, half co-ordinated series of searches and fire-fights. What, he was wondering, had become of the second wave of 233 men who were supposed to join him by air? By now, dusk was approaching. The anarchy of Kolwezi was not the best place for a night jump. By radio, Erulin learned of the latest logistical problem. For some reason, there had been difficulties in transferring the men from one type of aircraft at the Kamina staging-post into the Hercules which were to carry them to Kolwezi. The drop was postponed until the following morning. So the second wave jumped at first light on 20 May, at about the same time that the Belgian paras were descending by a somewhat easier method. They simply alighted comfortably, like tourists, from aircraft which landed at Kolwezi airfield a mere four miles from the town. The airport had been occupied since 17 May by friendly Zaïrean parachute soldiers, a full thirty-six hours before Erulin and his first wave made their hazardous descent on the town itself. Furthermore, the Transall being used as the French airborne command post was the supply ship for the same friendly forces: hence the ammunition on board.

It seemed possible, to begin with, on 20 May that the Legion paras might be drawn into unwitting combat with their Belgian and Zaïrean allies, so total was the breakdown in communication. As Gras put it in *Historia Special No. 414 bis*:

> They immediately began, without warning us, to penetrate into 2 REP's zone of action. It was absolutely necessary to avoid interference between the two units which carried the risk of grave misunderstanding. I took myself to Kolwezi at 0738 hrs to meet the Belgian commander, Colonel Depoorter. Our meeting was cordial, contrary to what others have tried to suggest, but it appeared that our missions were different. That of 2 REP was to restore the security of Kolwezi; that of the Belgians to recover as fast as possible their nationals who wanted to leave the town.

The legionnaires now concentrated on hunting Katangans in the black townships around Kolwezi while the Belgians swept up all Europeans at the scene, whether they wished to leave or not, and flew them out of the doomed town. A company of the second wave of legionnaires, meanwhile, had at last discovered a force of Katangans, estimated to be around 300, in a metal factory six miles from the town. Initially, the contact was made by a mere section of legionnaires which, outnumbered, found itself under spirited counter-attack. The section was withdrawn until reinforced by a company under Captain Coevoet, who put down a brisk mortar barrage and then launched an assault on the place. The Katangans fled in fifteen lorries, leaving sixty dead behind them.

On the evening of the following day, 21 May, the Belgians departed. Gras grumbled: 'They left as they had come, without warning us.' Now 2 REP returned to the town, a town of the dead whose streets were littered with 900 corpses; a town without water, food or electricity. The black townships, by contrast, were still crowded, and were thought to conceal Katangans whose native province this had been before independence, secession, civil war and exile. In particular, Manika was thought to harbour many of the men responsible for the atrocities and it was to this area that the legionnaires turned their attention.

During the following days, a multi-national African force was brought into the region to restore normal life. The men of 2 REP spread their influence throughout the surrounding Shaba province, in an effort to reassure both black and white that stability had returned. The regiment had lost five dead and twenty men wounded; the French Military Mission lost six in action and untraced; the Zaïre paras of 311 battalion – who had seized Kolwezi airfield before any ally arrived on the scene – lost fourteen dead and eight wounded. Civilian casualties comprised 120 Europeans dead and 500 Zaïrois. The bodies of 247 Katangans were also identified.

The operation could not be regarded as an unqualified success. France's determination to go it alone when a friendly host army had already established the key foothold in the combat zone, combined with the extemporary nature of the parachute operation – due to lack of aircraft and compatible parachute gear – led to an unnecessary loss of time and, it must be assumed, of life also.

For some legionnaires, 1978 was memorable for a less glamorous campaign; it marked their return to Chad. The first President of the country, Tombalbaye, had been assassinated in April 1975 in spite of French efforts to keep him alive and in power. His successor, General Félix Malloum, negotiated a short-lived peace with a leading dissident and former Paris law student, Hissen Habré. That arrangement broke down within days and in response to the capital's latest scream of (self-inflicted) agony, France launched 2,000 soldiers supported by Jaguar aircraft into a fresh adventure. The expedition included an armoured car squadron from 1 REC – the first of four to be sent to Chad during the next eighteen months – and a company of 2 REI, totalling in all perhaps 300 legionnaires. Yet it rapidly became apparent that not all President Giscard's men could prop up Malloum: the general went into exile in Nigeria in March 1979. The government which replaced Malloum's combined two mutually hostile northern tribal factions which had been united, hitherto, only in shared hatred of southern domination of Chad's political life . . . and therefore in their rejection of the French also. The leaders of these two factions were Habré, the ex-law student, and General Goukouni Ouedeye.

While a news blackout was being imposed in France as well as Chad itself, the legionnaires were serving remarkably short tours in this campaign, not least because of the frightening spread of hepatitis and other tropical diseases. There was also, inevitably, some effect on operational efficiency resulting from a political spider's web in which yesterday's enemies were miraculously transformed into today's allies, and vice versa.

The legionnaires were sometimes attached to Chad's armed forces as instructors. They did not relish passing on their expertise to people who, within a few weeks and another change of political dancing partners in N'Djamena, could use that knowledge to kill them. Legionnaires are no longer politically innocent. In Chad they knew that in promoting France's influence in this way they were taking part in a larger quadrille, one in which France and Libya sweated to elbow one another aside. Chad might not be a healthy place but, lying in the dead ground between Libya and black Africa, it was of great strategic importance. So while President Gaddafi boldly proclaimed a unification of his dictatorship with Chad, France sought to control Chad less obviously, through local surrogates. The legionnaire's more immediate problem was not lack of action but to determine on whose side it should be taken.

In April 1978 the crew of a Legion armoured car operating in conjunction with some of France's black berets, arrived at Salal after a long cross-country journey in the dark. The town, 250 miles north of the capital, was now held by a stout enemy force, so the briefing said, and sure enough, here came an unwary BTR – a Warsaw Pact vehicle – which one of the Legion gunners blew up from the rear with a 90mm shell. The town was reoccupied by government forces (that is to say, Goukouni troops, who had been rebels during the first French intervention in 1969) only after the armoured cars had hit the town with hundreds of rounds of 90mm at short range, with devastating results.

A month later, on 19 May, a training team sent from 2 REP to stiffen resistance in the little town of Mongo learned that neighbouring Ati was now occupied by hostile troops. When the team attempted to take Ati they came under vigorous attack and invoked air strikes from armoured helicopters and fast jets. Next morning, the Legion paras summoned reinforcements from their cavalry brethren 190 miles away.

As the armoured cars pounded along the desert road at fifty miles per hour, one drove off the road in a dust-cloud and crashed, fatally injuring a crewman. Out of a squadron of armoured cars starting the journey, only two arrived intact. In spite of that the counter-attack went in next morning. Over the next few days the same joint team recaptured the township of Djedda oasis following a two-day battle. But the cost of this grubby little war was rising fast: soon after the modest victory at Djedda, a French air force Jaguar aircraft – unit cost £4 million – was shot down by an enemy SAM-7 missile worth no more than about £5,000.

In the summer of 1978 the 2 REP detachment and some cavalrymen returned to Europe after just four months, to be replaced by 2 REI's 7th Company and the 4th Squadron of 1 REC. The Legion infantry soon found themselves engaged in close-quarter actions with well-armed, battle-hardened guer-rillas. At Geria in November, one legionnaire was killed and three wounded in a two-day small-arms battle. For the Legion, this second French intervention in Chad ended in September 1979 at a time when Goukouni, long an ally of Libya, was in command of the capital and Habré, under sentence of death, was in exile. The remaining French forces were extracted a few months later in May 1980. A mere nine months after that, Gaddafi publicly declared Libya and Chad to be one country.

From Chad's political gloom, France's army of intervention – increasingly a mobile exhibition to make a political statement about France's independence from the superpowers – was thrust into the pitiless, unnaturally illuminated theatre of Lebanon and with it, in its due turn, went the Legion. The first French troops put into Beirut, in fact, were paras of the 'Marine' infantry of the Rapid Action Force who joined the international peacekeepers in the Levant in 1978. It was August 1982 before legionnaires of 2 REP disembarked in the world's most feverish and politically violent city. The role of 'peacekeeping' does not fit the legion-naire's image or personality. Expert UN studies reveal that the slow, near-civilian reactions of Scandinavian and Irish soldiers have proved most effective in lowering macho Mediterranean temperatures on hot afternoons. Legionnaires, by contrast, are not noted for turning the other cheek. But the choice of 2 REP in August 1982 to act as a safe-conduct party for warriors of the

PLO and their leader Yasser Arafat from Beirut, celebrating defeat as if it were a great victory, was not unreasonable. Potential trouble-makers had to be convinced that the 'neutrals' guarding the route to the port were not so neutral as to be bystanders, hesitating to shoot if attacked. In the event, the shooting was all into the air on the part of the Palestinians.

On 13 September, 2 REP was withdrawn prematurely on the orders of the French government, following the election of a Phalange, non-Muslim president, Gemayel. He was assassinated almost immediately. The Palestinian camps, without the protection of independent outsiders, and still occupied by PLO families, were the scenes of sickening massacres by Phalange irregulars, under the noses of Israeli occupying forces. Arafat appealed for France to restore its presence. It did so, but not with the Legion.

By the time legionnaires returned to Lebanon in May 1983, they came as part of 31 Brigade, an air-transportable armoured force specially created in 1980 for overseas operations. The new formation included 2 REI (in armoured troop carriers) and 1 REC. To begin with, the French force enjoyed a brief honeymoon with West Beirut while nonchalant, unidentified groups of militiamen studied their positions and movements. By the time they left four months later, to be relieved by 11 Para Divison, it was after days spent sheltering from heavy calibre shellfire to which no rational military response was possible, for political reasons. When a water-supply truck was hit, for example, killing one legionnaire and wounding another, there was nothing to do except write the usual note to next-of-kin. This bruising experience was rounded off by 1 REC's farewell parade. As the men formed up in their best Number Ones, an air bursting shell exploded above them, seriously injuring three senior NCOs one of whom lost an arm.

France's third foray into the political quagmire of post-independence Chad was launched under the code-name 'Operation Manta' a few weeks before the unhappy farewell to Beirut, and again the combination of 1 REC's mobility and 90mm firepower gave the *Royale Étranger* a first-class ticket to the war, such as it was. One could not blame any legionnaire by now for failing to understand who was on whose side in Chad. In 1981, under pressure from President Mitterrand, General Goukouni (then head of state) ordered the Libyans to leave his capital. This they did with reluctance, sabotaging as many facilities as possible before they departed. Their disappearance was taken by Hissen Habré as a signal to take up arms once again in a new civil war. He did so with such effect that by June 1982 he had driven Goukouni out of N'Djamena. Ex-President Goukouni applied a well-tried formula: exile in neighbouring Cameroun; courtship of Gaddafi in Libya; guerrilla war against the new government supported by Libyan regulars. This time the support included an air force flying Mirage bombers which France had sold to Libya. So it was that the Legion returned to Chad in August 1983, with other intervention groups, to fight on behalf of the recent enemy, Habré, against the recent ally, Goukouni.

Operation Manta lasted little over a year. If the intention was to enhance France's political and diplomatic standing among its former African colonies, it was a disaster. The French arrived at N'Djamena this time, to find nothing of the infrastructure upon which they depended in working order. There was no aviation fuel and no means of transporting or storing it; no communications with the outside world beyond ordinary commercial telephone links; no motor vehicles in working order; even drinking water now had to be flown in. All the life-support systems upon which a fighting force of 3,300 men, including fast jet aircraft and helicopters, would depend had to be installed almost from scratch. Legionnaires sent back to a town they had conquered in 1978 described themselves, only half-jokingly, as the 'Damned of Salal'. At a higher level, planning staff depended upon American satellite photographs for information about enemy movements (and even then were not granted access to the original prints).

In January 1984, as the Libyans pushed south and captured the town of Ziguey, French Jaguars flew over the scene in a show of strength, but were obliged to follow unclear, politically-manicured rules of engagement. One Jaguar was promptly shot down and the pilot killed. As Libyan forces gradually advanced deeper into Chad, Gaddafi boasted: 'We will inflict on France a worse defeat than Dien Bien Phu.'

The following month, Mitterrand and Gaddafi agreed both would withdraw their troops. By now most French troops, including the legionnaires, were being pulled out anyway. The total number of casualties was eleven dead, most of them army paras killed in a single accident. The entire tragi-comedy was summarized by *The Economist* in December 1984:

> The tale of how a French president was taken in by Libya's Colonel Gaddafi, a man from whom most other people would not buy a used promise, could have been scripted by Feydeau. Act one, scene one: Mr Charles Hernu, the French defence minister, said boldly this summer: 'We will not leave Chad so long as there is one Libyan soldier south of the Aozou strip' (the northern slice of Chad, all but annexed by Libya). Scene two: in September, Libya and France surprisingly agreed that both of them would pull their forces out.
>
> Act two, scene one: the French withdrew, while the Libyans stayed put. President Mitterrand, with furrowed brow, met Colonel Gaddafi in Crete last month, to remind him of his promise. Scene two: Mr Cheysson, then France's foreign minister, claimed a week later that the Libyans had, indeed, gone. Scene three: after harrumphs from the United States, whose Awacs watchers-in-the-sky knew what was happening (and not happening) in Chad, the French admitted that there were still some 3,000 Libyans equipped with tanks and helicopters in the supposedly evacuated country.

This was, yet again, an example of France's dangerous wish-fulfilment at work, a process in which, as usual, the professional soldier took the risks. But in a shrinking world, in which no one's political back-garden was any longer screened from the neighbours, French unreality no longer went unremarked. No surprise, then, that learned strategists started to look more closely at France's recent activities in Africa. One of these, Mr John Chipman, NATO Fellow at the International Institute for Strategic Studies, identified seventeen high profile military interventions by France in black Africa between 1959 and 1984. These included efforts to keep some heads of state in office (e.g., President Senghor in Mali) and, by way of a change, Operation Barracuda, destabilizing the regime of President Bokassa (Central African Republic) in 1979.

If the risk carried by the interventionist legionnaire resulting from political incompetence combined with insufficient funding is as obvious as ever, the perils of garrison duty (other than cirrhosis of the liver) are less evident. The Legion continues its pioneering role in building works which, on any other drawing board, would be fantasy. The trans-Amazonian highway through the dense, dangerous rain forest on which 3 REI has worked for years in French Guiana, while simultaneously supporting the Ariane space base, is one example. Another is the scope of civil engineering by 5 REI in the Pacific in support of France's nuclear tests. Entire atolls have been built over and roads constructed even under the sea, to say nothing of fall-out shelters for the islanders in an environment (such as that of Fantagataufa atoll) sometimes so contaminated that fishing for crayfish is prohibited. This is an aspect of French grandeur which is not exposed much to public view, but it is there, and those most consistently exposed to the radiation risk, like the soldiers set to guard the malaria-prone swamps of Mexico by General Forey in 1863, are the legionnaires. France does not change. She still sees herself at the centre of a great empire, a superpower at the centre of the earth. Exaggeration? Consider the following statement:

> The geographic and political situation of France places it at the centre point of the two great axes around which modern international relations are articulated – North-South relations on the one hand. East-West ones on the other. That is the reason why the policy of the President of the Republic is established around these axes.

The reader might be forgiven for believing that the sentiment was expressed by a nineteenth-century French worthy in some provincial town on market day. In fact, the statement was made in all seriousness by socialist Defence Minister Charles Hernu in December 1981. France's unreality, one of the two themes of this book, matches that of the legionnaire himself. The difference between the two is that the legionnaire defiantly lives, or more often dies, with the consequences of his dream.

The romantic view of such soldiers is expressed by A. E. Housman's 'Epitaph On An Army Of Mercenaries':

> What God abandoned, these defended,
> And saved the sum of things for pay.

In fact, in truth and in extremis they *are* the 'abandoned of God' as well as their former selves, enjoying the dignity of danger and

accepting the integrity of pain as an antidote to political lies. As
the averagely successful legionnaire sees it, the contract with his
own mortality he signed the day he joined the Legion is the most
important thing he will ever do except for dying itself. Meanwhile he embraces life, unafraid to show off in smart uniforms,
which is one reason why the French politician and bureaucrat in
their drab grey suits ultimately hate him. But then courage and
the freedom it earns are not learned in offices.

APPENDIX I
Foreign Legion Campaign Chronology

1831	Foundation and start of Algerian Conquest
1835–39	Spanish Civil War (First Foreign Legion assigned to Spain)
1835	New Foreign Legion founded: joins Armée d'Afrique in Algeria
1839	Survivors of Spanish campaign join the new Legion
1854–55	Crimea
1859	Northern Italy
1863–67	Mexico
1870–71	Orléans, Alpine France, Paris
1882–1907	Saharan Morocco ('South Oranais')
1883	Tonkin, Indo-China
1885	Formosa
1892	Dahomey
1893	Sudan
1895	Madagascar
1907–14	Morocco
1914–18	Western Front (France) Eastern Front (Dardanelles; Serbia)
1918–20	Northern Russia
1918–33	Morocco
1917–27	Syria

1940		Battle of France prior to surrender of May 1940
1940		Norway, 13 Demi-Brigade (13 DBLE)
1940–45	Free French legionnaires of 13 DBLE supporting de Gaulle after French surrender of May 1940	Dakar Eritrea Lebanon ⎫ Syria ⎬ Opposing Vichy French forces including 6 Foreign Legion Infantry Regiment

1940–45		Bir Hakeim, Western Desert El Himeimat (Alamein flank) Tunisia Italy Southern France Alsace Western France (Gironde) Strasbourg Colmar French Alps
1940–42	Legionnaires loyal to Vichy France	North Africa Indo-China French West Africa Syria ⎱ Opposing Lebanon ⎰ Allied Forces including 13 DBLE
(1942	Vichy overrun by Germany following Vichy's surrender to Allied landing in North Africa. France changes sides.)	
1942–45	Legion other than Free French and Indo-Chinese garrison	Tunisia (Opposing Axis forces) Southern France Vosges, Eastern France Colmar Karlsruhe, Germany Stuttgart Arlberg, Austria
1940–45	5 Foreign Legion Infantry Regiment	Indo-China: Neutral during Japanese occupation of French Indo-China
March 1945	Japanese attack Legion bases	Legion survivors of Japanese massacres march into China; return after Japanese surrender. 5 Foreign Legion Infantry Regiment then disbanded.
August 1945	Japan surrenders to Ho Chi Minh's Viet Minh resistance movement	
September 1945	Ho Chi Minh's Vietnamese Republic declared. Hostilities between French and Vietnamese.	

September
1945–54	Indo-China
1954–62	Algeria, War of Independence
1961–	Irregular criminal activity by some legionnaires supporting Secret Army Organization opposed to Algerian independence and de Gaulle's U-turn on this issue
1969–71	Chad
1976	Djibouti (hostage rescue)
1978	Kolwezi, Zaïre
1978–80	Chad
1982–83	Beirut (with multi-national peacekeeping force)
1983–84	Chad (confrontation with Libya)

Legion's current deployments: Mainland France
Corsica
Djibouti, Gulf of Aden
Mayotte, Indian Ocean
French Guiana
French Polynesia

APPENDIX II
The Amazing Sergeant 'Brückler'

In an unpublished personal memoir, Jim Worden – former RAF pilot and Legion caporal-chef – recounts the extraordinary story of the German Sergeant 'Brückler'. 'Brückler', a Legion veteran when he transferred to Infantry Regiment Afrika 361, was concussed and taken prisoner by the British in the Western Desert. After treatment at Shallufa Military Hospital, Egypt, he was recruited by a British intelligence officer for a combined French-Palestinian-British attack on the Luftwaffe airfield at Derna. He almost certainly became one of the short-lived Special Interrogation Group described by Barrie Pitt in *The Crucible of War: Year of Alamein, 1942*. A fifteen-strong Free French team sent to attack an enemy airfield in Cyrenaica in the summer of that year "ran into total disaster".

Pitt wrote:

> To help them through an area believed to be swarming with German troops, they had taken with them members of the group known as SIG composed of Germans with strong anti-Nazi opinions. Many of the group were Jewish refugees from Nazi Germany, whose courage in undertaking such a mission was extraordinary, but on this occasion they also included two German prisoners-of-war who had persuasively professed sympathy with their views, but who in fact broke away at the first opportunity and reported the presence of the party to their own side. In the resultant battle, fourteen of the Frenchmen were killed or taken prisoner.

This version tallies closely with 'Brückler's' own description of the episode after World War II, when he was back in the Legion, serving with the Englishman Worden. 'Brückler' said that he was recruited to participate in a raid with Free French forces because, as an ex-legionnaire, he was assumed to be reliable. During the operation he arranged to go forward, unaccompanied, on a lone reconnaissance. When he reached the airfield control tower, dressed as a British sergeant, he told an astonished duty officer: "The Free French are here! Raise the alarm!"

Back in German uniform, 'Brückler' was decorated by General Rommel in person for this exploit, then posted out of harm's way to Tunisia. So he remained, until the Americans landed and he became a prisoner of war a second time. He was released by the French, he said, from a prison camp at Sétif, Algeria, in May 1945 as one of a number of men willing to help fight Algerian nationalists. (See chapter 13.) By this route he rejoined the Legion. But twenty years later he was still uneasy about what had happened. He confided in Worden, for Worden had coincidentally been in Shallufa Hospital at the same time as Brückler. Worden had also bombed Germany while flying with the RAF and made no secret of the fact. In an odd way, it was a bond between the two Legionnaires, a case of "There but for the grace of God. . ." Brückler's secret fear, as he admitted to the Englishman, was that "the British might still be after me as a war criminal."

BIBLIOGRAPHY
Titles in English

DMS Market Intelligence, *Rapid Deployment Force*. DMS Inc., 1980.

International Institute for Strategic Studies, *The Military Balance, 1985–1986*.

Pentagon Task Force, *The Pentagon Papers, The Defense Department history of United States Decisionmaking on Vietnam, Volume One*. Boston: Beacon Press, 1971.

Behr, Edward, *The Algerian Problem*. London: Hodder and Stoughton, 1961.

Chipman, John, *French Military Policy and African Security*. London: International Institute for Strategic Studies, 1985.

Cobban, Alfred, *A History of Modern France, Vol. 2: 1799–1871*. Harmondsworth: Penguin Books, 1965.

Garrett, Richard, *General Gordon*. London: Arthur Barker, 1974.

George, Sir Arthur, *Life of Lord Kitchener*. London: Macmillan, 1920.

Goebbels, Dr J., *The Goebbels Diaries, 1939–41*. London: Hamish Hamilton, 1982.

Gooch, G. P., *History of Modern Europe 1871–1919*. London: Cassell, 1923.

Grant, A. J. C. and H. Temperley, *Europe in the Nineteenth and Twentieth Centuries (1789–1939)*. London: Longmans, Green & Co., 1940.

Grauwin, Paul, *Doctor at Dien Bien Phu*. London: Hutchinson, 1955.

Guedella, Philip, *The Two Marshals*. London: Hodder and Stoughton, 1943.

Halliday, E. M., *The Ignorant Armies – The Anglo-American Archangel Expedition 1918–19*. London: Weidenfeld and Nicolson, 1960.

Hamilton, Iain, *Koestler, a Biography*. London: Secker and Warburg, 1982.

Hirst David, *The Gun and the Olive Branch – The Roots of Violence in the Middle East*. London: Faber and Faber, 1977.

Horne, Alistair, *The French Army and Politics*. London: Macmillan, 1984.

Ironside, Lord, *Archangel 1918–19*. London: Constable, 1953.

John, Colin, *Nothing to Lose*. London: Cassell, 1955.

Johnson, Paul, *A History of the Modern World (from 1917 to the 1980s)*. London: Weidenfeld and Nicolson, 1983.

Kingsford, C. L., *The Story of the Royal Warwickshire Regiment*. London: George Newnes, 1921.

McLeave, Hugh, *The Damned Die Hard*. Farnborough: Saxon House, D. C. Heath, 1974.

Maurice, J. F., et al., *The Franco-German War 1870–71 by Generals and Other Officers who took part in the Campaign*. London: A. Sonnenschein & Co., 1900.

Mockler, Anthony, *Our Enemies the French*. London: Leo Cooper, 1976.

Moorehead, Alan, *African Trilogy*. London: Lansborough, 1959.

Murray, Simon, *Legionnaire – An Englishman in the French Foreign Legion*. London: Sidgwick and Jackson, 1978.

Osburn, Arthur, *Unwilling Passenger*. London: Faber and Faber, 1932.

Paxton, Robert O., *Parades and Politics at Vichy*. Princeton University Press, 1966.

Pitt, Barrie, *The Crucible of War – Year of Alamein, 1942*. London: Jonathan Cape, 1982.

Porch, Douglas, *The Conquest of the Sahara*. London: Jonathan Cape, 1985.

Shaplen, Robert, *The Lost Revolution – Vietnam 1945–65*. London: André Deutsch, 1966.

Tombs, Robert, *The War Against Paris 1871*. Cambridge: Cambridge University Press, 1981.

Windrow, Martin, *Uniforms of the French Foreign Legion 1831 –1981*. Poole: Blandford Press, 1982.

Wood, H. F., *Adventure in North Russia: Allied operations*

against the Bolsheviks, 1919. Canadian Army Journal, Vol. 11, No. 4.

Yost, David S., *France's Deterrent Posture and Security in Europe.* London: International Institute for Strategic Studies, 1985.

Young, John Robert, et al., *The French Foreign Legion.* London: Thames and Hudson, 1984.

Young, Brig. Peter, *A Dictionary of Battles (1816–1976).* London: New English Library, 1977.

Zeldin, Theodore, *The French.* London: Collins, 1983.

Titles in French

'Mémorial de Nos Compagnons – Lieutenant Jean Deve, dit "Dewey"', *Journal de la Treizième Demi-Brigade,* 1984.

Képi Blanc editorial team, *La Légion Étrangère à 150 Ans.* Aubagne: Service Information et Historique de la Légion Étrangère, 1981.

Documents Diplomatiques Français, 1871–1914, Tome XI. Serie 2. Imp. Nationale.

d'Andoque, Nicolas, *1955–1962 Guerre et Paix en Algérie – L'épopée silencieuse des SAS.* Paris: Société de Production Littéraire, 1977.

Bonnecarré, Paul, *La Guerre Cruelle – La Légion Étrangère en Algérie.* Paris: Fayard, 1972.

Chastenet, Jacques, *Jours Inquiets et Jours Sanglants – Histoire de la Troisième Republique.* Paris: Hachette, 1955.

Courriere, Yves, *La Guerre d'Algérie.* Vol. 1: *Les Fils de la Toussaint;* Vol. 2: *Le Temps des Léopards;* Vol. 3: *L'heure des Colonels;* Vol. 4: *Les Feux du Désespoir.* Paris: Fayard, 1968.

Decoux, Adml., *A la Barre de l'Indo-Chine.* Paris: Plon, 1949.

La Délégation Française auprès de la Commission Allemande de l'Armistice, Tomes II and III. Paris: Imp. Nationale, 1950. 1952.

Devillers, Phillipe, *Histoire du Viet-Nam de 1940 à 1952*. Paris: Editions du Seuil, 1952.

De Vivie, Francois-Xavier, et al., *La Légion Étrangère 150e anniversaire. Historia Special*, No. 414 bis. Paris: Librairie Jules Tallandier 1981; *Les Paras. Historia Special*, No. 391 bis. 1979.

El-Kader, Abd, *Lettre aux Français* (translated from the Arabic by Réné R. Khawam). Paris: Editions Phebus, 1977.

Fleury, Georges, *Mourir à Lang Son*. Paris: Editions Grasset et Fasquelle, 1985.

Gandy, Alain, *Royale Étranger – Légionnaires Cavaliers au Combat 1921–1984*. Paris: Presses de la Cité, 1985.

Gauchon, Pascal and Patrick Buisson. *OAS – Jean Pied Noir*. Bievres, France, 1984.

Huré, Gen. R., et al., *L'Armée d'Afrique, 1830–1962*. Paris-Limoges: Charles-Lavauzelle, 1977.

Jauffret, J.-Ch., *Armée et pouvoir politique. La question des troupes spéciales chargées du maintien de l'ordre en France de 1871 à 1914*. Paris: Revue Historique, Presses Universitaires de France, 1983.

Koenig, Gen. Pierre, *Ce Jour-là: Bir Hakeim*. Paris: Editions Robert Laffont, 1971.

Lasserre, Jean, et al., *Bir Hakeim*. Orly: Icare, 1971.

Le Mire, Col. Henri, *Histoire Militaire de la Guerre d'Algérie*. Paris: Albin Michel, 1982.

Massu, Gen. Jacques, *La Vraie Bataille d'Alger*. Paris: Plon, 1971.

Mordal, Jacques, *Bir Hakeim*. Paris: Presses de la Cité, 1970.

Sabattier, G., *Le Destin de l'Indochine*. Paris: Plon, 1952.

Saint-Hillier, Gen. de CA, *Bir Hakeim 26 mai – 11 juin 1942*. Paris: Almanach du Combattant. 1982.

Sergent, Pierre, *Paras-Legion – le 2eme BEP en Indochine*. Paris: Presses de la Cité, 1982.

——*Je Ne Regrette Rien – La poignante histoire des légionnaires parachutistes du 1er REP*. Paris: Librairie Artheme Fayard, 1972.

——*Ma Peau au Bout de mes Idées*. Paris: La Table Ronde, 1967.

——*La Légion*. Paris: Graphiques Lafayette, 1985.

Spartacus, Col., *Operation Manta – Tchad 1983–1984*. Paris: Plon, 1985.

Villaume, Col., et al., *Légion Étrangère 1831–1981: Revue Historique des Armées, No. Special 1981*. Vincennes: Service Historiques des Armées, 1980.

Yacono, Xavier, *Que Sais-je: Histoire de la colonisation française*. Paris: Presses Universitaires de France, 1984.

Ysquierdo, Antoine, *Une Guerre Pour Rien – Le 1er REP cinq ans après*. Paris: La Table Ronde, 1966.

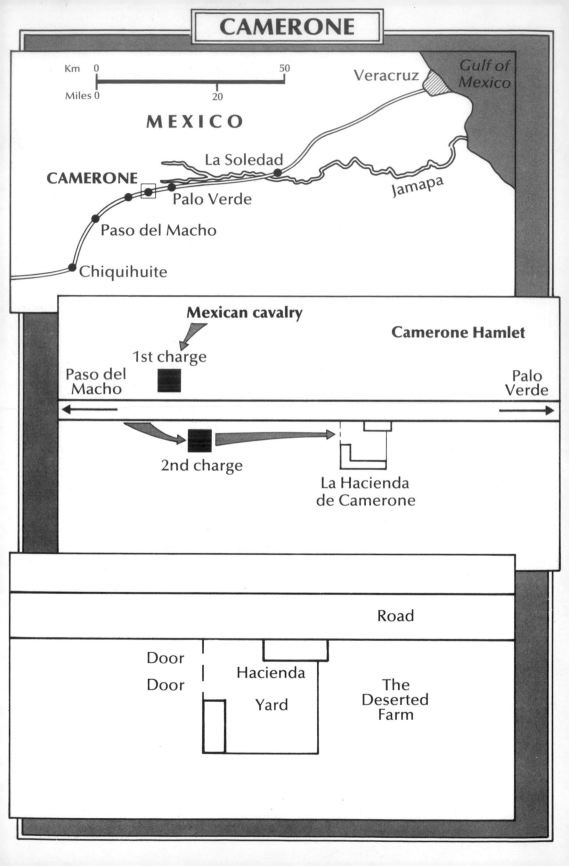

CAMERONE

Km 0   50
Miles 0   20

Veracruz

Gulf of Mexico

MEXICO

La Soledad

CAMERONE

Palo Verde

Jamapa

Paso del Macho

Chiquihuite

Mexican cavalry

1st charge

Camerone Hamlet

Paso del Macho

Palo Verde

2nd charge

La Hacienda de Camerone

Road

Door

Door

Hacienda

Yard

The Deserted Farm

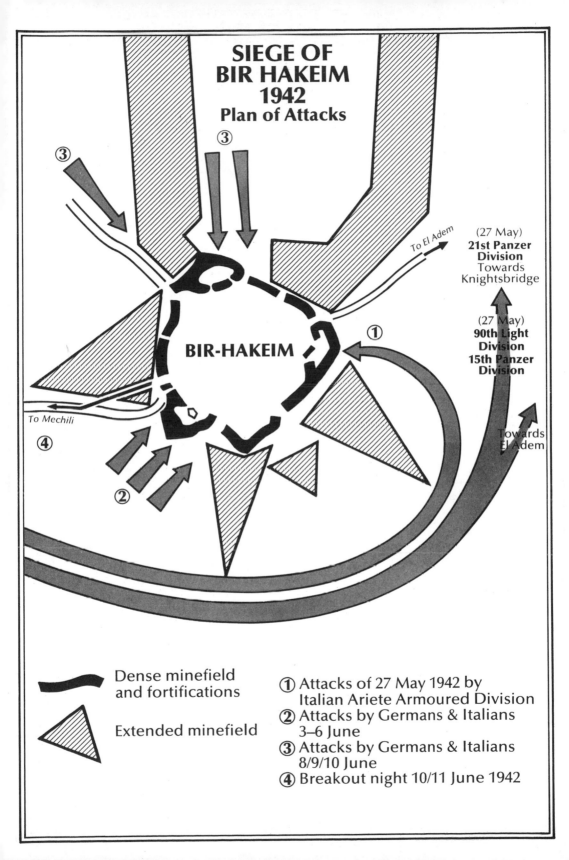

SIEGE OF BIR HAKEIM 1942
Plan of Attacks

③

③

BIR-HAKEIM

To El Adem

(27 May)
**21st Panzer
Division**
Towards
Knightsbridge

(27 May)
**90th Light
Division
15th Panzer
Division**

Towards
El Adem

To Mechili

①

④

②

**Dense minefield
and fortifications**

Extended minefield

① Attacks of 27 May 1942 by
Italian Ariete Armoured Division
② Attacks by Germans & Italians
3–6 June
③ Attacks by Germans & Italians
8/9/10 June
④ Breakout night 10/11 June 1942

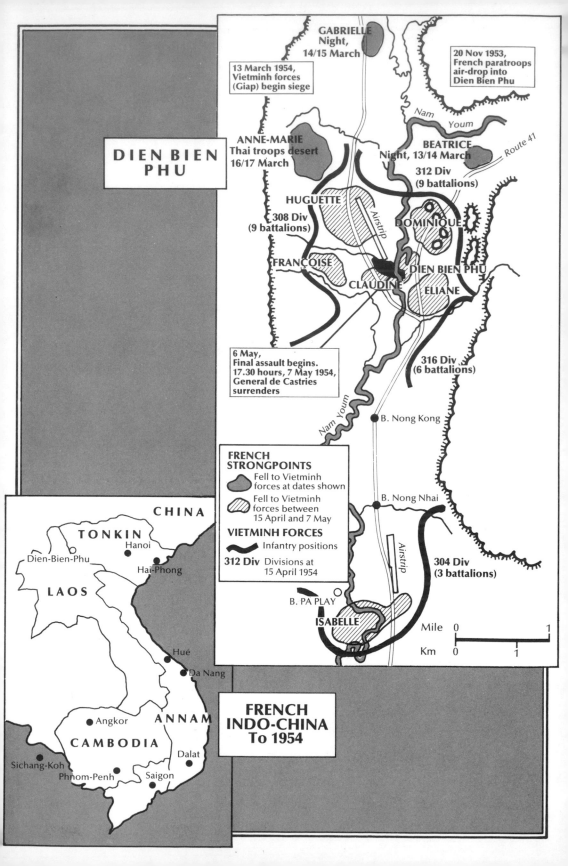

GABRIELLE
Night,
14/15 March

20 Nov 1953,
French paratroops
air-drop into
Dien Bien Phu

13 March 1954,
Vietminh forces
(Giap) begin siege

DIEN BIEN PHU

Nam Youm

ANNE-MARIE
Thai troops desert
16/17 March

BEATRICE
Night, 13/14 March
312 Div
(9 battalions)

Route 41

HUGUETTE
308 Div
(9 battalions)

Airstrip

DOMINIQUE

FRANÇOISE

DIEN BIEN PHU

CLAUDINE

ELIANE

316 Div
(6 battalions)

6 May,
Final assault begins.
17.30 hours, 7 May 1954,
General de Castries
surrenders

Nam Youm

B. Nong Kong

FRENCH STRONGPOINTS

Fell to Vietminh
forces at dates shown

Fell to Vietminh
forces between
15 April and 7 May

VIETMINH FORCES

Infantry positions

312 Div Divisions at
15 April 1954

B. Nong Nhai

Airstrip

304 Div
(3 battalions)

B. PA PLAY

ISABELLE

Mile 0   1

Km 0   1

CHINA

TONKIN

Hanoi

Dien-Bien-Phu

Hai-Phong

LAOS

Hué

Da Nang

Angkor

ANNAM

CAMBODIA

Dalat

Sichang-Koh

Phnom-Penh

Saigon

FRENCH INDO-CHINA To 1954

INDEX

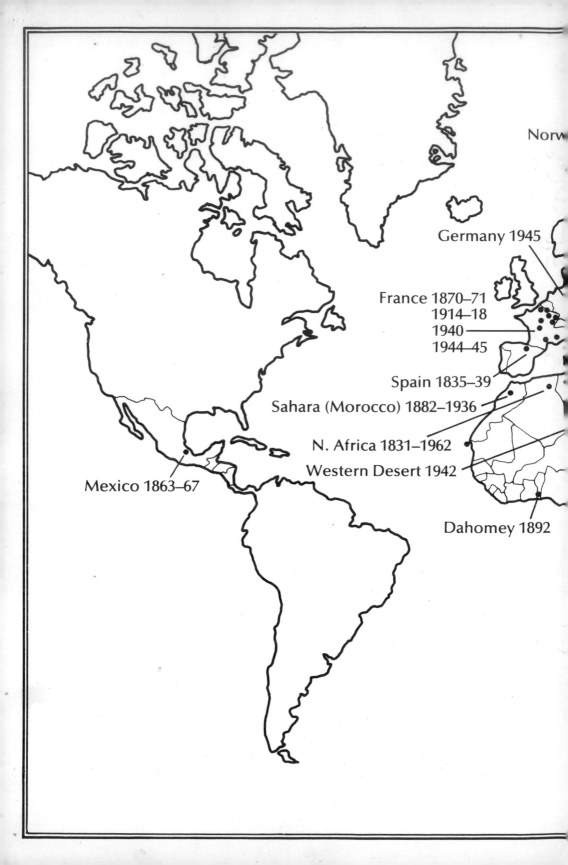